Quantifying the User Experience

Quantifying the User Experience

Practical Statistics for User Research

2nd Edition

Jeff Sauro

James R. Lewis

AMSTERDAM • BOSTON • HEIDELBERG • LONDON
NEW YORK • OXFORD • PARIS • SAN DIEGO
SAN FRANCISCO • SINGAPORE • SYDNEY • TOKYO
Morgan Kaufmann is an imprint of Elsevier

Morgan Kaufmann is an imprint of Elsevier
50 Hampshire Street, 5th Floor, Cambridge, MA 02139, United States

Library of Congress Cataloging-in-Publication Data
A catalog record for this book is available from the Library of Congress

British Library Cataloguing-in-Publication Data
A catalogue record for this book is available from the British Library

ISBN: 978-0-12-802308-2

For information on all Morgan Kaufmann publications
visit our website at https://www.elsevier.com/

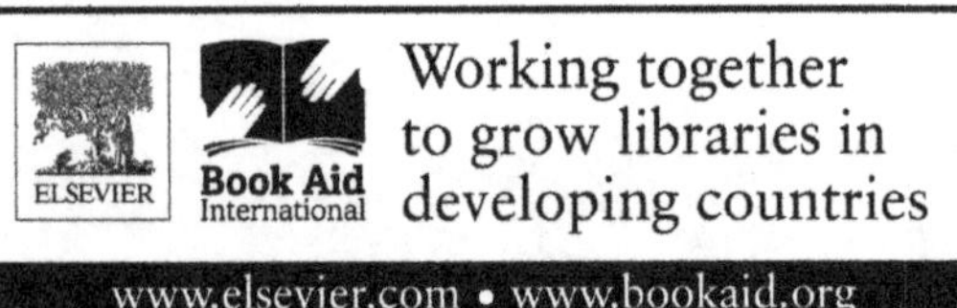

Acquisitions Editor: Todd Green
Editorial Project Manager: Lindsay Lawrence
Production Project Manager: Mohana Natarajan
Cover Designer: Mark Rogers

Typeset by Thomson Digital

To my wife Shannon: For the love and the life between the logarithms
-Jeff

To Cathy, Michael, and Patrick
-Jim

Contents

Biographies

JEFF SAURO

Dr Jeff Sauro is a six-sigma trained statistical analyst and founding principal of MeasuringU, a customer experience research firm based in Denver. For over 15 years he's been conducting usability and statistical analysis for companies such as Google, eBay, Walmart, Autodesk, Lenovo, and Dropbox or working for companies such as Oracle, Intuit, and General Electric.

Jeff has published over 20 peer-reviewed research articles and 5 books, including Customer Analytics for Dummies. He publishes a weekly article on user experience and measurement online at measuringu.com.

Jeff received his PhD in Research Methods and Statistics from the University of Denver, his Masters in Learning, Design and Technology from Stanford University, and BS in Information Management & Technology and BS in Television, Radio and Film from Syracuse University. He lives with his wife and three children in Denver, CO.

JAMES R. (JIM) LEWIS

Dr James R. (Jim) Lewis is a senior human factors engineer (at IBM since 1981) with a current focus on the measurement and evaluation of the user experience. He is a Certified Human Factors Professional with a PhD in Experimental Psychology (Psycholinguistics), an MA in Engineering Psychology, and an MM in Music Theory and Composition. Jim is an internationally recognized expert in usability testing and measurement, contributing (by invitation) the chapter on usability testing for the third and fourth editions of the *Handbook of Human Factors and Ergonomics*, presenting tutorials on usability testing and metrics at various professional conferences, and serving as the keynote speaker at HCII 2014. He was the lead interaction designer for the product now regarded as the first smart phone, the Simon, and is the author of *Practical Speech User Interface Design.*

Jim is an IBM Master Inventor Emeritus with 88 patents issued to date by the US Patent Office. He serves on the editorial board of the *International Journal of Human-Computer Interaction*, is co-editor in chief of the *Journal of Usability Studies*, and is on the scientific advisory board of the Center for Research and Education on Aging and Technology Enhancement (CREATE). He is a member of the Usability Professionals Association (UPA), the Human Factors and Ergonomics Society (HFES), the ACM Special Interest Group in Computer-Human Interaction (SIGCHI), past-president of the Association for Voice Interaction Design (AVIxD), and is a fifth degree black belt and certified instructor with the American Taekwondo Association (ATA).

Foreword

Joseph Dumas
User Experience Consultant

When the first edition of *Quantifying the User Experience* was announced in 2012, I ordered a copy. I knew the authors, Jeff and Jim, as frequent contributors to the User Experience (UX) research literature and they were both reviewing editors for the *Journal of Usability Studies* while I was its Editor in Chief. I always sent them the manuscripts to review that made heavy use of statistics.

Waiting for the book to arrive, I began to think: Do we in the User Experience (UX) profession need our own book on basic statistical methods? There are literally dozens of recent books on statistics written for psychologists, social scientists, engineers, market and medical researchers, etc. Why not just pick one of the best of those? How many ways can you explain how to compute a *t*-test?

Then I realized I was asking the wrong question. The issue is why *are* there so many books on statistics? The answer, I believe, is that statistical concepts and formulas are abstract concepts when approached without a context. Knowing when it's best to compute a *t*-test and which kind to compute come from that context. That insight is especially true today because there are so many software tools that do the computations for us.

A related factor is the fear that many students have about learning statistical concepts. I had that fear as an undergraduate. If I had had a teacher from another discipline using a book written for that discipline, it would have been harder to learn the concepts. So I believe that having a book that applies statistical concepts in a UX context would make learning easier.

How well then does this book put statistical concepts in context? My answer from reading this second edition and using the first one is that it does very well. In almost every paragraph the authors focus on using a statistic to shed light on a UX issue. For example, a section about *t*-tests focuses on comparing the means of two rating scales or usability test task times. The chapters on determining sample sizes are organized around different stages of product development: formative or summative. There are no abstract discussions of formulas without context.

The authors also have made good use of a set of organizational tools to support students and teachers. The first chapter has a set of decision maps that graphically provide a context for what follows in subsequent chapters. Chapter 1 also has a set of tables that tie those decisions to the sections in the book that cover them. I wish those tools had been available when I was teaching statistics. There are also summaries of key points, and review questions with answers at the end of chapters. These guys have taken the time to provide a structure that facilitates understanding. It shows that they take seriously the word "practical" in the subtitle.

I like the writing style. The authors convey the sense that they are UX professionals writing for UX professionals rather than experts writing for novices. There are "From the files of ..." call-out boxes throughout in which each author speaks about an issue that he has a personal anecdote about. Those call-outs are written in an informal style. I found them fun to read. Their content adds richness and personality and feels like the author is having a conversation with me.

The authors have added some new material to this second edition. The first edition contained great chapters on subjective measures. There is no more thorough discussion of posttask and posttest rating scales anywhere in the UX literature. In the second edition they have included additional scales that have appeared since the first edition. There is no longer any need to create your own rating scale as many of us did in the past. The publication of the 10 item Software Usability Scale (SUS) in 1996 stimulated interest in assessing posttest user satisfaction with a short set of ratings. It appeared at a time when usability testing had become the most visible empirical usability evaluation method. SUS has become the most popular posttest scale and it has provoked interest in developing even shorter ones. There are now several short posttask and posttest scales with demonstrated reliability. Jeff and Jim not only describe all of those scales, they compare and contrast them.

The authors have added a new chapter to the second edition, Chapter 10. It covers correlation, regression, and ANOVA. It's ironic, as the authors point out, that those statistics are among the oldest in the history of measurement. What I really like about the way the chapter has been put together is that it integrates the three statistics and shows how they are related to one another. When I was learning and later teaching statistics those methods were in separate chapters and ANOVA was treated as unrelated to correlation and regression. Chapter 10 is a major addition to the book.

There is one more question I asked myself about the book: why now? Someone could have written a statistics book for our profession 10 or 15 years ago. I believe that the wait was worth it. It is a sign of the maturity of the methods we use and the accumulation of research about them that makes the book more relevant now. We understand more about the context onto which the statistics are mapped. In addition, the profession has evolved in a number of ways since about the year 2000. It is no secret that the Internet changed everything. Websites and web pages have become a study in themselves. And it has made new methods possible, such as remote and unattended testing. There are new measures, such as click paths and conversion rates, as well as a renewed interest in A/B testing, all of which are covered in the book.

The Internet also was a major influence on the broadening of the way we think about human–computer interaction. Our earlier focus on usability, productivity, and problem identification has widened to user experience, which has stimulated the development of new measures. Those measures are included in the book and brought up to date in this second edition. Here, for example, you will find a discussion of the Net Promoter Score of customer loyalty, the hedonic scale of pleasure, and Usability Magnitude Estimation of the total user experience.

I have no more questions. I will use this second edition as a reference when I need to find the latest thinking about UX measurement and when I teach statistics again it will be my first choice. If this is your first book on the topic, trust me, you are in good hands.

Preface to the Second Edition

Welcome to the second edition of *Quantifying the User Experience*! In this edition we've maintained our focus on providing practical, up-to-date, and pragmatic information on how to measure and analyze user research data. The main changes in this edition are as follows:

- We've reviewed the appropriate literatures since 2012 and have updated content and references as needed.
- The topic in our book that has had the most new research published since 2012 is standardized usability questionnaires, so we have thoroughly refreshed Chapter 8.
- A consistent suggestion about the first edition was to cover correlation, so the second edition includes a completely new chapter introducing correlation, regression, and analysis of variance.
- Due to the inclusion of this new chapter, we have reworked the decision trees in Chapter 1 to guide readers to these topics as appropriate.

One of our primary goals in writing this book has been to make practical assessment of the user experience accessible to a broad range of practitioners and researchers. We start with an understanding of the kinds of data that user researchers typically encounter, and then provide analytical methods appropriate for those data, including tests of significance, confidence intervals, and sample size estimation. Some of the methods are conventional, such as the *t*-test, whereas other methods are the ones we wished had been taught in our intro to stats classes, but weren't (such as the adjusted-Wald binomial confidence interval).

Where we can, we provide recommendations and rationales for which method to use in which context. When we can't make a recommendation, we strive to provide the information needed to make and defend informed decisions. All of this is to support the creation of better products and services, which benefits the people who use them and the enterprises that provide them.

Acknowledgments

Thanks to the team at Morgan Kaufmann for inviting us to prepare a second edition. Many thanks to Lynda Finn, Linda Lior, and Phil Kortum for their thoughtful reviews of various draft chapters of this book. We deeply appreciate their time and helpful comments.

***

This book represents 10 years of research, resampling, and reading dozens of journal articles from many disciplines to help answer questions in an exciting field. Through the process not only am I satisfied with the answers I've found but also with what I've learned and the people whom I've met, most notably my coauthor Jim Lewis. Thank you to my family for the patience and encouragement through the process.

Jeff

Thanks to everyone who has made my career in usability and user experience so interesting and enjoyable—from my co-author Jeff Sauro to the user experience teams at IBM and State Farm to those who chose to pursue careers in teaching and under whom I had the great fortune to study. As always, thanks to my family for their encouragement and support.

Jim

CHAPTER 1

INTRODUCTION AND HOW TO USE THIS BOOK

INTRODUCTION

The last thing many designers and researchers in the field of user experience think of is statistics. In fact, we know many practitioners who find the field appealing because it largely avoids those impersonal numbers. The thinking goes that if usability and design are qualitative activities, it's safe to skip the formulas and numbers.

Although design and several usability activities are certainly qualitative, the impact of good and bad designs can easily be quantified in conversions, completion rates, completion times, perceived satisfaction, recommendations, and sales. Increasingly, usability practitioners and user researchers are expected to quantify the benefits of their efforts. If they don't, someone else will—unfortunately that someone else might not use the right metrics or methods.

THE ORGANIZATION OF THIS BOOK

This book is intended for those who measure the behavior and attitudes of people as they interact with interfaces. This book is not about abstract mathematical theories for which you may someday find a partial use. Instead, this book is about working backwards from the most common questions and problems you'll encounter as you conduct, analyze, and report on user research projects. In general, these activities fall into four areas:

1. Summarizing data and computing margins of error (Chapter 3)
2. Determining if there is a statistically significant difference, either in comparison to a benchmark (Chapter 4) or between groups (Chapters 5 and 10)
3. Finding the appropriate sample size for a study (Chapters 6, 7, and 10)
4. Investigating relationships among variables (Chapter 10).

We also provide:

- Background chapters with an overview of common ways to quantify user research (Chapter 2) and a quick introduction/review of many fundamental statistical concepts (Appendix)
- A comprehensive discussion of standardized usability questionnaires (Chapter 8)
- A discussion of enduring statistical controversies of which user researchers should be aware and able to articulate in defense of their analyses (Chapter 9)
- A wrap-up chapter with pointers to more information on statistics for user research (Chapter 11)

Each chapter ends with a list of key points and references. Most chapters also include a set of problems and answers to those problems so you can check your understanding of the content.

Quantifying the User Experience. http://dx.doi.org/10.1016/B978-0-12-802308-2.00001-1

HOW TO USE THIS BOOK

Despite there being a significant proportion of user research practitioners with advanced degrees, about 7% have PhDs (UXPA, 2014), for most people in the social sciences statistics is the only quantitative course they have to take. For many, statistics is a subject they know they should understand, but it often brings back bad memories of high-school math, poor teachers, and an abstract and difficult topic.

While we'd like to take all the pain out of learning and using statistics, there are still formulas, math, and some abstract concepts that we just can't avoid. Some people want to see how the statistics work, and for them we provide the math. If you're not terribly interested in the computational mechanics, then you can skip over the formulas and focus more on how to apply the procedures.

Readers who are familiar with many statistical procedures and formulas may find that some of the formulas we use differ from those taught in college statistics courses. Part of this is from recent advances in statistics (especially for dealing with binary data). Another part is due to our selecting the best procedures for practical user research, focusing on procedures that work well for the types of data and sample sizes you'll likely encounter.

Based on teaching many courses at industry conferences and at companies, we know the statistics background of the readers of this book will vary substantially. Some of you may have never taken a statistics course whereas others probably took several in graduate school. As much as possible, we've incorporated relevant discussions around the concepts as they appear in each chapter with plenty of examples using actual data from real user research studies.

In our experience, one of the hardest things to remember in applying statistics is what statistical test to perform when. To help with this problem, we've provided the following decision maps (Figs. 1.1–1.4) to help you get to the right statistical test and the sections of the book that discuss it.

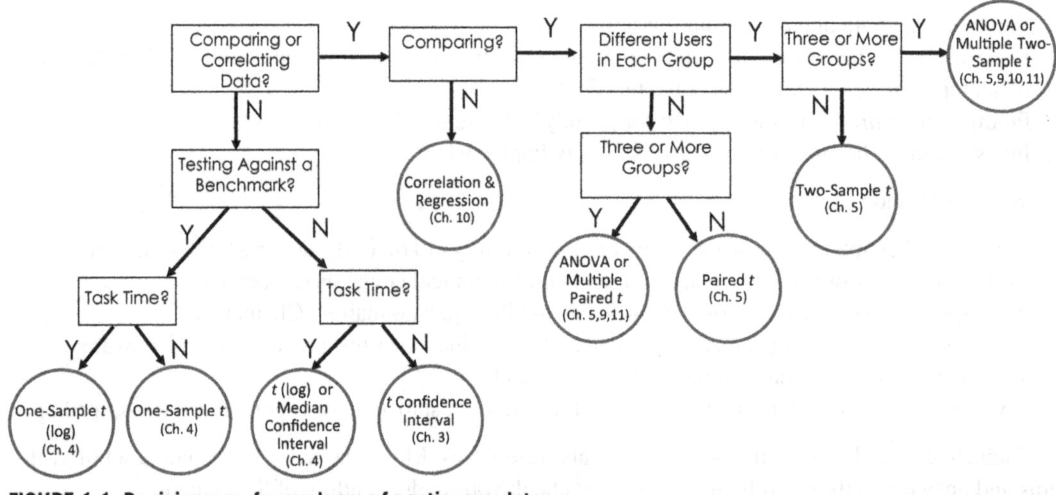

FIGURE 1.1 Decision map for analyses of continuous data

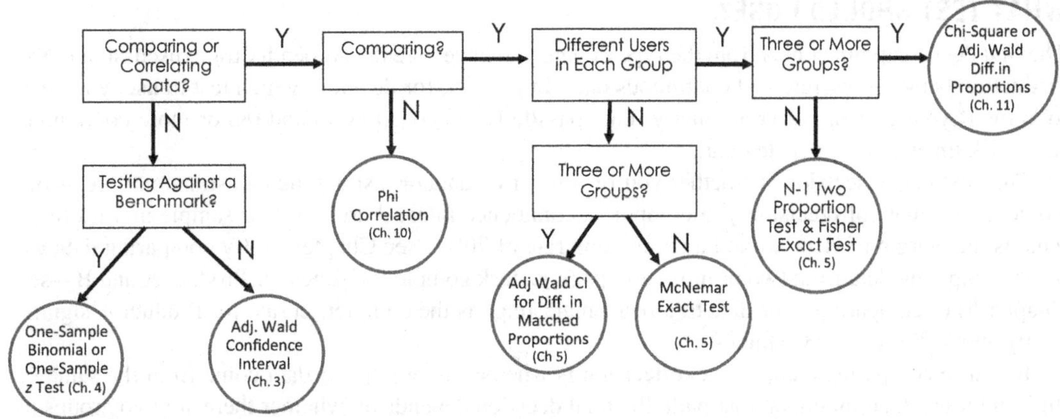

FIGURE 1.2 Decision map for analysis of discrete-binary data

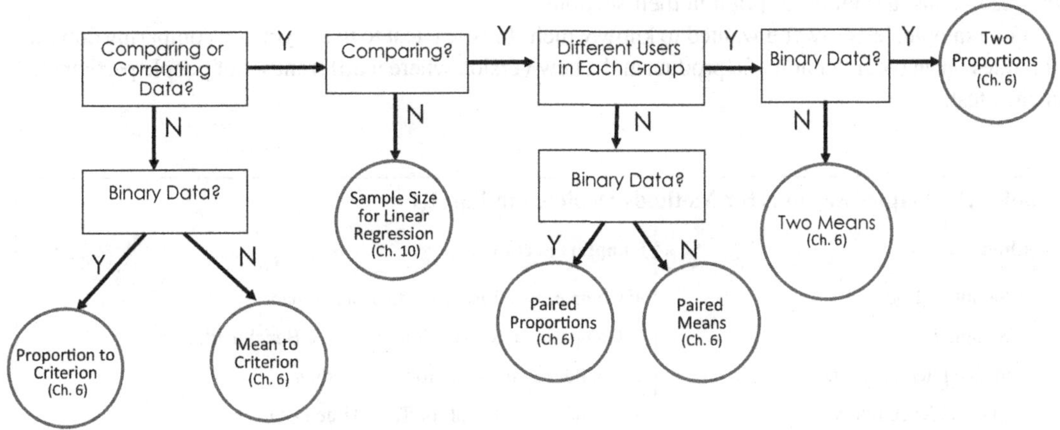

FIGURE 1.3 Decision map for sample sizes when comparing data

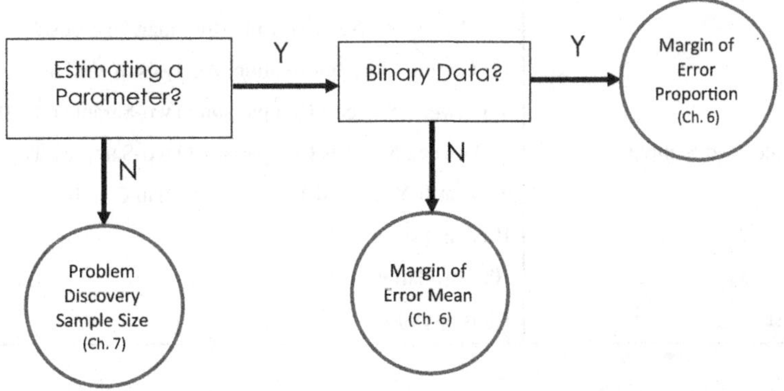

FIGURE 1.4 Decision map for sample sizes for estimating precision or detection

WHAT TEST SHOULD I USE?

The first decision point comes from the type of data you have. See the Appendix for a discussion of the distinction between discrete and continuous data. In general, for deciding which test to use, you need to know if your data are discrete-binary (e.g., pass/fail data coded as 1s and 0s) or more continuous (e.g., task times or rating scale data).

The next major decision is whether you're comparing data or just getting an estimate of precision. To get an estimate of precision you compute a confidence interval around your sample metrics (e.g., what is the margin of error around a completion rate of 70%—see Chapter 3). By comparing data we mean comparing data from two or more groups (e.g., task completion times for Product A and B—see Chapter 5) or comparing your data to a benchmark (e.g., is the completion rate for Product A significantly above 70%?—see Chapter 4).

If you're comparing data, the next decision is whether the groups of data come from the same or different users. Continuing on that path, the final decision depends on whether there are two groups to compare or more than two groups.

To find the appropriate section in each chapter for the methods depicted in Figures 1.1 and 1.2, consult Tables 1.1 and 1.2. Note that methods discussed in Chapter 11 are outside the scope of this book, and receive just a brief description in their sections.

For example, let's say you wanted to know which statistical test to use if you are comparing completion rates on an older version of a product and a new version where a different set of people participated in each test.

Table 1.1 Chapter Sections for Methods Depicted in Fig. 1.1

Method	Chapter: Section
One-Sample *t* (Log)	4: Comparing a Task Time to a Benchmark
One-Sample *t*	4: Comparing a Satisfaction Score to a Benchmark
Confidence Interval around Median	3: Confidence Interval around a Median
t (Log) Confidence Interval	3: Confidence Interval for Task-Time Data
t Confidence Interval	3: Confidence Interval for Rating Scales and Other Continuous Data
Paired *t*	5: Within-Subjects Comparison (Paired *t*-Test)
ANOVA or Multiple Paired *t*	5: Within-Subjects Comparison (Paired *t*-Test)
	9: What If You Need To Run More than One Test?
	11: Getting More Information: Analysis of Variance
Two-Sample *t*	5: Between-Subjects Comparison (Two-Sample *t*-Test)
ANOVA or Multiple Two-Sample *t*	5: Between-Subjects Comparison (Two-Sample *t*-Test)
	9: What If You Need To Run More than One Test?
	10: Analysis of Variance
Correlation	10: Correlation
Regression Analysis	10: Regression

Table 1.2 Chapter Sections for Methods Depicted in Fig. 1.2

Method	Chapter: Section
One-Sample Z-Test	4: Comparing a Completion Rate to a Benchmark—Large Sample Test
One-Sample Binomial	4: Comparing a Completion Rate to a Benchmark—Small Sample Test
Adjusted Wald Confidence Interval	3: Adjusted-Wald: Add Two Successes and Two Failures
McNemar Exact Test	5: McNemar Exact Test
Adjusted Wald Confidence Interval for Difference in Matched Proportions	5: Confidence Interval around the Difference for Matched Pairs
$N-1$ Two Proportion Test and Fisher Exact Test	5: $N-1$ Two Proportion Test; Fisher Exact Test
Adjusted Wald Difference in Proportion	5: Confidence for the Difference between Proportions
Correlation	10: Correlation—Computing the Phi Correlation
Chi Square	11: Getting More Information—Analysis of Many-Way Contingency Tables

1. Because completion rates are discrete-binary data (1 = Pass and 0 = Fail), we should use the decision map in Fig. 1.2.
2. At the first box "Comparing or Correlating Data" select "Y" because we're planning to compare data (rather than exploring relationships with correlation or regression).
3. At the next box "Comparing Data?" select "Y" because we are comparing a set of data from an older product with a set of data from a new product.
4. This takes us to the "Different Users in Each Group" box—we have different users in each group, so we select "Y."
5. Now we're at the "Three or More Groups" box—we have only two groups of users (before and after) so we select "N."
6. We stop at the "$N-1$ Two Proportion Test & Fisher Exact Test" (Chapter 5).

WHAT SAMPLE SIZE DO I NEED?

Often the first collision a user researcher has with statistics is in planning sample sizes. Although there are many "rules of thumb" on how many users you should test or how many customer responses you need to achieve your goals, there really are precise ways of estimating the answer. The first step is to identify the type of test for which you're collecting data. In general, there are three ways of determining your sample size:

1. Estimating a parameter with a specified precision (e.g., if your goal is to estimate completion rates with a margin of error of no more than 5%, or completion times with a margin of error of no more than 15 s)
2. Comparing two or more groups or comparing one group to a benchmark
3. Problem discovery, specifically, the number of users you need in a usability test to find a specified percentage of usability problems with a specified probability of occurrence.

Table 1.3 Chapter Sections for Methods Depicted in Figs. 1.3 and 1.4

Method	Chapter: Section
Two Proportions	6: Sample Size estimation for Chi-Squared Tests (Independent Proportions)
Two Means	6: Comparing Values—Example 6
Paired Proportions	6: Sample Size Estimation for McNemar Exact Tests (Matched Proportions)
Paired Means	6: Comparing Values—Example 5
Proportion to Criterion	6: Sample Size for Comparison with a Benchmark Proportion
Mean to Criterion	6: Comparing Values—Example 4
Margin of Error Proportion	6: Sample Size Estimation for Binomial Confidence Intervals
Margin of Error Mean	6: Estimating Values—Examples 1–3
Problem Discovery Sample Size	7: Using a Probabilistic Model of Problem Discovery to Estimate Sample Sizes for Formative User Research
Sample Size for Correlation	10: Sample Size Estimation for *r*
Sample Size for Linear Regression	10: Sample Size Estimation for Linear Regression

To find the appropriate section in each chapter for the methods depicted in Figs. 1.3 and 1.4, consult Table 1.3.

For example, let's say you wanted to compute the appropriate sample size if the same users will rate the usability of two products using a standardized questionnaire that provides a mean score.

1. Because the goal is to compare data, start with the sample size decision map in Fig. 1.3.
2. At the "Comparing or Correlating Data?" box, select Y because you're planning to compare data (rather than exploring their relationship with correlation or regression).
3. At the "Comparing?" box, select "Y" because there will be two groups of data, one for each product.
4. At the "Different Users in each Group?" box, select "N" because each group will have the same users.
5. Because rating-scale data are not binary, select "N" at the "Binary Data?" box.
6. Stop at the "Paired Means" procedure (Chapter 6).

YOU DON'T HAVE TO DO THE COMPUTATIONS BY HAND

We've provided sufficient detail in the formulas and examples that you should be able to do all computations in Microsoft Excel. If you have an existing statistical package like SPSS, Minitab, or SAS, you may find some of the results will differ (like confidence intervals and sample size computations) or they don't include some of the statistical tests we recommend, so be sure to check the notes associated with the procedures.

We've created an Excel calculator that performs all the computations covered in this book. It includes both standard statistical output (*p*-values and confidence intervals) and some more user-friendly output that, for example, reminds you how to interpret that ubiquitous *p*-value and which you can paste right into reports. It is available for purchase online at: www.measuringu.com/products/expandedStats.

For detailed information on how to use the Excel calculator (or a custom set of functions written in the R statistical programming language) to solve the over 100 quantitative examples and exercises that appear in this book, see Lewis and Sauro (2016).

KEY POINTS

- The primary purpose of this book is to provide a statistical resource for those who measure the behavior and attitudes of people as they interact with interfaces.
- Our focus is on methods applicable to practical user research, based on our experience, investigations, and reviews of the latest statistical literature.
- As an aid to the persistent problem of remembering what method to use under what circumstances, this chapter contains four decision maps to guide researchers to the appropriate method and its chapter in this book.

CHAPTER REVIEW QUESTIONS

1. Suppose you need to analyze a sample of task-time data against a specified benchmark. For example, you want to know if the average task time is less than two min. What procedure should you use?
2. Suppose you have some conversion-rate data and you just want to understand how precise the estimate is. For example, in examining the server log data you see 10,000 page views and 55 clicks on a registration button. What procedure should you use?
3. Suppose you're planning to conduct a study in which the primary goal is to compare task completion times for two products, with two independent groups of participants providing the times. Which sample size estimation method should you use?
4. Suppose you're planning to run a formative usability study—one where you're going to watch people use the product you're developing and see what problems they encounter. Which sample size estimation method should you use?

ANSWERS TO CHAPTER REVIEW QUESTIONS

1. Task-time data are continuous (not binary-discrete), so start with the decision map in Fig. 1.1. Because you're testing against a benchmark rather than comparing or correlating groups of data, follow the N path from "Comparing or Correlating Data?" At "Testing Against a Benchmark?", select the Y path. Finally, at "Task Time?", take the Y path, which leads you to "One-Sample *t* (Log)." As shown in Table 1.1, you'll find that method discussed in Chapter 4 in the section "Comparing a Task Time to a Benchmark" section on p. 52.
2. Conversion-rate data are binary-discrete, so start with the decision map in Fig. 1.2. You're just estimating the rate rather than comparing a set of rates, so at "Comparing or Correlating Data," take the N path. At "Testing Against a Benchmark?", also take the N path. This leads you to "Adjusted Wald Confidence Interval," which, according to Table 1.2, is discussed in Chapter 3 in the section "Adjusted-Wald: Add Two Successes and Two Failures" section on p. 22.

3. Because you're planning a comparison of two independent sets of task times, start with the decision map in Fig. 1.3. At "Comparing or Correlating Data?", select the Y path. At "Comparing", select the Y path. At Different Users in each Group?", select the Y path. At "Binary Data?", select the N path. This takes you to "Two Means," which, according to Table 1.3, is discussed in Chapter 6 in the section "Comparing Values—Example 6." See Example 6 on p. 114.
4. For this type of problem discovery evaluation, you're not planning any type of comparison, so start with the decision map in Fig. 1.4. You're not planning to estimate any parameters such as task times or problem occurrence rates, so at "Estimating a Parameter?", take the N path. This leads you to "Problem Discovery Sample Size" which, according to Table 1.3, is discussed in Chapter 7 in the section "Using a Probabilistic Model of Problem Discovery to Estimate Sample Sizes for Formative User Research" section on p. 143.

REFERENCES

Lewis, J.R., Sauro, J., 2016. Excel and R Companion to the Second Edition of "Quantifying the User Experience: Practical Statistics for User Research": Rapid Answers to over 100 Examples and Exercises. Create Space Publishers, Denver.

UXPA., 2014. The User Experience Professionals Association salary survey. Available from: https://uxpa.org/system/files/public/UXPASalarySurvey2014_Final.pdf.

CHAPTER 2

QUANTIFYING USER RESEARCH

WHAT IS USER RESEARCH?

For a topic with only two words, "user research" implies different things to different people. Regarding the "user" in user research, Edward Tufte (Bisbort, 1999) famously said: "Only two industries refer to their customers as 'users': computer design and drug dealing."

This book focuses on the first of those two types of customers. This user can be a paying customer, internal employee, physician, call-center operator, automobile driver, cell-phone owner, or any person attempting to accomplish some goal—typically with some type of software, website, or machine.

The "research" in user research is both broad and nebulous—a reflection of the amalgamation of methods and professionals that fall under its auspices. Robert Schumacher (2010, p. 6) offers one definition:

> *User research is the systematic study of the goals, needs and capabilities of users so as to specify design, construction, or improvement of tools to benefit how users work and live.*

Our concern is less with defining the term and what it covers than with quantifying the behavior of users—which is in the purview of usability professionals, designers, product managers, marketers, and developers.

DATA FROM USER RESEARCH

Although the term user research may eventually fall out of favor, the data that come from user research won't. Throughout this book we will use examples from usability testing, customer surveys, A/B testing, and site visits, with an emphasis on usability testing. Our emphasis on usability testing data is for three reasons.

1. Usability testing remains a central way of determining whether users are accomplishing their goals.
2. Both authors have conducted and written extensively about usability testing.
3. Usability testing uses many of the same metrics as other user research techniques (e.g., completion rates can be found just about everywhere).

Quantifying the User Experience. http://dx.doi.org/10.1016/B978-0-12-802308-2.00002-3

USABILITY TESTING

Usability has an international standard definition in ISO 9241 pt 11 (ISO, 1998), which defined usability as the extent to which a product can be used by specified users to achieve specified goals with effectiveness, efficiency, and satisfaction in a specified context of use. Although there are no specific guidelines on how to measure effectiveness, efficiency, and satisfaction, a large survey of almost 100 summative usability tests (Sauro and Lewis, 2009) reveals what practitioners typically collect. Most tests contain some combination of completion rates, errors, task times, task-level satisfaction, test-level satisfaction, help access, and lists of usability problems (typically including frequency and severity).

There are generally two types of usability tests: finding and fixing usability problems (formative tests) and describing the usability of an application using metrics (summative tests). The terms "formative" and "summative" come from education (Scriven, 1967) where they are used in a similar way to describe tests of student learning (formative—providing immediate feedback to improve learning vs. summative—evaluating what was learned).

The bulk of usability testing is formative. It is often a small-sample qualitative activity where the data take the form of problem descriptions and design recommendations. Just because the goal is to find and fix as many problems as you can does not mean there is no opportunity for quantification. You can quantify the problems in terms of frequency and severity, track which users encountered which problems, measure how long it took them to complete tasks, and determine whether they completed the tasks successfully.

There are typically two types of summative tests: Benchmark and Comparative. The goal of a Benchmark Usability Test is to describe how usable an application is relative to a set of benchmark goals. Benchmark tests provide input on what to fix in an interface and also provide an essential baseline for the comparison of post-design changes.

A Comparative Usability Test, as the name suggests, involves more than one application. This can be a comparison of a current with a prior version of a product or comparison of competing products. In comparative tests, the same users can attempt tasks on all products (within-subjects design) or different sets of users can work with each product (between-subjects design).

SAMPLE SIZES

There is an incorrect perception that sample sizes must be large (typically above 30) to use statistics and interpret quantitative data. We discuss sample sizes extensively in Chapters 6 and 7 and throughout this book show how to reach valid statistical conclusions with sample sizes less than 10. Don't let the size of your sample (even if you have as few as two to five users) preclude you from using statistics to quantify your data and to inform your design decisions.

REPRESENTATIVENESS AND RANDOMNESS

Somewhat related to the issues of sample sizes is that of the makeup of the sample. Often the concern with a small sample size is that the sample isn't "representative" of the parent population. Sample size and representativeness are actually different concepts. You can have a sample size of 5 that is representative of the population and you can have a sample size of 1000 that is not representative. One of the more famous examples of this distinction comes from the 1936 Literary Digest Presidential Poll. The magazine polled its readers on who they intended to vote for and received 2.4 million responses but incorrectly predicted the winner of the presidential election. The problem was not one of sample size but of representativeness. The people who responded tended to be individuals with higher incomes and education levels—not representative of the ultimate voters (see http://en.wikipedia.org/wiki/The_Literary_Digest).

The most important thing in user research, whether the data are qualitative or quantitative, is that the sample of users you measure represents the population about which you intend to make statements. Otherwise, you have no logical basis for generalizing your results from the sample to the population. No amount of statistical manipulation can correct for making inferences about one population if you observe a sample from a different population. Taken to the extreme, it doesn't matter how many men are in your sample if you want to make statements about female education levels or salaries. If you want to gain insight into how to improve the design of snowshoes, it's better to have a sample of 5 Arctic explorers than a sample of 1000 surfers. In practice, this means if you intend to draw conclusions about different types of users (e.g., new versus experienced, older versus younger) you should plan on having all groups represented in your sample.

One reason for the confusion between sample size and representativeness is that if your population is composed of, say, 10 distinct groups and you have a sample of 5, then there aren't enough people in the sample to have a representative from all 10 groups. You would deal with this by developing a sampling plan that ensures drawing a representative sample from every group that you need to study—a method known as stratified sampling. For example, consider sampling from different groups if you have reason to believe:

- There are potential and important differences among groups on key measures (Dickens, 1987).
- There are potential interactions as a function of group (Aykin and Aykin, 1991).
- The variability of key measures differs as a function of group.
- The cost of sampling differs significantly from group to group.

Gordon and Langmaid (1988) recommended the following approach to defining groups:

1. Write down all the important variables.
2. If necessary, prioritize the list.
3. Design an ideal sample.
4. Apply common sense to combine groups.

For example, suppose you start with 24 groups, based on the combination of six demographic locations, two levels of experience, and the two levels of gender. You might plan to (1) include equal numbers of males and females over and under 40 years of age in each group, (2) have separate groups for novice and experienced users, and (3) drop intermediate users from the test. The resulting plan requires sampling for two groups. A plan that did not combine genders and ages would require sampling eight groups.

Ideally your sample is also selected randomly from the parent population. In practice this can be very difficult. Unless you force your users to participate in a study you will likely suffer from at least some form on nonrandomness. In usability studies and surveys, people decide to participate and this group can have different characteristics than people who choose not to participate. This problem isn't unique to user research. Even in clinical trials in which life and death decisions are made about drugs and medical procedures, people with and without the medical condition under study who choose to participate could be different from those who do not choose to do so. Many of the principles of human behavior that fill psychology text books disproportionally come from college undergrads—a potential problem of both randomness and representativeness.

It's always important to understand the biases in your data and how that limits your conclusions. In applied research we are constrained by budgets and user participation but products still must ship, so we make the best decisions we can given the data we are able to collect. Where possible seek to minimize systematic bias in your sample but remember that representativeness is more important than randomness. In other words, you'll make better decisions if you have a less-than-perfectly random sample from the right population than if you have a perfectly random sample from the wrong population.

THREE TYPES OF STUDIES FOR USER RESEARCH

One of the primary goals of conducting user research is to establish some causal relationship between a design and a behavior or attitude (Sauro, 2013). Typically, we want to see if a design element or changes to an interface lead to a more usable experience (experiment) or if more desirable outcomes are associated with some aspect of our designs (correlation). Under the broad umbrella of experimentation, there are three major types of studies: experimental, quasi-experimental, and correlational. The types vary with regard to their internal validity (confidence in the causal relationship between our design and outcome variable) and external validity (confidence that we can extrapolate our findings to real user settings with other users and situations).

Experimental study: The hallmark of this type of study is the random assignment of participants to different treatments. This provides the strongest control against the influence of extraneous variables and, consequently, the highest level of internal validity. Truly random selection from the population of interest also provides the highest level of external validity. But what happens if you cannot randomly assign participants?

Quasi-experimental study: When an experiment is conducted without random assignment, it is quasi-experimental. For example, if you compare perceived usability using an instrument like the System Usability Scale (see Chapter 8) between users of an existing version of a product and those who have chosen to use a beta version, the differences you find could be due to differences in types of people rather than differences in the versions of the product. Due to the confounding of these variables (type of user and product version), the internal validity of the study is relatively weak. For naturally segmented groups, the external validity is relatively strong.

Correlational study: In a correlational study you examine the relationship between two variables, for example, the relationship between perceived usability and likelihood to recommend (LTR). This relationship tends to be strong and positive (people with higher perceived usability tend to provide higher LTR ratings (see the Chapter 8 sidebar "Relationship between the SUS and NPS"). For correlations, the external validity depends on proper selection from the population(s) of interest. The internal validity is quite weak, however, since correlation by itself cannot prove causation. For this example, it is more reasonable to assume that higher perceived usability causes propensity to recommend than the reverse, but it is important to keep this in mind that this you can't claim to have proved causality when all you have is a correlation.

DATA COLLECTION

Usability data can be collected in a traditional lab-based moderated session where a moderator observes and interacts with users as they attempt tasks. Such test setups can be expensive and time consuming and require collocation of users and observers (which can prohibit international testing). These types of studies often require the use of small-sample statistical procedures because the cost of each sample is high.

More recently, remote moderated and unmoderated sessions have become popular. In moderated remote sessions, users attempt tasks on their own computer and software from their location while a moderator observes and records their behavior using screen sharing software. In unmoderated remote sessions, users attempt tasks (usually on websites), while software records their clicks, page views, and time. For an extensive discussion of remote methods see *Beyond the Usability Lab* (Albert et al., 2010).

For a comprehensive discussion of usability testing, see the chapter "Usability Testing" in the *Handbook of Human Factors and Ergonomics* (Lewis, 2012). For practical tips on collecting metrics in usability tests, see *A Practical Guide to Measuring Usability* (Sauro, 2010) and *Measuring the User Experience* (Tullis and Albert, 2013).

In our experience, although the reasons for human behavior are difficult to quantify, the outcome of the behavior is easy to observe, measure, and manage. Following are descriptions of the more common metrics collected in user research, inside and outside of usability tests. We will use these terms extensively throughout the book.

COMPLETION RATES

Completion rates, also called success rates, are the most fundamental of usability metrics (Nielsen, 2001). They are typically collected as a binary measure of task success (coded as a 1) or task failure (coded as 0). You report completion rates on a task by dividing the number of users who successfully complete the task by the total number who attempted it. For example, if eight out of ten users complete a task successfully, the completion rate is 0.8 and usually reported as 80%. You can also subtract the completion rate from 100% and report a failure rate of 20%.

It is possible to define criteria for partial task success, but we prefer the simpler binary measure because it lends itself better for statistical analysis. When we refer to completion rates in this book, we will be referring to binary completion rates.

The other nice thing about a binary rate is that they are used throughout the scientific and statistics literature. Essentially the presence or absence of anything can be coded as 1s and 0s and then reported as a proportion or percentage. Whether this is the number of users completing tasks on software, patients cured from an ailment, number of fish recaptured in a lake, or customers purchasing a product, they can all be treated as binary rates.

USABILITY PROBLEMS (UI PROBLEMS)

If a user encounters a problem while attempting a task and it can be associated with the interface, it's a user interface problem (UI problem). UI problems, typically organized into lists, have names, a description, and often a severity rating that takes into account the observed problem frequency and its impact on the user.

The usual method for measuring the frequency of occurrence of a problem is to divide the number of occurrences within participants by the number of participants. A common technique (Rubin, 1994; Dumas and Redish, 1999) for assessing the impact of a problem is to assign impact scores according to whether the problem (1) prevents task completion, (2) causes a significant delay or frustration, (3) has a relatively minor effect on task performance, or (4) is a suggestion.

Table 2.1 Example of a UI Problem Matrix

	User 1	User 2	User 3	User 4	User 5	User 6	Total	Percent
Problem 1	X	X			X	X	4	0.67
Problem 2	X						1	0.167
Problem 3	X	X	X	X	X	X	6	1
Problem 4				X	X		2	0.33
Problem 5					X		1	0.167
Total	3	2	1	2	4	2	**14**	**p = 0.47**

The Xs represent users who encountered a problem. For example, User 4 encountered problems 3 and 4.

When considering multiple types of data in a prioritization process, it is necessary to combine the data in some way. One approach is to combine the data arithmetically. Rubin (1994) described a procedure for combining four levels of impact (using the criteria described above with 4 assigned to the most serious level) with four levels of frequency (4: frequency ≥ 90%; 3: 51–89%; 2: 11–50%; 1: ≤ 10%) by adding the scores. For example, if a problem had an observed frequency of occurrence of 80% and had a minor effect on performance, its priority would be 5 (a frequency rating of 3 plus an impact rating of 2). With this approach, priority scores can range from a low of 2 to a high of 8.

A similar strategy is to multiply the observed percentage frequency of occurrence by the impact score (Lewis, 2012). The range of priorities depends on the values assigned to each impact level. Assigning 10 to the most serious impact level leads to a maximum priority (severity) score of 1000 (which can optionally be divided by 10 to create a scale that ranges from 1 to 100). Appropriate values for the remaining three impact categories depend on practitioner judgment, but a reasonable set is 5, 3, and 1. Using those values, the problem with an observed frequency of occurrence of 80% and a minor effect on performance would have a priority of 24 (80 × 3/10).

From an analytical perspective, a useful way to organize UI problems is to associate them with the users who encountered them, as shown in Table 2.1.

Knowing the probability with which users will encounter a problem at each phase of development can become a key metric for measuring usability activity impact and ROI. Knowing which user encountered which problem allows you to better predict sample sizes, problem discovery rates, and the number of undiscovered problems (as described in detail in Chapter 7).

TASK TIME

Task time is how long a user spends on an activity. It is most often the amount of time it takes users to successfully complete a predefined task scenario but can be total time on a webpage or call length. It can be measured in milliseconds, seconds, minutes, hours, days, or years and is typically reported as an average (see Chapter 3 for a discussion on handling task-time data). There are many ways of measuring and analyzing task duration:

1. *Task completion time*: Time of users who completed the task successfully.
2. *Time till failure*: Time on task until users give up or complete the task incorrectly.
3. *Total time on task*: The total duration of time users are spending on a task.

ERRORS

Errors are any unintended action, slip, mistake, or omission a user makes while attempting a task. Error counts can go from 0 (no errors) to technically infinity (although it is rare to record more than 20 or so in one task in a usability test). Errors provide excellent diagnostic information on why users are failing tasks and, where possible, are mapped to UI problems. Errors can also be analyzed as binary measures: the user encountered an error (1 = yes) or (0 = no).

SATISFACTION RATINGS

Questionnaires that measure the perception of the ease of use of a system can be completed immediately after a task (post-task questionnaires), at the end of a usability session (post-test questionnaires), or outside of a usability test. Although you can write your own questions for assessing perceived ease of use, your results will likely be more reliable if you use one of the currently available standardized questionnaires (Sauro and Lewis, 2009). See Chapter 8 for a detailed discussion of usability questionnaires.

COMBINED SCORES

Although usability metrics significantly correlate (Sauro and Lewis, 2009), they don't correlate strongly enough that one metric can replace another. In general, users who complete more tasks tend to rate tasks as easier and to complete them more quickly. Some users, however, fail tasks and still rate them as being easy, or others complete tasks quickly and report finding them difficult. Collecting multiple metrics in a usability test is advantageous because this provides a better picture of the overall user experience than any single measure can. However, analyzing and reporting on multiple metrics can be cumbersome, so it can be easier to combine metrics into a single score. A combined usability metric can be treated just like any other metric and can be used advantageously as a component of executive dashboards or for determining statistical significance between products (Chapter 5). For more information on combining usability metrics into single scores see Sauro and Kindlund (2005), Sauro and Lewis (2009), and the "Can You Combine Usability Metrics into Single Scores?" section in Chapter 9.

A/B TESTING

A/B testing, also called split-half testing, is a popular method for comparing alternate designs on web pages. Popularized by Amazon, users randomly work with one of the two deployed design alternatives. The difference in design can be as subtle as different words on a button or a different product image, or can involve entirely different page layouts and product information.

CLICKS, PAGE VIEWS, AND CONVERSION RATES

For websites and web applications, it is typical practice to automatically collect clicks and page views, and in many cases these are the only data you have access to without conducting your own study. Both these measures are useful for determining conversion rates, purchase rates, or feature usage, and are used extensively in A/B testing, typically analyzed like completion rates.

To determine which design is superior, you count the number of users who were presented with each design and the number of users that clicked through. For example, if 1000 users experienced

Design A and 20 clicked on "Sign-Up," and 1050 users saw Design B and 48 clicked "Sign-Up," the conversion rates are 2 and 4.5%, respectively. To learn how to determine if there is a statistical difference between designs, see Chapter 5.

SURVEY DATA

Surveys are one of the easiest ways to collect attitudinal data from customers. Surveys typically contain some combination of open-ended comments, binary yes/no responses, and Likert-type rating scale data.

RATING SCALES

Rating scale items are characterized by closed-ended response options. Typically respondents are asked to agree or disagree to a statement (often referred to as Likert-type items). For numerical analysis, the classic five-choice Likert response options can be converted into numbers from 1 to 5 (as shown in Table 2.2).

Once you've converted the responses to numbers you can compute the mean and standard deviation and generate confidence intervals (Chapter 3) or compare responses to different products (Chapter 5). See Chapter 8 for a detailed discussion of questionnaires and rating scales specific to usability, and the "Is it OK to Average Data from Multipoint Scales?" section in Chapter 9 for a discussion of the arguments for and against computing means and conducting standard statistical tests with this type of data.

NET PROMOTER SCORES

Even though questions about customer loyalty and future purchasing behavior have been around for a long time, a recent innovation is the Net Promoter Question and scoring method used by many companies and in some usability tests (Reichheld, 2003, 2006). The popular Net Promoter Score is based on a single question about customer loyalty: How likely is it that you'll recommend this product to a friend or colleague? The response options range from 0 to 10 and are grouped into three segments:

Promoters: Responses from 9 to 10
Passives: Responses from 7 to 8
Detractors: Responses from 0 to 6

By subtracting the percentage of detractor responses from the percentage of promoter responses you get the Net Promoter Score which ranges from −100% to 100%, with higher numbers indicating a better loyalty score (more promoters than detractors). Although it can be analyzed just like any other rating scale item (using the mean and standard deviation) its segmentation scoring requires slightly different statistical treatments (see Chapters 5 and 8).

Table 2.2 Mapping of the Five Classic Likert Response Options to Numbers

This →	Strongly Disagree	Disagree	Neutral	Agree	Strongly Agree
Becomes This →	1	2	3	4	5

Table 2.3 Example of a UI Behavior Matrix

	User 1	User 2	User 3
Behavior 1	X	X	
Behavior 2	X		
Behavior 3	X	X	X

COMMENTS AND OPEN-ENDED DATA

Analyzing and prioritizing comments is a common task for the user researcher. Open-ended comments take all sorts of forms.

- Reasons why customers are promoters or detractors for a product
- Customer insights from field studies
- Product complaints to calls to customer service
- Why a task was difficult to complete

Just as usability problems can be counted, comments and most open-ended data can be turned into categories, quantified, and subjected to statistical analysis (Sauro, 2011). You can then further analyze the data by generating a confidence interval to understand what percent of all users likely feel this way (See Chapter 3).

REQUIREMENTS GATHERING

Another key function of user research is to identify features and functions of a product. While it's rarely as easy as asking customers what they want, there are methods of analyzing customer behaviors that reveal unmet needs. As shown in Table 2.3, these behaviors can be observed at home or workplace and then quantified in the same way as UI problems. Each behavior gets a name and description, then you record which users exhibited the particular behavior in a grid like the one below.

You can easily report on the percentage of customers who exhibited a behavior and generate confidence intervals around the percentage in the same way you do for binary completion rates (see Chapter 3). You can also apply statistical models of discovery to estimate required sample sizes, requirement discovery rates, and the number of undiscovered requirements (see Chapter 7).

KEY POINTS

- User research is a broad term that encompasses many methodologies that generate quantifiable outcomes, including usability testing, surveys, questionnaires, and site visits.
- Usability testing is a central activity in user research and typically generates the metrics of completion rates, task times, errors, satisfaction data, and user interface problems.

- Binary completion rates are both a fundamental usability metric and a metric applied to all areas of scientific research.
- You can quantify data from small sample sizes and use statistics to draw conclusions.
- Even open-ended comments and problem descriptions can be categorized and quantified.

REFERENCES

Albert, W., Tullis, T., Tedesco, D., 2010. Beyond the Usability Lab. Morgan Kaufmann, Burlington, MA.

Aykin, N.M., Aykin, T., 1991. Individual differences in human–computer interaction. Comput. Ind. Eng. 20, 373–379.

Bisbort, A. (1999). Escaping flatland. Available from: http://www.edwardtufte.com/tufte/advocate_1099

Dickens, J., 1987. The fresh cream cakes market: the use of qualitative research as part of a consumer research programme. In: Bradley, U. (Ed.), Applied Marketing and Social Research. John Wiley, New York, NY, pp. 23–68.

Dumas, J., Redish, J.C., 1999. A Practical Guide to Usability Testing. Intellect, Portland, OR.

Gordon, W., Langmaid, R., 1988. Qualitative Market Research: A Practitioner's and Buyer's Guide. Gower Publishing, Aldershot, Hampshire, England.

ISO, 1998. Ergonomic Requirements for Office Work with Visual Display Terminals (VDTs)—Part 11: Guidance on Usability (ISO 9241-11:1998(E)). Author, Geneva, Switzerland.

Lewis, J.R., 2012. Usability testing. In: Salvendy, G. (Ed.), Handbook of Human Factors and Ergonomics. fourth ed. John Wiley, New York, NY, pp. 1267–1312.

Nielsen, J. (2001). Success rate: The simplest usability metric. Available from: http://www.useit.com/alertbox/20010218.html

Reichheld, F.F., 2003. The one number you need to grow. Harvard Bus. Rev. 81, 46–54.

Reichheld, F., 2006. The Ultimate Question: Driving Good Profits and True Growth. Harvard Business School Press, Boston MA.

Rubin, J., 1994. Handbook of Usability Testing: How to Plan, Design, and Conduct Effective Tests. John Wiley, New York, NY.

Sauro, J., 2010. A Practical Guide to Measuring Usability. Measuring Usability LLC, Denver, CO.

Sauro, J., 2011. How to quantify comments. Available from: http://www.measuringusability.com/blog/quantify-comments.php

Sauro, J., 2013. 4 experiment types for user research. Available from: http://www.measuringu.com/blog/experimenting-ux.php

Sauro, J., Kindlund, E., 2005. A method to standardize usability metrics into a single score. Proceedings of CHI 2005. ACM, Portland, OR, pp. 401–409.

Sauro, J., Lewis, J.R., 2009. Correlations among prototypical usability metrics: evidence for the construct of usability. Proceedings of CHI 2009. ACM, Boston, MA, pp. 1609–1618.

Schumacher, R., 2010. The Handbook of Global User Research. Morgan Kaufmann, Burlington, MA.

Scriven, M., 1967. The methodology of evaluation. In: Tyler, R.W., Gagne, R.M., Scriven, M. (Eds.), Perspectives of Curriculum Evaluation. Rand McNally, Chicago, IL, pp. 39–83.

Tullis, T., Albert, B., 2013. Measuring the User Experience: Collecting, Analyzing, and Presenting Usability Metrics, second ed. Morgan Kaufmann, Waltham, MA.

CHAPTER

HOW PRECISE ARE OUR ESTIMATES? CONFIDENCE INTERVALS

3

INTRODUCTION

In usability testing, like most applied research settings, we almost never have access to the entire user population. Instead we have to rely on taking samples to estimate the unknown population values. If we want to know how long it will take users to complete a task or what percent will complete a task on the first attempt, we need to estimate from a sample. The sample means and sample proportions (called statistics) are estimates of the values we really want—called the population parameters.

When we don't have access to the entire population, even our best estimate from a sample will be close but not exactly right, and the smaller the sample size, the less accurate it will be. We need a way to know how good (precise) our estimates are.

To do so, we construct a range of values that we think will have a specified chance of containing the unknown population parameter. These ranges are called confidence intervals. For example, what is the average time it takes you to commute to work? Assuming you don't telecommute, even your best guess (say 25 min) will be wrong by a few minutes or seconds. It would be more correct to provide an interval. For example, you might say on most days it takes between 20 and 30 min.

CONFIDENCE INTERVAL = TWICE THE MARGIN OF ERROR

If you've seen the results of a poll reported on TV along with a margin of error, then you are already familiar with confidence intervals. Confidence intervals are used just like margins of errors. In fact, a confidence interval is twice the margin of error. If you hear that 57% of likely voters approve of proposed legislation (95% margin of error ±3%) then the confidence interval is six percentage points wide, falling between 54% and 60% (57 − 3% and 57 + 3%).

In the above example, the question was about approval, with voters giving only a binary "approve" or "not-approve" response. It is coded just like a task-completion rate (0's and 1's) and we calculate the margins of errors and confidence intervals in the same way.

CONFIDENCE INTERVALS PROVIDE PRECISION AND LOCATION

A confidence interval provides both a measure of location and precision. That is, we can see that the average approval rating is around 57%. We can also see that this estimate is reasonably precise. If we want to know whether the majority of voters approve the legislation we can see that it is very unlikely (less than a 2.5% chance) that fewer than half the voters approve. Precision, of course, is relative. If another poll has a margin of error of ±2%, it would be more precise (and have a narrower confidence interval),

Quantifying the User Experience. http://dx.doi.org/10.1016/B978-0-12-802308-2.00003-5

whereas a poll with a margin of error of 10% would be less precise (and have a wider confidence interval). Few user researchers will find themselves taking surveys about attitudes toward government. The concept and math performed on these surveys, however, is exactly the same as when we construct confidence intervals around completion rates.

THREE COMPONENTS OF A CONFIDENCE INTERVAL

Three things affect the width of a confidence interval: the confidence level, the variability of the sample, and the sample size.

Confidence level

The confidence level is the "advertised coverage" of a confidence interval—the "95%" in a 95% confidence interval. This part is often left off of margin of error reports in television polls. A confidence level of 95% (the typical value) means that if you were to sample from the same population 100 times, you'd expect the interval to contain the actual mean or proportion 95 times. In reality the actual coverage of a confidence interval dips above and below the nominal confidence level (discussed later). Although a researcher can choose a confidence level of any value between 0% and 100%, it is usually set to 95% or 90%.

Variability

If there is more variation in a population, each sample taken will fluctuate more and therefore create a wider confidence interval. The variability of the population is estimated using the standard deviation from the sample.

Sample size

Without lowering the confidence level, the sample size is the only thing a researcher can control in affecting the width of a confidence interval. The confidence interval width and sample size have an inverse square root relationship. This means if you want to cut your margin of error in half, you need to quadruple your sample size. For example, if your margin of error is ±20% at a sample size of 20 you'd need a sample size of approximately 80 to have a margin of error of ±10%.

CONFIDENCE INTERVAL FOR A COMPLETION RATE

One of the most fundamental of usability metrics is whether a user can complete a task. It is usually coded as a binary response: 1 for a successful attempt and 0 for an unsuccessful attempt. We saw how this has the same form as many surveys and polls that have only yes or no responses. When we watch ten users attempt a task and eight of them are able to successfully complete it, we have a sample completion rate of 0.80 (called a proportion) or, expressed as a percent, 80%.

If we were somehow able to measure all our users, or even just a few thousand of them, it is extremely unlikely that exactly 80% of all users would be able to complete the task. To know the likely range of the actual unknown population completion rate, we need to compute a binomial confidence interval around the sample proportion. There is a strong agreement on the importance of using confidence intervals in research. Until recently, however, there was not a terribly good way of computing binomial confidence intervals for small sample sizes.

CONFIDENCE INTERVAL HISTORY

It isn't necessary to go through the history of a statistic to use it, but we'll spend some time on the history of the binomial confidence interval for three reasons:

1. They are used very frequently in applied research.
2. They are covered in every statistics text (and you might even recall one formula).
3. There have been some relatively new developments in the statistics literature.

As we go through some of the different ways to compute binomial confidence intervals, keep in mind that statistical confidence means confidence in the method of constructing the interval—not confidence in a specific interval.

One of the first uses of confidence intervals was to estimate binary success rates (like the one used for completion rates). It was proposed by Simon Laplace 200 years ago (Laplace, 1812) and is still commonly taught in introductory statistics textbooks. It takes the following form:

$$\hat{p} \pm z_{\left(1-\frac{\alpha}{2}\right)}\sqrt{\frac{\hat{p}(1-\hat{p})}{n}}$$

where $\hat{p}$ is the sample proportion,
n is the sample size, and
$z_{\left(1-\frac{\alpha}{2}\right)}$ is the critical value from the normal distribution for the level of confidence (1.96 for 95% confidence).

For example, if we observe 7 out of 10 users completing a task, we get the following 95% confidence interval around our sample completion rate of 70% (7/10).

$$0.70 \pm 1.96\sqrt{\frac{0.70(1-0.70)}{10}} = 0.70 \pm 1.96\sqrt{0.021} = 0.70 \pm 0.28$$

According to this formula, we can be 95% confident that the actual population completion rate is somewhere between 42% and 98%. Despite Laplace's original use, it has come to be known as the Wald interval, named after the 20th century statistician Abraham Wald.

WALD INTERVAL: TERRIBLY INACCURATE FOR SMALL SAMPLES

The problem with the Wald interval is that it is terribly inaccurate at small sample sizes (less than about 100) or when the proportion is close to 0 or 1—conditions that are very common with small sample usability data and in applied research. Instead of containing the actual proportion 95 times out of 100, it contains it far less, often as low as 50–60% of the time (Agresti and Coull, 1998). In other words, when you think you're reporting a 95% confidence interval using the Wald method, it is more likely a 70% confidence interval. Because this problem is greatest with small sample sizes and when the proportion is far from 0.50, most introductory texts recommend large sample sizes to compute this confidence interval (usually at least 30). This recommendation also contributes to the widely held but incorrect notion that you need large sample sizes to use inferential statistics. As usability practitioners, we know that we often do not have the luxury of large sample sizes, but we also know that large sample sizes are not always required.

EXACT CONFIDENCE INTERVAL

Over the years there have been proposals to make confidence interval formulas more precise for all sample sizes and all ranges of the proportion. A class of confidence intervals known as exact intervals works well for even small sample sizes (Clopper and Pearson, 1934) and have been discussed in the usability literature (Lewis, 1996; Sauro, 2004). Exact intervals have two drawbacks: They tend to be overly conservative and are computationally intense, as shown in the Clopper–Pearson formula:

$$\left[1+\frac{n-x+1}{xF_{2x,2(n-x+1),1-\alpha/2}}\right]^{-1} < p < \left[1+\frac{n-x}{(x+1)F_{2(x+1),2(n-x),\alpha/2}}\right]^{-1}$$

For the same 7 out of 10 completion rate, an exact 95% confidence interval ranges from 35% to 93%.

As was seen with the Wald interval, a stated confidence level of, say 95%, is no guarantee of an interval actually containing the proportion 95% of the time. Exact intervals are constructed in a way that guarantees that the confidence interval provides AT LEAST 95% coverage. To achieve that goal, however, exact intervals tend to be overly conservative, containing the population proportion closer to 99 times out of 100 (as opposed to the nominal 95 times out of 100). In other words, when you think you're reporting a 95% confidence interval using an exact method, it is more likely a 99% interval. The result is an unnecessarily wide interval. This is especially the case when sample sizes are small, as they are in most usability tests.

ADJUSTED-WALD: ADD TWO SUCCESSES AND TWO FAILURES

Another approach to computing confidence intervals, known as the Score or Wilson interval, tends to strike a good balance between the exact and Wald in terms of actual coverage (Wilson, 1927). Its major drawback is it is rather tedious to compute and is not terribly well known, so it is thus often left out of introductory statistics texts. Recently, a simple alternative based on the work originally reported by Wilson, named the adjusted-Wald method by Agresti and Coull (1998), simply requires, for 95% confidence intervals, the addition of two successes and two failures to the observed number of successes and failures, and then uses the well-known Wald formula to compute the 95% binomial confidence interval.

Research (Agresti and Coull, 1998; Sauro and Lewis, 2005) has shown that the adjusted-Wald provides good coverage for most values of the sample completion rate (denoted $\hat{p}$), even when the completion rate approaches 0 or 1. The "add two successes and two failures" (or adding 2 to the numerator and 4 to the denominator) is derived from the critical value of the normal distribution for 95% intervals (1.96, which is approximately 2 and, when squared, is about 4).

$$\hat{p}_{\text{adj}} = \frac{x+\frac{z^2}{2}}{n+z^2} = \frac{x+\frac{1.96^2}{2}}{n+1.96^2} = \frac{x+1.92}{n+3.84} \approx \frac{x+2}{n+4}$$

where x is the number who successfully completed the task, and
n is the number who attempted the task (the sample size).

We find it easier to think of and explain this adjustment by rounding up to the whole numbers (2 successes and 2 failures) but since we almost always use software to compute confidence intervals we use the more precise 1.96 in the subsequent examples. Unless you're doing the computations on the back of napkin (see Fig. 3.1), we recommend using 1.96—it will also make the transition easier when

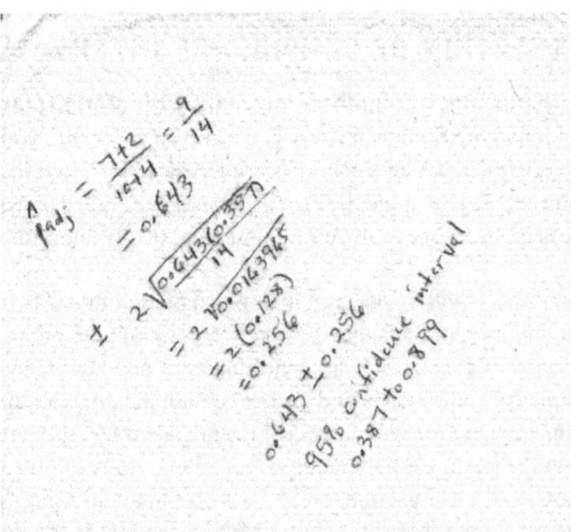

FIGURE 3.1 Back of Napkin Adjusted-Wald Binomial Confidence Interval

you need to use a different level of confidence than 95% (e.g., a 90% confidence level uses 1.64 and a 99% confidence level uses 2.57).

The standard Wald formula is updated with the new adjusted values of $\hat{p}_{\text{adj}}$ and n_{adj}.

$$\hat{p}_{\text{adj}} \pm z_{\left(1-\frac{\alpha}{2}\right)}\sqrt{\frac{\hat{p}_{\text{adj}}\left(1-\hat{p}_{\text{adj}}\right)}{n_{\text{adj}}}}$$

For example, if we compute a 95% adjusted-Wald interval for 7 out of 10 users completing a task, we first compute the adjusted proportion ($\hat{p}_{\text{adj}}$):

$$\hat{p}_{\text{adj}} = \frac{7+\frac{1.96^2}{2}}{10+1.96^2} = \frac{7+1.92}{10+3.84} = \frac{8.92}{13.84} = 0.645$$

Then substitute the adjusted proportion $\hat{p}_{\text{adj}}$ and the adjusted sample size n_{adj} into the Wald equation:

$$0.645 \pm 1.96\sqrt{\frac{0.645\ (1-0.645\ )}{13.84}} = 0.645 \pm 1.96\sqrt{0.0165} = \ 0.645 \pm 0.25$$

If 7 out of 10 users complete a task we can be 95% confident the actual completion rate is between 39% and 90% (pretty close to the back-of-napkin estimate in Fig. 3.1). Table 3.1 shows the intervals for all three methods.

Table 3.1 Comparison of Three Methods for Computing Binomial Confidence Intervals

CI Method	Low (%)	High (%)	Interval Width (%)	Comment
Wald	42	98	57	Inaccurate
Exact	35	93	59	Too wide
Adjusted-Wald	39	90	50	Just right

All computations performed at measuringu.com/wald.htm

ON THE STRICT INTERPRETATION OF CONFIDENCE INTERVALS

What you need to know when discussing confidence intervals with statisticians

We love confidence intervals. You should use them whenever you can. When you do, you should watch out for some conceptual hurdles. In general you should know that a confidence interval will tell you the most likely range of the unknown population mean or proportion. For example, if 7 out of 10 users complete a task, the 95% confidence interval is 39% to 90%. If we were able to measure everyone in the user population, this is our best guess as to the percent of users that can complete the task.

It is incorrect to say "There is a 95% *probability* the population completion rate is between 39% and 90%." While we (Jeff and Jim) will understand what you mean, others may be quick to point out the problem with that statement.

We are 95% confident *in the method* of generating confidence intervals and not in any given interval. The confidence interval we generated from the sample data either does or does not contain the population completion rate. If we ran 100 tests each with 10 users from the same population and computed confidence intervals each time, on average 95 of those 100 confidence intervals will contain the unknown population completion rate. We don't know if the one sample of 10 we had is one of those 5 that doesn't contain the completion rate. So it's best to avoid using "probability" or "chance" when describing a confidence interval and remember that we're 95% or 99% confident in the process of generating confidence intervals and not any given interval. Another way to interpret a confidence interval is to use Smithson's (2003, p. 177) plausibility terminology: "Any value inside the interval could be said to be a plausible value; those outside the interval could be called implausible."

Because it provides the most accurate confidence intervals over time, we recommend the adjusted-Wald interval for binomial confidence intervals for all sample sizes. At small sample sizes the adjustment makes a major improvement in accuracy. For larger sample sizes the effect of the adjustment has little impact but does no harm. For example, at a sample size of 500, adding two successes and two failures has much less of an impact on the calculation than when the sample size is 5.

There is one exception to our recommendation. If you *absolutely* must guarantee that your interval will contain the population completion rate no less than 95% of the time (or whatever level of confidence you have specified), then use the exact method.

BEST POINT ESTIMATES FOR A COMPLETION RATE

With small sample sizes in usability testing it is a common occurrence to have either all participants complete a task or all participants fail (100% and 0% completion rates). Although it is always possible that every single user will complete a task or every user will fail it, it is more likely when the estimate comes from a small sample size. In our experience such claims of absolute task success also tend to make stakeholders dubious of the small sample size. While the sample proportion is often the best estimate of the population completion rate, we have found some conditions where other estimates tend to be slightly better (Lewis and Sauro, 2006). Two other noteworthy estimates of the completion rate are:

- Laplace method: Add one success and one failure
- Wilson method: Add two successes and two failures (used as part of the adjusted-Wald interval).

Guidelines on reporting the best completion rate estimate

If you find yourself needing the best possible point estimate of the population completion rate consider the following rules on what to report (in addition to the confidence interval):

If you conduct usability tests in which your task completion rates typically take a wide range of values, uniformly distributed between 0% and 100%, then you should use the Laplace method. The smaller your sample size and the farther your initial estimate of the population completion rate is from 50%, the more you will improve your estimate of the actual completion rate.

If you conduct usability tests in which your task completion rates are roughly restricted to the range of 50–100% (the more common situation in usability testing), then the best estimation method depends on the value of the sample completion rate:

If the sample completion rate is:

1. *Less than or equal to 50%*: Use the Wilson method (which you get as part of the process of computing an adjusted-Wald binomial confidence interval).
2. *Between 50% and 90%*: Stick with reporting the sample proportion. Any attempt to improve on it is as likely to decrease as to increase the estimate's accuracy.
3. *Greater than 90% but less than 100%*: Apply the Laplace method. DO NOT use Wilson in this range to estimate the population completion rate, even if you have computed a 95% adjusted-Wald confidence interval.
4. *Equal to 100%*: Use the Laplace method.

Always use an adjustment when sample sizes are small ($n < 20$). It does no harm to use an adjustment when sample sizes are larger. Keep in mind that even these guidelines will only slightly improve the accuracy of your estimate of the completion rate, so this is no substitution for computing and reporting confidence intervals.

How accurate are point estimates from small samples?

Even the best point estimate from a sample will differ by some amount from the actual population completion rate. To get an idea of the typical amount of error, we created a Monte Carlo simulator. The simulator compared thousands of small sample estimates to an actual population completion rate. At a sample size of five, on average, the completion rate differed by around 11 percentage points from the population completion rate. Seventy-five percent of the time the completion differed by less than 21 percentage points (see www.measuringu.com/blog/memory-math.php).

The results of this simulation tell us that even a very small sample completion rate isn't useless even though the width of the 95% confidence interval is rather wide (typically 30+ percentage points). But given any single sample you can't know ahead of time how accurate your estimate is. The confidence interval will provide a definitive range of plausible values. From a practical perspective, keep in mind that the values in the middle of the interval are more likely than those near the edges. If 95% confidence intervals are too wide to support decision making, then it is may be appropriate to lower the confidence level to 90% or 80%. See "What are reasonable criteria" in Chapter 6 for a discussion of appropriate statistical criteria for industrial decision making.

CONFIDENCE INTERVAL FOR A PROBLEM OCCURRENCE

The adjusted-Wald binomial confidence interval is one of the researcher's most useful tools. Any measure that can be coded as binary can benefit from this confidence interval. In addition to a completion rate, another common measure of usability is the number of users likely to encounter a problem.

Even in primarily qualitative formative usability tests, simple counts of user-interface problems are taken. For example, 3 out of 5 users might experience the same problem with a design. Understanding the actual percent of users affected by the problem can guide the prioritization of problems and reduce some of the skepticism that comes with small sample sizes.

Using the adjusted-Wald formula, if 3 out 5 users experience a problem with a design, we can be 95% confident between 23% and 88% of all users are likely to experience the same problem. Although there is more uncertainty with small samples (the interval in this example is 65 percentage points wide), the confidence interval is still very informative. Specifically, it tells us we can be fairly certain that, if left uncorrected, one-fifth or more of all users would encounter the problem.

CONFIDENCE INTERVAL FOR RATING SCALES AND OTHER CONTINUOUS DATA

The best approach for constructing a confidence interval around numeric rating scales is to compute the mean and standard deviation of the responses then use the *t*-distribution. If you're used to treating rating scale responses as discrete frequencies see Chapter 9 ("Is it OK to average data from multipoint scales?"). The *t*-distribution is like the normal (also called *z*-distribution) except that it takes the sample size into account. With smaller sample sizes, our estimate of the population variance is rather crude and will fluctuate more from sample to sample. The *t*-distribution adjusts for how good our estimate is by making the intervals wider as the sample sizes get smaller. As the sample size increases (especially at or above a sample size of 30), the *t*-confidence interval converges on the normal *z*-confidence interval. After a sample size exceeds 100 or so, the difference between confidence intervals using the *z* and *t* is only a fraction of a point. In other words, the *t*-distribution will provide the best interval regardless of your sample size, so we recommend using it for all sample sizes.

The *t*-confidence interval takes the following form:

$$\bar{x} \pm t_{\left(1-\frac{\alpha}{2}\right)} \frac{s}{\sqrt{n}}$$

where $\bar{x}$ is the sample mean,
n is the sample size,
s is the sample standard deviation, and
$t_{\left(1-\frac{\alpha}{2}\right)}$ is the critical value from the *t*-distribution for $n-1$ degrees of freedom and the specified level of confidence.

The confidence interval formula can appear intimidating. A simplified way of thinking about it is to think of the confidence interval as two margins of error around the mean. The margin of error is approximately two standard errors, and the standard error is how much we expect sample means to fluctuate given the sample size (Fig. 3.2).

To construct the interval, we need the mean, standard error, sample size, and critical value from the *t*-distribution, using the appropriate value of *t* for our sample size and desired confidence level. We can obtain the mean and standard deviation from our sample data.

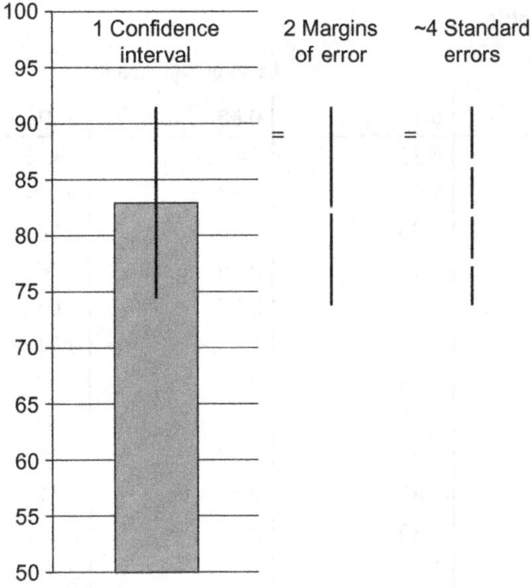

FIGURE 3.2 Diagram of Confidence Interval

Example 1

For example, let's use the following scores from the System Usability Scale (SUS), collected when users rated the usability of a CRM application.

$$90, 77.5, 72.5, 95, 62.5, 57.5, 100, 95, 95, 80, 82.5, 87.5$$

From this data we can generate the three basic ingredients needed to generate the *t*-confidence interval.

Mean: 82.9
Standard deviation: 13.5
Sample size: 12

The standard error is our estimate of how much the average sample means will fluctuate around the true population mean. It is the standard deviation divided by the square root of the sample size:

$$\text{Standard error} = \frac{s}{\sqrt{n}} = \frac{13.5}{\sqrt{12}} = 3.9$$

In a normal distribution, we'd expect 95% of sample means to fall within 1.96 standard errors of the mean (see the Crash Course in the Appendix for a refresher on this relationship). The standard error is the same thing as the standard deviation of the sampling distribution of means. It is called the standard error to differentiate it from the standard deviation of the raw data and remind us that every sample mean has some error in estimating the population mean.

Because our sample size is fairly small, 95% of sample means will actually fluctuate *more* than two standard errors. The exact number depends on our sample size, found by looking up values from the

Table 3.2 Abbreviated *t*-table

	Level of Significance				
df	0.2	0.1	0.05	0.01	0.001
1	3.08	6.31	12.71	63.66	636.62
2	1.89	2.92	4.30	9.92	31.60
3	1.64	2.35	3.18	5.84	12.92
4	1.53	2.13	2.78	4.60	8.61
5	1.48	2.02	2.57	4.03	6.87
6	1.44	1.94	2.45	3.71	5.96
7	1.41	1.89	2.36	3.50	5.41
8	1.40	1.86	2.31	3.36	5.04
9	1.38	1.83	2.26	3.25	4.78
10	1.37	1.81	2.23	3.17	4.59
11	1.36	1.80	2.20	3.11	4.44
12	1.36	1.78	2.18	3.05	4.32
13	1.35	1.77	2.16	3.01	4.22
14	1.35	1.76	2.14	2.98	4.14
15	1.34	1.75	2.13	2.95	4.07

t-distribution in a statistics text book, the Excel function = TINV(0.05,11) or the online calculator at: *www.usablestats.com/calcs/tinv*.

To find the *t*-critical value, we need alpha and the degrees of freedom. Alpha is the Greek symbol for the level of significance used in the study, typically 0.05. It is also one minus the confidence level, which is typically 95% (1−0.95 = 0.05).

The degrees of freedom (df) for this type of confidence interval is the sample size minus 1 (12−1 = 11). Below (Table 3.2) is an abbreviated *t*-table similar to ones you would find in a textbook. We first find 11 df and move to the right in the table until we reach our desired significance level (0.05).

We find the critical value of 2.20. Such a result is typically written as ($t_{0.05}$, 11) = 2.20. It tells us at a sample size of 12 we can expect 95% of sample means to fall within 2.2 standard deviations of the population mean. We then express this as the margin of error:

$$\text{Margin of error} = 2.2\frac{s}{\sqrt{n}} = 2.2 \times 3.9 = 8.6$$

The confidence interval is twice the margin of error, with upper and lower bounds computed by adding it to and subtracting it from our sample mean.

$$\text{Confidence interval} = 82.9 - 8.6 \text{ to } 82.9 + 8.6$$
$$= 74.3 \text{ to } 91.5$$

Thus, we can be 95% confident that the true score is between 74.3 and 91.5.

Example 2

Fifteen users were asked to find information about a Mutual Fund on a Financial Services company website. After attempting the task, users answered a single 7-point Likert question about how difficult the task was. A rating of 1 corresponds to the response "Very Difficult" and a 7 "Very Easy".

The responses were:

$$3, 5, 3, 7, 1, 6, 2, 5, 1, 1, 3, 2, 6, 2, 2$$

From this data, we can generate the three basic ingredients we need to generate the *t*-confidence interval.

Mean: 3.27
Standard deviation: 2.02
Sample size: 15

The critical value from the *t*-distribution is ($t_{0.05}$, 14) = 2.14. Plugging the values in the formula, we get:

$$\bar{x} \pm t_{\left(1-\frac{\alpha}{2}\right)} \frac{s}{\sqrt{n}} = 3.27 \pm 2.14 \frac{2.02}{\sqrt{15}} = 3.27 \pm 1.1$$

Thus, we can be 95% confident that the population rating on this question is between 2.2 and 4.4.

CONFIDENCE INTERVAL FOR TASK-TIME DATA

Measuring time on task is a good way to assess task performance. Although it is an ideal continuous metric because it can be measured at very small increments, there is a complication with task time. Users cannot take any less than a fraction of a second to complete a typical usability task, but can take many minutes or hours, so task-time data has a tendency to be positively skewed (see Fig. 3.3).

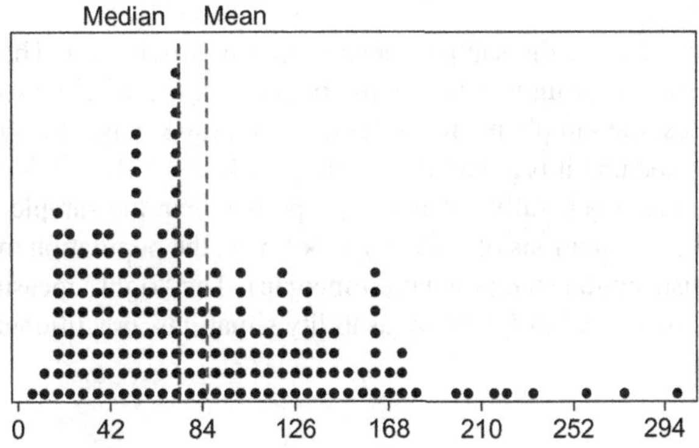

FIGURE 3.3 Positively Skewed Task-Time Data

Sample task from an unattended usability test with 192 users who completed the task. The median is 71 and the arithmetic mean is 84.

Confidence intervals, like many statistical procedures, assume the underlying data has at least an approximately symmetrical distribution. Fig. 3.3 shows a nonsymmetrical distribution, so the mean is no longer a good measure of the center of the distribution. A few long task times have a strong pull on the mean, and for positively skewed data, the mean will always be higher than the center. Before we consider computing the best confidence interval around task time averages, we need to discuss the best average time.

MEAN OR MEDIAN TASK TIME?

Up to this point we've been using the arithmetic mean as the measure of central tendency for rating scale data and referring to it as the average. The confidence intervals are providing the most likely boundary of the population mean. For many positively skewed datasets like home-prices or employee salaries, the median is a better measure of the center. By definition, the median provides the center point of the data—the point at which half the values are above the point and half are below. We suspect this is what most practitioners are trying to get at when they report an "average" task time.

For example, the task times of 100, 101, 102, 103, and 104 have a mean and median of 102. Adding an additional task time of 200 skews the distribution, making the mean 118.33 and the median 102.5.

It would seem that using the median would be the obvious choice for reporting the average task time, and this is indeed what many textbooks teach and what many practitioners do. There are, however, two major drawbacks to the median: variability and bias.

Variability

The strength of the median in resisting the influence of extreme values is also its weakness. The median doesn't use all the information available in a sample. For odd samples, the median is the central value; for even samples, it's the average of the two central values. Consequently, the medians of samples drawn from a continuous distribution are more variable than their means (Blalock, 1972). The increased variability of the median relative to the mean is amplified when sample sizes are small because with the introduction of each new value, the median can jump around a lot. Even though the underlying distribution is continuous, the sample values are not—they are essentially discrete.

Bias

One of the desirable properties of the sample mean is that it is unbiased. That is, any sample mean is just as likely to overestimate or underestimate the population mean. The median doesn't share this property. At small samples, the sample median of completion times tends to consistently overestimate the population median—meaning it is a biased statistic (Cordes, 1993).

Although the sample mean generally has better properties than the sample median, we know that due to the skewness of the distributions of usability task times, the population mean will be larger than the center value of the distribution (the population median). The "right" measure of central tendency depends on the research question, but for many usability situations, practitioners want to estimate the center of the distribution.

GEOMETRIC MEAN

To find the best estimate of the middle task time for small sample usability data, we conducted an analysis of several alternatives for average task times (such as the arithmetic mean, median, geometric

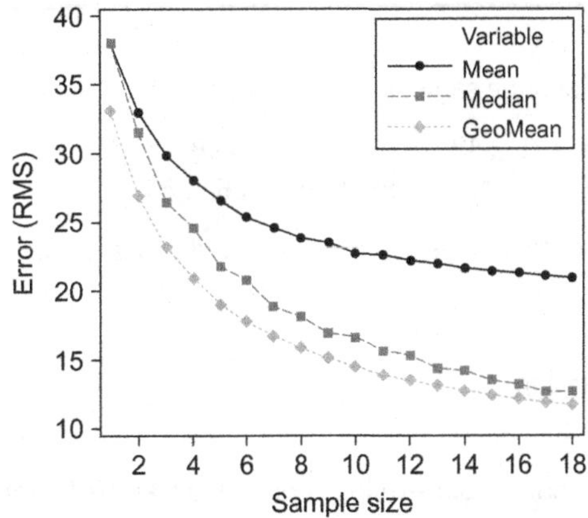

FIGURE 3.4 Comparison of Central Tendency of Mean, Median, and Geometric Mean for Task-Time Data as a Function of Sample Size

mean, and trimmed means). We used a large set of usability tasks and found the geometric mean to be a better estimate of the center than any of the other types of averages we assessed, including the sample median (Sauro and Lewis, 2010). For sample sizes less than 25, the geometric mean has less error and bias than the median or mean (see Fig. 3.4). Because this average is not familiar to most usability practitioners, we explain it in more detail below.

Computing the geometric mean

To find the geometric mean, first convert raw task times using a log-transformation, find the mean of the transformed values, and then convert back to the original scale by exponentiating. The log-transformation can be done using the Excel function =LN(), using the ln button on most hand calculators, or using the web calculator at: www.measuringu.com/time_intervals.php.

For example, the following ten raw task times: 94, 95, 96, 113, 121, 132, 190, 193, 255, 298 get transformed into the log values: 4.54, 4.55, 4.56, 4.73, 4.80, 4.88, 5.25, 5.26, 5.54, 5.70. The arithmetic mean of these log values is 4.98. We can then exponentiate this value using the Excel function =EXP() or the e^x button on a calculator to get the geometric mean of 146 s.

The raw times have an arithmetic mean of 159 s and median of 127 s. Over time the geometric mean will be the better estimate of the center for sample sizes less than around 25. For larger sample sizes, the sample median will be a better estimate of the population median. When possible, we recommend that practitioners use the geometric mean with small samples along with the confidence intervals around this average, computing the upper and lower bounds using the transformed data, then exponentiating those bounds to get back to the original time scale.

Log transforming confidence intervals for task-time data

We can also generate the confidence intervals for task times using the log-values. Once the data have been converted to their logs, we use the same procedure we did for confidence intervals around rating scale data, and then transform the data back to the original scale.

$$\bar{x}_{\log} \pm t_{\left(1-\frac{\alpha}{2}\right)} \frac{s_{\log}}{\sqrt{n}}$$

Example 1

Here are raw completion times and the same times expressed as their natural log:

Raw times: 94, 95, 96, 113, 121, 132, 190, 193, 255, 298
Log times: 4.54, 4.55, 4.56, 4.73, 4.80, 4.88, 5.25, 5.26, 5.54, 5.70

Next we follow the same steps to find the standard error and critical value from the *t*-distribution to generate the margin of error.

Mean of the logs: 4.98
Standard deviation of logs: 0.426
Sample size: 10

We use the standard deviation and sample size to generate the standard error of the mean (our estimate of how much sample means will vary at this sample size).

$$\text{Standard error} = \frac{s}{\sqrt{n}} = \frac{0.426}{\sqrt{10}} = 0.135$$

We look up the critical value from the *t*-distribution for 9 df (10−1) and get ($t_{0.05}$, 9) = 2.26. Next we plug in our values to get the margin of error.

$$\text{Margin of error} = 2.26\ \frac{s}{\sqrt{n}} = 2.26 \times 0.135 = 0.305$$

The confidence interval is twice the margin of error and is expressed by adding and subtracting it from the log-mean.

$$\text{Log confidence interval} = 4.98 - 0.305 \text{ to } 4.98 + 0.305$$
$$= 4.68 \text{ to } 5.29$$

The final step is to convert this log-confidence interval back to the original scale by exponentiating the values.

$$\text{Confidence interval} = e^{(4.68)} \text{ to } e^{(5.29)}$$
$$= 108 \text{ to } 198 \text{ s}$$

We can then be 95% confident the population *median* task time is between 108 and 198 s.

Example 2

The following eleven task times come from users who completed a task in a contact-manager software program:

Raw times: 40, 36, 53, 56, 110, 48, 34, 44, 30, 40, 80
Log times: 3.689, 3.584, 3.970, 4.025, 4.700, 3.871, 3.526, 3.784, 3.401, 3.689, 4.382
Mean of the logs: 3.87
Standard deviation of logs: 0.384
Sample size: 11

The critical value from the t-distribution is ($t_{0.05}$, 10) = 2.23.

$$\bar{x}_{\log} \pm t_{\left(1-\frac{\alpha}{2}\right)} \frac{s_{\log}}{\sqrt{n}} = 3.87 \pm 2.23 \frac{0.384}{\sqrt{11}} = 3.87 \pm 0.258$$

$$\begin{aligned}\text{Log confidence interval} &= 3.87 - 0.258 \text{ to } 3.87 + 0.258\\ &= 3.62 \text{ to } 4.13\\ &= e^{(3.62)} \text{ to } e^{(4.13)}\\ &= 37 \text{ to } 62 \text{ s}\end{aligned}$$

We can then be 95% confident the population *median* task time is between 37 and 62 s.

CONFIDENCE INTERVAL FOR LARGE SAMPLE TASK TIMES

As the sample size gets larger (especially above 25) the sample median does a better job of estimating the population median and should be used as the best average task time (Fig. 3.4). For large sample task times it also makes sense to compute a confidence interval around the median. The procedure for doing this is explained in the next section.

CONFIDENCE INTERVAL AROUND A MEDIAN

Certain types of data such as task times, reaction times or salary data tend to be skewed and the median tends to be a better estimate of the middle value than the mean. For small sample task-time data the geometric mean estimates the population median better than the sample median. As sample sizes get larger (especially above 25) the median tends to be the best estimate of the middle value.

When providing the median as the estimate of the average you should also include confidence intervals. The computations for a confidence interval around the median involve more than just inserting the median in place of the mean.

As with all confidence interval formulas there are a number of ways to compute them. Below is a method that uses the binomial distribution to estimate the intervals and should work well for most large sample situations.

The median is the point where 50% of values are above a value and 50% are below it. We can think of it as being at the 50th percentile. The point where 25% of values fall below a point is called the 25th percentile (also the 1st quartile) and the 75th percentile is higher than 75% of all values (the 3rd quartile).

The following formula constructs a confidence interval around any percentile. The median (0.5) would be the most common but it could also be used with any percentile such as 0.05, 0.97, or 0.25.

$$np \pm z_{\left(1-\frac{\alpha}{2}\right)} \sqrt{np(1-p)}$$

where n is the sample size,
p is the percentile expressed as a proportion (0.5 for the median),
$z_{\left(1-\frac{\alpha}{2}\right)}$ is the critical value from the normal distribution (1.96 for a 95% confidence level), and
$\sqrt{np(1-p)}$ is the standard error.

The results of the equation are rounded up to the next integer and the boundary of the confidence interval is between the two values in the ordered dataset.

Example 1

The following task times come from 30 users who successfully completed a task in a desktop accounting package:

167	158	136
124	77	317
85	65	120
136	80	186
110	95	109
330	96	116
76	100	248
57	122	96
173	115	137
76	152	149

The median task time is 118 s. The 95% confidence interval around the median is

$$np \pm Z_{\left(1-\frac{\alpha}{2}\right)}\sqrt{np(1-p)}$$
$$= 30(0.5) \pm 1.96\sqrt{30 \times 0.5(1-0.5)}$$
$$= 15 \pm 1.96 \times 2.74$$
$$= 15 \pm 5.36 = 9.63 \text{ and } 20.37 = 10 \text{ to } 21$$

So we need to find the 10th and 21st value (given in bold) in our ordered dataset

57	100	**137**
65	109	149
76	110	152
76	115	158
77	116	167
80	120	173
85	122	186
95	124	248
96	136	317
96	136	330

The 95% confidence interval around the median of 118 s ranges from 96 to 137 s.

Example 2

The following task times come from 27 users who successfully completed a task in a desktop accounting package. Arranged from the shortest to longest times, they are:

82	118	141
96	118	150
100	127	161
104	132	178
105	133	201
110	134	201
111	134	211
117	139	223
118	141	256

The median task time for these 27 users is 133 s.

$$np \pm z_{\left(1-\frac{\alpha}{2}\right)}\sqrt{np(1-p)}$$
$$= 27(0.5) \pm 1.96\sqrt{27 \times 0.5(1-0.5)}$$
$$= 13.5 \pm 1.96 \times 2.6$$
$$= 13.5 \pm 5.1 = 8.4 \text{ and } 18.6 = \text{the 9th and 19th times}$$

The 95% confidence interval around the median of 133 s ranges from 118 to 141 s.

KEY POINTS

- Due to sampling error, even the best point estimate from a sample will usually be wrong.
- You should use confidence intervals around all point estimates to understand the most likely range of the unknown population mean or proportion.
- Computing a confidence interval requires four things: an estimate of the mean, an estimate of the variability (derived from the sample standard deviation), the desired confidence level (typically 95%) and the sample size.
- Use the adjusted-Wald binomial confidence interval for completion rates. For rough estimates of 95% adjusted-Wald binomial confidence intervals, add 2 successes and 2 failures to the observed completion rate.
- For satisfaction data using rating scales use the *t*-confidence interval (which takes the sample size into account).
- The geometric mean is the best estimate of the middle task time from small sample sizes (less than 25).
- Task-time data is positively skewed and should be log-transformed prior to using the *t*-confidence interval.
- For large-sample task-time data (≥25) the median is the best point estimate of the middle task time, so you should compute a confidence interval around the median using the method for a confidence interval around a percentile.
- Table 3.3 provides a list of formulas used in this chapter.

Table 3.3 List of Chapter 3 Formulas

Type of Evaluation	Basic Formula	Notes
Wald binomial confidence interval	$\hat{p} \pm z_{\left(1-\frac{\alpha}{2}\right)}\sqrt{\frac{\hat{p}(1-\hat{p})}{n}}$	Commonly taught, but not recommended for small sample sizes—use z for desired level of confidence
Adjusted-Wald binomial confidence interval	$\hat{p}_{adj} \pm z_{\left(1-\frac{\alpha}{2}\right)}\sqrt{\frac{\hat{p}_{adj}(1-\hat{p}_{adj})}{n_{adj}}}$	Relatively new procedure, recommended for all samples sizes—see below for formulas for p_{adj} and n_{adj}
Adjustment of p for adjusted-Wald binomial confidence interval	$\hat{p}_{adj} = \frac{x+\frac{z^2}{2}}{n+z^2}$	Need to compute this to use in formula for adjusted-Wald binomial confidence interval
Adjustment of n for adjusted-Wald binomial confidence interval	$n_{adj} = n + z^2$	Need to compute this to use in formula for adjusted-Wald binomial confidence interval
Confidence interval for continuous data	$\bar{x} \pm t_{\left(1-\frac{\alpha}{2}\right)}\frac{s}{\sqrt{n}}$	Use t for the appropriate degrees of freedom and confidence level
Confidence interval around a percentile	$np \pm z_{\left(1-\frac{\alpha}{2}\right)}\sqrt{np(1-p)}$	For large sample sizes only—to use as confidence interval around the median, set $p = 0.5$.

CHAPTER REVIEW QUESTIONS

1. Find the 95% confidence interval around the completion rate from a sample of 12 users where 10 completed the task successfully.
2. What is the 95% confidence interval around the median time for the following 12 task times: 198, 220, 136, 162, 143, 130, 199, 99, 136, 188, 199
3. What is the 90% confidence interval around the median time for the following 32 task times:

251	21	60
108	43	34
27	47	48
18	15	219
195	37	338
82	46	78
222	107	117
38	19	62
81	178	40
181	95	52
140	130	

4. Find the 95% confidence interval around the average SUS score for the following fifteen scores from a test of an automotive website: 70, 50, 67.5, 35, 27.5, 50, 30, 37.5, 65, 45, 82.5, 80, 47.5, 32.5, 65
5. With 90% confidence, if 2 out of 8 users experience a problem with a registration element in a web-form, what percent of all users could plausibly encounter the problem should it go uncorrected?

ANSWERS TO CHAPTER REVIEW QUESTIONS

1. Use the adjusted-Wald binomial confidence interval. The adjustment is 11.9/15.84 = .752:

$$\hat{p}_{adj} \pm z_{\left(1-\frac{\alpha}{2}\right)}\sqrt{\frac{\hat{p}_{adj}\left(1-\hat{p}_{adj}\right)}{n_{adj}}} = 0.752 \pm 1.96\sqrt{\frac{0.752(1-0.752)}{15.84}}$$
$$= 0.752 \pm 0.212 = 95\% \text{ CI between } 54.0\% \text{ and } 96.4\%$$

2. The log times are: 5.288, 5.394, 4.913, 5.088, 4.963, 4.868, 5.293, 4.595, 4.913, 5.236, 5.293 which makes the geometric mean = $e^{(5.08)}$ = 160.24 s. The 95% CI is:

$$\bar{x}_{log} \pm t_{\left(1-\frac{\alpha}{2}\right)}\frac{s_{log}}{\sqrt{n}} = 5.08 \pm 2.23\frac{0.246}{\sqrt{11}} = 5.08 \pm 0.166$$
$$= e^{(4.91)} \text{ to } e^{(5.24)} = 136 \text{ to } 189 \text{ s}$$

3. The sample median is 70 s. The critical value from the normal distribution is 1.64 for a 90% level of confidence.

$$np \pm z_{\left(1-\frac{\alpha}{2}\right)}\sqrt{np(1-p)}$$
$$= 32(0.5) \pm 1.64\sqrt{32 \times 0.5(1-0.5)}$$
$$= 16 \pm 1.64 \times 2.83$$
$$= 16 \pm 4.64 = 11.36 \text{ and } 20.64 = \text{the 12th and 21st times}$$
$$= 90\% \text{ CI between 47 and 107 s}$$

4. A *t*-confidence interval should be constructed using a critical value of ($t_{0.05}$, 14) = 2.14. The mean and standard deviation are 52.3 and 18.2 respectively.

$$\bar{x} \pm t_{\left(1-\frac{\alpha}{2}\right)}\frac{s}{\sqrt{n}} = 52.3 \pm 2.14\frac{18.2}{\sqrt{15}} = 52.3 \pm 10.1$$

The 95% confidence interval for the average SUS score of 52.3 is between 42.2 and 62.4.

5. Compute a 90% adjusted-Wald binomial confidence interval. For 90% confidence, the value of z is 1.64. The adjusted proportion is 3.35/10.71 = 0.313.

$$\hat{p}_{adj} \pm z_{\left(1-\frac{\alpha}{2}\right)}\sqrt{\frac{\hat{p}_{adj}\left(1-\hat{p}_{adj}\right)}{n_{adj}}} = 0.313 \pm 1.64\sqrt{\frac{0.313(1-0.313)}{10.71}}$$
$$= 0.313 \pm 0.233$$

We can be 90% confident between 8.0% and 54.6% of all users will encounter this problem if 2 out of 8 encountered it in the lab.

REFERENCES

Agresti, A., Coull, B., 1998. Approximate is better than 'exact' for interval estimation of binomial proportions. Am. Stat. 52, 119–126.

Blalock, H.M., 1972. Social Statistics. McGraw-Hill, New York, NY.

Clopper, C.J., Pearson, E., 1934. The use of confidence intervals for fiducial limits illustrated in the case of the binomial. Biometrika 26, 404–413.

Cordes, R., 1993. The effects of running fewer subjects on time-on-task measures. Int. J. Hum. Comput. Int. 5 (4), 393–403.

Laplace, P.S., 1812. Theorie Analytique Des Probabilitites. Courcier, Paris, France.

Lewis, J.R., 1996. Binomial confidence intervals for small sample usability studies. In: Salvendy, G., Ozok, A. (Eds.), Advances in Applied Ergonomics: Proceedings of the 1st International Conference on Applied Ergonomics—ICAE '96. USA Publishing, Istanbul, Turkey, pp. 732–737.

Lewis, J.R., Sauro, J., 2006. When 100% really isn't 100%: Improving the accuracy of small-sample estimates of completion rates. J. Usability Stud. 3 (1), 136–150.

Sauro, J. (2004). Restoring confidence in usability results. From Measuring Usability, Available from: http://www.measuringu.com/conf_intervals.htm.

Sauro, J., Lewis, J.R. (2005). Estimating completion rates from small samples using binomial confidence intervals: Comparisons and recommendations. In: Proceedings of the Human Factors and Ergonomics Society Forty-Ninth Annual Meeting (pp. 2100–2104). Santa Monica, CA: HFES.

Sauro, J., Lewis, J.R. (2010). Average task times in usability tests: What to report? In: Proceedings of CHI 2010 (pp. 2347–2350). Atlanta, GA: ACM.

Smithson, M. (2003). Confidence intervals. Sage University Papers Series on Quantitative Applications in the Social Science, 07-140. Thousand Oaks, CA: Sage.

Wilson, E.B., 1927. Probable inference, the law of succession, and statistical inference. J. Am. Stat. Assoc. 22, 209–212.

CHAPTER

DID WE MEET OR EXCEED OUR GOAL?

4

INTRODUCTION

Confidence intervals are an excellent way for showing both the location and precision of an estimate. All other things being equal, estimates based on larger sample sizes will have a more precise estimate of the unknown population mean or proportion.

Once you get used to using confidence intervals with small sample sizes you may start to notice that the boundaries of the interval can be rather wide. For example, if eight out of nine users complete a task, we can be 95% confident that actual population completion rate is between 54.3% and 99.9%. While this interval is informative (e.g., there's a very small chance the completion rate will be less than 50%) there is still a lot of uncertainty. In fact, the interval is almost 50 percentage points wide, which reflects a margin of error of plus or minus 23%. Many people familiar with televised poll results with margins of error of less than 5% may believe a margin of error close to 25% is rather unhelpful.

ERRATA SHEET EFFECTIVENESS: A RISK ASSESSMENT—FROM THE FILES OF JIM LEWIS

When arguing for change, the width of the interval doesn't matter as much as the specific endpoints

In the early 1990s, my lab received a request to test a critical change to the documentation of a new computer. Because it would have been expensive to update the content of the installation guide at the time of the discovery of the need to change the instructions (many copies had already been printed), our assignment was to assess the effectiveness of inserting an errata sheet at the top of the packaging where customers would see it first upon opening the box. The words "DO THIS FIRST" appeared at the top of the sheet in 24-point bold type (Fig. 4.1). Despite its location and prominent heading, six of eight participants installing the computer ignored the errata sheet, setting it aside without attempting to use its instructions. Because we ran this test before the development of the adjusted-Wald binomial confidence interval, we reported the exact binomial confidence interval. The observed failure rate was 75%, with a 95% exact confidence interval ranging from 35% to 97%. Although we wound up with a very wide confidence interval (spanning 62 percentage points) due to the small sample size and had not established a criterion before running the test, we argued that the lower limit of the confidence interval indicated that it was very unlikely that the true failure rate in the population would be less than 35%. Development was unwilling to accept that level of risk, and spent the money needed to update the documentation rather than relying on the errata sheet.

Quantifying the User Experience. http://dx.doi.org/10.1016/B978-0-12-802308-2.00004-7

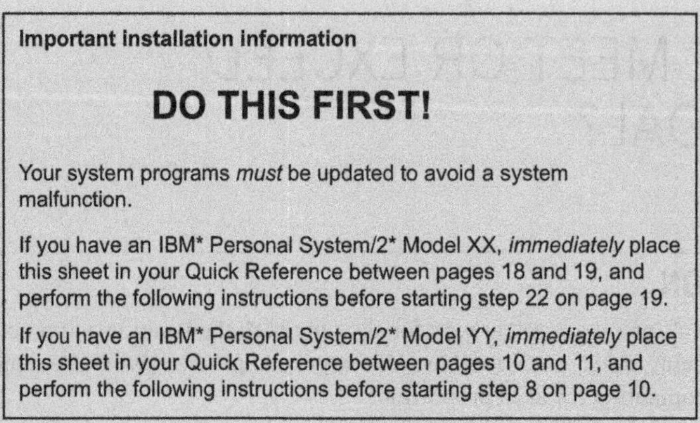

Important installation information

DO THIS FIRST!

Your system programs *must* be updated to avoid a system malfunction.

If you have an IBM* Personal System/2* Model XX, *immediately* place this sheet in your Quick Reference between pages 18 and 19, and perform the following instructions before starting step 22 on page 19.

If you have an IBM* Personal System/2* Model YY, *immediately* place this sheet in your Quick Reference between pages 10 and 11, and perform the following instructions before starting step 8 on page 10.

FIGURE 4.1 Test errata sheet

Such high margins of error are the consequences of small sample studies. All is not lost however; often with statistics it is a matter of reframing the results. One of the best ways to reframe the results is to compare them to a specific benchmark or goal. For example, as stated earlier, we can be at least 95% confident more than half the users will complete the task. We are able to make that statement because the lower boundary of the confidence interval does not dip below 54%, and therefore anything below 54% becomes an improbable result (having less than a 2.5% chance of occurring over the long-run—Fig. 4.2).

Using the boundaries of the confidence interval is a simple way to determine whether you've met or exceeded a goal. If you wanted to be sure at least half the users can complete the task before you move to the next design iteration (or release the software) then you have statistically significant evidence from just nine users.

Perhaps 50% is too low of a bar. Can we be sure at least 60% of users can complete the same task? Because the confidence interval boundary goes below 60% we can't be 95% confident at least 60% of users can complete the task (Fig. 4.3).

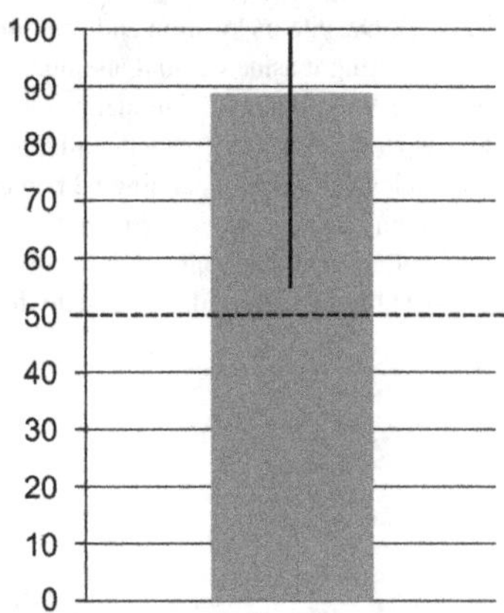

FIGURE 4.2 Fifty percent is an improbable result

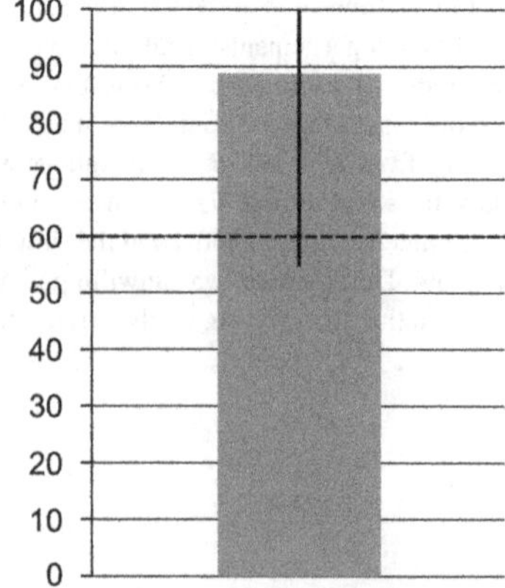

FIGURE 4.3 Sixty percent is a plausible result

Instead of just eye-balling the boundaries of confidence intervals to determine whether we've exceeded a benchmark there are statistical ways to get more precise answers. As we've seen with the confidence interval computations, the method we use will depend on the type of data (discrete-binary vs. continuous) as well as the sample size. We will first cover the methods for comparing completion rates and then proceed to the continuous measures of satisfaction scores and task times.

WHERE DO CRITERIA COME FROM?

There are a variety of sources of varying quality

Some approaches to the development of criteria are as follows:

1. Base criteria on historical data obtained from previous tests that included the task.
2. Base criteria on findings reported in published scientific or marketing research.
3. Use task modeling such as GOMS or KLM to estimate expert task-time performance (Sauro, 2009).
4. Negotiate criteria with the stakeholders who are responsible for the product.

Ideally, the goals should have an objective basis and shared acceptance among stakeholders such as Marketing and Development (Lewis, 1982). The best objective basis for measurement goals is data from previous usability studies of predecessor or competitive products. For maximum generalizability, the source of historical data should be studies of similar types of participants completing the same tasks under the same conditions (Chapanis, 1988). If this type of information is not available (or really, even if it is), it is important for test designers to recommend objective goals and to negotiate with the other stakeholders for the final set of shared goals.

Whatever approach you take, don't let analysis paralysis prevent you from specifying goals. "Defining usability objectives (and standards) isn't easy, especially when you're beginning a usability program. However, you're not restricted to the first objective you set. The important thing is to establish some specific objectives immediately, so that you can measure improvement. If the objectives turn out to be unrealistic or inappropriate, you can revise them" (Rosenbaum, 1989, p. 211). If you find yourself needing to make these types of revisions, try to make them in the early stages of gaining experience and taking initial measurements with a product. Do not change reasonable goals to accommodate an unusable product.

WHAT IS A GOOD SUCCESSFUL TASK COMPLETION RATE?—FROM THE FILES OF JEFF SAURO

Evidence from 1189 tasks conducted in 115 usability tests

An analysis of almost 1200 usability tasks shows that the average task-completion rate is 78% (Sauro, 2011). When setting a goal for task completion rate, context matters. If the costs for task failure are high (loss of money, loss of life) then you need to aim for 100%. If the consequences are less impactful, then you can relax the rate a bit. I've often seen walk-up-and-use consumer web-applications with a 70% completion rate target. That is, a task is considered good enough for now if there is evidence from testing that at least 70% completed the task on their first attempt.

Even though context matters, it can help to have an idea about how well your task completion rate stacks up against others taken during a usability test. I've been collecting task-completion rate data for several years—from business software, consumer software, and websites. In total I have data from 1189 tasks taken from both lab-based (90%) and unmoderated usability tests (10%). The data come from 115 usability tests from 3472 users across over a dozen organizations. Based on these data, Lah and Lewis (in press) created a curved grading scale for successful task completion rates (shown in Table 4.1, modeled after the curved grading scale for System Usability Scale (SUS) scores in Chapter 8).

The upper 15% of the distribution are As and the lower 15% of scores are Fs. Normally, one might further divide the top 15% into A + , A, and A−, but about 15% of the tasks in this distribution had successful completion rates of 100%, so there is no way to establish A+ or A−, to be an A (top 15%), the completion rate has to be 100%. If you don't have historical data to guide criteria setting for successful task completion rates, you can use Table 4.1 to either set the criterion or to inform discussions with stakeholders. For example, if you want to target a grade A user experience, you need to set your target to 100%. If that seems too radical for your situation, you might shoot for an above average experience by setting the target to 87%.

Table 4.1 Curved Grading Scale for Successful Task Completion Rates

Successful Completion Rate	Grade	Percentile Range
100	A	85–100
96.9–99.9	B+	80–84
90.3–96.8	B	70–79
86.7–90.2	B−	65–69
83.1–86.6	C+	60–64
67.3–83.0	C	41–59
61.4–67.2	C−	35–40
33.6–61.3	D	15–34
0–33.5	F	0–14

The top 15% of tasks had 100% successful completions, so it is not possible to define A− or A+ within the overall A range—the only way to get an A is to have 100% successful completions

ONE-TAILED AND TWO-TAILED TESTS

In Chapter 3 we used confidence intervals to describe the most likely range of an unknown population parameter (a completion rate or average task time). For that purpose, the usual practice is to build the interval so the sum of the probabilities of greater and smaller values is equal to one minus the level of confidence. For example, if it's a symmetrical 95% confidence interval, then the probability of values below the lower limit is 2.5% and the probability of values above the upper limit is also 2.5%. In addition to providing information about the most likely range of the parameter, this confidence interval implies a two-sided test with α equal to 0.05. It's a two-sided test because you care about both sides of the confidence interval. Any time you care about outcomes that can be either significantly higher than a criterion or might just as well be significantly lower (e.g., when testing one product against another without any preconception of which is better), you'd use a two-sided test.

The topic of this chapter, however, is on testing against a benchmark. When testing against a benchmark, you usually only care about one side of the outcome. For example, if you've established a maximum defect rate, then you have reached your benchmark only if the observed defect rate is significantly lower than the target. The same is true for task times—you've beat the benchmark if the times you measure are significantly faster than the target time. For percent successful completions, you've achieved your goal only when the success rate you measure is significantly greater than the benchmark (Fig. 4.4).

As we go through the methods and examples in this chapter, we'll cover two ways to conduct one-sided tests of significance for assessing an observed outcome against a pre-established benchmark. The traditional way is to estimate the likelihood of having obtained the observed result if the benchmark is true. Another way is to construct a confidence interval and then to compare, as appropriate, the upper or lower limit of the interval with the benchmark. For successful completions, you would compare the lower limit with the benchmark—if the lower limit is higher than the benchmark, then the result indicates

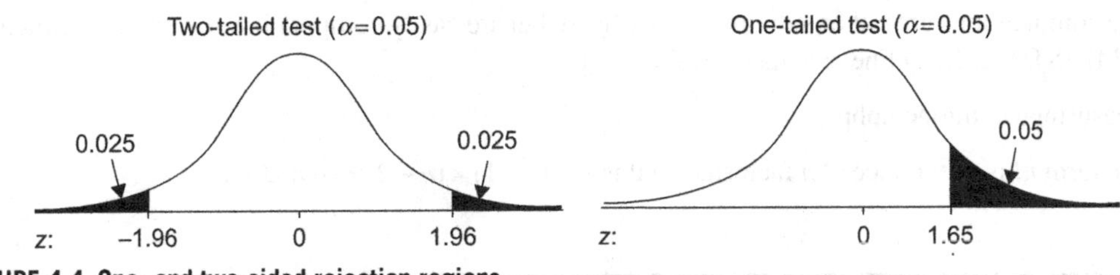

FIGURE 4.4 One- and two-sided rejection regions

statistical significance. For completion times you'd compare the upper limit with the benchmark—if the upper limit is lower than the benchmark, then you have evidence of a statistically significant outcome.

There is, however, a trick to doing one-sided testing with confidence intervals. You no longer care about what happens on one side of the interval, so you need to put all of the rejection area on one side of the confidence interval. You do that by doubling the value of α that you're going to use for the test, then subtract that from 100% to determine the confidence level you should use for the confidence interval. For example, if you're going to set α to 0.05 (5%), then you need to build a 90% confidence interval. If you're going to use a more liberal value for α, say, 10%, then you'd need to construct an 80% confidence interval. If this seems a little confusing right now, don't worry, there will be plenty of examples showing how to do this.

COMPARING A COMPLETION RATE TO A BENCHMARK

To determine whether there is sufficient evidence that more than a set percent of users can complete a task we perform one of two statistical tests depending on whether we have a small or large sample size. In this case small sample sizes are a function of both the number of users tested and the observed completion rate and failure rate. The closer the observed completion rate and failure rates are to 50%, the larger is the sample size needed to achieve a set level of precision and confidence. As a general rule (Agresti and Franklin, 2007), the sample size is "small" when the number of users tested times the proportion (p) or times one minus the proportion (q) is less than 15 ($np < 15$ or $nq < 15$). Put another way you need at least 15 failures and 15 successes for the sample to be considered "large." For example, if eight out of nine users complete a task ($p = 0.89$), the small sample method would be used since the value of $np = 9(0.89) = 8$ (and there aren't at least 15 successes and 15 failures). In practice, you should plan on using the small sample method if the total number of users tested is less than 30. In lab-based testing it is unusual to have a sample size much larger than this so we'll cover it first.

SMALL SAMPLE TEST

For small sample sizes we use the exact probabilities from the binomial distribution to determine whether a sample completion rate exceeds a particular benchmark. The formula for the binomial distribution is

$$p(x) = \frac{n!}{x!(n-x)!} p^x (1-p)^{(n-x)}$$

where x is the number of users who successfully completed the task,
n is the sample size.

The computations are rather tedious to do by hand, but are easily computed using the Excel function BINOMDIST() or the online calculator available at:

measuringu.com/onep.php

The term $n!$ is pronounced "n factorial" and is $n \times (n-1) \times (n-2) \times \cdots \times 2 \times 1$.

Example 1

During an early stage design test eight out of nine users successfully completed a task. Is there sufficient evidence to conclude that at least 70% of all users would be able to complete the same task?

We have an observed completion rate of 8/9 = 88.9%. Using the exact probabilities from the binomial we can find the probability of obtaining eight or more successes out of nine trials if the population completion rate is 70%. To do so we find the probability of getting exactly eight successes and the probability of getting exactly nine successes.

$$p(8) = \frac{9!}{8!(9-8)!} 0.70^8 (1-0.70)^{(9-8)} = \frac{9!}{8!(1!)} 0.0576(0.30)^{(1)} = 9(0.01729) = 0.1556$$

$$p(9) = \frac{9!}{9!(9-9)!} 0.70^9 (1-0.70)^{(9-9)} = \frac{9!}{9!(1)} 0.04035(0.30)^{(0)} = 0.04035(1) = 0.04035$$

In Excel:

=BINOMDIST(8,9,0.70,FALSE) = 0.1556
=BINOMDIST(9,9,0.70,FALSE) = 0.04035

So the probability of eight or nine successes out of nine attempts is 0.1556 + 0.04035 = 0.1960. In other words, there is an 80.4% chance the completion rate exceeds 70%. Whether this is sufficient evidence largely depends on the context of the test and the consequences of being wrong. This result is not suitable for publication. For many early design tests, however, this is sufficient evidence that efforts are better spent on improving other functions.

The probability we computed here is called an "exact" probability—"exact" not because our answer is exactly correct but because the probabilities are calculated exactly, rather than approximated as they are with many statistical tests such as the *t*-test. Exact probabilities with small sample sizes tend to be conservative—meaning they overstate the long-term probability and therefore understate the actual chances of having met the completion-rate goal.

Mid-probability

One reason for the conservativeness of exact methods with small sample sizes is that the probabilities have a finite number of possible values instead of taking on any number of values (such as with the *t*-test). One way to compensate for this discreteness is to simulate a continuous result by using a point in between the exact probabilities—called a midprobability.

In the previous example we'd only use half the probability associated with the observed number of successes plus the entire probability of all values *above* what we observed. The probability of observing eight out of nine successes given a population probability of 70% is 0.1556. Instead of using 0.1556 we'd use $\frac{1}{2}(0.1556) = 0.07782$. We add this half-probability to the probability of nine out of nine successes (0.07782 + 0.04035) which gets us a mid-*p* value of 0.1182. We would now state that there is an 88.2% chance the completion rate exceeds 70%. Compare this result to the exact *p*-value of 0.1960 (an 80.4% chance the completion rate exceeds 70%). Due to its method of computation, the mid-*p* will always look better than the exact-*p* result.

Although mid-*p* values tend to work well in practice they are not without controversy (as are many techniques in applied statistics). Statistical mathematicians don't think much of the mid-*p* value because taking half a probability doesn't appear to have a good mathematical foundation—even though it tends to provide better results. Rest assured that its use is not just some fudge factor that tends to work. Its use is justified as a way or correcting for the discreteness in the data like other continuity corrections in statistics. For more discussion on continuity corrections see Gonick and Smith (1993, pp. 82–87).

A balanced recommendation is to compute both the exact-*p* and mid-*p* values but emphasize the mid-*p* (Armitage et al., 2002). When you need just one *p*-value in applied user research settings, we recommend using the less conservative mid-*p* value unless you must guarantee that the reported *p*-value is greater than or equal to the actual long-term probability. This is the same recommendation we gave when computing binomial confidence intervals (see Chapter 3)—use an exact method when you need to be absolutely sure you've not understated the actual probability (and just know you're probably overstating it). For almost all applications in usability testing or user research, using just the mid-*p* value will suffice. Online calculators often provide the values for both methods (e.g., measuringu.com/onep.php—Fig. 4.5).

Use this calculator to generate both a one-sample confidence interval and to test against a criteria or benchmark.

# Passed	Total Tested		Test Proportion
8	9	Is Greater Than	0.70

Submit

Results

The probability the observed proportion 0.89 comes from a population greater than 0.70 is **88.18%** .

Exact Binomial P-Value is 0.196

95% Adjusted-Wald CI (54.31, 100)

FIGURE 4.5 ***p*** **and mid-*p* results for eight successes out of nine attempts compared to criterion of 70% success**

Example 2

The results of a benchmarking test showed that 18 out of 20 users were able to complete the task successfully. Is it reasonable to report that at least 70% of users can complete the task?

We have an observed completion rate of 18/20 = 90%. Using the exact probabilities from the binomial we can find the probability of obtaining 18 or more successes out of 20 trials if the population completion rate is 70%. To do so we find the probability of getting exactly 18, 19, and 20 successes.

$$p(18) = \frac{20!}{18!(20-18)!}0.70^{18}(1-0.70)^{(20-18)} = 0.02785$$

$$p(19) = \frac{20!}{19!(20-19)!}0.70^{19}(1-0.70)^{(20-19)} = 0.00684$$

$$p(20) = \frac{20!}{20!(20-20)!}0.70^{20}(1-0.70)^{(20-20)} = 0.000798$$

The exact p-value is 0.02785 + 0.00684 + 0.000798 = 0.0355.

The mid-p value is 0.5(0.02785) + 0.00684 + 0.000798 = 0.0216.

Both p-values are below the common α threshold of 0.05 and so both provide compelling evidence that at least 70% of users can complete the task. It's also a result that's suitable for publication.

It is generally a good idea to compute a confidence interval with every statistical test because the confidence interval will give you an idea about the precision of your metrics in addition to statistical significance. To compute the confidence interval for a one-sided test, set the confidence level to 90% (because you only care about one tail, this is a one-sided test with α equal to 0.05) and compute the interval—if the interval lies about 0.70, then you've provided compelling evidence that at least 70% of users can complete the task. As shown in Fig. 4.6, using the adjusted-Wald confidence interval we get a 90% confidence interval between 73.0% and 97.5%.

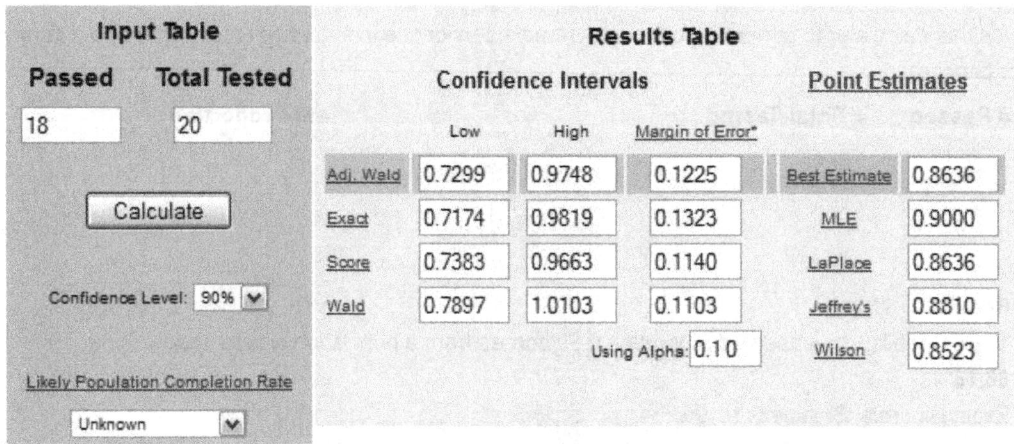

FIGURE 4.6 Ninety percent confidence intervals for 18 of 20 successful task completions

LARGE SAMPLE TEST

The large sample test is based on the normal approximation to the binomial and uses a z-score to generate a p-value. It is only appropriate when there are at least 15 successes and 15 failures in the sample. For example, if 24 out of 41 users complete a task successfully there are 24 successes and 16 failures making the large sample test the appropriate choice.

While many of the assumptions that come with statistical tests are flexible, such as violating the normality assumption with a t-test, when tests use only one-tailed p-values they tend to be particularly vulnerable to inaccuracies. Because we use a one-sided test when we want to know whether a completion rate exceeds a benchmark (and therefore one-tailed p-values), it is important to use the small sample binomial test unless there are at least 15 successes and 15 failures.

The large-sample test statistic takes the following form:

$$z = \frac{\hat{p} - p}{\sqrt{\frac{p(1-p)}{n}}}$$

where $\hat{p}$ is the observed completion rate expressed as a proportion (e.g., 0.90 indicates a 90% completion rate),
p is the benchmark (e.g., 0.70),
n is the number of users tested.

Example 1

The results from a remote-unmoderated test of a website task found that 85 out of 100 users were able to successfully locate a specific product and add it to their shopping cart. Is there enough evidence to conclude that at least 75% of all users can complete this task successfully?

There are at least 15 successes and 15 failures so using the large sample method is appropriate. Filling in the values we get

$$z = \frac{\hat{p} - p}{\sqrt{\frac{p(1-p)}{n}}} = \frac{0.85 - 0.75}{\sqrt{\frac{0.75(1-0.75)}{100}}} = \frac{0.10}{0.0433} = 2.309$$

We look up the obtained z-score of 2.309 using a normal table of values or use the Excel function =NORMSDIST(2.309) to get the cumulative distribution of z up to 2.309 (which is 0.9895), then subtract that from 1 to get the one-tailed p-value of 0.0105. This means that there is around a 1% chance of seeing an 85% completion rate from a sample of 100 users if the actual completion rate is less than 75%. Put more succinctly we can say there is around a 99% chance at least 75% of users can complete the task. The 95% adjusted-Wald confidence interval is between 76.6% and 90.8%.

Example 2

If 233 out of 250 users were able to complete a task in an unmoderated usability test, is there enough evidence to conclude at least 90% of all users can complete the task?

There are at least 15 successes and 15 failures so using the large sample method is appropriate.

$$z = \frac{\hat{p} - p}{\sqrt{\frac{p(1-p)}{n}}} = \frac{0.932 - 0.90}{\sqrt{\frac{0.90(1-0.90)}{250}}} = \frac{0.032}{0.019} = 1.687$$

We look up the obtained z-score of 1.687 using a normal table of values or use the Excel function =NORMSDIST(1.687) = 0.9541 and subtract that from 1 to get the one-tailed p-value of 0.0459, which indicates a statistically significant result. We can be 95.4% sure at least 90% of users can complete the task given that 233 out of 250 did. The 90% adjusted-Wald confidence interval is between 90.1% and 95.4%. ■

COMPARING A SATISFACTION SCORE TO A BENCHMARK

Post-test questionnaires like the SUS are popular for both lab-based and unmoderated usability tests as they provide some idea about what users think about the usability of the product or website tested. For practical statistical evaluation, questionnaire data can be treated as continuous data so we can use a one-sample t-test for both small and large sample sizes (see Chapter 9 for a discussion of the controversy of using parametric statistics on questionnaire data).

A SUS score, like most questionnaire data, is hard to interpret without some meaningful comparison. Bangor et al. (2008) and Lewis and Sauro (2009) have published some benchmarks for the SUS across different products (for details, see Chapter 8). For example, an average SUS score for cell phones is around 67. We can use this value to determine whether a current cell-phone usability test exceeds this benchmark. To test the benchmark we will use the one-sample t-test. The t-distribution is also used when constructing confidence intervals (see Chapter 3) and comparing two means for satisfaction data (see Chapter 5). The test statistic looks like the following:

$$t = \frac{\hat{x} - \mu}{\frac{s}{\sqrt{n}}}$$

where $\hat{x}$ is the sample mean,
μ is the benchmark being tested,
s is the sample standard deviation, and
n is the sample size.

The fraction $\frac{s}{\sqrt{n}}$ is called the standard error of the mean (sem). The result of the equation will tell us how many standard errors there are between our sample mean and the benchmark. The more standard errors there are the more evidence we will have that our sample exceeds the benchmark.

Example 1

Twenty users were asked to complete some common tasks (dialing, adding contacts, and texting) on a new cell-phone design. At the end of the test the users responded to the 10 item SUS questionnaire. The mean SUS score was 73 and the standard deviation was 19. Is there enough evidence to conclude that the perceived usability of this cell phone is better than the industry average of 67 as reported by Bangor et al. (2008)?

$$t = \frac{\hat{x} - \mu}{\frac{s}{\sqrt{n}}} = \frac{73 - 67}{\frac{19}{\sqrt{20}}} = \frac{6}{4.24} = 1.41$$

The observed difference of six SUS points is 1.41 standard errors from the benchmark. To know how likely this difference is from a sample size of 20 we look up the one-tailed probability value in a *t*-table (the degrees of freedom for this type of *t*-test is $n-1$, in this case, 19), the online calculator available at usablestats.com/calcs/tdist or use the Excel function =TDIST(1.41, 19,1).

USING THE EXCEL TDIST FUNCTION WHEN *T* IS NEGATIVE—FROM THE FILES OF JEFF SAURO

Working around a puzzling limitation

For some reason, the Excel TDIST function does not work with negative values of t. There are a couple of ways to work around this limitation. You can either reverse the observed value and the benchmark in the numerator, or you can use the absolute value function inside TDIST, for example, =TDIST(ABS(−0.66),10,1) when the value of t is −0.66, there are 10 degrees of freedom, and you're running a one-sided test. It took me a while to figure out why Excel sometimes wasn't producing *p*-values—it happened when t was negative.

The parameters are the test statistic (1.41), the degrees of freedom (19), and a one-tailed test (1). We get the probability of 0.0874, meaning we can be around 91% confident this cell phone has an average score greater than the industry average of 67. For most development environments this is sufficient evidence to conclude the cell phone is above average.

We can generate a two-sided 80% confidence interval around our sample mean with the data we have here (the 80% confidence interval would correspond to a one-tailed test at an α of 0.10). The only additional information we need is the critical value from the *t*-distribution for a confidence level of 0.80 and 19 degrees of freedom. Using the Excel function =TINV(0.20,19), the critical value of t is 1.33.

$$\bar{x} \pm t_{\left(1-\frac{\alpha}{2}\right)} \frac{s}{\sqrt{n}} = 73 \pm 1.33 \frac{19}{\sqrt{20}} = 73 \pm 5.6$$

The margin of error is 5.6 points, so we can be 80% confident the population's true SUS score is between 67.4 and 78.6. The lower boundary of the 80% confidence interval does not dip below 67.

Example 2

In a recent unmoderated usability test 172 users attempted tasks on a rental-car website and then answered the SUS questionnaire. The mean response was 80 and the standard deviation was 23. Can we conclude the average SUS score for the population is greater than 75?

$$t = \frac{\hat{x} - \mu}{\frac{s}{\sqrt{n}}} = \frac{80 - 75}{\frac{23}{\sqrt{172}}} = \frac{5}{1.75} = 2.85$$

The observed difference of five SUS points is 2.85 standard errors from the benchmark. Finding the probability associated with this difference we get a *p*-value of 0.002 (=TDIST(2.85, 171,1)). There is less than a 1% chance that a mean of 80 for a sample size of 172 would come from a population with a mean less than 75. In other words we can be more than 99% confident that the average score for all users of this website exceeds 75.

The 90% confidence interval around the average SUS score is

$$\bar{x} \pm t_{\left(1-\frac{\alpha}{2}\right)} \frac{s}{\sqrt{n}} = 80 \pm 1.65 \frac{23}{\sqrt{172}} = 80 \pm 2.9$$

The two-sided 90% confidence interval is between the SUS scores of 77.1 and 82.9.

DO AT LEAST 75% AGREE? CONVERTING CONTINUOUS RATINGS TO DISCRETE

As is the case with any continuous measure like satisfaction ratings you can always "downgrade" the results into discrete-binary responses. This is what happens when managers look at "top-box" or "top-two-box" scores. For example, on a 5-point rating scale you can report the number of users who "agreed" by converting 4s and 5s into 1s and 1–3 into 0s. You could then answer the question, do at least 70% of users "agree" with the statement "I feel confident conducting business with this website." You would then analyze the data using the binary completion rate method (for both large and small sample sizes) instead of the continuous method.

For example, following are the responses from 12 users who completed two tasks on the Walmart.com website and responded to the item "I feel confident conducting business with this website" at the end of the test. A 1 is Strongly Disagree and a 5 is Strongly Agree. Can we conclude at least 75% of users feel confident conducting business on Walmart.com (ratings of 4 or 5)?

4,4,5,5,5,5,3,5,1,5,5,5

Converting these responses to binary we get

1,1,1,1,1,1,0,1,0,1,1,1

We have 10 out of 12 users who agreed with the statement. The small-sample binomial mid-*p* value is 0.275, which indicates a 72.5% chance that 75% of all users agree with the statement. For most applications that's not a high level of certainty so it would be difficult to confidently conclude that at least 75% of all users agree with the statement "I feel confident conducting business with this website." The 80% adjusted-Wald confidence interval around the percentage of users who agree is between 65.3% and 93.4%. The interval contains the benchmark of 75%, which isn't even near the lower limit of 65.3%, also reinforcing the point that we don't have convincing evidence that at least 75% of users agree.

Disadvantages to converting continuous ratings to discrete

When you convert continuous ratings to discrete data you lose information. During the process both a 4 and a 5 become a 1. You no longer have as precise a measure of the intensity of agreement or disagreement. The disadvantage of losing the intensity of agreement is that it becomes harder to measure improvements. It will take a larger sample size to detect improvements and achieve benchmarks. For example, using the same 12 ratings from the Walmart.com website the average response is a 4.33 (standard deviation =1.23). Instead of testing whether a certain percentage of agree's (top-2-box) exceeds a benchmark, you could use 4 as the lower boundary of "agree" and compute a one-sample *t*-test to answer the same question, this time taking into account the intensity of the agreement.

$$t = \frac{\hat{x} - \mu}{\frac{s}{\sqrt{n}}} = \frac{4.33 - 4}{\frac{1.23}{\sqrt{12}}} = \frac{0.33}{0.355} = 0.929$$

The value of t for this one-tailed test is 0.929 with 11 degrees of freedom ($p = 0.186$), so there is an 81.4% chance that the mean for all users exceeds 4. Although we generally recommend using the original raw continuous data when testing claims, there are many times when reporting on company dashboards requires conforming to a top-box or top-2-box approach with specific criteria such as 90% must "agree."

Net Promoter Score

Another common example of converting continuous rating scale data into discrete top-2-box scoring is the popular Net Promoter Score (netpromoter.com/np/calculate.jsp). The NPS is a measure of loyalty that uses only a single question "How likely are you to recommend this product to a friend?" and is measured on an 11-point scale (0 = Not at all Likely to 10 = Extremely Likely). Promoters are those who rate a 9 or 10 (top-2-box), detractors are those who rate 0 to 6 and passive responders are those who respond 7 or 8. The "Net" in Net Promoter Score comes from the scoring process whereby you subtract the percent of detractors from the percent of promoters. In fact, usability explains a lot of the variability in the NPS (Sauro, 2010—for more details, see Chapter 8).

For example, 15 users attempted to make travel arrangements the website expedia.com. At the end of the usability test they were asked the Net Promoter question. Here are their responses:

$$10,7,6,9,10,8,10,10,9,8,7,5,8,0,9$$

When we convert these responses to detractors (0–6), passive (7–8), and promoters (9–10) we have seven promoters and three detractors generating a Net Promoter Score of 4/15 = 26.7%.

WHAT IS A GOOD NET PROMOTER SCORE?—FROM THE FILES OF JEFF SAURO

Evidence from 17 consumer and productivity software products

The appeal of top box scoring approaches like the Net Promoter Score is that they appear easier to interpret than a mean. Many executives are comfortable working with percentages. So knowing there is a higher percentage of customers likely to recommend your product than dissuade others from using it may be more helpful than just knowing the mean responses is a 7.5. Despite this appeal, one still needs to know what a "good" score is beyond a negative versus positive proportion. A leading competitor, the industry average, or historical data for the same product are all helpful—but are usually difficult to obtain. One of the first adopters of the Net Promoter Score was Intuit, the software company that makes QuickBooks and TurboTax. It's not surprising that many software companies now use the NPS as a key corporate metric. I commissioned a study in March 2011 to survey the sentiments of customers of 17 consumer and productivity software products. I found the average NPS score was a 21% with a range of -−26% to 56%—with the best showing coming for customers of TurboTax. For more details on the study see www.measuringu.com/software-benchmarks.php. The average and high Net Promoter scores for your industry can be used as valid benchmarks if the comparisons are meaningful for your product.

COMPARING A TASK TIME TO A BENCHMARK

Task-time data are a continuous metric like satisfaction data. However, as was explored in Chapter 3, task-time data tend to be positively skewed (having a long right tail). One of the assumptions underlying most statistical procedures is that the data are approximately symmetrical and bell-shaped (t-confidence intervals in Chapter 3, two-sample t-tests in Chapter 5). Fortunately many statistical tests are "robust" to violations of this normality assumption. Unfortunately, a one-sided one-sample t-test is particularly vulnerable to this violation (Agresti and Franklin, 2007). To remedy this problem we will use the same procedure we used in Chapter 3. We first convert the raw task times to log times and perform the same one-sample t-test we used for the questionnaire data.

$$t = \frac{\ln(\mu) - \hat{x}_{\ln}}{\frac{s_{\ln}}{\sqrt{n}}}$$

where $\hat{x}_{\ln}$ is the mean of the log values and
$S_{\ln}$ is their standard deviation.

One slight difference in this formula is that we subtract the observed time from the benchmark (in the expectation that our sample mean is less than the benchmark we want to test). This is not always the case as we'll see in the first example taken from an actual scenario.

HOW LONG SHOULD A TASK TAKE?—FROM THE FILES OF JEFF SAURO

It depends on the context of the task

As soon as you start collecting time on task in a usability test you will want to know what an acceptable time is. Task times are highly dependent on the context of the task. Even slight variations in the same task scenario can substantially change task times and makes finding a comparison difficult. For example, a common task in customer relationship management (CRM) software is adding a sales contact to the database. An acceptable time will differ if the required information is just an email address versus an email, phone, street address, and sales notes. There isn't a single solution to this issue. In my experience, I've had the most luck having the same participants attempt the same tasks on the older version of the interface (the products are presented in alternating orders). This provides both a benchmark on the old interface, using the exact same task, and immediately tells you if the users can perform the task faster (or at least as fast) on the new interface. See Chapter 5 for more information on comparing task times for a within-subjects design. For more information see www.measuringu.com/blog/task-times.php.

Another common method for determining ideal task times is to identify the expert or fastest task time and set the unacceptable time to 1.5 times (or another multiple) this time for each task. However, it's unclear what a good multiple should be (Sauro and Kindlund, 2005). More research is needed to make this approach more meaningful, so use it as a last resort.

Example 1

As shown in Fig. 4.7, the rental-car website Budget.com has posted the slogan "Rent a car in just 60 s."

Twelve users in a lab-based usability test were all able to successfully rent a car from Boston's Logan International Airport.

Task times: 215, 131, 260, 171, 187, 147, 74, 170, 131, 165, 347, 90
Geometric mean task time: 160 s

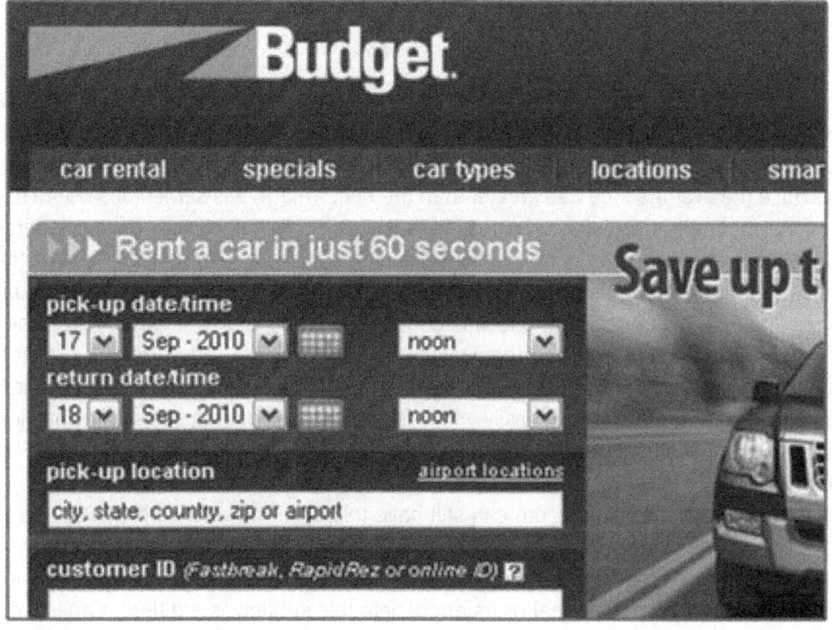

FIGURE 4.7 Rent a car in just 60 s

Is there evidence to suggest that the average task time is **LESS THAN** 60 s?

First we log-transformed the values using the Excel function =LN().

Log transformed times: 5.37, 4.88, 5.56, 5.14, 5.23, 4.99, 4.30, 5.14, 4.88, 5.11, 5.85, 4.50
Mean of log times: 5.08
Standard deviation of log times: 0.423
Log of benchmark: 4.09

$$t = \frac{\log(\mu) - \log(\hat{x})}{\frac{\log(s)}{\sqrt{n}}} = \frac{4.09 - 5.08}{\frac{0.423}{\sqrt{12}}} = \frac{-0.98}{0.122} = -8.057$$

The test statistic is negative because our sample geometric mean (see Chapter 3) is 160 s. When the sample average takes longer than the benchmark you know right away that there's less than a 50% chance that we can claim that the average task time is less than the benchmark. In this example the average time was almost three times the benchmark! When we look up the probability associated with this *t*-statistic we get the *p*-value of 0.9999965. In other words there's far less than a 1% chance of obtaining an average time of 160 s if the population average time is less than 60 s. The 95% confidence interval (*t*-critical value = 2.2) for the average task time is

$$\bar{x}_{\log} \pm t_{\left(1-\frac{\alpha}{2}\right)} \frac{s_{\log}}{\sqrt{n}} = 5.08 \pm 2.2 \frac{0.423}{\sqrt{12}} = 5.08 \pm 0.269$$

$$\text{Confidence interval} = e^{(4.81)} \text{ to } e^{(5.35)}$$
$$= 123 - 210\,\text{s}$$

Using the geometric mean as a proxy for the median (given a sample size of 12), we can be about 95% confident the median task time is between 123 and 210 s (Sauro and Lewis, 2010).

Even though we knew right away that we have little evidence that the average time to rent a car is less than 60 s (because the average time was greater than the benchmark) it is sometimes useful to go through the motions of computing the statistics. The reason is that some might wrongly have the perception that an average time from only 12 users is not meaningful. The statistical result tells us in fact that we have strong evidence that the average user time will exceed 60 s. If someone was concerned about the small sample size used to test this benchmark and was considering increasing the sample size, these data tell us there's less than 1 chance in a million the average time could be less than 60 s—even if the sample size is 10 times as large! This is a reoccurring theme in usability testing with small samples—you can determine an interface is unusable very easily with a small sample size, but to show statistically that an interface is usable; you need a large sample size (see Chapter 6 on failure rates and Chapter 7 on problem discovery rates).

If you were wondering how Budget.com can still have this claim on their website, the reason is that it is referring to users who are part of their loyalty program, have their information prepopulated, and most importantly the claim doesn't mention anything about an "average time." It could be referring to the fastest possible completion time. Whether casual users appreciate this subtlety is a different question and is why it made for a good test case at the Comparative Usability Evaluation-8 at the 2009 UPA Conference (Molich et al., 2009).

MY FAVORITE MEANINGLESS CLAIM—FROM THE FILES OF JIM LEWIS

Up to 98% accuracy—or more!

Not surprisingly, marketing claims generally have looser guidelines than peer-reviewed publications. My favorite claim came from an off-the-shelf dictation package, advertising "Up to 98% accuracy—or more!"—which is a claim that actually says you'll get somewhere between 0 and 100% accuracy. I'm sure the next year, it said, "Up to 99% accuracy—or more!" Even if the product hadn't changed, it would still be true.

Example 2

Eleven users completed a common task in a financial application (a journal entry). Can we be at least 90% sure users can enter this journal entry in less than 100 s?

Raw task times: 90, 59, 54, 55, 171, 86, 107, 53, 79, 72, 157
Geometric mean: 82.3 s
Log times: 4.50, 4.08, 3.99, 4.01, 5.14, 4.45, 4.67, 3.97, 4.37, 4.28, 5.06
Mean of log times: 4.41
Standard deviation of log times: 0.411
Log of benchmark: 4.61

$$t = \frac{\log(\mu) - \log(\hat{x})}{\frac{\log(s)}{\sqrt{n}}} = \frac{4.61 - 4.41}{\frac{0.411}{\sqrt{11}}} = \frac{0.19}{0.124} = 1.53$$

We look up the probability of this t-statistic on 10 degrees of freedom for a one-tailed test =TDIST(1.53, 10,1) = 0.0785. The probability of seeing an average time of 82.3 s if the actual population time is greater than 100 s is around 7.85%. In other words we can be about 92.15% confident users can complete this task in less than 100 s.

The 80% confidence interval (t-critical value = 1.37) for the average task time is between:

$$\bar{x}_{\log} \pm t_{\left(1-\frac{\alpha}{2}\right)} \frac{s_{\log}}{\sqrt{n}} = 4.41 \pm 1.37 \frac{0.411}{\sqrt{11}} = 4.41 \pm 0.17$$

$$\text{Confidence interval} = e^{(4.24)} \text{ to } e^{(4.58)}$$
$$= 69\text{–}98 \text{ s}$$

If we were able to test all users on this task and application, we can be about 80% confident the median task time will be between 69 and 98 s (using the geometric mean as a proxy for the median). As discussed earlier in the chapter we report the two-tailed 80% confidence interval because we're interested in a one-tailed test with an α of 0.10.

■

KEY POINTS

- The statistical test you use for completion rates depends on the sample size: A sample size is considered small unless you have more than 15 successes and 15 failures.
- For determining whether a certain percentage of users can complete a task *for small sample sizes* use the midprobability from the binomial distribution.
- For determining whether a certain percentage of users can complete a task *for large sample sizes* use the normal approximation to the binomial.
- You can always convert continuous rating scale data into discrete-binary data and test a percentage that agrees with a statement, but in so doing, you lose information.
- For comparing a set of satisfaction scores from a survey or questionnaire with a benchmark, use the one-sample t-test for all sample sizes.
- For determining whether a task time falls below a benchmark, log-transform the times and then perform a one-sample t-test for all sample sizes.
- Table 4.2 provides a list of formulas used in this chapter.

CHAPTER REVIEW QUESTIONS

1. Out of 26 users, 25 were able to create an expense report in a financial application. Is there enough evidence to conclude that at least 90% of all users can complete the same task?
2. In an unmoderated usability test of an automotive website, 150 out of 180 participants correctly answered a qualifying question at the end of a task to demonstrate they'd successfully completed the task. Can at least 75% of users complete the task?

Table 4.2 List of Chapter 4 Formulas

Type of Evaluation	Basic Formula	Notes
Binomial probability formula	$p(x)=\frac{n!}{x!(n-x)!}p^x(1-p)^{(n-x)}$	Used in exact and mid-*p* binomial tests (small sample)
Normal approximation to the binomial (Wald)	$z=\frac{\hat{p}-p}{\sqrt{\frac{p(1-p)}{n}}}$	Used for large-sample binomial tests (large sample if at least 15 successes and 15 failures)
One-sample *t*-test	$t=\frac{\hat{x}-\mu}{\frac{s}{\sqrt{n}}}$	Used to test continuous data (e.g., satisfaction scores, completion times)
t-based confidence interval around the mean	$\bar{x}\pm t_{\left(1-\frac{\alpha}{2}\right)}\frac{s}{\sqrt{n}}$	Used to construct confidence interval as alternative test against a criterion for continuous data

3. An “average” score for websites using the SUS is 70 (Bangor et al., 2008). After completing two tasks on the Travelocity.com website, the average SUS score from 15 users was a 74.7 (sd = 12.9). Is this website’s usability significantly above average?
4. Twelve users attempted to locate a toy on the toysrus.com website and rated the difficulty of the task an average of 5.6 (sd = 1.4) on a 7-point scale (where a 7 means very easy). Is there evidence that the average rating is greater than 5?
5. Six participants called an interactive voice response system to find out the appropriate replacement head for an electric shaver and the nearest location to pick one up. All participants completed the task successfully, with the following task completion times (in minutes): 3.4, 3.5, 1.7, 2.9, 2.5, and 3.2. Do the data support the claim that callers, on average, can complete this task in less than 3 min?

ANSWERS TO CHAPTER REVIEW QUESTIONS

1. Out of 26 users, 25 successfully completed the task. There are fewer than 15 successes and 15 failures, so this is a small sample. Using the Excel =BINOMDIST function to compute the exact probably for getting 25/26 successes and 26/26 successes and adding them together to get the probability of the observed or greater number of successes, we get

$$=\text{BINOMDIST}(26,26,0.9,\text{FALSE})=0.065$$
$$=\text{BINOMDIST}(25,26,0.9,\text{FALSE})=0.187$$
$$P(25\text{ or }26\text{ successes}\,|\,26\text{ trials and }p=0.90)=0{,}065+0.187=0.2513$$

So, the likelihood of getting 25 or 26 successes if the true success rate is 90% is about 0.25, which is not terribly compelling. Taking 1 −0.25 = 0.75, there is a 75% likelihood that the completion rate exceeds 90%.

Things look a little better if you use the recommended mid-*p* approach, using half of the probability for *P*(25), which is 0.093, for a combined probability (*p*(25, 26)) of 0.158, indicating an 84% likelihood that the completion rate exceeds 90%—better, but still not compelling.

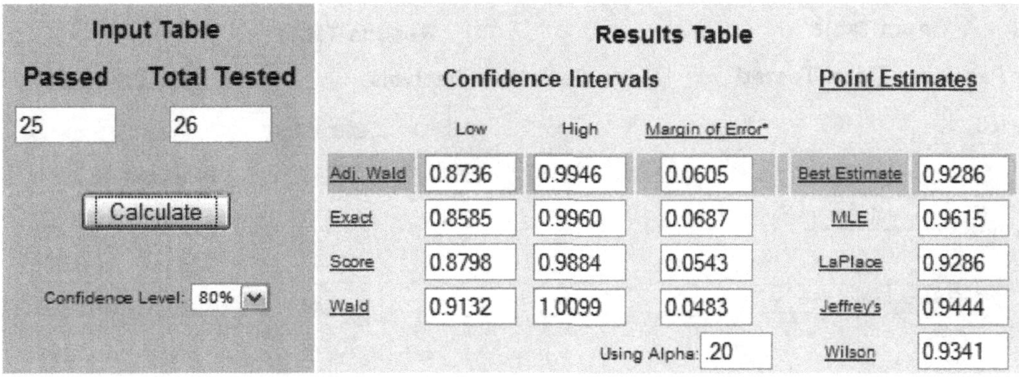

Input Table		Results Table					
Passed	Total Tested	Confidence Intervals				Point Estimates	
25	26		Low	High	Margin of Error*		
		Adj. Wald	0.8736	0.9946	0.0605	Best Estimate	0.9286
Calculate		Exact	0.8585	0.9960	0.0687	MLE	0.9615
		Score	0.8798	0.9884	0.0543	LaPlace	0.9286
Confidence Level: 80%		Wald	0.9132	1.0099	0.0483	Jeffrey's	0.9444
				Using Alpha:	.20	Wilson	0.9341

FIGURE 4.8 Results of adjusted-Wald confidence interval for Question 1

A third approach to answering this question is to use the calculator at measuringu.com/wald.htm to compute an 80% adjusted-Wald binomial confidence interval, using 80% confidence to achieve a one-sided test with α set to 0.10—a reasonable set of criteria for a single-shot industrial test (see Chapter 6, "What are Reasonable Criteria?"), as shown in Fig. 4.8.

The confidence interval approach provides a conclusion consistent with the exact- and mid-*p* methods. Because the adjusted-Wald interval contains the benchmark of 0.90, there is insufficient evidence to conclude that in the tested population at least 90% of users could successfully complete the task. An advantage of computing the confidence interval is that you get an idea about what benchmarks the data in hand would support. For example, because the lower limit of the interval is 87.36%, the data would support the claim that at least 85% of users could successfully complete the task.

2. For this test, 150 out of 180 participants completed the task successfully, and the question is whether this provides compelling evidence that at least 75% of users from the tested population would also successfully complete the task. Because there are more than 15 successes and more than 15 failures, it is OK to use the large sample method—the normal approximation to the binomial— to answer the question. The observed success rate is 150/180 = 0.833, the sample size is 180, and the benchmark is 0.75, so

$$z=\frac{\hat{p}-p}{\sqrt{\frac{p(1-p)}{n}}}=\frac{0.833-0.75}{\sqrt{\frac{0.75(1-0.75)}{180}}}=\frac{0.083}{0.0323}=2.582$$

If the success rate in the population is actually equal to 0.75, then the probability of getting a *z*-score of 2.582 is 0.0049.

$$=\text{NORMSDIST}(2.582)=0.9951$$
$$p=1-0.9951=0.0049$$

To get a better mental picture of what this means, use the calculator at measuringu.com/wald.htm to compute a 98% adjusted-Wald binomial confidence interval, using 98% confidence to achieve a one-sided test with α set to 0.01. As shown in Fig. 4.9, the lower limit of the adjusted-Wald

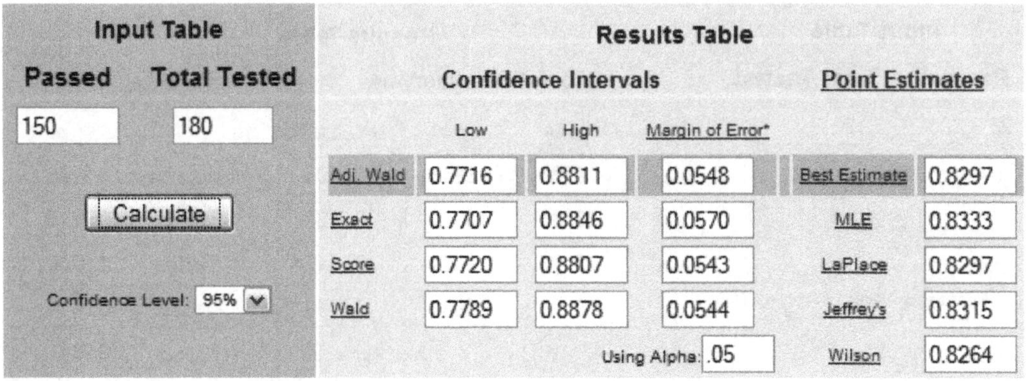

Input Table

Passed	Total Tested
150	180

Calculate

Confidence Level: 95%

Results Table

	Confidence Intervals				Point Estimates	
	Low	High	Margin of Error*			
Adj. Wald	0.7716	0.8811	0.0548		Best Estimate	0.8297
Exact	0.7707	0.8846	0.0570		MLE	0.8333
Score	0.7720	0.8807	0.0543		LaPlace	0.8297
Wald	0.7789	0.8878	0.0544		Jeffrey's	0.8315
		Using Alpha:	.05		Wilson	0.8264

FIGURE 4.9 Results of adjusted-Wald confidence interval for Question 2

confidence interval exceeds the benchmark, which provides compelling evidence of having met the benchmark.

3. Here we need to determine if the observed SUS mean of 74.7, given a sample size of 15 (so there are 14 degrees of freedom) and standard deviation of 12.9, is significantly greater than the benchmark of 70. Applying the formula for a one-sided one-sample *t*-test:

$$t = \frac{\hat{x} - \mu}{\frac{s}{\sqrt{n}}} = \frac{74.7 - 70}{\frac{12.9}{\sqrt{15}}} = \frac{4.7}{3.33} = 1.41$$

The result of this test is $t(14) = 1.41$, $p = 09$.

$$=\text{TDIST}(1.41,14,1) = p = 0.09$$

To run the statistical test using a confidence interval, use confidence of 80% to set the one-sided α to 0.10. The critical value of *t* for 80% confidence and 14 degrees of freedom is 1.345. The standard error of the mean, as shown in the aforementioned equation, is 3.33. The critical difference for the confidence interval, therefore, is 1.345×3.33, or about 4.5, so the confidence interval ranges from 70.2 to 79.2. Because the lower limit of the confidence interval barely exceeds the benchmark, there is reasonable, though not overwhelming, evidence of having met the benchmark.

4. In this problem we need to determine if the observed mean of 5.6, given a sample size of 12 (so there are 11 degrees of freedom) and standard deviation of 1.4, is significantly greater than the benchmark of 5. Applying the formula for a one-sided one-sample *t*-test:

$$t = \frac{\hat{x} - \mu}{\frac{s}{\sqrt{n}}} = \frac{5.6 - 5}{\frac{1.4}{\sqrt{12}}} = \frac{0.6}{0.404} = 1.48$$

The result of this test is $t(11) = 1.48$, $p = 08$.

$$=\text{TDIST}(1.48,11,1) = p = 0.08$$

Just like Question 3, to run the statistical test using a confidence interval, use confidence of 80% to set the one-sided α to 0.10. The critical value of *t* for 80% confidence and 11 degrees of freedom is 1.363. The standard error of the mean, as shown in the aforementioned equation, is 0.404. The critical difference for the confidence interval, therefore, is 1.363 × .404, or about 0.55, so the confidence interval ranges from 5.05 to 6.15. Again, as in Question 3, the lower limit of the confidence interval barely exceeds the benchmark, so there is reasonable, but not overwhelming, evidence of having met the benchmark.

5. The data in this problem are task times, so it's a good idea to start by calculating their natural log values (in Excel, =LN()), which are 1.22, 1.25, 0.53, 1.06, 0.92, and 1.16. For these six values, the mean is 1.025, the standard deviation is 0.271, the standard error of the mean is 0.111, and the criterion is 1.10 (LN(3) = 1.10). Using these values to compute *t*:

$$t = \frac{\mu - \hat{x}}{\frac{s}{\sqrt{n}}} = \frac{1.10 - 1.025}{\frac{0.271}{\sqrt{6}}} = \frac{0.075}{0.111} = 0.676$$

For this test $t(5)$ =0.676, $p = 0.26$. This is far from compelling evidence of having beaten the benchmark.

To run the statistical test using a confidence interval, set the confidence to 80% for a one-sided α of 0.10. The critical value of *t* for 80% confidence and 5 degrees of freedom is 1.476. The standard error of the mean, as shown in the aforementioned equation, is 0.111. The critical difference for the confidence interval, therefore, is 1.476(0.111), or about 0.164, so the confidence interval of the log values ranges from 0.861 to 1.189. Using the EXP function to convert these natural log values back to times in minutes, the confidence interval ranges from 2.4 to 3.3 min. The upper bound of the confidence limit exceeds the criterion of three min, so the results do not support the claim that most callers would complete the task in less than three min. The confidence interval does suggest that, given the data in hand, most callers would complete the task in less than 3.5 min.

REFERENCES

Agresti, A., Franklin, C.A., 2007. Statistics: The Art and Science of Learning from Data. Pearson, New York, NY.

Armitage, P., Berry, G., Matthews, J.N.S., 2002. Statistical Methods in Medical Research, fourth ed. Blackwell Science, Oxford, UK.

Bangor, A., Kortum, P.T., Miller, J.T., 2008. An empirical evaluation of the System Usability Scale. Int. J. Hum.-Comput. Interact. 6, 574–594.

Chapanis, A., 1988. Some generalizations about generalization. Hum. Factors 30, 253–267.

Gonick, L., Smith, W., 1993. Cartoon Guide to Statistics. Collins Reference, New York, NY.

Lah, U., & Lewis, J.R., 2016. How expertise affects a digital-rights-management-sharing application's usability. IEEE Software 33(3), 76–82.

Lewis, J.R., 1982. Testing small system customer set-up. Proceedings of the Human Factors Society 26th Annual Meeting. Human Factors Society, Santa Monica, CA, pp. 718–720.

Lewis, J.R., Sauro, J., 2009. The factor structure of the System Usability Scale. In: Kurosu, M. (Ed.), Human Centered Design, HCII 2009 94-103. Springer-Verlag, Berlin, Germany.

Molich, R., Kirakowski, J., Sauro, J., Tullis, T., 2009. Comparative usability task measurement workshop (CUE-8). At the UPA 2009 Conference. UPA, Portland, OR.

Rosenbaum, S., 1989. Usability evaluations versus usability testing: When and why? IEEE Trans. Prof. Commun. 32, 210–216.

Sauro, J., 2009. Estimating productivity: composite operators for keystroke level modeling. In: Jacko, J.A. (Ed.), In: Proceedings of the 13th International Conference on Human-Computer Interaction, HCII 2009. Springer-Verlag, Berlin, Germany. pp. 352–361.

Sauro, J., 2010. Does better usability increase customer loyalty? From Measuring U. Available from: http://www.measuringu.com/usability-loyalty.php

Sauro, J. (2011). What is a good task-completion rate? From Measuring U. Available from: http://www.measuringu.com/blog/task-completion.php

Sauro, J., Kindlund E., 2005. How long should a task take? Identifying specification limits for task times in usability tests. Proceedings of the Human Computer Interaction International Conference (HCII 2005), Las Vegas, USA.

Sauro, J., Lewis, J.R., 2010. Average task times in usability tests: What to report? Proceedings of CHI 2010. ACM, Atlanta, GA, 2347–2350.

CHAPTER

IS THERE A STATISTICAL DIFFERENCE BETWEEN DESIGNS?

5

INTRODUCTION

Many researchers first realize the need for statistics when they have to compare two designs or products in an A/B test or competitive analysis. When stakes are high (or subject to scrutiny) just providing descriptive statistics and declaring one design better is insufficient. What is needed is to determine whether the difference between designs (such as between conversion rates, task times, or ratings) is greater than what we'd expect from chance. This chapter is all about determining whether a difference is statistically significant and how large or small of a difference likely exists in the untested population.

COMPARING TWO MEANS (RATING SCALES AND TASK TIMES)

A central theme in this book is to understand the role of chance in our calculations. When we can't measure every user to compute a mean likelihood to recommend or a median task time, we have to estimate these averages from a sample.

Just because a sample of users from Product A has a higher average System Usability Scale (SUS) score than a sample from Product B does not mean the average SUS score for all users is higher on Product A than Product B. Chance plays a role in every sample selection and we need to account for that when comparing means. See Sauro (2011a) for more detail on using the SUS for comparing interface usability.

To determine whether SUS scores, Net Promoter Scores, task times, or any two means from continuous variables are significantly different (such as comparing different versions of the same product over time or against a competitive product), you first need to identify whether the same users were used in each test (within-subjects design) or whether there was a different set of users tested on each product (between-subjects design).

WITHIN-SUBJECTS COMPARISON (PAIRED *t*-TEST)

When the same users are in each test group you have removed a major source of variation between your sets of data. In such tests you should alternate which product users encounter first to minimize carryover effects. If all users encounter Product A first, this runs the risk of unfairly biasing users—either for or against Product A. The advantages are that you can attribute differences in measurements to differences between products, and you can detect smaller differences with the same sample size.

Quantifying the User Experience. http://dx.doi.org/10.1016/B978-0-12-802308-2.00005-9

To determine whether there is a significant difference between means of continuous or rating scale measurements, use the following formula:

$$t = \frac{\bar{D}}{\frac{s_D}{\sqrt{n}}}$$

where $\bar{D}$ is the mean of the difference scores,
S_D is the standard deviation of the difference scores,
n is the sample size (the total number of users), and
t is the test statistic (look-up using the t-distribution based on the sample size for *two-sided area*). See Technical Note 1.

Example 1: Comparing two System Usability Scale (SUS) means

For example, in a test between two expense-reporting applications, 26 users worked (in random order) with two web applications (A and B). They performed several tasks on both systems and then completed the 10-item SUS questionnaire, with the results shown in Table 5.1 (subtracting the score for B from the score for A to get the difference score).

Product A had a mean SUS score of 82.2 and Product B had a mean SUS score of 52.7. The mean of the difference scores was 29.5 with a standard deviation of 14.125. Plugging these values in the formula, we get

$$t = \frac{29.5}{\frac{14.125}{\sqrt{26}}}$$

$$t = 10.649$$

We have a test statistic (t) equal to 10.649. To determine whether this is significant, we need to look up the p-value using a t-table, the Excel function =TDIST(), or the calculator available at http://www.usablestats.com/calcs/tdist.

The degrees of freedom for this type of test is equal to $n - 1$, so we have 25 degrees of freedom (26−1). Because this is a two-sided test (see Technical Note 1), the p-value is =TDIST(10.649,25,2) = .0000000001. Because this value is so small, we can conclude that there's less than a one in a billion chance that the population mean SUS scores are equal to each other. Put another way, we can be over 99.999% sure products A and B have different SUS scores. Product A's SUS score of 82.2 is statistically significantly higher than product B's of 52.7, so we can conclude users perceive Product A as easier to use.

Technical Note 1: We're using the two-sided area (instead of the one-sided area that was used in comparing a mean to a benchmark in Chapter 4) because we want to see whether the difference between SUS means is equal to 0, which is a two-sided research question. It is tempting to look at the results and see that Product A had a higher mean and then use just a one-sided test. Although it wouldn't matter in

Table 5.1 Pairs of SUS Scores and Their Differences for Example 1

User	A	B	Difference
1	77.5	60	17.5
2	90	62.5	27.5
3	80	45	35
4	77.5	20	57.5
5	100	80	20
6	95	42.5	52.5
7	82.5	32.5	50
8	97.5	80	17.5
9	80	52.5	27.5
10	87.5	60	27.5
11	77.5	42.5	35
12	87.5	87.5	0
13	82.5	52.5	30
14	50	10	40
15	77.5	67.5	10
16	82.5	40	42.5
17	80	57.5	22.5
18	65	32.5	32.5
19	72.5	67.5	5
20	85	47.5	37.5
21	80	45	35
22	100	62.5	37.5
23	80	40	40
24	57.5	45	12.5
25	97.5	65	32.5
26	95	72.5	22.5
Mean	**82.2**	**52.7**	**29.5**

this example, it can happen that the one-sided test generates a significant *p*-value but the corresponding two-sided *p*-value is not significant. Waiting until after the test has been conducted to determine whether to use a one -or two-sided test improperly capitalizes on chance. We strongly recommend sticking with the two-sided test when comparing two means (also see Chapter 9, "Should You Always Conduct a Two-Tailed Test?").

Confidence interval around the difference

With any comparison we also want to know the size of the difference (often referred to as the effect size). The p-value we get from conducting the paired t-test tells us only that the difference is significant. A significant difference could mean just a one-point difference in SUS scores, which would not be of much practical importance. As sample sizes get large (above 100), as is common in remote unmoderated testing, it becomes more likely to see a statistically significant difference when the actual effect size is not practically significant. The confidence interval around the difference helps us distinguish between trivial (albeit statistically significant) differences and differences users would likely notice.

To generate a confidence interval around the difference scores to understand the likely range of the true difference between products, use the following formula:

$$\bar{D} \pm t_a \frac{s_D}{\sqrt{n}}$$

where $\bar{D}$ is the mean of the difference scores (as was used in computing the test statistic),
n is the sample size (the total number of users),
S_D is the standard deviation of the difference scores (also used in computing the test statistic), and
t_a is the critical value from the t-distribution for $n-1$ degrees of freedom and the specified level of confidence.

For a 95% confidence interval and sample size of 26 (25 degrees of freedom), the critical value is 2.06. See http://www.usablestats.com/calcs/tdist to obtain critical values from the t-distribution, or in Excel use =TINV(0.05,25).

Plugging in the values we get

$$29.5 \pm 2.06 \frac{14.125}{\sqrt{26}}$$

$$29.5 \pm 5.705$$

We can be 95% confident the actual difference between product SUS scores is between 23.8 and 35.2.

Practical significance

The difference is statistically significant, but is it practically significant? To answer this question depends on how we interpret the lowest and highest plausible differences. Even the lowest estimate of the difference of 23.8 points puts Product A at 45% higher than Product B. It also helps to know something about SUS scores. A difference of 23.8 points crosses a substantial range of products and places Product A's perceived usability much higher than Product B's relative to hundreds of other product scores (Sauro, 2011a; also see Chapter 8, Tables 8.5 and 8.7). Given this information it seems reasonable to conclude that users would notice the difference in the usability and it suggests that the difference is both statistically and practically meaningful.

Technical Note 2: For the confidence interval formula we use the convention that t_a represents a two-sided confidence level. Many, but not all, statistics books use the convention $t_{\left(1-\frac{\alpha}{2}\right)}$ which is based on a table of values that is one-sided. We find this approach more confusing because in most cases you'll be working with two-sided rather than one-sided confidence intervals. It is also inconsistent with the Excel TINV function, which is a very convenient way to get desired values of t when computing confidence intervals.

COMPARING TASK TIMES

In earlier chapters we saw how task times have a strong positive skew from some users taking a long time to complete a task. This skew makes confidence intervals (Chapter 3) and tests against benchmarks (Chapter 4) less accurate. In those situations we applied a log transformation to the raw times to improve the accuracy of the results. When analyzing difference scores, however, the two-tailed paired t-test is widely considered robust to violations of normality, especially when the skew in the data takes the same shape in both samples (Agresti and Franklin, 2007; Box, 1953; Howell, 2002). Although sample mean task times will differ from their population median, we can still accurately tell whether the difference between means is greater than what we'd expect from chance alone using the paired t-test, so there is no need to complicate this test with a transformation.

Example 2: Comparing two task times

In the same test of two accounting systems used in Example 1, task times were also collected. One task asked users to create an expense report. Of the 26 users who attempted the task, 21 completed it successfully on both products. These 21 task times and their difference scores appear in Table 5.2. Failed task attempts are indicated with a minus sign and not included in the calculation.

The mean *difference* score is −77 s and the standard deviation of the difference scores is 61 s. Plugging these values in the formula we get

$$t = \frac{\hat{D}}{\frac{s_D}{\sqrt{n}}}$$

$$t = \frac{-77}{\frac{61}{\sqrt{21}}}$$

$$t = -5.78$$

We have a test statistic (t) equal to −5.78 with 20 ($n - 1$) degrees of freedom and the decision prior to running the study to conduct a two-sided test. To determine whether this is significant we need to look up the p-value using a t-table, the Excel function =TDIST(), or the calculator available at http://www.usablestats.com/calcs/tdist. Using =TDIST(5.78,20,2), we find $p = 0.00001$, so there is strong evidence to conclude that users take less time to complete an expense report on Product A. If you follow the steps from the previous example, you'll find that the 95% confidence interval for this difference ranged from about 49–104 s—a difference that users are likely to notice.

Table 5.2 Pairs of Completion Times and Their Differences for Example 2

User	A	B	Difference
1	223	—	
2	140	—	
3	178	184	−6
4	145	195	−50
5	256	—	
6	148	210	−62
7	222	299	−77
8	141	148	−7
9	149	184	−35
10	150	—	
11	133	229	−96
12	160	—	
13	117	200	−83
14	292	549	−257
15	127	235	−108
16	151	210	−59
17	127	218	−91
18	211	196	15
19	106	162	−56
20	121	176	−55
21	146	269	−123
22	135	336	−201
23	111	167	−56
24	116	203	−87
25	187	247	−60
26	120	174	−54
Mean	**158**	**228**	**−77**

In this example, the test statistic is negative because we subtracted the typically longer task time (from Product B) from the shorter task time (Product A). We would get the same *p*-value if we subtracted the smaller time from the larger time, changing the sign of the test statistic. When using the Excel TDIST function, keep in mind that it only works with positive values of *t*.

Normality assumption of the paired t-test

As we've seen with the paired *t*-test formula, the computations are performed on the difference scores. We therefore are only working with one sample of data which means the paired *t*-test is really just the one-sample *t*-test from Chapter 4 with a different name.

The paired *t*-test therefore has the same normality assumption as the one-sample *t*-test. For large sample sizes (above 30) normality isn't a concern because the sampling distribution of the mean is normally distributed (see Chapter 9). For smaller sample sizes (less than 30) and for two-tailed tests, the one-sample *t*-test/paired *t*-test is considered robust against violations of the normality assumption. That is, data can be non-normal (as with task-time data) but still generate accurate *p*-values (Box, 1953) when using a paired *t*-test.

BETWEEN-SUBJECTS COMPARISON (TWO-SAMPLE *t*-TEST)

When a different set of users is tested on each product there is variation both between users and between designs. Any difference between the means (e.g., questionnaire data, task times) must be tested to see whether it is greater than the variation between the different users.

To determine whether there is a significant difference between means of independent samples of users, we use the two-sample *t*-test (also called *t*-test on independent means). It uses the following formula:

$$t = \frac{\hat{x}_1 - \hat{x}_2}{\sqrt{\frac{s_1^2}{n_1} + \frac{s_2^2}{n_2}}}$$

where $\hat{x}_1$ and $\hat{x}_2$ are means from samples 1 and 2,
s_1 and s_2 are standard deviations from samples 1 and 2,
n_1 and n_2 are the sample size from samples 1 and 2, and
t is the test statistic (look-up using the *t*-distribution based on the sample size for *two-sided area*)

Example 1: Comparing two SUS scores

For example, in a test between two CRM applications, the following SUS scores were obtained after 11 users attempted tasks on Product A and 12 different users attempted the same tasks on Product B for a total of 23 different users tested (Table 5.3).

Product A had a mean SUS score of 51.6 (sd = 4.07) and Product B had a mean SUS score of 49.6 (sd = 4.63). Plugging these values in the formula we get

$$t = \frac{51.6 - 49.6}{\sqrt{\frac{4.07^2}{11} + \frac{4.63^2}{12}}}$$

$$t = 1.102$$

Table 5.3 Data for Comparison of SUS Scores from Independent Groups

A	B
50	50
45	52.5
57.5	52.5
47.5	50
52.5	52.5
57.5	47.5
52.5	50
50	50
52.5	50
55	40
47.5	42.5
	57.5
51.6	**49.6**

The observed difference in SUS scores generates a test statistic (*t*) equal to 1.102. To determine whether this is significant, we need to look up the *p*-value using a *t*-table, the Excel function =TDIST, or the calculator available at http://www.usablestats.com/calcs/tdist.

We have 20 degrees of freedom (see the sidebar on "Degrees of Freedom for the Two-sample *t*-test") and want the ***two-sided*** area, so the *p*-value is =TDIST(1.102,20,2) = 0.2835. Because this value is rather large (and well above 0.05 or 0.10) we can't conclude that the difference is greater than chance. A *p*-value of 0.2835 tells us the probability that this difference of two points is due to chance is 28.35%. Put another way, we can be only about 71.65% sure that products A and B have different SUS scores—a level of certainty that is better than 50–50 but that falls well below the usual criterion for claiming a significant difference. Product A's SUS score of 51.6, while higher, is not statistically distinguishable from Product B's score of 49.6 at this sample size.

If we had to pick one product, there's more evidence that Product A has a higher SUS score, but in reality it could be that the two are indistinguishable in the minds of users or, less likely, that users think Product B is more usable. In most applied research settings, having only 71.65% confidence that the products are different is not sufficient evidence for a critical decision.

With time and budget to collect more data, you can use the estimates of the standard deviation and the observed difference to compute sample size needed to detect a two-point difference in SUS scores (see Chapter 6). Given a sample standard deviation of 4.1 and a difference of two points (95% confidence and 80% Power), you'd need a sample size of 136 (68 in each group) to reliably detect a difference this small.

DEGREES OF FREEDOM FOR THE TWO-SAMPLE *t*-TEST

It's a little more complicated than the one-sample test, but that's what computers are for

It's simple to calculate the degrees of freedom for a one-sample *t*-test—just subtract 1 from the sample size ($n - 1$). There's also a simple formula for computing degrees of freedom for a two-sample *t*-test, which appears in many statistics books—add the independent sample sizes together and subtract 2 ($n_1 + n_2 - 2$).

Instead of using that simple method for the two-sample *t*-test, in this book we use a modification called the Welch–Satterthwaite procedure (Satterthwaite, 1946; Welch, 1938). It provides accurate results even if the variances are unequal (one of the assumptions of the two-sample *t*-test) by adjusting the number of degrees of freedom using the following formula:

$$\mathrm{df} = \frac{\left(\frac{s_1^2}{n_1} + \frac{s_2^2}{n_2}\right)^2}{\frac{\left(\frac{s_1^2}{n_1}\right)^2}{n_1 - 1} + \frac{\left(\frac{s_2^2}{n_2}\right)^2}{n_2 - 1}}$$

where s_1 and s_2 are the standard deviations of the two groups, and
n_1 and n_2 are the group's sample sizes.

For fractional results, round the degrees of freedom (df) down to the nearest integer. For the data in Table 5.3, the computation of the degrees of freedom is

$$\mathrm{df} = \frac{\left(\frac{4.07^2}{11} + \frac{4.63^2}{12}\right)^2}{\frac{\left(\frac{4.07^2}{11}\right)^2}{11 - 1} + \frac{\left(\frac{4.63^2}{12}\right)^2}{12 - 1}} = \frac{10.8}{0.52} = 20.8, \text{ which rounds down to } 20$$

The computations are a bit tedious to do by hand, but most software packages compute it automatically, and it's fairly easy to set up in Excel. If, for some reason, you don't have access to a computer and the variances are approximately equal, you can use the simpler formula ($n_1 + n_2 - 2$). If the variances are markedly different (e.g., the ratio of the standard deviations is greater than 2), as a conservative shortcut you can subtract 2 from the smaller of the two sample sizes.

Confidence interval around the difference

With any comparison, we also want to know the size of the difference (the effect size). The *p*-value we get from conducting the two-sample *t*-test only tells us that a significant difference exists. For example, a significant difference could mean just a one-point difference in SUS scores (which would not be of much practical importance) or a 20-point difference, which would be meaningful.

There are several ways to report an effect size, but for practical work, the most compelling and easiest-to-understand is the confidence interval. We can use the following formula to generate a confidence interval around the difference scores to understand the likely range of the true difference between products:

$$(\hat{x}_1 - \hat{x}_2) \pm t_a \sqrt{\frac{s_1^2}{n_1} + \frac{s_2^2}{n_2}}$$

where $\hat{x}_1$ and $\hat{x}_2$ are means from samples 1 and 2,
s_1 and s_2 are standard deviations from samples 1 and 2,

n_1 and n_2 are the sample size from samples 1 and 2, and
t_a is the critical value from the t-distribution for a specified level of confidence and degrees of freedom. For a 95% confidence interval and 20 degrees of freedom, the critical value is 2.086. See http://www.usablestats/calcs/tdist for obtaining critical values from the t-distribution.

Plugging in the values we get

$$51.6-49.6 \pm 2.086\sqrt{\frac{4.07^2}{11}+\frac{4.63^2}{12}}$$

$$2.0 \pm 3.8$$

So, we can be 95% confident that the actual difference between product SUS scores is between −1.8 and 5.8. Because the interval crosses zero, we can't be 95% sure that a difference exists; as stated previously, we're only 71.65% sure. Although Product A appears to be a little better than Product B, the confidence interval tells us that there is still a modest chance that Product B has a higher SUS score (by as much as 1.8 points).

Example 2: Comparing two task times

Twenty users were asked to add a contact to a CRM application. Eleven users completed the task on the existing version and nine different users completed the same task on the new enhanced version. Is there compelling evidence to conclude that there has been a reduction in the mean time to complete the task? The raw values (in seconds) appear in Table 5.4.

The mean task time for the 11 users of the old version was 37 s with a standard deviation of 22.4 s. The mean task time for the nine users of the new version was 18 s with a standard deviation of 13.4 s. Plugging in the values we get

$$t=\frac{\hat{x}_1-\hat{x}_2}{\sqrt{\frac{s_1^2}{n_1}+\frac{s_2^2}{n_2}}}$$

$$t=\frac{37-18}{\sqrt{\frac{22.4^2}{11}+\frac{13.4^2}{9}}}$$

$$t=2.33$$

The observed difference in mean times generates a test statistic (t) equal to 2.33. To determine whether this is significant we need to find the p-value using a t-table, the Excel function =TDIST, or the calculator available at http://www.usablestats.com/calcs/tdist.

We have 16 degrees of freedom (see the sidebar on "Degrees of Freedom for the Two-sample t-test") and want the *two-sided* area, so the p-value is =TDIST(2.33,16,2) = 0.033. Because this value is rather small (less than 0.05) there is reasonable evidence that the two task times are different. We can conclude users take less time with the new design. From this sample we can estimate the likely range of the difference

Table 5.4 Data for Comparison of Task Times from Independent Groups

Old	New
18	12
44	35
35	21
78	9
38	2
18	10
16	5
22	38
40	30
77	
20	

between mean times by generating a confidence interval. For a 95% confidence interval with 16 degrees of freedom, the critical value of *t* is 2.12. See http://www.usablestats.com/calcs/tdist for obtaining critical values from the *t*-distribution.

Plugging the values into the formula we get

$$(\hat{x}_1 - \hat{x}_2) \pm t_a \sqrt{\frac{s_1^2}{n_1} + \frac{s_2^2}{n_2}}$$

$$37 - 18 \pm 2.12\sqrt{\frac{22.4^2}{11} + \frac{13.4^2}{9}}$$

$$19 \pm 17.2$$

We can be 95% confident the difference in mean times is between about 2 and 36 s.

ASSUMPTIONS OF THE *t*-TESTS

The two-sample *t*-test has four assumptions:

1. Both samples are representative of their parent populations (representativeness).
2. The two samples are unrelated to each other (independence).
3. Both samples are approximately normally distributed (normality).
4. The variances in both groups are approximate equal (homogeneity of variances).

As with all statistical procedures, the first assumption is the most important. The *p*-values, confidence intervals, and conclusions are only valid if the sample of users is representative of the population about which you are making inferences. In user research this means having the right users attempt the right tasks on the right interface.

Meeting the second assumption is usually not a problem in user research as the values from one participant are unlikely to affect the responses of another. The latter two assumptions, however, can cause some consternation and are worth discussing.

Normality

Like the one-sample *t*-test, paired *t*-test, and most parametric statistical tests, there is an underlying assumption of normality. Specifically, this test assumes that the sampling distribution of the mean differences (not the distribution of the raw scores) is approximately normally distributed. When this distribution of mean differences is not normal, the *p*-values can be off by some amount. For large samples (above 30 for all but the most extreme distributions) the normality assumption isn't an issue because the sampling distribution of the mean is normally distributed according to the Central Limit Theorem (see Chapter 9).

Fortunately, even for small sample sizes (less than 30), the *t*-test still generates reliable results even when the data are not normally distributed. For example, Box (1953) showed that a typical amount of error is a manageable 2%. For example, if you generate a *p*-value of 0.02, the long-term actual probability might be 0.04. This is especially the case when the sample sizes in both groups are equal so, if possible, you should plan for equal sample sizes in each group, even though you might end up with uneven sample sizes.

Equality of variances

The third assumption is that the variances (and equivalently the standard deviations) are approximately equal in both groups. As a general rule, you should only be concerned about unequal variances when the ratio between the two standard deviations is greater than 2 (e.g., a standard deviation of 4 in one sample and 12 in the other is a ratio of 3) (Agresti and Franklin, 2007). The robustness of the two-sample *t*-test also extends to violations of this assumption, especially when the sample sizes are roughly equal (Agresti and Franklin, 2007; Box, 1953; Howell, 2002). For a method of adjusting degrees of freedom to help compensate for unequal variances, see the sidebar: "Degrees of Freedom for the Two-sample *t*-test."

Don't worry too much about violating assumptions (except representativeness)

Now that we've covered the assumptions for the two-sample *t*-test, we want to reassure you that you shouldn't concern yourself with them too much for most practical work—except of course representativeness. No amount of statistical manipulations can overcome the problem of measuring the wrong users performing the wrong tasks.

We've provided the detail on the other assumptions here so you can be aware that they exist. You might have encountered warnings about non-normal data and heterogeneous variances in statistics books, or from colleagues critical of the use of *t*-tests with typical continuous or rating-scale usability metrics. It is our opinion that the two-sample *t*-test, especially when used with two-sided probabilities and (near) equal sample sizes, is a workhorse that will generate accurate results for statistical comparisons in user research. It is, however, always a good idea to examine your data, ideally graphically to look for outliers or unusual observations that could have arisen from coding errors or errors users made while responding. These types of data quality errors can have a real effect on your results—an effect that properly conducted statistics cannot fix.

COMPARING COMPLETION RATES, CONVERSION RATES, AND A/B TESTING

A binary response variable takes on only two values: yes/no, convert/didn't convert, purchased/didn't purchase, completed the task/failed the task, and so on. These are coded into values of 1 and 0, respectively. Even continuous measures can be degraded into binary measures: proportion of users taking less than a minute to complete a task, proportion of responses scoring 9 or 10 on an 11-point scale. These types of binary measures appear extensively in user research.

As with the continuous method for comparing task times and satisfaction scores, we need to consider whether the two samples being compared have different users in each group (between-subjects) or use the same people (within-subjects).

BETWEEN-SUBJECTS

Comparing the two outcomes of binary variables for two independent groups happens to be one of the most frequently computed procedures in applied statistics. Surprisingly, there is little agreement on the best statistical test for this situation. For large sample sizes, the chi-square test is typically recommended. For small sample sizes, the Fisher exact test (also called the Fisher–Irwin test) is typically recommended. However, there is disagreement on what constitutes a "small" or "large" sample size and what version of these tests to use. A recent survey of medical and general statistics textbooks by Campbell (2007) found that only 2 of 14 books agreed on what procedure to recommend for comparing two independent binary outcomes.

The latest research suggests that a slight adjustment to the standard chi-square test, and equivalently to the two-proportion test, generates the best results for almost all sample sizes. The adjustment is simply subtracting 1 from the total sample size and using it in the standard chi-square or two-proportion test formulas (shown later in this chapter). Because there is so much debate on this topic we spend the next few pages describing the alternatives which you are likely to encounter (or were taught) and then present the recommended $N-1$ chi-square test and $N-1$ two-proportion test. You can skip to the $N-1$ chi-square section if you have no interest in understanding the alternative formulas and their drawbacks.

Chi-square test of independence

One of the oldest methods and the one typically taught in introductory statistics books is the chi-square test. Karl Pearson, who also developed the most widely used correlation coefficient, proposed the chi-square test in 1900 (Pearson, 1900).

It uses an intuitive concept of comparing the observed counts in each group with what you would expect from chance. The chi-square test makes no assumptions about the parent population in each group, so it is a distribution-free nonparametric test. It uses a 2 × 2 table (pronounced two by two) with the nomenclature shown in Table 5.5.

Table 5.5 Nomenclature for Chi-Square Tests of Independence

	Pass	Fail	Total
Design A	a	b	m
Design B	c	d	n
Total	r	s	N

To conduct a chi-square test, compare the result of the following formula to the chi-square distribution with 1 degree of freedom.

$$\chi^2 = \frac{(ad - bc)^2 N}{mnrs}$$

> **DEGREES OF FREEDOM FOR CHI-SQUARE TESTS**
>
> **For a 2 × 2 table, it's always 1**
>
> The general formula for calculating the degrees of freedom for a chi-square test of independence is to multiply one less than the number of rows by one less than the number of columns.
>
> $$df = (r - 1)(c - 1)$$
>
> In a 2 × 2 table, there are two rows and two columns, so all chi-square tests conducted on these types of tables have 1 degree of freedom.

For example, if 40 out of 60 (67%) users complete a task on Design A, can we conclude it is statistically different from Design B where 15 out of 35 (43%) users passed? Setting this up in Table 5.6 and filling the values in the formula, we get

$$\chi^2 = \frac{(40 \times 20 - 20 \times 15)^2 \times 95}{60 \times 35 \times 55 \times 40}$$

$$\chi^2 = 5.1406$$

We use a table of chi-square values or the Excel function =CHIDIST(5.1406, 1), and get the *p*-value of 0.0234. Because this value is low, we conclude the completion rates are statistically different. Design A has the higher completion rate and so it is statistically higher than B's.

Small sample sizes

The chi-square test tends to generate accurate results for large sample sizes, but is not recommended when sample sizes are small. As mentioned earlier, both what constitutes a small sample size and what alternative procedure to use is the subject of continued research and debate.

Table 5.6 Data for Chi-Square Test of Independence

	Pass	Fail	Total
Design A	40	20	60
Design B	15	20	35
Total	55	40	95

The most common sample size guideline is to use the chi-square test when the expected cell counts are greater than 5 (Cochran, 1952, 1954). This rule appears in most introductory statistics text despite being somewhat arbitrary (Campbell, 2007). The expected counts are different than the actual cell counts, computed by multiplying the row and column totals for each cell and then dividing by the total sample size. From the aforementioned example, this generates the following expected cell counts:

$$\frac{(r \times m)}{N} = \frac{(55 \times 60)}{95} = 34.74$$

$$\frac{(s \times m)}{N} = \frac{(40 \times 60)}{95} = 25.26$$

$$\frac{(r \times n)}{N} = \frac{(55 \times 35)}{95} = 20.26$$

$$\frac{(s \times n)}{N} = \frac{(40 \times 35)}{95} = 14.74$$

The minimum expected cell count for the data in the example is 14.74 which is greater than 5 and so, according to the common sample size guideline, the normal chi-square test is appropriate.

Here is another example comparing conversion rates on two designs with a total sample size of 22 and some expected cell counts less than 5. The cell nomenclature appears in parentheses in Table 5.7. Eleven out of 12 users (92%) completed the task on Design A; 5 out of 10 (50%) completed it on Design B.

Filling in these values we get

$$\chi^2 = \frac{(ad - bc)^2 N}{mnrs}$$

$$\chi^2 = \frac{(11 \times 5 - 1 \times 5)^2 \times 22}{12 \times 10 \times 16 \times 6}$$

$$\chi^2 = 4.7743$$

Looking up this value in a chi-square table or using the Excel function =CHIDIST(4.7743, 1) we get the p-value of 0.0288, so we conclude there is a statistically significant difference between conversion rates for these designs.

Table 5.7 Conversion Rates for Two Designs

	Pass	Fail	Total
Design A	11 (*a*)	1 (*b*)	12 (*m*)
Design B	5 (*c*)	5 (*d*)	10 (*n*)
Total	16 (*r*)	6 (*s*)	22 (*N*)

However, in examining the expected cell frequencies we see that two are less than 5.

$$\frac{(r \times m)}{N} = \frac{(16 \times 12)}{22} = 8.73$$

$$\frac{(s \times m)}{N} = \frac{(6 \times 12)}{22} = 3.27$$

$$\frac{(r \times n)}{N} = \frac{(16 \times 10)}{22} = 7.27$$

$$\frac{(s \times n)}{N} = \frac{(6 \times 10)}{22} = 2.73$$

With low expected cell counts, most statistics textbooks warn against using the chi-square test and instead recommend either the Fisher exact test (aka Fisher Irwin test) or the chi-square test with Yates correction. Before covering those alternative methods, however, we should mention the two-proportion test.

Two-proportion test

Another common way for comparing two proportions is the two-proportion test. It is mathematically equivalent to the chi-square test. Agresti and Franklin (2007) have suggested a rule of thumb for its minimum sample size that there should be at least 10 successes and 10 failures in each sample.

It generates a test statistic that is looked up using the normal (z) distribution to find the p-values. It uses the following formula and will be further discussed in a subsequent section ($N-1$ two-proportion test).

$$z = \frac{(\hat{p}_1 - \hat{p}_2)}{\sqrt{PQ \times \left(\frac{1}{n_1} + \frac{1}{n_2}\right)}}$$

Fisher exact test

The Fisher exact test uses exact probabilities instead of approximations as is done with the chi-square distribution and t distributions. As with the exact binomial confidence interval method used in Chapter 4, exact methods tend to be conservative and generate p-values that are higher than they should be and therefore require larger differences between groups to achieve statistical significance.

The Fisher exact test computes the p-values by finding the probabilities of all possible combinations of 2×2 tables that have the same marginal totals (the values in cells m, n, r, and s) that are equal to or more extreme than the ones observed. These values are computed for each 2×2 table using the following formula:

$$p = \frac{m!n!r!s!}{a!b!c!d!N!}$$

The computations are very tedious to do by hand and, because they involve factorials, can generate extremely large numbers. Software is used in computing the p-values because there are typically dozens of tables that have the same marginal or more extreme marginal totals (m, n, r, and s) even for modest sample sizes. An online Fisher exact test calculator is available at www.measuringu.com/fisher.php.

The two-tailed p-value generated from the calculator is 0.0557. Using 0.05 as our threshold for significance, strictly speaking, we would conclude there is NOT a statistically significant difference between designs using the Fisher exact test. In applied use, we'd likely come to the same conclusion if we have 94.4% confidence or 95% confidence—namely that it's unlikely that the difference is due to chance. For more discussion of this topic, see "Can You Reject the Null Hypothesis When $p > 0.05$?" in Chapter 9.

Yates correction

The Yates correction attempts to approximate the p-values from the Fisher exact test with a simple adjustment to the original chi-square formula.

$$\chi^2_{\text{yates}} = \frac{\left(|ad - bc| - \frac{N}{2}\right)^2 N}{mnrs}$$

Using the same aforementioned example, we get the Yates chi-square test statistic of

$$\chi^2_{\text{yates}} = \frac{\left(|11 \times 5 - 1 \times 5| - \frac{22}{2}\right)^2 \times 22}{12 \times 10 \times 16 \times 6}$$

$$\chi^2_{\text{yates}} = 2.905$$

Looking up this value in a chi-square table or using the Excel function =CHIDIST(2.905, 1) we get the p-value of 0.0883. Using 0.05 as our threshold for significance, we would conclude there is NOT a statistically significant difference between designs using the Yates correction (although, as with the Fisher test, this outcome would probably draw our attention to the possibility of a significant difference).

For this example, the p-value for the Yates correction is *higher* than the Fisher exact test, which is a typical result. In general, the Yates correction tends to generate p-values higher than the Fisher exact test and is therefore even more conservative, overstating the true long-term probability of a difference. For this reason and because most software programs can easily calculate the Fisher exact test, we do not recommend the use of the chi-square test with the Yates correction.

N−1 Chi-square test

Pearson also proposed an alternate form of the chi-square test in his original work (Campbell, 2007; Pearson, 1900). Instead of multiplying the numerator by N (the total sample size), it is multiplied by $N-1$.

$$\chi^2 = \frac{(ad - bc)^2 (N-1)}{mnrs}$$

Campbell (2007) has shown this simple adjustment to perform better than the standard chi-square, Yates variant, and Fisher exact tests for almost all sample sizes. It tends *not* to work well when the minimum expected cell count is less than 1. Fortunately, having such low expected cell counts doesn't happen a lot in user research, and when it does, the Fisher exact test is an appropriate substitute. Using the $N-1$ chi-square test, we get the following p-value from the example data used previously:

$$\chi^2 = \frac{(11\times5-1\times5)^2\times21}{12\times10\times16\times6}$$

$$\chi^2 = 4.557$$

Looking up this value in a chi-square table or using the Excel function =CHIDIST(4.557, 1) we get the p-value of 0.0328. Using 0.05 as our threshold for significance, we would conclude there is a statistically significant difference between designs.

N−1 Two-proportion test

An alternative way of analyzing a 2 × 2 table is to compare the differences in proportions. Similar to the two-sample t-test where the difference between the means was compared to the t-distribution, the $N-1$ chi-square test is equivalent to an $N-1$ two-proportion test. Instead of using the chi-square distribution to generate the p-values, we use the normal (z) distribution.

Many readers may find this approach more intuitive for three reasons.

1. It is often easier to think in terms of completion rates or conversion rates (measured as proportions) rather than the number of users that pass or fail.
2. We use the more familiar and readily available normal distribution as the reference distribution for finding p-values and don't need to worry about degrees of freedom.
3. The confidence interval formula uses the difference between the two proportions and makes for an easier transition in computation and understanding.

The $N-1$ two-proportion test uses the standard large sample two-proportion formula (as shown in the previous section) except that it is adjusted by a factor of $\sqrt{\frac{N-1}{N}}$. This adjustment is algebraically equivalent to the $N-1$ chi-square adjustment. The resulting formula is

$$z = \frac{(\hat{p}_1-\hat{p}_2)\sqrt{\frac{N-1}{N}}}{\sqrt{PQ\times\left(\frac{1}{n_1}+\frac{1}{n_2}\right)}}$$

where

$\hat{p}_1$ and $\hat{p}_2$ are the sample proportions

$P=\left(\frac{x_1+x_2}{n_1+n_2}\right)$, where x_1 and x_2 are the numbers completing or converting, and n_1 and n_2 are the numbers attempting

$Q=1-P$

N is the total sample size in both groups

Table 5.8 Summary of *p*-values Generated from Sample Data for Chi-Square and Fisher Tests

Method	*P*-value	Notes
$N-1$ chi-square/$N-1$ two-proportion test	0.0328	Recommended: When expected cell counts are all >1
chi-square/ two-proportion test	0.0288	Not Recommended: Understates true probability for small sample sizes
chi-square with Yates correction	0.0883	Not Recommended: Overstates true probability for all sample sizes
Fisher exact test	0.0557	Recommended: When any expected cell count is <1

Using the example data we have 11 out of 12 (91.7%) completing on Design A and 5 out of 10 (50.0%) completing on Design B for a total sample size of 22.

First we compute the values for P and Q and substitute them in the larger equation.

$$P=\left(\frac{11+5}{12+10}\right)=0.727 \quad \text{and} \quad Q=1-0.727=0.273$$

$$z=\frac{(0.917-0.50)\sqrt{\frac{22-1}{22}}}{\sqrt{0.727\times0.273\times\left(\frac{1}{12}+\frac{1}{10}\right)}}$$

$$z=2.135$$

We can use a normal (z) table to look up the two-sided p-value or the Excel function =(1-NORMSDIST(2.135))*2 which generates a two-sided p-value of 0.0328—the same p-value we got from the $N-1$ chi-square test, demonstrating their mathematical equivalence.

Table 5.8 summarizes the p-values generated from the sample data for all approaches and our recommended strategy.

Confidence interval for the difference between proportions

As with all tests of statistical comparisons, in addition to knowing whether the difference is significant, we also want to know how large of a difference likely exists. To do so for this type of comparison, we generate a confidence interval around the difference between two proportions. The recommended formula is an adjusted-Wald confidence interval similar to that used in Chapter 4, except that it is for a difference between proportions (Agresti and Caffo, 2000) instead of around a single proportion (Agresti and Coull, 1998).

The adjustment is to add a quarter of a squared z-critical value to the numerator and half a squared z-critical value to the denominator when computing each proportion. For a 95% confidence level the two-sided z-critical value is 1.96. This is like adding two pseudo observations to each sample—one success and one failure—as shown in the following:

$$\hat{p}_{\text{adj}}=\frac{x+\frac{z^2}{4}}{n+\frac{z^2}{2}}=\frac{x+\frac{1.96^2}{4}}{n+\frac{1.96^2}{2}}=\frac{x+.9604}{n+1.92}\approx\frac{x+1}{n+2}$$

This adjustment is then inserted into the more familiar (to some) Wald confidence interval formula.

$$(\hat{p}_{\text{adj1}} - \hat{p}_{\text{adj2}}) \pm z_{\alpha}\sqrt{\frac{\hat{p}_{\text{adj1}}(1-\hat{p}_{\text{adj1}})}{n_{\text{adj1}}} + \frac{\hat{p}_{\text{adj2}}(1-\hat{p}_{\text{adj2}})}{n_{\text{adj2}}}}$$

z_{α} = two-sided z critical value for the level of confidence (e.g., 1.96 for a 95% confidence level)

With the same example data we've used so far, we will compute a 95% confidence interval. First we compute the adjustments.

For Design A, 11 out of 12 users completed the task, and these become our x and n, respectively.

$$\hat{p}_{\text{adj1}} = \frac{x + \frac{z^2}{4}}{n + \frac{z^2}{2}} = \frac{11 + \frac{1.96^2}{4}}{12 + \frac{1.96^2}{2}} = \frac{11 + 0.9604}{12 + 1.92} = \frac{11.96}{13.92} = 0.859$$

For Design B, five out of ten users completed the task, and these become our respective x and n.

$$\hat{p}_{\text{adj2}} = \frac{x + \frac{z^2}{4}}{n + \frac{z^2}{2}} = \frac{5 + \frac{1.96^2}{4}}{10 + \frac{1.96^2}{2}} = \frac{5 + 0.9604}{10 + 1.92} = \frac{5.96}{11.92} = 0.50$$

Note: When the sample proportion is 0.5, the adjusted p will also be 0.50, as seen in this example.

Plugging these adjustments into the main formula we get

$$(0.859 - 0.50) \pm 1.96\sqrt{\frac{0.859(1-0.859)}{13.92} + \frac{0.50(1-0.50)}{11.92}}$$

$$0.359 \pm 0.338$$

By adding and subtracting 0.338 to the difference between proportions of 0.359, we get a 95% confidence interval that ranges from 0.022 to 0.697. That is, we can be 95% confident that the actual difference between design completion rates is between 2% and 70%.

Example 1: Comparing two completion rates

A new version of a CRM software application was created to improve the process of adding contacts to a distribution list. Four out of nine users (44.4%) completed the task on the old version and 11 out of 12 (91.7%) completed it on the new version. Is there enough evidence to conclude the new design improves completion rates? We will use the $N-1$ two-proportion test.

$$z = \frac{(\hat{p}_1 - \hat{p}_2)\sqrt{\frac{N-1}{N}}}{\sqrt{PQ \times \left(\frac{1}{n_1} + \frac{1}{n_2}\right)}}$$

$$P=\left(\frac{x_1+x_2}{n_1+n_2}\right)$$

Filling in the values we get

$$P=\left(\frac{4+11}{9+12}\right)=0.714 \quad \text{and} \quad Q=1-0.714=0.286$$

$$z=\frac{(0.917-0.444)\sqrt{\frac{21-1}{21}}}{\sqrt{0.714\times0.286\times\left(\frac{1}{9}+\frac{1}{12}\right)}}$$

$$z=2.313$$

We can use a normal (z) table to look up the two-sided p-value or the Excel function NORMSDIST for the test statistic of 2.313. To use NORMSDIST, you need to copy the formula =(1-NORMSDIST(2.313))*2, which generates a p-value of 0.0207. Because this value is low, we have reasonable evidence to conclude the completion rate on the new CRM design has improved. To estimate the actual improvement in the completion rate for the entire user population, we now generate a 95% confidence interval around the difference in proportions using the adjusted-Wald procedure.

$$\hat{p}_{\text{adj1}}=\frac{x+\frac{z^2}{4}}{n+\frac{z^2}{2}}=\frac{4+\frac{1.96^2}{4}}{9+\frac{1.96^2}{2}}=\frac{4+0.96}{9+1.92}=\frac{4.96}{10.92}=0.454$$

$$\hat{p}_{\text{adj2}}=\frac{x+\frac{z^2}{4}}{n+\frac{z^2}{2}}=\frac{11+\frac{1.96^2}{4}}{12+\frac{1.96^2}{2}}=\frac{11+0.96}{12+1.92}=\frac{11.96}{13.92}=0.859$$

The critical value of z for a 95% confidence level is 1.96.

$$(0.859-0.454)\pm1.96\sqrt{\frac{0.859(1-0.859)}{13.92}+\frac{0.454(1-0.454)}{10.92}}$$

$$0.405\pm0.347$$

The 95% confidence interval is 0.058 to 0.752, that is, we can be 95% confident the actual improvement in completion rates on the new task design is between 6% and 75%.

Example 2: A/B testing

An A/B test was conducted live on an e-commerce website for two weeks to determine which product page converted more users to purchase a product. Concept A was presented to 455 users and 37 (8.13%) purchased the product. Concept B was presented to 438 users and 22 (5.02%) purchased the product. Is there evidence that one concept is statistically better than the other? Using the $N-1$ two-proportion test we get

$$P = \left(\frac{37+22}{455+438}\right) = 0.066 \quad \text{and} \quad Q = 1 - 0.066 = 0.934$$

$$z = \frac{(0.0813-0.0502)\sqrt{\frac{893-1}{893}}}{\sqrt{0.066 \times 0.934 \times \left(\frac{1}{455}+\frac{1}{438}\right)}}$$

$$Z = 1.87$$

Looking up the test statistic 1.87 in a normal table, we get a two-sided p-value of 0.06. The probability the two concepts have the same conversion rate is around 6%. That is, there is about a 94% probability the completion rates are different. The 90% confidence interval around the difference in conversion rates (which uses the critical value of 1.64) is

$$\hat{p}_{\text{adj1}} = \frac{x+\frac{z^2}{4}}{n+\frac{z^2}{2}} = \frac{37+\frac{1.64^2}{4}}{455+\frac{1.64^2}{2}} = \frac{37+0.68}{455+1.35} = \frac{37.68}{456.35} = 0.083$$

$$\hat{p}_{\text{adj1}} = \frac{x+\frac{z^2}{4}}{n+\frac{z^2}{2}} = \frac{22+\frac{1.64^2}{4}}{438+\frac{1.64^2}{2}} = \frac{22+0.68}{438+1.35} = \frac{22.68}{439.35} = 0.052$$

$$(0.083-0.052) \pm 1.64\sqrt{\frac{0.083(1-0.083)}{466.35}+\frac{0.052(1-0.052)}{439.35}}$$

$$0.031 \pm 0.027$$

The 90% confidence interval around the observed difference of 0.031 ranges from 0.004 to 0.058. That is, if Concept A was used on all users (assuming the two week period was representative) we could expect it to convert between 0.4% and 6% more users than Concept B. As with any confidence interval, the actual long-term conversion rate is more likely to be closer to the middle value of 3.1% than to either of the extreme end points. For many large-volume e-commerce websites, however, even the small lower limit estimated advantage of 0.4% for Concept A could translate into a lot more revenue.

WITHIN-SUBJECTS

When the same users are used in each group the test design is within-subjects (also called matched pairs). As with the continuous within-subjects test (the paired t-test) the variation between users has been removed and you have a better chance of detecting differences (higher power) with the same sample size as a between-subjects design.

To determine whether there is a significant difference between completion rates, conversion rates, or any dichotomous variable we use the McNemar exact test and generate p-values by testing whether the proportion of discordant pairs is greater than 0.5 (called the sign test) for all sample sizes.

McNemar exact test

The McNemar exact test uses a 2×2 table similar to those in the between-subjects section, but the primary test metric is the number of participants who switch from pass to fail or fail to pass—the discordant pairs (McNemar, 1969).

Unlike the between-subjects chi-square test, we cannot setup our 2×2 table just from the summary data of the participants who passed and failed. We need to know the number who had a different outcome on each design—the discordant pairs of responses. Table 5.9 shows the nomenclature used to represent the cells of the 2×2 table for this type of analysis.

We want to know if the proportion of discordant pairs (cells b and c) is greater than what we'd expect to see from chance alone. For this type of analysis, we set chance to 0.50. If the proportion of pairs that are discordant is different from 0.50 (higher or lower), then we have evidence that there is a difference between designs.

To test the observed proportion against a test proportion, we use the nonparametric binomial test. This is the same approach we took in Chapter 4 (Comparing Small Sample Completion Rates to a Criterion). When the proportion tested is 0.50, the binomial test goes by the special name "the sign test."

The sign test uses the following binomial probability formula:

$$p(x) = \frac{n!}{x!(n-x)!} p^x (1-p)^{(n-x)}$$

where
x is the number of positive or negative discordant pairs (cell c *or* cell b, whichever is smaller),
n is the total number of discordant pairs (cell b + cell c), and
$p = .50$.

Note: The term $n!$ is pronounced "n factorial" and is $n \times (n-1) \times (n-2) \times \cdots \times 2 \times 1$.

As discussed in Chapter 4, we will again use mid-probabilities as a less conservative alternative to exact probabilities, which tend to overstate the value of p, especially when sample sizes are small.

Table 5.9 Nomenclature for McNemar Exact Test

	Design B Pass	Design B Fail	Total
Design A	a	b	m
Design B	c	d	n
Total	r	s	N

Example 1: Completion rates

For example, 15 users attempted the same task on two different designs. The completion rate on Design A was 87% and on Design B was 53%. Table 5.10 shows how each user performed, with 0s representing failed task attempts and 1s for passing attempts.

Next we total the number of concordant and discordant responses in a 2 × 2 table (Table 5.11).

Table 5.10 Sample Data for McNemar Exact Test

User	Design A	Design B
1	1	0
2	1	1
3	1	1
4	1	0
5	1	0
6	1	1
7	1	1
8	0	1
9	1	0
10	1	1
11	0	0
12	1	1
13	1	0
14	1	1
15	1	0
Comp rate	87%	53%

Table 5.11 Concordant and Discordant Responses for Example 1

	Design B Pass	Design B Fail	Total
Design A Pass	7 (*a*)	6 (*b*)	13 (*m*)
Design A Fail	1 (*c*)	1 (*d*)	2 (*n*)
Total	8 (*r*)	7 (*s*)	15 (*N*)

Concordant pairs

- Seven users completed the task on both designs (cell *a*)
- One user failed on Design A and failed on Design B (cell *d*)

Discordant pairs

- Six users completed on Design A but failed on Design B (cell *b*)
- One user failed on Design A and passed on Design B (cell *c*)

Table 5.12 shows the discordant users along with a sign (positive or negative) to indicate whether they performed better (plus sign) or worse (negative sign) on Design B. By the way, this is where this procedure gets its name the "sign test"—we're testing whether the proportion of pluses to minuses is significantly different from 0.50.

In total, there were seven discordant pairs (cell *b* + cell *c*). Most users who performed differently performed better on Design A (six of seven). We will use the smaller of the discordant cells to simplify the computation, which is the one person in cell *c* who failed on Design A and passed on Design B. (Note that you will get the same result if you used the larger of the discordant cells, but it would be more work.) Plugging these values in the formula, we get

$$p(0) = \frac{7!}{0!(7-0)!} 0.5^0 (1-0.5)^{(7-0)} = 0.0078$$

$$p(1) = \frac{7!}{1!(7-1)!} 0.5^1 (1-0.5)^{(7-1)} = 0.0547$$

The one-tailed exact-*p* value is these two probabilities added together, 0.0078 + 0.0547 = 0.0625, so the two-tailed probability is double this (0.125). The mid-probability is equal to half the exact probability for the value observed plus the cumulative probability of all values less than the one observed. In this case, the probability of all values less than the one observed is just the probability of 0 discordant pairs, which is 0.0078:

$$\text{Mid } p = \frac{1}{2} 0.0547 + 0.0078$$

$$\text{Mid } p = 0.0352$$

Table 5.12 Discordant Performance from Example 1

User	Relative Performance on B
1	−
4	−
5	−
8	+
9	−
13	−
15	−

The one-tailed mid-*p* value is 0.0352, so the two-tailed mid-*p* value is double this (0.0704). Thus, the probability of seeing one out of seven users perform better on Design A than B if there really was no difference is 0.0704. Put another way, we can be about 93% sure Design A has a better completion rate than Design B.

The computations for this two-sided mid-*p* value are rather tedious to do by hand, but are fairly easy to get using the Excel function =2*(BINOMDIST(0,7,0.5,FALSE) + 0.5*BINOMDIST(1,7,0.5, FALSE)).

If you need to guarantee that the reported *p*-value is greater than or equal to the actual long-term probability, then you should use the exact-*p* values instead of the mid-*p* values. This is similar to the recommendation we gave when comparing the completion rate to a benchmark and when computing binomial confidence intervals (see Chapter 4). For most applications in user research, the mid-*p* value will work better (lead to more correct decisions) over the long run (Agresti and Coull, 1998).

Alternate approaches

As with the between-subjects chi-square test, there isn't much agreement among statistics texts (or statisticians) on the best way to compute the within-subjects *p*-value. This section provides information about additional approaches you might have encountered. You may safely skip this section if you trust our recommendation (or if you're not interested in more geeky technical details).

Chi-square statistic

The most common recommendation in statistics text books for large sample within-subject comparisons is to use the chi-square statistic. It is typically called the McNemar chi-square test (McNemar, 1969), as opposed to the McNemar exact test which we presented in the earlier section. It uses the following formula:

$$\chi^2 = \frac{(c-b)^2}{c+b}$$

You will notice that the formula only uses the discordant cells (*b* and *c*). You can look up the test statistic in a chi-square table with 1 degree of freedom to generate the *p*-value, or use the Excel CHIDIST function. Using the data from Example 1 with seven discordant pairs we get a test statistic of

$$\chi^2 = \frac{(1-6)^2}{7} = 3.571$$

Using the Excel function =CHIDIST(3.571, 1), we get the *p*-value of 0.0587, which, for this example, is reasonably close to our mid-*p* value of 0.0704.

However, to use this approach, the sample size needs to be reasonably large to have accurate results. As a general guide, it is a large enough sample if the number of discordant pairs ($b + c$) is greater than 30 (Agresti and Franklin, 2007).

You can equivalently use the *z*-statistic and corresponding normal table of values to generate a *p*-value instead of the chi-square statistic, by simply taking the square root of the entire equation.

$$Z = \frac{c-b}{\sqrt{c+b}}$$

$$Z = \frac{6-1}{\sqrt{6+1}} = \frac{5}{\sqrt{7}} = 1.89$$

Using the Excel NORMSDIST function (=2*NORMSDIST(1.89)), we get $p = 0.0587$, demonstrating the mathematical equivalence of the methods.

Yates correction to the chi-square statistic

To further complicate matters, some texts recommend using a Yates corrected chi-square for all sample sizes (Bland, 2000). As shown in the following, the Yates correction is

$$\chi^2 = \frac{(|c-b|-1)^2}{b+c}$$

Using the data from Example 1 with seven discordant pairs we get

$$\chi^2 = \frac{(|1-6|-1)^2}{7} = 2.29$$

We look up this value in a chi-square table of values with 1 degree of freedom or use the Excel function =CHIDIST(2.29, 1) to get the *p*-value of 0.1306. For this example, this value is even higher than the exact-*p* value from the sign test, which we expect to overstate the magnitude of *p*. A major criticism of the Yates correction is that it will likely exceed the *p*-value from the sign test. Recall that this overcorrection also occurs with the Yates correction of the between-subjects chi-square test. For this reason, we do not recommend the use of the Yates correction.

Table 5.13 provides a summary of the *p*-values generated from the different approaches and our recommendations.

Confidence interval around the difference for matched pairs

To estimate the likely magnitude of the difference between matched pairs of binary responses, we recommend the appropriate adjusted-Wald confidence interval (Agresti and Min, 2005). As described in Chapter 3 for confidence intervals around a single proportion, this adjustment uses the same concept as that for the between-subjects confidence interval around two proportions.

When applied to a 2 × 2 table for a within-subjects setup (as shown in Table 5.14), the adjustment is to add 1/8th of a squared critical value from the normal distribution for the specified level of confidence

Table 5.13 Summary of *p*-values Generated from Sample Data for McNemar Tests

Method	*P*-value	Notes
McNemar exact test using mid-probabilities	0.0704	Recommended: For all sample sizes will provide best average long-term probability, but some individual tests may understate actual probability
McNemar exact test using exact probabilities	0.125	Recommended: For all sample sizes when you need to guarantee the long-term probability is greater than or equal to the *p*-value (a conservative approach)
McNemar chi-square test/*z* test	0.0587	Not Recommended: Understates true probability for sample sizes and is unclear about what constitutes a large sample size
McNemar chi-square test with Yates correction	0.1306	Not Recommended: Overstates true probability for all sample sizes

Table 5.14 Framework for Adjusted-Wald Confidence Interval

	Design B Pass	Design B Fail	Total
Design A Pass	a_{adj}	b_{adj}	m_{adj}
Design A Fail	c_{adj}	d_{adj}	n_{adj}
Total	r_{adj}	s_{adj}	N_{adj}

to each cell in the 2 × 2 table. For a 95% level of confidence, this has the effect of adding two pseudo observations to the total number of trials (*N*).

Using the same notation from the 2 × 2 table with the "adj" meaning to add $\frac{z_\alpha^2}{8}$ to each value, we have the formula:

$$(\hat{p}_{2adj} - \hat{p}_{1adj}) \pm z_\alpha \sqrt{\frac{(\hat{p}_{12adj} + \hat{p}_{21adj}) - (\hat{p}_{21adj} - \hat{p}_{12adj})^2}{N_{adj}}}$$

where

$$\hat{p}_{1adj} = \frac{m_{adj}}{N_{adj}}$$

$$\hat{p}_{2adj} = \frac{r_{adj}}{N_{adj}}$$

$$\hat{p}_{12adj} = \frac{b_{adj}}{N_{adj}}$$

$$\hat{p}_{21adj} = \frac{c_{adj}}{N_{adj}}$$

z_α = two-sided *z* critical value for the level of confidence (e.g., 1.96 for a 95% confidence level)

$\frac{z_\alpha^2}{8}$ = The adjustment added to each cell (e.g., for a 95% confidence level this is $\frac{1.96^2}{8} = 0.48$)

The formula is similar to the confidence interval around two independent proportions. The key difference here is how we generate the proportions from the 2 × 2 table.

Table 5.15 shows the results from Example 1 (so you don't need to flip back to the original page).

Table 5.15 Results from Example 1

	Design B Pass	Design B Fail	Total
Design A Pass	7 (*a*)	6 (*b*)	13 (*m*)
Design A Fail	1 (*c*)	1 (*d*)	2 (*n*)
Total	8 (*r*)	7 (*s*)	15 (*N*)

Table 5.16 Adjusted Values for Computing Confidence Interval

	Design B Pass	Design B Fail	Total
Design A Pass	7.5 (a_{adj})	6.5 (b_{adj})	14 (m_{adj})
Design A Fail	1.5 (c_{adj})	1.5 (d_{adj})	3 (n_{adj})
Total	9 (r_{adj})	8 (s_{adj})	17 (N_{adj})

Table 5.16 shows the adjustment of 0.5 added to each cell.

You can see that the adjustment has the effect of adding two pseudo users to the sample as we go from a total of 15–17. Filling these values in the formula for a 95% confidence interval (which has a critical z-value of 1.96) we get

$$\hat{p}_{1adj} = \frac{14}{17} = 0.825$$

$$\hat{p}_{2adj} = \frac{9}{17} = 0.529$$

$$\hat{p}_{12adj} = \frac{6.5}{17} = 0.383$$

$$\hat{p}_{21adj} = \frac{1.5}{17} = 0.087$$

$$\left(\hat{p}_{2adj} - \hat{p}_{1adj}\right) \pm z_{\alpha}\sqrt{\frac{\left(\hat{p}_{12adj} + \hat{p}_{21adj}\right) - \left(\hat{p}_{21adj} - \hat{p}_{12adj}\right)^2}{N_{adj}}}$$

$$(0.529 - 0.825) \pm 1.96\sqrt{\frac{(0.383 + 0.087) - (0.087 - 0.383)^2}{17}}$$

$$-0.296 \pm 0.295$$

The 95% confidence interval around the difference in completion rates between designs is −59.1% to −0.1%. The confidence interval goes from negative to positive because we subtracted the design with the better completion rate from the one with the worse completion rate.

There's nothing sacred about the order in which you subtract the proportions. We can just as easily subtract Design B from Design A, which would generate a confidence interval of 0.1– 59.1%. Neither confidence interval quite crosses 0, so we can be about 95% confident there is a difference. It is typically easier to subtract the smaller proportion from the larger when reporting confidence intervals, so we will do that through the remainder of this section.

The mid-p value from the McNemar exact test was 0.0704 which gave us around 93% confidence that there was a difference—just short of the 95% confidence indicated by the adjusted-Wald confidence interval (which is based on a somewhat different statistical procedure), but likely confident enough for many early stage designs to move on to the next research question (or make any indicated improvements to the current design and move on to testing the next design).

In most applied settings, the difference between 94% confidence and 95% confidence shouldn't lead to different decisions. If you are using a rigid cutoff of 0.05, such as for a publication, then use the *p*-value to decide whether to reject the null hypothesis. Keep in mind that most statistical calculations approximate the role of chance. Both the approximation and the choice of the method used can result in *p*-values that fluctuate by a few percentage points (as we saw in Table 5.13) so don't get too hung up on what the "right" *p*-value is. If you are testing in an environment where you need to guarantee a certain *p*-value (medical device testing come to mind), then increasing your confidence level to 99% and using the exact-*p* values instead of the mid-*p* values will significantly reduce the probability of identifying a chance difference as significant.

Example 2: Completion rates

In a comparative usability test, 14 users attempted to rent the same type of car in the same city on two different websites (Avis.com and Enterprise.com). All 14 users completed the task on Avis.com but only 10 of 14 completed it on Enterprise.com. The users and their task results appear in Table 5.17 and Table 5.18. Is there sufficient evidence that more users could complete the task on Avis.com than on Enterprise.com (as designed at the time of this study)?

Table 5.17 Completion Data from CUE-8 Task

User	Avis.com	Enterprise.com
1	1	1
2	1	1
3	1	0
4	1	0
5	1	1
6	1	1
7	1	1
8	1	0
9	1	1
10	1	1
11	1	1
12	1	0
13	1	1
14	1	1
Comp rate	100%	71%

Table 5.18 Organization of Concordant and Discordant Pairs from CUE-8 Task

	Enterprise.com Pass	Enterprise.com Fail Pass	Total
Avis.com Pass	10 (*a*)	4 (*b*)	14 (*m*)
Avis.com Fail	0 (*c*)	0 (*d*)	0 (*n*)
Total	10 (*r*)	4 (*s*)	14 (*N*)

Table 5.19 Discordant Performance from CUE-8 Task

User	Relative Performance on Enterprise.com
3	—
4	—
8	—
12	—

In total there were four discordant users (cell *b* + cell *c*), all of which performed better on Avis.com. Table 5.19 shows the improvement performance difference for the four users on Enterprise.com.

Plugging the appropriate values in the formula we get

$$p(x) = \frac{n!}{x!(n-x)!} p^x (1-p)^{(n-x)}$$

$$p(0) = \frac{4!}{0!(4-0)!} 0.5^0 (1-0.5)^{(4-0)} = 0.0625$$

The one-tailed exact-*p* value is 0.0625, so the two-tailed probability is double this (0.125). The mid-probability is equal to half the exact probability for the value observed plus the cumulative probability of all values less than the one observed. Because there are no values less than 0, the one-tailed mid-probability is equal to half of 0.0625:

$$\text{Mid-}p = \frac{1}{2}(0.0625)$$

$$\text{Mid-}p = 0.0313$$

The one-tailed mid-*p* value is 0.0313, so the two-tailed mid-*p* value is double this (0.0625). Thus, the probability of seeing zero out of four users perform worse on Enterprise.com if there really was no difference is 0.0625. Put another way, we can be around 94% sure Avis.com had a better completion rate than Enterprise.com on this rental car task at the time of this study.

■

COMPARING RENTAL CAR WEBSITES

Why Enterprise.com had a worse completion rate— from the files of Jeff Sauro

In case you were wondering why Enterprise.com had a worse completion rate, the task required users to add a GPS system to the rental car reservation. On Enterprise.com, this option only appeared AFTER you entered your personal information. It thus led four users to spend a lot of time hunting for that option and either giving up or saying they would call customer service. Allowing users to add that feature (which changes the total rental price) would likely increase the completion rate (and rental rate) for Enterprise.com.

The 95% confidence interval around the difference is found by first adjusting the values in each interior cell of the 2 × 2 table by 0.5 $\left(\frac{1.96^2}{8} = 0.48 \approx 0.5\right)$, as shown in Table 5.20.

Finding the component parts of the formula and entering the values we get

$$(\hat{p}_{2\text{adj}} - \hat{p}_{1\text{adj}}) \pm z_\alpha \sqrt{\frac{(\hat{p}_{12\text{adj}} + \hat{p}_{21\text{adj}}) - (\hat{p}_{21\text{adj}} - \hat{p}_{12\text{adj}})^2}{N_{\text{adj}}}}$$

$$\hat{p}_{1\text{adj}} = \frac{m_{\text{adj}}}{N_{\text{adj}}} = \frac{15}{16} = 0.938$$

$$\hat{p}_{2\text{adj}} = \frac{r_{\text{adj}}}{N_{\text{adj}}} = \frac{11}{16} = 0.688$$

$$\hat{p}_{12\text{adj}} = \frac{b_{\text{adj}}}{N_{\text{adj}}} = \frac{4.5}{16} = 0.281$$

$$\hat{p}_{21\text{adj}} = \frac{c_{\text{adj}}}{N_{\text{adj}}} = \frac{0.5}{16} = 0.03$$

Table 5.20 Adjusted Counts for CUE-8 Task

	Design B Pass	Design B Pass	Total
Design A Pass	10.5 (a_{adj})	4.5 (b_{adj})	15 (m_{adj})
Design A Fail	0.5 (c_{adj})	0.5 (d_{adj})	1 (n_{adj})
Total	11 (r_{adj})	5 (s_{adj})	16 (N_{adj})

$$(0.938-0.688)\pm 1.96\sqrt{\frac{(0.281+0.03)-(0.03-0.281)^2}{16}}$$

$$0.250\pm 0.245$$

We can be 95% confident the difference between proportions is between 0.5% and 49.5%. This interval does not cross zero which tells us we can be 95% confident the difference is greater than zero. It is another example of a significant difference seen with the confidence interval but not with the *p*-value. We didn't plan on both examples having *p*-values so close to 0.05. They are a consequence of using data from actual usability tests. Fortunately, you are more likely to see *p*-values and confidence intervals point to the same conclusion.

KEY POINTS

- When comparing two designs or products, you need to account for chance differences between sample data by generating a *p*-value from the appropriate statistical test.
- To understand the likely range of the difference between designs or products, you should compute a confidence interval around the difference.
- To determine which statistical test you need to use, you need to identify whether your outcome measure is binary or continuous and whether you have the same users in each group (within-subjects) or a different set of users (between-subjects).
- For comparing data from two continuous means such as questionnaire data or task times:
  - *For between-subjects:* Use the two-sample *t*-test if different users are in each sample. The procedure can handle non-normal data and unequal variances. Compute a *t*-confidence interval around the difference between means.
  - *For within-subjects:* Use the paired *t*-test if the same users are in each sample. The procedure can handle non-normal data. Compute a *t*-confidence interval around the difference between means.
- There is surprisingly little agreement in the statistics literature on the best statistical approach for comparing binary measures. Our recommendations appear the most promising given the current research.
- For comparing a binary outcome measure such as task completion rates or conversion rate (as used in A/B testing):
  - *For between-subjects:* Use the $N-1$ two-proportion test if different users are in each sample and compute an adjusted-Wald confidence interval around the difference in the proportions.
  - *For within-subjects:* Use the McNemar exact test (using the mid-probability variant) if the same users are in each sample. Compute an adjusted-Wald confidence interval around the difference in the matched proportions.
- Table 5.21 provides a list of the formulas used in this chapter.

Table 5.21 Formulas Used in this Chapter

Name of Formula	Formula	Notes
Paired t-test (dependent means)	$t = \frac{\hat{D}}{\frac{s_D}{\sqrt{n}}}$	Used for all sample sizes when the same users are used in both groups.
Confidence interval around the difference between paired means	$\bar{D} \pm t_a \frac{s_D}{\sqrt{n}}$	Used for all sample sizes.
Two-sample t-test (independent means)	$t = \frac{\hat{x}_1 - \hat{x}_2}{\sqrt{\frac{s_1^2}{n_1} + \frac{s_2^2}{n_2}}}$	Used for all sample sizes when different users are in each sample. It is robust to violations of normality and unequal variances especially when using the Welch–Satterthwaite procedure to adjust the degrees of freedom.
Welch–Satterthwaite adjustment to degrees of freedom	$\text{df} = \frac{\left(\frac{s_1^2}{n_1} + \frac{s_2^2}{n_2}\right)^2}{\frac{\left(\frac{s_1^2}{n_1}\right)^2}{n_1 - 1} + \frac{\left(\frac{s_2^2}{n_2}\right)^2}{n_2 - 1}}$	Adjusts the degrees of freedom used in a two-sample t-test which makes the test more robust to violations of normality and unequal variances.
Confidence interval around two independent means	$(\hat{x}_1 - \hat{x}_2) \pm t_a \sqrt{\frac{s_1^2}{n_1} + \frac{s_2^2}{n_2}}$	Used for all sample sizes.
$N-1$ chi-square test for comparing two independent proportions (equal to the $N-1$ two-proportion test)	$\chi^2 = \frac{(ad - bc)^2 (N-1)}{mnrs}$	The test is the same as the standard chi-square test except it is adjusted by multiplying the numerator by $N-1$. The test is algebraically equivalent to the $N-1$ two proportion test. It works well as long as the expected cell counts are greater than 1 (otherwise use the Fisher exact test).
$N-1$ two-proportion test for comparing two independent proportions	$z = \frac{(\hat{p}_1 - \hat{p}_2)\sqrt{\frac{N-1}{N}}}{\sqrt{PQ \times \left(\frac{1}{n_1} + \frac{1}{n_2}\right)}}$	The test is the same as the standard two-proportion test except it is adjusted by multiplying the numerator by $\sqrt{\frac{N-1}{N}}$. The test is algebraically equivalent to the $N-1$ chi-square test. It works well as long as the expected cell counts are greater than 1 (otherwise use the Fisher exact test).
Fisher exact test on two independent proportions	$p = \frac{m!n!r!s!}{a!b!c!d!N!}$	Only recommended when expected cell counts are less than 1 (which doesn't happen a lot). Software computes the p-values by finding all possible combinations of tables equal to or more extreme than the marginal totals observed.

Table 5.21 Formulas Used in this Chapter (*cont.*)

Name of Formula	Formula	Notes
Adjusted-Wald confidence interval for the difference between independent proportions	$(\hat{p}_{\text{adj1}} - \hat{p}_{\text{adj2}}) \pm z_\alpha \sqrt{\frac{\hat{p}_{\text{adj1}}(1-\hat{p}_{\text{adj1}})}{n_{\text{adj1}}} + \frac{\hat{p}_{\text{adj2}}(1-\hat{p}_{\text{adj2}})}{n_{\text{adj2}}}}$	The adjustment is to add a quarter of a squared z-critical value to the numerator and half a squared z-critical value to the denominator when computing each proportion.
McNemar exact test for matched proportions	$p(x) = \frac{n!}{x!(n-x)!} p^x (1-p)^{(n-x)}$	This is the binomial probability formula which is used on the proportion of discordant pairs. See the chapter for the process of using this and the mid-p value.
Adjusted-Wald confidence interval for difference between matched proportions	$(\hat{p}_{2\text{adj}} - \hat{p}_{1\text{adj}}) \pm z_\alpha \sqrt{\frac{(\hat{p}_{12\text{adj}} + \hat{p}_{21\text{adj}}) - (\hat{p}_{21\text{adj}} - \hat{p}_{12\text{adj}})^2}{N_{\text{adj}}}}$	The interval is adjusted by adding $\frac{z_\alpha^2}{8}$ to each cell. For a 95% confidence level this is about 0.5.

CHAPTER REVIEW QUESTIONS

1. Ten users completed the task to find the best priced nonstop roundtrip ticket on JetBlue.com. A different set of 14 users attempted the same task on AmericanAirlines.com. After each task attempt, the users answered the seven-point Single Ease Question (SEQ, see Sauro, 2011b). Higher responses indicate an easier task. The mean response of JetBlue was 6.1 (sd = .88) and the mean response on American Airlines was 4.86 (sd = 1.61). Is there enough evidence from the sample to conclude that users think booking a flight on American Airlines is more difficult than on JetBlue? What is the likely range of the difference between mean ratings using a 90% level of confidence?
2. Two designs were tested on a website to see which would convert more users to register for a webinar. Is there enough evidence to conclude one design is better?
   Design A: 4 out of 109 converted
   Design B: 0 out of 88 converted
   Compute a 90% confidence interval around the difference.
3. A competitive analysis of travel websites was conducted. One set of 31 users completed tasks on Expedia.com and another set of 25 users completed the same tasks on Kayak.com. Users rated how likely they would be to recommend the website to a friend on an 11-point scale (0 to 10) with 10 being extremely likely. The mean score on Expedia.com was 7.32 (sd = 1.87) and the mean score on Kayak.com was 5.72 (sd = 2.99). Is there evidence that more people would likely recommend Expedia over Kayak.com? What is the likely range for the difference between means using a 95% confidence level?
4. Using the same set of data from question 3, the responses were segmented into promoters, passives, and detractors as shown in Table 5.22. This process degrades a continuous measure into a discrete binary one (which is the typical approach when computing the Net Promoter Score).

Table 5.22 Data for Review Question 4

Website	Segment	Response Range	No. of Responses
Expedia	Promoters	9–10	7
	Passive	7–8	14
	Detractors	0–6	10
Kayak	Promoters	9–10	5
	Passive	7–8	8
	Detractors	0–6	12

Is there evidence to conclude that there is a difference in the proportion of promoters (the top-2-box scores) between websites?

5. The same 14 users attempted to rent a car on two rental car websites: Budget.com and Enterprise.com. The order of presentation of the websites was counterbalanced, so half of the users worked with Budget first, and the other half with Enterprise. Table 5.23 shows which users were successful on which website. Is there enough evidence to conclude that the websites have different completion rates? How much of a difference, if any, likely exists between the completion rates (use a 90% level of confidence)?

Table 5.23 Data for Review Question 5

User	Budget.com	Enterprise.com
1	1	1
2	1	1
3	1	0
4	1	0
5	0	1
6	1	1
7	1	1
8	0	0
9	1	1
10	1	1
11	1	1
12	1	0
13	1	1
14	1	1
Comp rate	86%	71%

Table 5.24 Data for Review Question 6

User	Budget	Enterprise	Difference
1	90.0	65.0	25
2	85.0	82.5	2.5
3	80.0	55.0	25
4	92.5	67.5	25
5	82.5	82.5	0
6	80.0	37.5	42.5
7	62.5	77.5	−15
8	87.5	67.5	20
9	67.5	35.0	32.5
10	92.5	62.5	30
11	65.0	57.5	7.5
12	70.0	85.0	−15
13	75.0	55.0	20
14	95.0	60.0	35
Mean (sd)	80 (11)	64 (15)	16.8 (18)

6. After completing five tasks on both Budget.com and Enterprise.com, the 14 users from question 5 completed the SUS (Table 5.24). The mean SUS scores were 80.4 (sd = 11) for Budget.com and 63.5 (sd = 15) for Enterprise.com. Is there enough evidence to conclude that the SUS scores are different? How large of a difference likely exists in the entire user population using a 95% confidence interval?

ANSWERS TO CHAPTER REVIEW QUESTIONS

1. A two-sample t-test should be conducted using the following formula:

$$t = \frac{\hat{x}_1 - \hat{x}_2}{\sqrt{\frac{s_1^2}{n_1} + \frac{s_2^2}{n_2}}} = \frac{6.1 - 4.86}{\sqrt{\frac{0.88^2}{10} + \frac{1.61^2}{14}}} = 2.42$$

The degrees of freedom for this test are as follows:

$$\text{df} = \frac{\left(\frac{0.88^2}{10} + \frac{1.61^2}{14}\right)^2}{\frac{\left(\frac{0.88^2}{10}\right)^2}{10-1} + \frac{\left(\frac{1.61^2}{14}\right)^2}{14-1}} = \frac{0.068954}{0.003303} = 20.9, \text{ which rounds down to } 20$$

Looking up the test statistic in a *t*-table with 20 degrees of freedom we get a *p*-value of 0.025. There is sufficient evidence for us to conclude that users find completing the task on American Airlines more difficult. For a 90% level of confidence with 20 degrees of freedom, the *t*-critical value is 1.72 and the formula is

$$(\hat{x}_1 - \hat{x}_2) \pm t_a \sqrt{\frac{s_1^2}{n_1} + \frac{s_2^2}{n_2}} = 1.24 \pm 1.72\sqrt{\frac{0.88^2}{10} + \frac{1.61^2}{14}} = 1.24 \pm 0.88$$

So we can be 90% confident the difference between mean ratings is 0.36–2.12 between the two airline websites.

2. Conduct an $N-1$ two-proportion test.

$$P = \left(\frac{x_1 + x_2}{n_1 + n_2}\right) = \left(\frac{4+0}{109+88}\right) = 0.02$$

$$z = \frac{(\hat{p}_1 - \hat{p}_2)\sqrt{\frac{N-1}{N}}}{\sqrt{PQ\left(\frac{1}{n_1} + \frac{1}{n_2}\right)}} = \frac{(0.367 - 0)\sqrt{\frac{197-1}{197}}}{\sqrt{0.02 \times 0.98 \times \left(\frac{1}{109} + \frac{1}{88}\right)}} = 1.81$$

Looking up the test statistic 1.81 in a normal table we get a two-tailed *p*-value of 0.07. This means there is about a 93% chance the designs are different, which is probably strong enough evidence for almost all circumstances. The 90% confidence interval around the difference is computed using the adjusted-Wald formula. First compute the adjustment for each proportion. The critical value of *z* for a 90% level of confidence is 1.64.

$$\hat{p}_{\text{adj1}} = \frac{x + \frac{z^2}{4}}{n + \frac{z^2}{2}} = \frac{4 + \frac{1.64^2}{4}}{109 + \frac{1.64^2}{2}} = \frac{4 + 0.68}{109 + 1.35} = \frac{4.68}{110.35} = 0.0423$$

$$\hat{p}_{\text{adj2}} = \frac{x + \frac{z^2}{4}}{n + \frac{z^2}{2}} = \frac{0 + \frac{1.64^2}{4}}{88 + \frac{1.64^2}{2}} = \frac{0 + 0.68}{88 + 1.35} = \frac{0.68}{89.35} = 0.0075$$

Then insert this adjustment into the confidence interval formula:

$$(0.0423 - 0.0075) \pm 1.64\sqrt{\frac{0.0423(1-0.0423)}{110.35} + \frac{0.0075(1-0.0075)}{89.35}}$$

The 90% interval is 0.00 to 0.07, which means we can be 90% confident the difference between conversion rates favors Design A somewhere between 0.0% and 7.0%.

3. Use a two-sample t-test because we have independent samples and a continuous response variable. Using the two-sample t-test formula we get

$$t = \frac{\hat{x}_1 - \hat{x}_2}{\sqrt{\frac{s_1^2}{n_1} + \frac{s_2^2}{n_2}}} = \frac{7.32 - 5.72}{\sqrt{\frac{1.87^2}{31} + \frac{2.99^2}{25}}} = 2.33$$

With the following degrees of freedom:

$$\text{df} = \frac{\left(\frac{1.87^2}{31} + \frac{2.99^2}{25}\right)^2}{\frac{\left(\frac{1.87^2}{31}\right)^2}{31-1} + \frac{\left(\frac{2.99^2}{25}\right)^2}{25-1}} = \frac{0.221283}{0.005753} = 38.5, \text{which rounds down to 38}$$

Looking up the test statistic 2.33 using a t-table with 38 degrees of freedom shows a p-value of 0.025. Thus, there is only a 2.5% probability that the difference between means is due to chance. Put another way, there is a 97.5% probability that the mean score on Expedia.com is higher than on Kayak.com. The t-critical value for a 95% confidence level with 38 degrees of freedom (http://www.usablestats.com/calcs/tinv) is 2.02.

$$(\hat{x}_1 - \hat{x}_2) \pm t_a \sqrt{\frac{s_1^2}{n_1} + \frac{s_2^2}{n_2}} = (7.32 - 5.72) \pm 2.02\sqrt{\frac{1.87^2}{31} + \frac{2.99^2}{25}} = 1.6 \pm 1.4$$

We can be 95% confident the difference between mean scores on the likelihood-to-recommend question is between 0.2 and 3.0 in favor of the Expedia.com website.

4. We have two independent proportions, so we use the $N-1$ two-proportion test.

$$P = \left(\frac{x_1 + x_2}{n_1 + n_2}\right) = \left(\frac{7+5}{31+25}\right) = 0.214$$

$$z = \frac{(\hat{p}_1 - \hat{p}_2)\sqrt{\frac{N-1}{N}}}{\sqrt{PQ \times \left(\frac{1}{n_1} + \frac{1}{n_2}\right)}} = \frac{(0.226 - 0.2)\sqrt{\frac{56-1}{56}}}{\sqrt{0.214 \times 0.786 \times \left(\frac{1}{31} + \frac{1}{25}\right)}} = 0.232$$

Looking up the test statistic of 0.232 in a normal (z) table, we get a two-sided p-value of 0.817. Given this sample there is only an 18.3% chance that the proportion of promoters is different between Expedia.com and Kayak.com. Note how the evidence for a difference has dropped when examining top-2-box scores compared to the difference between means in question 3. When we compared the means in question 3 we found a statistical difference. This illustrates that when you reduce a continuous measure to a binary outcome measure, you lose information. The result in this case is little evidence for a difference in top-2-box scores, an example of the loss of sensitivity due to the reduction of multipoint scale data to binary.

Table 5.25 Arrangement of Concordant and Discordant Data for Review Question 5

	Enterprise.com Pass	Enterprise.com Fail Pass	Total
Budget.com Pass	9 (*a*)	3 (*b*)	12 (*m*)
Budget.com Fail	1 (*c*)	1 (*d*)	2 (*n*)
Total	10 (*r*)	4 (*s*)	14 (*N*)

5. We need to conduct a McNemar exact test. First set up the 2 × 2 table, as shown in Table 5.25. We can see that four users had different outcomes (discordant pairs) between websites (from cells *b* and *c*). The minus signs in Table 5.26 indicate worse performance on Enterprise.com.

Three users performed worse on Enterprise.com and one performed better. To find the probability of having one out of four discordant pairs if the probability is really 0.50, we use the binomial probability formula to find the mid-*p* value. In Excel, the formula is =2*(BINOMDIST(0,4,0.5,FALSE) + 0.5*BINOMDIST(1,4,0.5,FALSE)), which generates a two-tailed mid-*p* value of 0.375. That is, there's only a 62.5% chance the completion rates are different given the data from this sample. Although the observed completion rates are different, they aren't different enough for us to conclude that Budget.com's completion rate on this task is significantly different from Enterprise.com's.

To compute the 90% confidence interval around the difference between proportions, we use the adjusted-Wald procedure. The critical value of *z* for a 90% level of confidence is 1.64, making the adjustment $\frac{1.64^2}{8} = 0.34$.

We update the 2 × 2 table with the 0.34 adjustment to each cell (Table 5.27).

Table 5.26 Discordant Data for Review Question 5

User	+ or − Difference
3	−
4	−
5	−
6	+

Table 5.27 Adjusted Data for Review Question 5

	Enterprise.com Pass	Enterprise.com Fail Pass	Total
Budget.com Pass	9.34 (a_{adj})	3.34 (b_{adj})	12.7 (m_{adj})
Budget.com Fail	1.34 (c_{adj})	1.34 (d_{adj})	2.7 (n_{adj})
Total	10.7 (r_{adj})	4.7 (s_{adj})	15.4 (N_{adj})

Finding the component parts of the formula and entering the values we get

$$\left(\hat{p}_{2\text{adj}}-\hat{p}_{1\text{adj}}\right)\pm z_{\alpha}\sqrt{\frac{\left(\hat{p}_{12\text{adj}}+\hat{p}_{21\text{adj}}\right)-\left(\hat{p}_{21\text{adj}}-\hat{p}_{12\text{adj}}\right)^2}{N_{\text{adj}}}}$$

$$\hat{p}_{1\text{adj}}=\frac{m_{\text{adj}}}{N_{\text{adj}}}=\frac{11.7}{15.4}=0.826$$

$$\hat{p}_{2\text{adj}}=\frac{r_{\text{adj}}}{N_{\text{adj}}}=\frac{10.7}{15.4}=0.695$$

$$\hat{p}_{12\text{adj}}=\frac{b_{\text{adj}}}{N_{\text{adj}}}=\frac{3.34}{15.4}=0.217$$

$$\hat{p}_{21\text{adj}}=\frac{c_{\text{adj}}}{N_{\text{adj}}}=\frac{1.34}{15.4}=0.087$$

$$(0.826-0.695)\pm 1.64\sqrt{\frac{(0.217+0.087)-(0.087-0.217)^2}{15.4}}$$

$$0.131\pm 0.225$$

The 90% confidence interval is −9.5 to 35.5%. Because the interval crosses 0, this also tells us there's less than a 90% chance that the completion rates are different.

6. We perform a paired t-test because the same users worked with each website. The test statistic is

$$t=\frac{\hat{D}}{\frac{s_{\text{D}}}{\sqrt{n}}}=\frac{16.8}{\frac{18}{\sqrt{14}}}=3.48$$

Looking up the test statistic of 3.48 in a t-table with 13 degrees of freedom or using the Excel function =TDIST(3.48,13,2), we get the two-sided p-value of 0.004. We have strong evidence to conclude that users think the Budget.com website is easier to use as measured by the SUS. The t-critical value with 13 degrees of freedom for a 95% level of confidence is 2.16, so the resulting 95% confidence interval is

$$\bar{D}\pm t_{\text{a}}\frac{s_{\text{D}}}{\sqrt{n}}$$

$$=16.8\pm 2.16\frac{18}{\sqrt{14}}$$

$$=16.8\pm 10.4$$

We can be 95% confident the mean difference for the entire user population is between 6.4 and 27.2.

REFERENCES

Agresti, A., Caffo, B., 2000. Simple and effective confidence intervals for proportions and differences of proportions result from adding two successes and two failures. Am. Stat. 54 (4), 280–288.

Agresti, A., Coull, B., 1998. Approximate is better than 'exact' for interval estimation of binomial proportions. Am. Stat. 52, 119–126.

Agresti, A., Franklin, C.A., 2007. Statistics: The Art and Science of Learning from Data. Prentice Hall, Upper Saddle River, NJ.

Agresti, A., Min, Y., 2005. Simple improved confidence intervals for comparing matched proportions. Stat. Med. 24, 729–740.

Bland, M., 2000. An Introduction to Medical Statistics, third ed. Oxford University Press, Oxford, UK.

Box, G.E.P., 1953. Non-normality and test on variance. Biometrika 40, 318–355.

Campbell, I., 2007. Chi-squared and Fisher–Irwin tests of two-by-two tables with small sample recommendations. Stat. Med. 26, 3661–3675.

Cochran, W.G., 1952. The χ^2 test of goodness of fit. Ann. Math. Stat. 23, 315–345.

Cochran, W.G., 1954. Some methods for strengthening the common χ^2 tests. Biometrics 10, 417–451.

Howell, D., 2002. Statistical Methods for Psychology, fifth ed. Thomson Learning, Andover, UK.

McNemar, Q., 1969. Psychological Statistics, fourth ed. Wiley, New York.

Pearson, K., 1900. On the criterion that a given system of deviations from the probable in the case of a correlated system of variables is such that it can be reasonably supposed to have arisen from random sampling. Phil. Mag. Ser. 5 (50), 157–175.

Satterthwaite, F.E., 1946. An approximate distribution of estimates of variances components. Biometrics Bull. 2, 110–114.

Sauro, J., 2011a. A Practical Guide to the System Usability Scale. CreateSpace, Denver, CO.

Sauro, J., 2011b. If you could only ask one question, use this one. Available from: http://www.measuringu.com/blog/single-question.php

Welch, B.L., 1938. The significance of the difference between two means when the population variances are unequal. Biometrika 29, 350–362.

CHAPTER

WHAT SAMPLE SIZES DO WE NEED? PART 1: SUMMATIVE STUDIES

6

INTRODUCTION

WHY DO WE CARE?

Before tackling the question of determining the sample sizes needed by usability practitioners, we should address the question of "why do we care?" The primary motive behind sample size estimation, as illustrated in Fig. 6.1, is economics.

If additional samples didn't cost anything—didn't take any additional time or cost any additional money—then we'd always conduct studies with very large samples. That is the case with some types of user research (e.g., Internet surveys delivered via email or conducted using Internet services such as Mechanical Turk, which has a low incremental cost typically ranging from $0.25 to 1.00 per participant). The reason that survey samples rarely contain fewer than several hundred respondents is due to the cost structure of surveys (Alreck and Settle, 1985). The fixed costs of the survey include activities such as determining information requirements, identifying survey topics, selecting a data collection method, writing questions, choosing scales, composing the questionnaire, and so on. For this type of research, the additional or marginal cost of including hundreds of additional respondents can be very small relative to the fixed costs.

This, however, is not the case for most moderated usability testing. Imagine the cost of adding participants to a usability study:

- in which there might be as little as a week or two between the availability of testable software and the deadline for providing recommendations for improvement
- when resources allow the observation of only one participant at a time
- with a set of tasks that takes two days to complete

Usability researchers have devoted considerable attention to sample size estimation due to the typically high cost of observing participants in moderated testing (and this is not unique to usability—medical studies involving functional magnetic resonance imaging are very expensive, with a substantial incremental cost for additional subjects).

THE TYPE OF USABILITY STUDY MATTERS

There are two major conceptions of usability: summative and formative (Lewis, 2012), based on methodological distinctions for assessment originally developed in the field of education (Scriven, 1967). The summative conception is that the primary focus of usability should be on measurements related to the accomplishment of global task goals (measurement-based evaluation). The formative conception

Quantifying the User Experience. http://dx.doi.org/10.1016/B978-0-12-802308-2.00006-0

FIGURE 6.1 You Don't Have to be Einstein to Figure out the Relationship Between Sample Size and Economics

is that practitioners should focus on the detection and elimination of usability problems (diagnostic evaluation). The different conceptions imply differences in the appropriate statistical models to use for sample size estimation.

Usability testing emerged from the experimental methods of psychology (in particular, cognitive and applied psychology) and human factors engineering (Dumas and Salzman, 2006). Experimenters conducting traditional experiments develop a careful plan of study that includes the exact number of participants to expose to the different experimental treatments. The more formative (diagnostic, focused on problem discovery) the focus of a usability test, the less it is like a traditional experiment. The more summative (focused on measurement) a usability test is, the more it should resemble the mechanics of a traditional experiment.

The focus of this chapter is on sample size estimation for summative usability studies. We will cover sample size estimation for formative usability studies in the next chapter.

BASIC PRINCIPLES OF SUMMATIVE SAMPLE SIZE ESTIMATION

Sometimes you might just want to estimate the value of a measure. For example, how satisfied are users with the usability of a given website? At other times you might want to compare a measure with a specific goal, or to compare alternatives. For example, can users complete a given task in less than two min; or can they complete the task more quickly with a new version of a program than they could with a competitor's version? Fig. 6.2 illustrates these three questions.

In Chapters 3–5, we've covered methods for conducting statistical tests to answer these questions. The purpose of this section is to show how to estimate the number of participants you will need to achieve specific measurement goals.

Traditional sample size estimation requires estimates of the variance of the measure of interest and a judgment of how precise the measurement must be, where precision includes the magnitude of the

FIGURE 6.2 Illustration of Three Traditional Statistical Questions

critical difference and the desired statistical confidence level (Walpole, 1976). Once you have that information, the rest is mathematical mechanics (typically, using the formula for the *t* statistic).

Estimates of variance can come from previous studies that used the same method (same or similar tasks and measures). If no historical estimate is available and it isn't possible to conduct a pilot study, another approach is to define the critical difference as a fraction of the standard deviation (Diamond, 1981), specifying the critical difference in standard units—in other words, as a critical effect size—rather than directly in units of the target measure.

All other things being equal, precise measurement is preferable to imprecise measurement. However, the more precise a measurement is, the more it will cost, which gets us back to the basic motivation for sample size estimation—that running more participants than necessary is wasteful of resources (Kraemer and Thiemann, 1987).

In addition to the economic incentive to estimate sample size, the process of carrying out sample size estimation can also lead to a realistic determination of how much precision is required to make the necessary decision(s) (Alreck and Settle, 1985). Consider using a "what if" approach to help stakeholders determine their required precision. Start by asking what would happen if the average value from the study was off the true value by 1%—usually a difference this small won't affect the final decision. If that amount of discrepancy doesn't matter, what if the measurement was off by 5%? If that level of imprecision is acceptable, continue until the stakeholders indicate that the measurement would be too imprecise to guide their decision making. Then start the process again, this time addressing the required level of statistical confidence. Note that statistically unsophisticated decision makers are likely to start out by expecting 100% confidence, which is possible only if you can sample every unit in the population, in which case you wouldn't need to use statistics to guide decision making. Presenting stakeholders with the sample sizes needed to achieve different levels of precision and confidence can help them achieve a realistic data collection plan, collecting just enough data to answer the question(s) at hand.

ESTIMATING VALUES

Before the middle of the eighteenth century there is little indication ... of a willingness of astronomers to combine observations; indeed ... there was sometimes an outright refusal to combine them ... the idea that accuracy could be increased by combining measurements made under different conditions was slow to come. They feared that errors in one observation would contaminate others, that errors would multiply, not compensate (Stigler, 1986, p. 4).

TRUE SCORE THEORY AND THE CENTRAL LIMIT THEOREM

Why averaging scores leads to greater accuracy as you increase the sample size

The fundamental theorem of True Score Theory is that every observed score (x) has two components—the true score (t) and some error (e), mathematically, $x_i = t + e_i$. Given unbiased measurement, the value of t will be consistent, but the value of e will vary randomly, in other words, will sometimes add to t and other times will subtract from it. As you increase the sample size and take the average, the true value will emerge because the randomly varying errors will cancel out. The roots of this argument reach back to 1755, when Thomas Simpson published a treatise entitled *An Attempt to Show the Advantage Arising by Taking the Mean of a Number of Observations in Practical Astronomy*. Simpson laid some of the foundations for the estimation of confidence intervals when he argued that positive and negative errors should be equally probable and that there were assignable limits within which errors would typically fall (Cowles, 1989).

The Central Limit Theorem also has a rich history, first proved by Simon Laplace in 1810, but with historical roots that go back to James Bernoulli's publication of *Ars Conjectandi* in 1713 (Cowles, 1989). The Central Limit Theorem states that as n approaches infinity, the cumulative distribution of the standardized sample mean (the distribution of z) approaches the cumulative standardized normal distribution (Bradley, 1976). In other words, for any actual distribution (normal or not), as the sample size increases, the sampling distribution of the mean becomes more and more normal, with the mean at the center of the sampling distribution and 95% of sample means within ±2 standard errors of the true mean. It is important to remember that this does not apply to the location of the true mean in the distribution of individual scores. If the true distribution is skewed, as is often the case for completion times, the mean will not be the best indicator of the center of the distribution. What the Central Limit Theorem does indicate is that as the sample size increases, the accuracy of the estimation of the mean will improve—in other words, that the errors in multiple observations compensate rather than multiply.

From True Score Theory and the Central Limit Theorem, we now know that combining observations sharpens rather than contaminates our estimates. For many of the situations encountered by usability practitioners, manipulating the one-sample t-test provides a path to determining how many observations it will take to achieve a desired accuracy for the estimate. It would be simpler to use the one-sample z-test, but for practical moderated usability testing, the sample sizes will almost always be too small to justify the use of z instead of t.

Just a quick reminder before we continue—many of the sample size estimation procedures described in this chapter are new, so it's important for us to document how we got from the formula for the test statistic to the sample size formula. If you don't care about the math, that's fine—just skip over the equations and go right to the examples. Now, back to the math.

The formula for computing t is:

$$t = \frac{d}{sem}$$

where d is an observed difference and sem is the standard error of the mean, which in turn is the standard deviation divided by the square root of the sample size, or:

$$sem = \frac{s}{\sqrt{n}}$$

Knowing this, we can use algebra to get n on the left side of the equation:

$$t = \frac{d}{s/\sqrt{n}}$$

$$t\left(\frac{s}{\sqrt{n}}\right) = d$$

$$\frac{s}{\sqrt{n}} = \frac{d}{t}$$

$$\frac{\sqrt{n}}{s} = \frac{t}{d}$$

$$\sqrt{n} = \frac{t(s)}{d}$$

$$n = \frac{t^2 s^2}{d^2}$$

Therefore, to calculate n, we need values for s^2, t, and d.

For s^2, we need an estimate of the variance (the square of the sample standard deviation) as described earlier—typically from a similar experiment (either a previous usability test or a pilot test). If no estimate of the variance is available, it is possible to define d as some proportion of s (Example 3) or, for certain kinds of measurements, to use a rule of thumb to estimate the variance (see the sidebar "Rules of Thumb for Estimating Unknown Variance").

d is the critical difference for the experiment—the smallest difference between the obtained and true value that you need to be able to detect. There is no mathematical approach to determining the appropriate value of d. This is a matter of judgment, either based on the experimenter's knowledge of the domain or using the "what if" approach described earlier.

t is the critical value of t for the desired level of statistical confidence. Again, the level of statistical confidence to use is a matter of judgment, but is often set between 80% and 99%, most often to either 90 or 95%. For more information on the considerations that affect this decision, see the sidebar "What are Reasonable Test Criteria?"

Using t in this process, though, introduces a complication. Unlike z, the value of t depends on its degrees of freedom (df), which in turn depends on the sample size—which is what we're trying to compute. For a one-sample t-test:

$$df = n - 1$$

Diamond (1981) described a way to get around this difficulty by using iteration. Returning to Fig. 6.2, assume that the person in the first panel, let's call him Bob, has timed his drive to work for one week. The times (in minutes) for Monday through Friday were 12, 14, 12, 20, and 16 (to keep this example simple, we'll ignore the possibility of systematically different traffic patterns as a function of the day of the week). The variance (s^2) for these five measurements is 11.2. Bob has always felt like it takes him about 15 min to get to work, so he decides that he will set his critical difference to 10% of the expected time, or 1.5 min (a completely arbitrary but reasonable decision). He also decides to set the statistical confidence to 95% (again, arbitrary but reasonable). In other words, using reasoning similar to that used for the construction of t-based confidence intervals, he wants to collect enough data to ensure that he can be 95% confident that the resulting estimate of his drive time will be within 1.5 min of his actual drive time. Bob now has all of the elements he needs to calculate the required sample size—the variability is 11.2 ($s = 3.35$), the confidence level is 95%, and the critical difference is 1.5. The steps are:

1. Start with the z-score for the desired level of confidence in place of t. For 95% confidence, this is 1.96.
2. Compute $n = (z^2s^2)/d^2$, which for this example is $n = (1.96^2)(11.2)/1.5^2$, which equals 19.1. Because Diamond (1981) advises rounding sample size estimates up to the next whole number, the initial estimate is $n = 20$.
3. Next, adjust the estimate by replacing the z-score with the t-score for a sample size of 20. For this estimate, use $n - 1$ (19 in this case) to compute the degrees of freedom (df) to use to find the value for t in the next iteration (which is 2.093). Note that the value of z will always be smaller than the appropriate value of t, making the initial estimate smaller than it should be.
4. Recalculate n using 2.093 in place of 1.96 to get 21.8, which rounds up to 22.
5. Because the appropriate value of t is now a little smaller than 2.093 (because the estimated sample size is now larger, with 22 − 1, or 21, degrees of freedom), calculate n again, this time using a t of 2.080. The new estimate of n is 21.5, which rounds up to 22.
6. Stop iterating when you get the same estimate of n on two iterations or you begin cycling between two values for n, in which case you should average the values (and, if necessary, round up). See Table 6.1 for the full set of iterations for this example. For Bob to achieve his goals, he will need to measure the duration of his drive to work 22 times.

Diamond (1981) pointed out that sometimes all you need is the initial estimate and one iteration, as long as you don't mind having a sample size that's a little larger than necessary. If the cost of each

Table 6.1 Sample Size Iteration Procedure for *t*-Tests

	Initial	1	2
t	1.96	2.093	2.08
t^2	3.84	4.38	4.33
s^2	11.2	11.2	11.2
d	1.5	1.5	1.5
d^2	2.25	2.25	2.25
df	19	21	21
Unrounded	19.1	21.8	21.5
Rounded up	20	22	22

sample is very high, though, it makes sense to iterate until reaching one of the stopping criteria. Note that the initial estimate establishes the lower bound for the sample size (20 in this example), and the first iteration establishes the upper bound (22 in this example).

SHOULD BOB HAVE USED THE GEOMETRIC MEAN?

Yes, but there's an important trick ...

In Chapter 3 we recommended using the geometric mean for estimates of typical completion times when the sample size is less than 25. Bob's driving times are a type of completion time, so should he have done his sample size calculations using the geometric mean, with natural logs of the driving times rather than their actual values? The natural logs of his driving times are 2.48490665, 2.63905733, 2.48490665, 2.995732274, and 2.772588722. The average of these log times is 2.675438325 with a variance of 0.046488657, so the geometric mean is 14.5 min (as expected, slightly less than the arithmetic mean of 14.8 min) and its standard deviation is about 1.24 min (less than half of the regular standard deviation of 3.35). But what should he use for d?

You might think that you should just take the natural log of the critical difference—for 1.5 the natural log is 0.405—but due to the nature of logarithms, that wouldn't work. Instead, you need to add the critical difference to the arithmetic mean, take the natural logarithm of that, then subtract the natural logarithm of the arithmetic mean (Lynda Finn, personal communication, Apr. 28, 2011). Expressed mathematically:

$$d_{\ln} = \ln(\bar{x} + d) - \ln(\bar{x})$$

For Bob's driving times, this would be:

$$d_{\ln} = \ln(14.8 + 1.5) - \ln(14.8) = \ln(16.3) - \ln(14.8) = 2.791165 - 2.694627 = 0.096538$$

If you use 0.046488657 for the variance and 0.096538 for the critical difference in place of the values shown in Table 6.1, it turns out that you arrive at the same conclusion—to achieve this measurement goal you'll need a total sample size of 22. Note, however, that these data are only slightly skewed. The more skewed the time data are, the greater the difference in the estimated sample sizes. Because the log transform applied to completion time data almost always reduces the estimate of the variance, it is often the case that you'll determine that you need a smaller sample size than you would if you used the raw (untransformed) data. If the cost of additional samples is low, then this won't matter much, but if it's high, then this could reduce the cost of the experiment without sacrificing any of the measurement goals. If you know you're going to use the log transform on your data, then you should consider computing your sample size estimation with this in mind, even though the resulting estimate will rarely differ substantially from the estimate made with raw time scores.

Example 1: A realistic usability testing example given an existing estimate of variability

This example illustrates the computation of a sample size requirement for the estimation of a value given an existing estimate of variability and realistic criteria. For speech recognition, it is important to track the recognizer's accuracy due to the usability problems that misrecognitions can cause. For this example, suppose:

- Recognition variability (variance) from a previous similar evaluation = 5.5 ($s = 2.345$)
- Critical difference (d) = 1.5%
- Desired level of confidence: 90% (so the initial value of $z = 1.645$)

Table 6.2 shows the iterative steps that lead to the final sample size estimation for this example. After three iterations, the process settles on a sample size of 9.

Table 6.2 Iterations for Example 1

	Initial	1	2	3
t	1.645	1.943	1.833	1.86
t^2	2.71	3.78	3.36	3.46
s^2	5.5	5.5	5.5	5.5
d	1.5	1.5	1.5	1.5
d^2	2.25	2.25	2.25	2.25
df	6	9	8	8
Unrounded	6.6	9.2	8.2	8.5
Rounded up	7	10	9	9

Example 2: An unrealistic usability testing example

Suppose a stakeholder wasn't satisfied with the criteria used in Example 1, and wanted a higher level of confidence and a smaller critical difference, such as:

- Recognition variability (variance) from a previous similar evaluation = 5.5 ($s = 2.345$)
- Critical difference (d) = 0.5%
- Desired level of confidence: 99% (so the initial value of $z = 2.576$)

The results appear in Table 6.3.

The initial estimate is 146 which goes up to 150 with the first iteration, then stays there. There might be some settings in which usability investigators would consider 146–150 participants a reasonable and practical sample size, but they are rare. Confronted with these results, the hypothetical stakeholder would very likely want to reconsider the criteria.

Table 6.3 Iterations for Example 2

	Initial	1	2
t	2.576	2.61	2.609
t^2	6.64	6.81	6.81
s^2	5.5	5.5	5.5
d	0.5	0.5	0.5
d^2	0.25	0.25	0.25
df	145	149	149
Unrounded	146.0	149.9	149.8
Rounded up	146	150	150

Example 3: No estimate of variability

Examples 1 and 2 had estimates of variance, either from a previous study or a quick pilot study. Suppose you don't have any idea what the measurement variability is and it isn't possible to run a pilot study to get an initial estimate (no time or too expensive). Diamond (1981) provided a method for getting around this problem but, to apply it, you need to give up the definition of the critical difference (d) in terms of the variable of interest and replace it with a definition in terms of a fraction of the standard deviation—in other words, to define d as an effect size.

The typical use of an effect size is as a standardized measure of the magnitude of an outcome, computed by dividing the difference (d) between the observed and hypothesized values of a parameter by the standard deviation. The motivation behind the development of the effect size was to have a measure of effect that, unlike the observed significance level (p), is independent of the sample size (Minium et al., 1993). Cohen (1988) suggested using 0.2, 0.5, and 0.8 as rule-of-thumb values for small, medium, and large effects.

Assume that with 80% confidence, you want to be able to detect a fairly small effect—specifically, you want to be able to detect effects that are equal to or greater than one-third of a standard deviation. In the previous examples, we used d as the symbol for the critical difference, so in this example we'll use e as the symbol for the effect size, which leads to:

$$e = \frac{d}{s}$$
$$d = e(s)$$

The measurement criteria are:

- Recognition variability from a previous similar evaluation = N/A
- Critical difference (d) = 0.33s
- Desired level of confidence: 80% (so the initial value of $z = 1.282$)

The initial sample size estimate is:

$$n = \frac{z^2s^2}{d^2} = \frac{1.282^2(s^2)}{(0.33s)^2} = \frac{1.282^2(s^2)}{0.33^2(s^2)} = \frac{1.64}{0.11} = 14.9$$

which rounds up to 15. The result of the first iteration, replacing 1.282 with t for 14 degrees of freedom and 80% confidence (1.345), results in a sample size estimation of 16.5, which rounds up to 17. Thus, the appropriate sample size is somewhere between 15 and 17. The next iteration confirms a final estimate of 17.

If you prefer an alternative approach when the variance is completely unknown, there are rules of thumb for the typical variability encountered for certain types of data. See the sidebar "Rules of Thumb for Estimating Unknown Variance."

RULES OF THUMB FOR ESTIMATING UNKNOWN VARIANCE

Strategies for when you don't have any other estimates of variance

If you have an idea about the largest and smallest values for a population of measurements but don't have all the data values that you would need to actually estimate the variability, you can estimate the standard deviation (s) by dividing the difference between the largest and smallest values by 6. This technique assumes that the population distribution is normal and then takes advantage of the fact that 99% of a normal distribution will lie in the range of plus or minus three standard deviations of the mean (Parasuraman, 1986).

Nielsen (1997) surveyed 36 published usability studies and found that the mean standard deviation for measures of expert performance was 33% of the mean value of the usability measure (in other words, if the mean completion time was 100 s, the mean standard deviation was about 33 s). For novice user learning (across 12 studies), the mean standard deviation was 46% of the measure of interest. For error rates (across 13 studies), it was 59%.

Churchill (1991) provided a list of typical variances for data obtained from rating-scale items (such as those used in the System Usability Scale). Because the number of points in a scale item affects the possible variance (more points increase reliability, but also allow for more variance), you need to take the number of scale points into account. For five-point scales, the typical variance is 1.2–2.0; for seven-point scales it is 2.4–4.0; and for 10-point scales it is 3.0–7.0. Because rating scale data tends to have a more uniform rather than normal distribution, Churchill suggested using a number nearer the high end of the listed range when estimating sample sizes.

COMPARING VALUES

Sometimes you need to do more than just estimate a value. You might also need to compare one value with another. That comparison could be an estimated value against a static benchmark, or it could be one estimated value against another. The following examples illustrate how to perform such comparisons with continuous data using confidence intervals based on t-scores.

Example 4: Comparison with a benchmark

For an example comparing a measurement to a benchmark, suppose that you have a product requirement that the SUS score for installation should be at least 75. In a preliminary evaluation, the mean SUS score was 65. Development has fixed a number of usability problems found in that preliminary study, so you're ready to measure the SUS for installation again, using the following measurement criteria:

- Variability from the previous evaluation = 5.0 ($s = 2.236$)
- Critical difference (d) = 1 point
- Desired level of confidence: 95% (so the initial value of $z = 1.645$)

The interpretation of these measurement criteria is that you want to be 95% confident that you can detect a difference as small as 1 point between the mean of the data gathered in the test and the benchmark you're trying to beat. In other words, the installation will pass if the observed mean SUS is 76 or higher because the sample size should guarantee a lower limit to the confidence interval that is no more than 1 point below the mean (as long as the observed variance is less than or equal to the initial estimate of the variance). As discussed in Chapter 4, this is a one-sided test, so the initial value of z given 95% confidence should be 1.645, not 1.96. Otherwise, the procedure for determining the sample size in this situation is the same as that of Example 1, with the computations shown in Table 6.4. The outcome of these iterations is an initial sample size estimation of 14, ending with an estimate of 16.

Table 6.4 Iterations for Example 4

	Initial	1	2
t	1.645	1.771	1.753
t^2	2.71	3.14	3.07
s^2	5	5	5
d	1	1	1
d^2	1	1	1
df	13	15	15
Unrounded	13.5	15.7	15.4
Rounded up	14	16	16

Example 5: Within-subjects comparison of an alternative

As discussed in Chapter 4, when you obtain two comparable measurements from each participant in a test (a within-subjects design), you can use a paired t-test to assess the results. Another name for this is a difference score t-test because you work with the mean and standard deviation of the difference scores rather than the raw scores. Suppose that you plan to obtain recognition accuracy scores from participants who have dictated test texts into your product under development and a competitor's current product using the following criteria:

- Difference score variability from a previous evaluation = 10.0 ($s = 3.162$)
- Critical difference (d) = 2.5%
- Desired level of confidence: 99% (so the initial value of $z = 2.576$)

This situation is similar to that of the previous example because the goal of a difference scores t-test is to determine if the average difference between scores is significantly different from 0. So, one way to think

Table 6.5 Iterations for Example 5

	Initial	1	2	3	4
t	2.576	3.169	2.921	3.012	2.977
t^2	6.64	10.04	8.53	9.07	8.86
s^2	10	10	10	10	10
d	2.5	2.5	2.5	2.5	2.5
d^2	6.25	6.25	6.25	6.25	6.25
df	10	16	13	14	14
Unrounded	10.6	16.1	13.6	14.5	14.2
Rounded up	11	17	14	15	15

about this test is that the usability criterion is 0 and you want to be 99% confident that if the true difference between system accuracies is 2.5% or more, you will be able to detect it because the confidence interval around the mean difference will not contain 0. This example differs, however, in that you're conducting a two-tailed test with 99% confidence because you're making no prior assumption about which system is better, so the initial value of z should be 2.576, not 2.236. Table 6.5 shows the iterations for this example, leading to $n = 15$.

Example 6: Between-subjects comparison of an alternative

So far, the examples have involved one group of scores, making them amenable to similar treatment. However, if you need to compare scores from two independent groups, things get a little more complicated. For example, you could have different sample sizes for each group. If you are dealing with that complex of a situation, or dealing with even more complex sample size estimation for multifactor or multivariable experiments typically analyzed with analysis of variance or other more advanced linear modeling, you will need to consult more advanced references such as Brown (1980), Kraemer and Thiemann (1987), or Winer et al. (1991).

To simplify things for this example (which should be fairly common in usability testing), assume that the groups are essentially equal (especially with regard to performance variability), which should be the case if the groups contain participants from a single population who have received random assignment to treatment conditions. In this case it is reasonable to believe that the variances (and thus the sample sizes) for both groups should be about equal. For this specific simplified situation, the degrees of freedom will be $2(n - 1)$ because there are two independent groups (each with $n - 1$ df), and the formula for the initial estimate of the sample size for each group is:

$$n = \frac{2z^2s^2}{d^2}$$

Table 6.6 Iterations for Example 6

	Initial	1	2
t	2.576	2.698	2.687
t^2	6.635	7.280	7.220
s^2	10	10	10
d	2.5	2.5	2.5
d^2	6.25	6.25	6.25
df	42	46	46
Unrounded	21.2	23.3	23.1
Rounded up	22	24	24

Note the similarity to the formula presented in Example 1, but with the numerator multiplied by 2. For example, suppose that you need to conduct the experiment described in Example 5 with independent groups of participants, keeping the measurement criteria the same:

- Difference score variability from a previous evaluation = 10.0 ($s = 3.162$)
- Critical difference (d) = 2.5%
- Desired level of confidence: 99% (so the initial value of $z = 2.576$)

As shown in Table 6.6, the iterations converge on a sample size of 24 participants per group, for a total sample size of 48. There is a well-known efficiency advantage for within-subjects designs over these types of between-subjects designs, illustrated in this example. Because participants act as their own controls in within-subjects experiments, their difference scores eliminate a substantial amount of variability relative to the raw scores, which leads to lower sample size requirements. For the same measurement precision, the estimated sample size for Example 5 was 15 participants, about 31% of the sample size requirement estimated for this example.

Example 7: Where's the power?

The power of a test refers to its ability to detect a difference between observed measurements and hypothesized values if one exists. The power of a test is not an issue when you're just estimating the value of a parameter, but it is an issue when testing a hypothesis (as in Examples 4–6)—either comparing a result to a benchmark or comparing alternatives. In traditional hypothesis testing, there is a null (H_0) and an alternative (H_a) hypothesis. The typical null hypothesis is that there is no difference between groups. The typical alternative hypothesis is that the difference is something greater than zero. When the alternative hypothesis is that the difference is nonzero, the test is two-tailed because you can reject the null hypothesis with either a sufficiently positive or a sufficiently negative result. As discussed in Chapter 4, if the only meaningful outcome is in one direction (e.g., when comparing a result against a benchmark), you can (and should) use a one-tailed test. Fig. 6.3 shows the

Decision	Reality: H_0 *is true*	Reality: H_0 *is false*
Evidence not strong enough to reject H_0 ($p>\alpha$)	Correctly failed to reject H_0 Confidence: $1-\alpha$	Made Type II error Acceptable probability: β
Evidence is strong enough to reject H_0 ($p<\alpha$)	Made Type I error Acceptable probability: α	Correctly rejected H_0 Power: $1-\beta$

FIGURE 6.3 Possible Outcomes of a Hypothesis Test

possible outcomes of a hypothesis test and shows the relationships among those outcomes and the concepts of confidence, power, and the acceptable probabilities of Type I and Type II errors.

In hypothesis testing, there are two ways to be right and two ways to be wrong. The two ways to be right are (1) to fail to reject the null hypothesis (H_0) when it is true, or (2) to reject the null hypothesis when it is false. The two ways to be wrong are (1) to reject the null hypothesis when it is true (Type I error—a false alarm), or (2) to fail to reject the null hypothesis when it is false (Type II error—a miss). Strictly speaking, you never accept the null hypothesis because the failure to acquire sufficient evidence to reject the null hypothesis could be due to (1) no significant difference between groups, or (2) a sample size too small to detect an existing difference. So, rather than saying that you accept the null hypothesis, you say that you have failed to reject it. Regardless of rejecting or failing to reject the null hypothesis based on the value of *p*, you should also report the effect size or, even better, provide a confidence interval.

The formula used in Example 5 for the initial sample size estimate was:

$$n = \frac{z^2 s^2}{d^2}$$

In the example, the *z*-score was set for 99% confidence (which means that $\alpha = 0.01$). To take power into account in this formula, we need to add another *z*-score to the formula—the *z*-score associated with the desired power of the test (as illustrated in Fig. 6.3). Thus the formula becomes:

$$n = \frac{(z_\alpha + z_\beta)^2 s^2}{d^2}$$

and for each iteration, you need to add together the values for the appropriate t_α and t_β depending on the different test criteria set for the desired levels of confidence and power.

You might wonder where the value for power was in Example 5. When beta (β) equals 0.5 (in other words, when the power is 50%), the one-sided value of z_β is 0, so z_β disappears from the formula. Note that when using this method for sample size estimation, the *z* and *t* values for β should always be one-sided, regardless of whether the test itself will be one- or two-sided (Diamond, 1981).

Table 6.7 Iterations for Example 7

	Initial	1	2	3
t_α	2.576	2.878	2.819	2.831
t_β	0.842	0.862	0.858	0.859
$t_{\alpha+\beta}$	3.418	3.740	3.677	3.690
$t_{\alpha+\beta^2}$	11.68	13.99	13.52	13.62
s^2	10	10	10	10
d	2.5	2.5	2.5	2.5
d^2	6.25	6.25	6.25	6.25
df	18	22	21	21
Unrounded	18.7	22.4	21.6	21.8
Rounded up	19	23	22	22

So, in Example 5 the implicit power was 50%. Suppose you want to increase the power of the test to 80% (reducing β to 0.2). What happens to the recommended sample size?

- Difference score variability from a previous evaluation = 10.0 (s = 3.162)
- Critical difference (d) = 2.5
- Desired level of confidence: 99% (so the initial value of $z_\alpha = 2.576$)
- Desired power: 80% (so the initial one-sided value of z_β is 0.842—you could use =ABS(NORMSINV(0.2)) to find this value in Excel)
- Sum of desired confidence and power: $z_\alpha + z_\beta = 3.418$

With this change, as shown in Table 6.7 the iterations converge on a sample size of 22 (compared to the previously estimated sample size of 15 when the target power was 50%). The sample size is larger, but this is the price paid to increase the power of the test without affecting its level of protection against Type I errors (false alarms).

Note that if this sample size turned out to be too large for the available testing resources, then you can get to a smaller sample size by making any or all of the following three changes to the criteria as part of the process of planning the test:

- increase the value of the critical difference
- reduce the power of the test
- reduce the confidence level

WHAT ARE REASONABLE TEST CRITERIA?

It depends ...

In scientific publishing the primary criterion for statistical significance is to set the permissible Type I error (α) equal to 0.05. Based on writings by Karl Pearson, "Student" (Gosset), and Wood and Stratton, this convention was apparently in use starting in the first decade of the 20th century (Cowles, 1989). In 1925, Sir Ronald Fisher was the first to explicitly cite 0.05 as a convenient limit for judging significance, "in the context of examples of how often deviations of a particular size occur in a given number of trials – that twice the standard deviation is exceeded about one in 22 trials, and so on" (Cowles, 1989, p. 175).

This practice is equivalent to having 95% confidence that the effect is real rather than random and has a strong focus on controlling the Type I error. There is no corresponding typical practice for the Type II error (β), although some suggest setting it to 0.20 (Diamond, 1981), and others have recommended making it equal to α (Kirakowski, 2005). The rationale behind the emphasis on controlling the Type I error in scientific publication is the belief that it is better to delay the introduction of good information into the scientific database (a Type II error) than to let in erroneous information (a Type I error).

In industrial evaluation, the appropriate values for Type I and II errors depend on the demands of the situation—specifically, whether the cost of a Type I or II error would be more damaging to the organization. Because usability practitioners are often resource-constrained, especially with regard to making timely decisions while competing in dynamic marketplaces, we've included examples that use 80 or 90% confidence rather than 95% and fairly large values for *d*—examples that illustrate a greater balance between Type I and II errors than is typical in work intended for scientific publication. As Nielsen (1997, p. 1544) suggested, "a confidence level of 95% is often used for research studies, but for practical development purposes, it may be enough to aim for an 80% level of confidence." For an excellent discussion of this topic for usability researchers, see Wickens (1998), and for other technical issues and perspectives, see Landauer (1997).

Another way to look at the issue is to ask the question, "Am I typically interested in small high-variability effects or large low-variability effects?" In usability testing, the customary emphasis is on the detection of large low-variability effects (either large performance effects or frequently occurring problems). You can prove the existence of large low-variability effects with fairly small sample sizes. Although it can be tempting to equate sample size with population coverage, that just isn't true. A small sample size drawn from the right population provides better evidence than a large sample size drawn from the wrong population. Furthermore, the statistics involved in computing *t*-based confidence intervals from small samples compensate for the potentially smaller variance in the small sample by forcing the confidence interval to be wider than that for a larger sample (specifically, the value of *t* is greater when samples are smaller).

WHAT CAN I DO TO CONTROL VARIABILITY?

When you design a study, you have full control over many of the variables. You can set the level of confidence (or alternatively, the value of α), the power of the study (or alternatively, the value of β), the magnitude of the critical difference (d), and the final sample size (n). The element in the equation over which you have the least control is the variability of a measurement (s^2). There are, however, some things you can do to keep measurement variance as small as possible, including:

- Make sure that your participants understand what they are supposed to do. Unless potential participant confusion is part of the evaluation (and it could be), it will only add to measurement variance.
- If appropriate, let participants get familiar with the testing situation by having them complete practice trials, but be careful that you do not unduly reveal study-relevant information.
- If appropriate, use expert rather than novice participants. By definition, expertise implies reduced performance variability (Mayer, 1997).
- If you need to include both expert and novice users, you should be able to get equal measurement precision for both groups with unequal sample sizes (fewer experts needed than novices—which is good because experts are usually harder to recruit as participants than novices).
- If appropriate, study simple rather than complex tasks.
- Use data transformations for measurements that tend to exhibit correlations between means and variances or standard deviations. For example, frequency counts often have proportional means and variances (treated with the square-root transformation), and time scores often have proportional means and standard deviations (treated with the logarithmic transformation) (Myers, 1979; Sauro and Lewis, 2010).

- For comparative studies, if possible, use within-subjects designs rather than between-subjects designs.
- Keep user groups as homogeneous as possible (but note that although this reduces variability, it can threaten a study's external validity if the test group is more homogenous than the population under study) (Campbell and Stanley, 1963).

IMPORTANT! Apply these tips only when they do not adversely affect the validity and generalizability of your study. Having a study that is valid and generalizable is far more important than reducing variance. That said, however, the smaller your variance, the more precise your measurement, and the smaller will be the required sample size for a target level of precision.

SAMPLE SIZE ESTIMATION FOR BINOMIAL CONFIDENCE INTERVALS

The methods for proportions are similar to those for *t*-tests. Rather than needing an estimate of the variance of the mean (s^2), you need an estimate of the expected proportion (p), where $p = x/n$ (the number of successes over the number of binomial trials). This is because the variance of a binomial measurement is $p(1 - p)$. If you do not have any prior expectation of the value of p (e.g., from a previous test), then the safest thing to do is to assume $p = 0.5$ because that's the value of p that has the largest variance (which will push you toward a relatively larger sample size). For example, when p is 0.5, $p(1 - p)$ is $0.5(0.5) = 0.25$; when p is 0.25, $p(1 - p)$ is $0.25(0.75) = 0.1875$, 75% of the maximum variance of 0.25.

BINOMIAL SAMPLE SIZE ESTIMATION FOR LARGE SAMPLES

The conditions that require a large sample size for a binomial test are the same as those that require a large sample size for a *t*-test: high confidence, high power, large variance, and a small critical difference. As presented in Chapter 3, the critical difference for the Wald (large sample) interval is:

$$d = z\sqrt{\frac{\hat{p}(1-\hat{p})}{n}}$$

The value of z depends on:

- The desired confidence level
- The desired level of power
- Whether the test is one- or two-sided

Following essentially the same algebraic steps as those shown earlier in the chapter to isolate n on the left side of the equation for the critical difference of a confidence interval based on a *t*-test, you get:

$$n = \frac{z^2(\hat{p})(1-\hat{p})}{d^2}$$

Note the similarity to:

$$n = \frac{z^2 s^2}{d^2}$$

They are identical, with the exception of substituting $(\hat{p})(1-\hat{p})$—the estimate of binomial variance—for s^2.

For example, assume you want to estimate the success rate of users logging into a website using a new login procedure, using the following criteria:

- Success rate from a previous evaluation is not available—so use $p = 0.5$
- Critical difference (d) = 0.05
- Desired level of confidence: 95% (so the value of $z = 1.96$)

Then the required sample size will be $((1.96^2)(0.5)(0.5))/0.05^2$, which is 385 (384.1 rounded up).

Consider another example, with everything the same except the estimate of p. Assume that you've collected login success data with your current login procedure and currently 90% ($p = 0.9$) of users successfully authenticate. You've made changes that you believe are very likely to improve the success rate to 95% ($p = 0.95$) and want to collect data to estimate the success rate. Under those conditions, your estimated sample size would be $((1.96^2)(0.95)(0.05))/0.05^2 = 72.99$, which rounds up to 73.

This illustrates a fact that user researchers must accept. Even with fairly modest goals—95% confidence ($z = 1.96$), 50% power ($z = 0$), and a critical difference of ±0.05, the required sample size will be larger than is common practice in moderated usability studies, although not out of line with the sample sizes typical in unmoderated user research. If you must work with small samples and you collect binomial data such as success rates, you must be prepared to deal with large binomial confidence intervals and to use interpretive strategies such as those discussed in Chapters 3 and 4 to make those intervals useful despite their large size (illustrated in the sidebar "User Assessment of the Value of a Disk Drive In-Use Indicator for Floor-Standing Personal Computers").

USER ASSESSMENT OF THE VALUE OF A DISK DRIVE IN-USE INDICATOR FOR FLOOR-STANDING PERSONAL COMPUTERS

Out of sight, out of mind?—from the files of Jim Lewis

In the late 1980s, my lab received word of a plan to remove the disk drive in-use indicator from the next version of our floor-standing personal computers. The designers had reasoned that because the unit was on the floor, typically under a desk, that they could save a little money on each unit by eliminating the LED that flashed when the disk drive was in use. To test this hypothesis we randomly selected 20 users of floor-standing computers at our site and got their permission to cover their existing in-use indicators with aluminum tape. We checked back with those users a week later, and found that seven of them (35%) had removed the tape because they found the absence of the in-use indicator so disturbing. This was well before the development of the adjusted-Wald binomial confidence interval (Agresti and Coull, 1998), so we assessed the result with a 95% exact binomial confidence interval, which ranged from 15–59%. From this result we argued that the best case was that about one out of every six users would have a strong negative reaction to the absence of the disk drive in-use indicator, and the worst case was that the proportion of disaffected users would be three out of five. The evidence from this user study did not support the designers' intuition. In this case, our discovery of the issue and consequent presentation of the results was too late to affect the design, but based on our study, there was an effort to monitor user reaction in the field—user reaction which was consistent with our results. For these reasons, the disk drive in-use indicator came back in all following floor-standing models in that product line.

BINOMIAL SAMPLE SIZE ESTIMATION FOR SMALL SAMPLES

In previous chapters, we've recommended using the adjusted-Wald binomial confidence interval rather than the standard Wald, especially with small samples ($n < 100$). From a historical perspective, the adjusted-Wald interval is fairly new, published by Agresti and Coull in 1998. We do not know of any published work describing sample size estimation for this type of binomial confidence interval, but due to its similarity with the standard Wald interval, we can provide some practical guidance.

We start with a review of how to adjust the Wald formula to get to the adjusted-Wald. After you decide on the required confidence level, you look up its corresponding value of z. For a given x and n (where $\hat{p} = x/n$), you add $z^2/2$ to x (to get x_{adj}) and z^2 to n (to get n_{adj}). Thus, the adjusted value of $\hat{p}$ is:

$$\hat{p}_{adj} = \frac{x + \frac{z^2}{2}}{n + z^2} = \frac{x_{adj}}{n_{adj}}$$

From this equation, we can see three things:

1. To get from the adjusted value of n used in the adjusted-Wald formula to the actual value of n, it's necessary to subtract z^2 from n_{adj}.
2. With one exception ($\hat{p} = 0.5$), the adjusted value of $\hat{p}$ will always differ from the value of $\hat{p}$ such that the binomial variance will increase, with a corresponding increase in the width of the confidence interval. When $\hat{p} = 0.5$, the adjusted value of $\hat{p}$ remains 0.5.
3. As the values of x and n increase, the effect of the adjustment on the value of $\hat{p}$ decreases, so this adjustment is more important for smaller than for larger sample sizes.

HOW DOES BINOMIAL VARIANCE WORK?

The more extreme the value of *p*, the lower the variance

At first it might seem a bit counterintuitive, but more moderate values of p correspond to higher variability in outcomes. The highest possible binomial variability occurs when $p = 0.5$—the statistical equivalent of a coin toss. When you toss a fair coin, you really have no idea on any given toss whether the outcome will be heads or tails. On the other hand, imagine a 10-sided die with nine gray faces and one white. You can be pretty sure that most tosses of that die will result in a gray face up—in fact, the probability of getting gray is 0.9. For the fair coin, the variability is 0.5(0.5) = 0.25; for the 10-sided die, the variability is 0.9(0.1) = 0.09—much less than 0.25 (Fig. 6.4).

Using the formula for sample size estimation for the standard Wald interval as a model, the formula for the adjusted-Wald is:

$$n_{adj} = \frac{z^2(\hat{p}_{adj})(1 - \hat{p}_{adj})}{d^2}$$

FIGURE 6.4 Examples of Moderate and Extreme Values of *p*

Substituting $n\hat{p}$ for x, the formula for $\hat{p}_{\text{adj}}$ is:

$$\hat{p}_{\text{adj}} = \frac{n\hat{p} + \frac{z^2}{2}}{n + z^2}$$

Because $n_{\text{adj}} = n + z^2$, then $n = n_{\text{adj}} - z^2$, so the final estimate of n is:

$$n = \frac{z^2(\hat{p}_{\text{adj}})(1 - \hat{p}_{\text{adj}})}{d^2} - z^2$$

We know the values of z and d because we select them. The value of $\hat{p}$ comes from a previous evaluation or, if unknown, gets set to 0.5 to maximize the variance and the resulting sample size estimate. The value of n, however, is unknown because that's what we're trying to estimate. To deal with that, we recommend a three-step process.

1. Get an initial estimate of n using the standard Wald formula from the previous section:

$$n = \frac{z^2(\hat{p})(1 - \hat{p})}{d^2}$$

2. Use that initial estimate to calculate $\hat{p}_{\text{adj}}$ using $\hat{p}_{adj} = \frac{n\hat{p} + \frac{z^2}{2}}{n + z^2}$
3. Then use $\hat{p}_{\text{adj}}$ in $n = \frac{z^2(\hat{p}_{\text{adj}})(1 - \hat{p}_{\text{adj}})}{d^2} - z^2$ to get the final estimate of n

For example, suppose you have reason to believe that the current success rate for a particular task is 0.75, and want to see if that's correct. You know you won't be able to conduct a large-scale study; in fact, you probably won't be able to test more than 20 people. For this reason, you realistically set your target precision to 0.20, and balance that by setting your confidence to 95% (so $z = 1.96$). To recap:

- Success rate from a previous evaluation $p = 0.75$
- Critical difference (d) = 0.20
- Desired level of confidence: 95% (so the value of $z = 1.96$)

First, compute the initial sample size estimate using the standard Wald formula:

$$n = \frac{z^2(\hat{p})(1 - \hat{p})}{d^2} = \frac{1.96^2(0.75)(1 - 0.75)}{0.2^2} = 18.01$$

Rounded up, the initial estimate of n is 19.

Next, use that initial estimate of n to compute the adjusted value of p:

$$\hat{p}_{\text{adj}} = \frac{n\hat{p} + \frac{z^2}{2}}{n + z^2} = \frac{19(0.75) + \frac{1.96^2}{2}}{19 + 1.96^2} = 0.708$$

And use that adjusted value of p to compute the final estimate of n:

$$n = \frac{z^2(\hat{p}_{\text{adj}})(1 - \hat{p}_{\text{adj}})}{d^2} - z^2 = \frac{1.96^2(0.708)(1 - 0.708)}{0.2^2} - 1.96^2 = 16.02$$

Rounded up, the final estimate of n is 17.

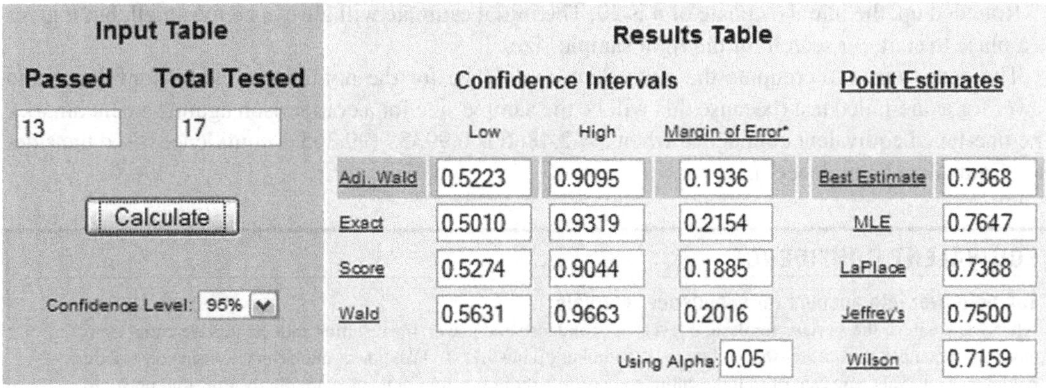

Input Table		Results Table					
Passed	Total Tested	Confidence Intervals				Point Estimates	
13	17		Low	High	Margin of Error*		
		Adj. Wald	0.5223	0.9095	0.1936	Best Estimate	0.7368
Calculate		Exact	0.5010	0.9319	0.2154	MLE	0.7647
		Score	0.5274	0.9044	0.1885	LaPlace	0.7368
Confidence Level: 95%		Wald	0.5631	0.9663	0.2016	Jeffrey's	0.7500
				Using Alpha:	0.05	Wilson	0.7159

FIGURE 6.5 Result of Sample Size Estimation Example for Adjusted-Wald Binomial Confidence Interval

If n is going to equal 17 and the expected value of p is 0.75, then the expected value of x is np, which is 17(0.75) = 12.75, which rounds to 13. We have to round the estimate up because x can only be a whole number. For this reason, the value of the resulting x/n will not usually equal the expected value of p, but it can get close—in this case it's 13/17 = 0.7647. If we put these values of x and n in the online calculator at www.measuringu.com/wald.htm, we find that the observed value of d is 0.1936, just 0.0064 less than the target value of 0.20 (Fig. 6.5).

SAMPLE SIZE FOR COMPARISON WITH A BENCHMARK PROPORTION

The general strategies for comparing a result with a benchmark target are the same for any test, whether based on continuous data and using t-tests or on count data and using binomial tests. To compute the required sample size, you need to:

- Determine the value of the benchmark.
- Set the desired levels of confidence and power assuming a one-tailed test.
- Decide on the required level of precision.

For example, suppose a first design of the installation process for a new dictation program had a success rate of 55%, so for the next version you want to show that you've improved the success rate to at least 65%. You decide to use the standard levels of 95% confidence and 80% power, which have corresponding one-sided z-scores of 1.645 and 0.8416 (and which sum to 2.4866) and to set the required level of precision to 20%. With a benchmark of at least 65% and precision of 20%, the target value of p to use for sample size estimation is 0.85 (0.65 + 0.20). Basically, you want to set up a test in which you can show beyond a reasonable doubt that you have achieved your goal for successful installation (if that is indeed the case), so you need to set your actual target to the benchmark plus the planned level of precision. To compute the recommended sample size for this scenario, use the following procedure based on the adjusted-Wald formula.

First, compute the initial sample size estimate using the standard Wald formula (for this scenario, with 95% confidence for a one-tailed test and 80% power, use $z = 2.4866$):

$$n = \frac{z^2(\hat{p})(1-\hat{p})}{d^2} = \frac{2.4866^2(0.85)(1-0.85)}{0.2^2} = 19.7$$

Rounded up, the initial estimate of n is 20. The initial estimate will always be too small, but it gives us a place to start our search for the right sample size.

The next step is to compute the equivalent confidence for the nominal levels of confidence and power for a one-tailed test (because this will be the sample size for a comparison against a benchmark). The one-tailed equivalent confidence when $z = 2.4866$ is 0.99355 (99.355% confidence—see the sidebar "Equivalent Confidence").

> **EQUIVALENT CONFIDENCE**
>
> **Taking power into account for confidence intervals**
>
> After you combine the z-scores for desired levels of confidence and power, the resulting sum could have come from any pair of component z-scores that add up to that number (Table 9.2). To take power into account when constructing confidence intervals, you can act as if the entire composite z-score was for confidence, implicitly adjusting power to 50% (for which $z_\beta = 0$). The value of the equivalent confidence depends on whether the resulting confidence interval is one- or two-tailed. For most uses, it should be two-tailed. For confidence intervals associated with benchmark tests, it should be one-tailed. For two-tailed equivalent confidence, you can insert the z-score into the Excel function =1-2*(1-NORMSDIST(Z)). For one-tailed equivalent confidence, you can use =NORMSDIST(Z).
>
> For example, suppose you decided to set confidence to 95% and power to 80% for a two-tailed test. The z for confidence (two-tailed) would be 1.96 and for power (always one-tailed) would be 0.8416, for a total z of 2.8016. Using this value of z in =1-2*(1-NORMSDIST(2.8016)) returns 0.9949, or 99.49% equivalent confidence. For the corresponding one-tailed situation, the z for 95% confidence would be 1.645 and for 80% power would be 0.8416, for a total z of 2.4866. Using that z in =NORMSDIST(2.4866) returns 0.99355, or 99.355% equivalent confidence.
>
> You normally won't need to worry about equivalent confidence, but it is useful when working out sample size estimates for testing outcomes against benchmarks. For a specified set of conditions, the confidence interval using equivalent confidence and the minimum acceptable sample size should just barely exclude the benchmark.

The last step is to set up a table of one-tailed adjusted-Wald confidence intervals starting with $n = 20$ and continuing until the lower bound of the confidence interval is higher than the criterion of 0.65. For x, multiply n by the target value of p (0.85 in this example) and round it to the nearest whole number. As shown in Table 6.8, when $n = 36$ the lower bound is just over 0.65 (although it is very close when $n = 35$), with $x = 31$.

As a check, what would happen if we got exactly 31 successes out of 36 attempts and applied the small-sample method from Chapter 4 for testing a rate against a benchmark? The mid-p likelihood of that outcome by chance is about 0.003 (for exact and large-sample tests it's about 0.004), so we would conclude that the evidence strongly supports an actual rate significantly higher than the criterion of 0.65. The strength of the result relative to setting $\alpha = 0.05$ is due to setting the power of the test to 80%. With a sample size of 36 and one-tailed $\alpha = 0.05$, you could tolerate up to seven failures and still have reasonably compelling evidence of an actual rate significantly higher than 0.65. For a small-sample test with $n = 36$, $x = 29$, and a true rate of 0.65, the likelihood of that result by chance would be 0.023. The likelihood of eight failures would be 0.053, just missing the preestablished cutoff of 0.05.

If you do not need the lower limit of the confidence interval to exceed the benchmark, you can use a more standard formula to compute an adequate sample size for a hypothesis test. Using Excel functions, that formula (Cohen, 1988) is:

$$=\text{CEILING}(2*((z_a + z_B) / (\text{SQRT}(2)*\text{ABS}(2*\text{ASIN}(\text{SQRT}(p)) - 2*\text{ASIN}(\text{SQRT}(b)))))\hat{}2,1)$$

Table 6.8 Estimating the Sample Size for Assessing a Rate Against a Benchmark of 0.65 and Critical Difference of 0.20 With 95% Confidence and 80% Power

If n =	x	p	x_{adj}	n_{adj}	p_{adj}	d_{adj}	Lower Bound
20	17	0.8500	20.0913	26.1826	0.7674	0.2053	0.5620
21	18	0.8571	21.0913	27.1826	0.7759	0.1989	0.5770
22	19	0.8636	22.0913	28.1826	0.7839	0.1928	0.5911
23	20	0.8696	23.0913	29.1826	0.7913	0.1871	0.6042
24	20	0.8333	23.0913	30.1826	0.7651	0.1919	0.5732
25	21	0.8400	24.0913	31.1826	0.7726	0.1866	0.5859
26	22	0.8462	25.0913	32.1826	0.7797	0.1817	0.5980
27	23	0.8519	26.0913	33.1826	0.7863	0.1769	0.6094
28	24	0.8571	27.0913	34.1826	0.7925	0.1724	0.6201
29	25	0.8621	28.0913	35.1826	0.7984	0.1682	0.6303
30	26	0.8667	29.0913	36.1826	0.8040	0.1641	0.6399
31	26	0.8387	29.0913	37.1826	0.7824	0.1683	0.6141
32	27	0.8438	30.0913	38.1826	0.7881	0.1644	0.6236
33	28	0.8485	31.0913	39.1826	0.7935	0.1608	0.6327
34	29	0.8529	32.0913	40.1826	0.7986	0.1573	0.6413
35	30	0.8571	33.0913	41.1826	0.8035	0.1539	0.6496
36	31	0.8611	34.0913	42.1826	0.8082	0.1507	**0.6574**

where b is the benchmark and p is the sum of the benchmark and the required level of precision. Due to its less stringent requirements, the estimated sample size using this formula will always be less than the equivalent confidence method. For this example, the estimated sample size using this formula is 28:

=CEILING(2*((2.486) / (SQRT(2)*ABS(2*ASIN(SQRT(0.85)) − 2*ASIN(SQRT(0.65)))))^2,1) = 28

SAMPLE SIZE ESTIMATION FOR CHI-SQUARED TESTS (INDEPENDENT PROPORTIONS)

In Chapter 5, we discussed the implications of the recent research by Campbell (2007) regarding when to use Fisher or chi-squared tests for small-sample studies and, if using chi-squared, which type to use. This research indicated that you should only use the Fisher test (specifically, the Fisher–Irwin test with two-sided tests carried out by Irwin's rule) only if you have at least one cell in the two-by-two table where the expected (the expected, not the observed) value is 0—which will not typically be the case in user research. In most cases, user researchers comparing two proportions using a two-by-two table should use the $N-1$ chi-squared test (the standard chi-squared test, but with N replaced by $N-1$).

The formula for computing chi-squared for a two-by-two table does not lend itself to easy conversion to a formula for computing the estimated sample size. Fortunately, Campbell (2007) pointed out that it is equivalent to the chi-squared test "to test the value of Z from the ratio of the difference in two proportions to the standard error of the difference" (p. 3672), modifying the standard formula for z by the factor $\{(N-1)/N\}^{1/2}$. This equivalence allows us to use a fairly direct approach to sample size estimation for $N-1$ chi-squared tests of two-by-two tables—one that is similar to the approach taken throughout this chapter.

To keep the computations manageable and for conceptual simplification, we're going to assume an equal sample size for each group. This is under the control of the investigator when conducting a designed experiment such as a usability study, but is not always under control for other types of user research. If you have no idea what your final sample sizes will be, it is reasonable to assume they will be the same. If you have some prior knowledge of how the sample sizes will be different, you can use online calculators such as the one at statpages.org (statpages.org/proppowr.html) to get the estimate, but bear in mind that at the time of writing this chapter, these calculators compute the sample size for a standard chi-squared test of two-by-two tables, not the currently recommended $N-1$ chi-squared test.

The formula for a standard z-test of the difference in two proportions assuming equal group sizes is:

$$z = \frac{d}{\sqrt{\frac{2pq}{n}}}$$

where d is the difference between the two proportions, p_1 and p_2;
$p_1 = x_1/n$ and $p_2 = x_2/n$,
where n is the sample size of each group, and
x_n represents the number of events of interest, for example, the number of successful task completions; and q is $1-p$.

To adjust this standard z-test to the one that is the same as the recommended $N-1$, multiply the previous formula by:

$$\sqrt{\frac{2n-1}{2n}}$$

We use $2n$ instead of N because the N in a chi-squared test is the total sample size for both groups. Under the assumption of equal group sizes, N is equal to $2n$. When we do this, we get:

$$z = \frac{d\sqrt{\frac{2n-1}{2n}}}{\sqrt{\frac{2pq}{n}}}$$

To convert this from a z-test to an equation for estimating sample size, we need to use algebra to get n on the left side of the equation. The steps are:

$$z\sqrt{\frac{2pq}{n}} = d\sqrt{\frac{2n-1}{2n}}$$

$$z^2 \frac{2pq}{n} = d^2 \frac{2n-1}{2n}$$

$$z^2(2pq) = \frac{d^2(2n-1)}{2}$$

$$2z^2(2pq) = d^2(2n-1)$$

$$\frac{4z^2pq}{d^2} = (2n-1)$$

$$2n = \left(\frac{4z^2pq}{d^2}\right) + 1$$

$$n = \frac{4z^2pq}{2d^2} + \frac{1}{2}$$

$$n = \frac{2z^2p(1-p)}{d^2} + \frac{1}{2}$$

So, to compute the estimated sample size for an $N - 1$ chi-squared test, we need values for:

- z: The sum of the two-tailed z-value for confidence and the one-tailed value for power—for example, 90% confidence and 80% power would correspond to respective z-values of 1.645 and 0.842, which sum to 2.487
- p: The average of the expected values of p_1 and p_2 (determined from previous experiments, pilot studies, or stakeholder consensus)
- d: The minimum practical difference that you need to detect, which is the difference between p_1 and p_2 (note that the closer these values are, the smaller d will be, which can dramatically increase the sample size required to discriminate between them with statistical significance)

Suppose you've recently run a test comparing successful completion rates for the installation of the current version of a product and a new version in which you've made changes to improve the ease of installation. In that previous study, the successful completion rate for the current version was 0.7 and for the new version was 0.8. You've made some additional changes that should eliminate some of the problems participants had with the new version—enough that you think you should get a successful completion rate of at least 0.9 (90% success). With this background information, you decide to see what sample size you would need, given:

- z: For 90% confidence and 80% power you get z-values of 1.645 and 0.842, which sum to 2.487
- p: The expected average of p_1 and p_2, which is 0.8 (the average of 0.7 and 0.9)
- d: The difference between p_1 and p_2 is 0.2

Plugging these values into the equation, you get:

$$n = \frac{2(2.487)^2(0.8)(0.2)}{0.2^2} + \frac{1}{2}$$

$$n = 49.98$$

For these levels of confidence, power, and precision, you'd need 50 participants in each group (100 in total). Assume that you don't have the time or money to run 100 participants, so you decide to relax your level of confidence to 80%. With 80% confidence and 80% power you get z-values of 1.282 and 0.842, which sum to 2.124. Everything else stays the same.

Now you get:

$$n = \frac{2(2.124)^2(0.8)(0.2)}{0.2^2} + \frac{1}{2}$$
$$n = 36.6$$

A group size of 37 is a little better, but a total sample size of 74 still stretches the resources of most moderated usability studies. So you try one more time, this time setting power to 50% (so its corresponding z-score is 0), and you get:

$$n = \frac{2(1.282)^2(0.8)(0.2)}{0.2^2} + \frac{1}{2}$$
$$n = 13.6$$

For these levels of confidence, power, and precision, you'll need 14 participants per group (28 in total).

Although some statisticians frown upon ever reusing data, you do already have data for the current version of the product. As long as your sample size from that previous study is equal to or greater than 14 and you can reasonably assume that you're drawing the old and new samples from the same population (in other words, that the test conditions are essentially equivalent despite the passage of time), you have data from which you could draw (if needed) a random selection of 14 participants. If you have fewer than 14 participants, you could run the difference to get your sample size up to 14. Regardless, you will need to run about 14 participants with the latest version of the product in development. With data from 28 participants (half using the current version, half using the most recent version), you can conduct your N − 1 chi-squared test (or, equivalently, an N − 1 two-proportion test).

On the other hand, if you determine that these levels of confidence, power, and precision are inadequate for your needs, you can cancel the study and use your resources for some other user research project that might be more likely to be productive. The point is that you are making this decision with a clear understanding of the potential risks and benefits of conducting the study with the estimated sample size.

SAMPLE SIZE ESTIMATION FOR MCNEMAR EXACT TESTS (MATCHED PROPORTIONS)

As discussed in Chapter 5, when you run a within-subjects study, the most appropriate test to use to assess differences in proportions (such as success rates) is the McNemar Exact Test. Like the chi-squared test, the McNemar Exact Test does not lend itself to easy conversion to a formula for computing the estimated sample size. Again, like the chi-squared test, there is an alternative approach using confidence intervals based on the direct comparison of proportions (Agresti and Min, 2005) that we can use to derive a formula for estimating the sample size requirement for this type of test. The standard Wald version of that confidence interval formula is:

$$(\hat{p}_{21} - \hat{p}_{12}) \pm z\sqrt{[(\hat{p}_{12} + \hat{p}_{21}) - (\hat{p}_{21} - \hat{p}_{12})^2]/n}$$

This is a bit more complicated than the confidence interval formula for estimating a single value of p. Table 6.9 provides the definitions of the various probabilities used in the previously mentioned confidence interval formula.

The various proportions in Table 6.9 are the cell counts divided by the number of participants. For example, the proportion associated with the discordant pairs in which participants succeed with Design A but fail with Design B is $\hat{p}_{12} = b/n$. The other proportion of discordant pairs, where participants succeed with Design B but fail with Design A, is $\hat{p}_{21} = c/n$. The success rate for Design A $(\hat{p}_1)$ is $(a + b)/n$, and the success rate for Design B $(\hat{p}_2)$ is $(a + c)/n$.

Note that the difference between proportions that appears in the confidence interval formula is $(\hat{p}_{21} - \hat{p}_{12})$, even though the most likely difference of interest is that between the success rates $(\hat{p}_2 - \hat{p}_1)$. It's okay, though, because in this type of test the difference between the success rates for the two designs is equal to the difference between the proportions of discordant pairs.

$$d = \hat{p}_1 - \hat{p}_2 = \frac{(a+c)}{n} - \frac{(a+b)}{n} = \frac{(a+c-a-b)}{n} = \frac{(c-b)}{n} = \frac{c}{n} - \frac{b}{n} = \hat{p}_{21} - \hat{p}_{12}$$

To derive a sample size formula from the standard Wald confidence interval formula, we need to set the critical difference (the part to the right of the ± sign) to d, then solve for N.

$$(\hat{p}_{21} - \hat{p}_{12}) \pm z\sqrt{[(\hat{p}_{12} + \hat{p}_{21}) - (\hat{p}_{21} - \hat{p}_{12})^2]/n}$$

$$d = z\sqrt{[(\hat{p}_{12} + \hat{p}_{21}) - (\hat{p}_{21} - \hat{p}_{12})^2]/n}$$

$$d^2 = \frac{z^2[(\hat{p}_{12} + \hat{p}_{21}) - (\hat{p}_{21} - \hat{p}_{12})^2]}{n}$$

$$nd^2 = z^2[(\hat{p}_{12} + \hat{p}_{21}) - (\hat{p}_{21} - \hat{p}_{12})^2]$$

$$n = \frac{z^2[(\hat{p}_{12} + \hat{p}_{21}) - (\hat{p}_{21} - \hat{p}_{12})^2]}{d^2}$$

$$n = \frac{z^2[(\hat{p}_{12} + \hat{p}_{21})^2 - (d)^2]}{d^2}$$

$$n = \frac{z^2(\hat{p}_{12} + \hat{p}_{21})}{d^2} - \frac{z^2(d^2)}{d^2}$$

$$n = \frac{z^2(\hat{p}_{12} + \hat{p}_{21})}{d^2} - z^2$$

The previous formula comes from the standard Wald formula for a binomial confidence interval for matched proportions. Agresti and Min (2005) explored a number of adjustment methods and showed that making an adjustment similar to the adjusted-Wald for a single proportion (Agresti and Coull, 1998) leads to more accurate estimation in the long run. Based on their results, we recommend adding the value of $z^2/8$ to each of the interior cells of the layout shown in Table 6.9. For a 95% confidence interval, the value of z is 1.96, so the value of z^2 is 3.8416, and the value of $z^2/8$ is 0.48—just about 0.5. Another way of conceptualizing this adjustment for a back-of-the-envelope 95% confidence

Table 6.9 Definitions for Test of Matched Proportions (McNemar Exact Test)

	Pass Design B	Fail Design B	Total
Pass Design A	$a(\hat{p}_{11})$	$b(\hat{p}_{12})$	$a+b(\hat{p}_1)$
Fail Design A	$c(\hat{p}_{21})$	$d(\hat{p}_{22})$	$c+d(1-\hat{p}_1)$
Total	$a+c(\hat{p}_2)$	$b+d(1-\hat{p}_2)$	n (1.0)

interval is that you're adding one success and one failure to the actually obtained counts, distributing them evenly across the four cells. Multiplying $z^2/8$ by 4, the value of $n_{adj} = n + z^2/2$.

Next, you can calculate adjusted values for the discordant proportions ($\hat{p}_{12}$, $\hat{p}_{21}$—keeping in mind that $b = \hat{p}_{12}n$ and $c = \hat{p}_{21}n$):

$$\hat{p}_{adj12} = \frac{\hat{p}_{12}n + \frac{z^2}{8}}{n + \frac{z^2}{2}}$$

$$\hat{p}_{adj21} = \frac{\hat{p}_{21}n + \frac{z^2}{8}}{n + \frac{z^2}{2}}$$

$$d_{adj} = \hat{p}_{adj21} - \hat{p}_{adj12}$$

Plugging these adjusted values into the standard Wald sample size formula, we get:

$$n_{adj} = \frac{z^2(\hat{p}_{adj12} + \hat{p}_{adj21})}{d_{adj}^2} - z^2$$

Because the adjusted value of n for this method is $n_{adj} = n + z^2/2$, then $n = n_{adj} - z^2/2$, therefore:

$$n = \frac{z^2(\hat{p}_{adj12} + \hat{p}_{adj21})}{d_{adj}^2} - z^2 - z^2/2$$

$$n = \frac{z^2(\hat{p}_{adj12} + \hat{p}_{adj21})}{d_{adj}^2} - 1.5z^2$$

Using a strategy similar to what we used for sample size estimation for a single proportion, sample size estimation for this type of test will have three steps.

1. Use the sample size formula derived from the standard Wald confidence interval for matched proportions to get an initial estimate of the required sample size. To do this, you will need to make decisions about the amount of confidence and power for the test and the minimum size of the difference that you need to be able to detect (d), and you will need estimates of the discordant proportions $\hat{p}_{12}$ and $\hat{p}_{21}$. If you don't have any idea about the expected values of $\hat{p}_{12}$ and

$\hat{p}_{21}$, then subtract $d/2$ from 0.5 for your estimate of $\hat{p}_{12}$ and add $d/2$ to 0.5 for your estimate of $\hat{p}_{21}$. Doing this will maximize the binomial variability for the selected value of d, which will in turn maximize the sample size estimate, ensuring an adequate sample size, but at the potential cost of running more participants than necessary.

2. Use the sample size estimate from Step 1 to get the adjusted values: $\hat{p}_{adj12}$, $\hat{p}_{adj21}$, and d_{adj}.
3. Use the sample size formula derived from the adjusted-Wald confidence interval for matched proportions to compute the final estimate of n (the number of participants required for the test).

For example, suppose you recently ran a pilot study in which you had 10 participants attempt to complete a car reservation with two websites using counterbalanced orders of presentation, with the overall success rates for websites A and B equal to 0.8 and 0.9, respectively. In that study, one participant was successful with website A but was unsuccessful with website B ($\hat{p}_{12} = 0.10$), and two were successful with website B but not with website A ($\hat{p}_{21} = 0.20$), so the difference in the proportions was 0.10. If these results remained stable, how many participants would you need to run to achieve statistical significance with 95% confidence ($\alpha = 0.05$) and 50% power ($\beta = 0.50$)?

For this confidence and power, the value of z is 1.96 (1.96 for 95% confidence and 0 for 50% power). First, use the standard Wald formula for matched proportions to get an initial estimate of n.

$$n = \frac{z^2(\hat{p}_{12} + \hat{p}_{21})}{d^2} - z^2$$

$$n = \frac{1.96^2(0.1 + 0.2)}{0.1^2} - 1.96^2 = 111.4$$

Rounded up, the initial estimate of n is 112. Using that estimate to adjust the discordant proportions and their difference:

$$\hat{p}_{adj12} = \frac{\hat{p}_{12}n + \frac{z^2}{8}}{n + \frac{z^2}{2}} = \frac{0.1(112) + \frac{1.96^2}{8}}{112 + \frac{1.96^2}{2}} = 0.102529$$

$$\hat{p}_{adj21} = \frac{\hat{p}_{21}n + \frac{z^2}{8}}{n + \frac{z^2}{2}} = \frac{0.2(112) + \frac{1.96^2}{8}}{112 + \frac{1.96^2}{2}} = 0.200843$$

$$d_{adj} = 0.200843 - 0.102529 = 0.098314$$

Finally, use the adjusted-Wald formula for matched proportions to get the final estimate of n.

$$n = \frac{z^2(\hat{p}_{adj12} + \hat{p}_{adj21})}{d_{adj}^2} - 1.5z^2$$

$$n = \frac{1.96^2(0.102529 + 0.200843)}{0.098314^2} - 1.5(1.96)^2 = 114.8$$

Rounded up, the final sample size estimate is 115 participants. As a practical matter, if you estimate an odd number of participants, you should add one more so you can evenly counterbalance the order in which participants use the two products, so the final planned sample size should be 116.

As a check, let's compute the resulting adjusted-Wald confidence interval. If one of the endpoints of the interval is close to 0 given this pattern of results, then the estimated sample size is appropriate. For $\hat{p}_1 = 0.8$, $\hat{p}_2 = 0.9$, $\hat{p}_{12} = 0.1$, and $\hat{p}_{21} = 0.2$ with a sample size of 116, the resulting 95% adjusted-Wald confidence interval ranges from −0.005 to 0.192, with the lower limit just below 0. Rounding to the nearest percentage, the interval for the difference in proportions ranges from 0% to 19%, confirming the adequacy of the estimated sample size for the given conditions.

THE IMPORTANCE OF SAMPLE SIZE ESTIMATION

From David Salsburg's *The Lady Tasting Tea*

The book The Lady Tasting Tea: How Statistics Revolutionized Science in the Twentieth Century (Salsburg, 2001) chronicles the personal and professional stories of the most influential statisticians of the 20th century. Salsburg, himself a practicing biostatistician who had met many of the subjects of his book, occasionally reveals insights from his own work, including this rationale for the importance of sample size estimation before conducting a study (p. 265):

> A careful examination of resources available often produces the conclusion that it is not possible to answer that question with those resources. I think that some of my major contributions as a statistician were when I discouraged others from attempting an experiment that was doomed to failure for lack of adequate resources. For instance, in clinical research, when the medical question posed will require a study involving hundreds of thousands of patients, it is time to reconsider whether that question is worth answering.

DEALING WITH MORE COMPLEX SAMPLE SIZE ESTIMATION

Consider using a tool like G*Power

We've covered quite a few cases in this chapter, but it is possible that you might encounter a more complex situation. For example, you might want to compare experts with novices, in which case you shouldn't be comfortable with the assumption of equal variance. Almost by definition, expert performance will be less variable than novice performance, which means that you can achieve equal levels of group precision with a smaller sample of experts than novices.

One of the most popular free programs for sample size estimation is G*Power, available at <www.gpower.hhu.de/>. G*Power has options to provide different sample size estimates for independent groups based on differences in variability and/or expected effect sizes. If you compare G*Power estimates with the estimates in the examples and exercises in this chapter, you will find that they will often be the same, but will sometimes differ very slightly (usually by no more than 1) due to differences in round-off strategies. The strategy proposed by Diamond (1981) to always round up appears to be a bit more conservative than the G*Power strategy. In most cases, any differences will be trivial, but if the cost of each sample is extremely expensive, you might want to use the slightly less conservative G*Power approach.

KEY POINTS

- Sample size estimation is an important part of planning a user study, especially when the cost of a sample is high.
- Different types of studies require different methods for sample size estimation. This chapter covers methods for user studies (such as summative usability studies) that use measurements

that are continuous (such as time on task), multipoint scale (such as usability questionnaires), or discrete (such as successful task completions).

- Different research goals (such as estimation of a value, comparison with a benchmark, or comparison among alternatives) require different methods for sample size estimation.
- To obtain a sample size estimation formula, take the formula for the appropriate test and solve for n.
- Sample size formulas for estimation of a value or comparison with benchmarks or alternatives require (a) an estimate of the expected measurement variance, (b) a decision about the required level of confidence, (c) a decision about the required power of the test, and (d) a decision about the smallest difference that is important for the test to be able to detect. Table 6.10 provides a list of the sample size formulas discussed in this chapter.

CHAPTER REVIEW QUESTIONS

1. Assume you've been using a single 100-point item as a post-task measure of ease-of-use in past usability tests. One of the tasks you routinely conduct is installation. For the most recent usability study of the current version of the software package, the variability of this measurement (s^2) was 25 ($s = 5$). You're planning your first usability study with a new version of the software, and all you want to do is to get an estimate of this measure with 90% confidence and to be within ±2.5 points of the true value. How many participants do you need to run in the study?
2. Continuing with the review question given earlier, what if your research goal is to compare your result with a benchmark of having a result greater than 75? Also, assume that for this comparison you want a test with 80% power and want to be able to detect differences that are at least 2.5 points above the benchmark. The estimated variability of measurement is still 25 ($s = 5$) and desired confidence is still 90%. How many participants do you need to run in the study?
3. Again continuing with this example, what if you have improved the installation procedures for the new version, and want to test it against the previous version in a study where each participant performs the installation task with both the current and new versions, with the ability to detect a difference of at least 2.5 points? Assume that power and confidence remain at 80 and 90%, respectively, and that the estimated variability is still 25 ($s = 5$). How many participants do you need to run in the study?
4. Next, assume that the installation procedure is so time consuming that you cannot get participants to perform installation with both products, so you'll have to have the installations done by independent groups of participants. How many participants do you need to run in the study? Assume that nothing else changes—power and confidence remain at 80 and 90%, respectively, variance is still 25, and the critical difference is still 2.5.
5. Continuing with the situation described in the previous question, suppose your resources (time and money) will only allow you to run a total of 20 participants to compare the alternative installation procedures. What can you do to reduce the estimated sample size?
6. Suppose that in addition to your subjective assessment of ease-of-use, you have also been measuring installation successes and failures using small-sample moderated usability studies. For the most recent usability study, the installation success rate was 65%. Using this as your best estimate of future success rates, what sample size do you need if you want to estimate with 90% confidence the new success rate within ±15 percentage points of the true value?

Table 6.10 List of Sample Size Formulas for Summative Testing

Type of Evaluation	Basic Formula	Notes
Estimation (nonbinary data)	$n = \frac{t^2 s^2}{d^2}$	Start by using the appropriate two-sided z-score in place of t for the desired level of confidence, then iterate to the final solution, as described in the text
Comparison with a benchmark (nonbinary data)	$n = \frac{(t_\alpha + t_\beta)^2 s^2}{d^2}$	Start by using the appropriate one-sided values of z for the values of t for the desired levels of confidence (α) and power (β), then iterate to the final solution, as described in the text
Comparison of alternatives (nonbinary data within-subjects)	$n = \frac{(t_\alpha + t_\beta)^2 s^2}{d^2}$	Start by using the appropriate values of z for the values of t for the desired levels of confidence (two-sided α) and power (one-sided β), then iterate as described in the text
Comparison of alternatives (nonbinary data between-subjects, assuming equal group sizes)	$n = \frac{2(t_\alpha + t_\beta)^2 s^2}{d^2}$	Start by using the appropriate values of z for the values of t for the desired levels of confidence (two-sided α) and power (one-sided β), then iterate to the final solution, as described in the text, to get the estimated sample size requirement for each group
Estimation (binary data, large sample)	$n = \frac{z^2(\hat{p})(1-\hat{p})}{d^2}$	Use for large sample studies, or as the first step in the process for small sample studies. For this and the rest of the equations given later, z^2 is the sum of z_α and z_β (confidence plus power)
Estimation (binary data, small sample)	$\hat{p}_{\text{adj}} = \frac{n\hat{p} + \frac{z^2}{2}}{n + z^2}$	Use for the second step in the process for small sample studies to get the adjusted estimate of p
Estimation (binary data, small sample)	$n_{\text{adj}} = \frac{z^2(\hat{p}_{\text{adj}})(1-\hat{p}_{\text{adj}})}{d^2} - z^2$	Use for the third step in the process for small sample studies to get the adjusted estimate of n
Comparison of alternatives (binary data, between-subjects)	$n = \frac{2z^2 p(1-p)}{d^2} + \frac{1}{2}$	Use to estimate group sizes for $N - 1$ chi-squared tests (independent proportions) with equal group sizes—the total sample size estimate is $2n$
Comparison of alternatives (binary data, within-subjects)	$n = \frac{z^2(\hat{p}_{12} + \hat{p}_{21})}{d^2} - z^2$	Use for the initial estimate of n for a McNemar Exact Test (matched proportions)
Comparison of alternatives (binary data, within-subjects)	$\hat{p}_{\text{adj12}} = \frac{p_{12}n + \frac{z^2}{8}}{n + \frac{z^2}{2}}, \hat{p}_{\text{adj21}} = \frac{p_{21}n + \frac{z^2}{8}}{n + \frac{z^2}{2}}$	Use for the second step in the process of estimating n for a McNemar Exact Test (matched proportions)
Comparison of alternatives (binary data, within-subjects)	$n = \frac{z^2(\hat{p}_{\text{adj12}} + \hat{p}_{\text{adj21}})}{d^2_{\text{adj}}} - 1.5z^2$	Use for the third step in the process of estimating n for a McNemar Exact Test (matched proportions)

7. You're pretty confident that your new installation process will be much more successful than the current process—in fact, you think you should have about 85% correct installation—much better than the current success rate of 65%. The current installation process is lengthy, typically taking two–three days to complete with verification of correct installation, so each participant will perform just one installation. You want to be able to detect the expected difference of 20 percentage points between the success rates with 80% confidence and 80% power, and are planning to run the same number of participants with the current and new installation procedures. How many participants (total including both groups) do you need to run?
8. For another product (Product B for "Before"), the current installation procedure is fairly short (about a half-hour), but that current process has numerous usability issues that have led to an estimated 50% failure rate on first attempts. You've tracked down the most serious usability issues and now have a prototype of an improved product (Product A for "After"). In a pilot study with 10 participants, you had 4 participants succeed with both products, 1 failed with both, 4 were successful with Product A but not B, and 1 was successful with Product B but not A. What are the resulting estimates for p_1, p_2, p_{12}, and p_{21}? If you want to run a larger-scale test with 95% confidence and 80% power, how many participants should you plan to run if you expect this pattern of results to stay roughly the same?

ANSWERS TO CHAPTER REVIEW QUESTIONS

1. The research problem in this exercise is to estimate a value without comparison to a benchmark or alternative. From the problem statement, the variability (s^2) is 25 ($s = 5$) and the critical difference (d) is 2.5. This situation requires iteration to get to the final sample size estimate, starting with the z-score associated with two-sided testing and 90% confidence, which is 1.645. As shown in Table 6.11, the final sample size estimate for this study is 13 participants.
2. Relative to Review Question 1, we're moving from a simple estimation problem to a comparison with a benchmark, which means that we now need to consider the power of the test and because we're testing against a benchmark, will use a one-sided rather than a two-sided test. Like the

Table 6.11 Iterations for Review Question 1

	Initial	1	2	3
t	1.645	1.812	1.771	1.782
t^2	2.71	3.29	3.14	3.18
s^2	25	25	25	25
d	2.5	2.5	2.5	2.5
d^2	6.25	6.25	6.25	6.25
df	10	13	12	12
Unrounded	10.8	13.1	12.5	12.7
Rounded up	11	14	13	13

Table 6.12 Iterations for Review Question 2

	Initial	1	2
t_α	1.282	1.330	1.328
t_β	0.842	0.862	0.861
$t_{\alpha+\beta}$	2.123	2.192	2.189
$t_{\alpha+\beta^2}$	4.51	4.81	4.79
s^2	25	25	25
d	2.5	2.5	2.5
d^2	6.25	6.25	6.25
df	18	19	19
Unrounded	18.0	19.2	19.2
Rounded up	19	20	20

previous exercise, this will require iteration, starting with the sum of the one-sided z-scores for 90% confidence and 80% power, which are, respectively, 1.282 and 0.842. As shown in Table 6.12, the final sample size estimate for this study is 20 participants.

3. Relative to Review Question 2, we're moving from comparison with a fixed benchmark to a within-subjects comparison between alternative designs, so the test should be two-sided rather than one-sided. The two-sided z-score for 90% confidence and one-sided for 80% power are 1.645 and 0.842, respectively. Table 6.13 shows the process of iterating for this situation, with a final sample size estimate of 27 participants.

Table 6.13 Iterations for Review Question 3

	Initial	1	2
t_α	1.645	1.711	1.706
t_β	0.842	0.857	0.856
$t_{\alpha+\beta}$	2.487	2.568	2.561
$t_{\alpha+\beta^2}$	6.18	6.59	6.56
s^2	25	25	25
d	2.5	2.5	2.5
d^2	6.25	6.25	6.25
df	24	26	26
Unrounded	24.7	26.4	26.2
Rounded up	25	27	27

Table 6.14 Iterations for Review Question 4

	Initial	1	2
t_α	1.645	1.661	1.660
t_β	0.842	0.842	0.842
$t_{\alpha+\beta}$	2.487	2.503	2.502
$t_{\alpha+\beta^2}$	6.185	6.263	6.261
s^2	25	25	25
d	2.5	2.5	2.5
d^2	6.25	6.25	6.25
df	98	100	100
Unrounded	49.5	50.1	50.1
Rounded up	50	51	51

4. Relative to Review Question 3, we're moving from a within-subjects experimental design to one that is between-subjects. That means that the formula for starting the iterative process starts with $n = 2z^2s^2/d^2$ rather than $n = z^2s^2/d^2$ (where z is the sum of the z-scores for confidence and power, z_α and z_β)—essentially doubling the required sample size at that point in the process. Furthermore, the estimation is for the size of one group, so we'll need to double it again to get the estimated sample size for the entire study. Table 6.14 shows the process of iterating for this situation, with a final sample size estimate of 51 participants per group, and a total sample size estimate of 102 participants.
5. Keeping many of the conditions of the situations the same, over the course of the first four review questions, we've gone from needing a sample size of 13 to simply estimate the ease-of-use score within a specified level of precision, to 20 to compare it against a benchmark, to 27 to perform a within-subjects usability test, to 102 to perform a between-subjects usability test. Clearly, the change that led to the greatest increase in the sample size estimate was the shift from a within- to a between-subjects comparison of alternatives, so one way to reduce the estimated sample size is to strive to run within-subjects studies rather than between-subjects when you must compare alternatives. The other aspects of experimental design that you can control are the choices for confidence level, power, and critical difference. Let's assume that you were able to change your plan to a within-subjects study. Furthermore, you have worked with your stakeholders to relax the requirement for the critical difference (d) from 2.5 to 3.5. As shown in Table 6.15, these two changes—switching from a between- to a within-subjects design and increasing the critical difference by just one point—lead to a study design for which you should only need 15 participants. Note that if the critical difference were relaxed to five points, the required sample size would be just eight participants. Also note that this is only one of many ways to reduce the sample size requirement, for example, you could have reduced the levels of confidence and power.

Table 6.15 Iterations for Review Question 5

	Initial	1	2
t_α	1.645	1.782	1.761
t_β	0.842	0.873	0.868
$t_{\alpha+\beta}$	2.487	2.655	2.629
$t_{\alpha+\beta^2}$	6.18	7.05	6.91
s^2	25	25	25
d	3.5	3.5	3.5
d^2	12.25	12.25	12.25
df	12	14	14
Unrounded	12.6	14.4	14.1
Rounded up	13	15	15

6. For this question, the variable of interest is a binomial pass/fail measurement, so the appropriate approach is the sample size method based on the adjusted-Wald binomial confidence interval. We have the three pieces of information that we need to proceed: the success rate from the previous evaluation (p) was 0.65, the critical difference (d) is 0.15, and the desired level of confidence is 90% (so the two-sided value of z is 1.645). We first compute an initial sample size formula using the standard Wald formula: $n = z^2p(1 - p)/d^2$; which for this problem is: $n = (1.645)^2(0.65)(0.35)/0.15^2 = 27.4$, which rounds up to 28. Next, we use that initial estimate of n to compute the adjusted value of p: $p_{adj} = (np + z^2/2)/(n + z^2)$; which for this problem is: $p_{adj} = ((28)(0.65) + 1.645^2/2)/(28 + 1.645^2) = 0.6368$. We next use the adjusted value of p and the initial estimate of n to compute the adjusted estimate of n: $(n_{adj} = (z^2(p_{adj})(1 - p_{adj})/d^2) - z^2)$, which for this problem is $((1.645)^2(0.6368)(0.3632)/0.15^2) - 1.645^2 = 25.11$, which rounds up to 26. As a check, we could set the expected number of successes (x) to 0.65(26), which rounds to 17. A 90% adjusted-Wald binomial confidence interval for 17/26 has an observed p of 0.654, an adjusted p of 0.639, and a margin of error of 0.147, just a little more precise than the target precision of 0.15.
7. Because in this problem you're planning to compare success rates between independent groups, the appropriate test is the $N - 1$ chi-squared test. From the conditions of the problem, we have information needed to do the sample size estimation: the expected values of p_1 and p_2 (0.65 and 0.85, respectively, for an average $p = 0.75$ and $d = 0.20$) and the sum of the z-scores for 80% confidence (two-sided $z = 1.282$) and 80% power (one-sided $z = 0.842$) of 2.124. Plugging these values into the appropriate sample size estimation formula, we get: $n = (2(2.124^2)(0.75)(0.25))/0.2^2 + 0.5 = 42.8$, which rounds up to 43 participants per group, for a total of 86 participants. This is outside the scope of most moderated usability tests. Relaxing the power to 50% (so its associated z-score would be 0, making the total value of $z = 1.282$) would reduce the estimate of n per group to 16 (total sample size of 32).

8. The appropriate statistical test for this type of study is the McNemar Exact Test (or, equivalently, a confidence interval using the adjusted-Wald method for matched proportions). From the pilot study, the estimates for the different key proportions are $p_1 = 0.8$, $p_2 = 0.5$, $p_{12} = 0.4$, and $p_{21} = 0.1$, so $d = 0.3$. Using the three-step process, first compute an initial estimate of n with the standard Wald formula, using $z = 2.8$ (the sum of 1.96 for two-tailed 95% confidence and 0.84 for one-tailed 80% power):

$$n = \frac{2.8^2(0.1+0.4)}{0.3^2} - 2.8^2 = 35.7$$

Rounded up, this initial estimate is 36. Next, compute the adjustments.

$$\hat{p}_{\text{adj12}} = \frac{0.1(36)+\frac{2.8^2}{8}}{36+\frac{2.8^2}{2}} = 0.114729$$

$$\hat{p}_{\text{adj21}} = \frac{0.4(36)+\frac{2.8^2}{8}}{36+\frac{2.8^2}{2}} = 0.385271$$

$$d_{\text{adj}} = 0.385271 - 0.114729 = 0.270541$$

Then compute the final sample size estimate which, after rounding up, is 42.

$$n = \frac{2.8^2(0.114729+0.385271)}{0.270541^2} - 1.5(2.8)^2 = 41.8$$

You can check this estimate by computing a confidence interval to see if it includes or excludes 0. Because the power of the test is 80%, you need to compute an equivalent confidence to use that combines the nominal power and confidence of the test (see the sidebar "Equivalent Confidence"). The composite z for this problem is 2.8, so the equivalent confidence to use for a two-sided confidence interval is 99.4915%. The closest integer values for a, b, c, and d are, respectively, 17, 17, 4, and 4, for the following values:

$$p_1 : 34/42 = 0.81$$
$$p_2 : 21/42 = 0.5$$
$$p_{12} : 17/42 = 0.405$$
$$p_{21} : 4/42 = 0.095$$

The resulting confidence interval ranges from −0.55 to −0.015—close to but not including 0. Using an n of 40, the expected values of p_1, p_2, p_{12}, and p_{21} are exactly 0.8, 0.5, 0.4, and 0.1, respectively, and the confidence interval ranges from −0.549 to 0.0025, just barely including 0. The bounds of these confidence intervals support the sample size estimate of 42, but if samples were expensive, 40 would probably be adequate.

REFERENCES

Agresti, A., Coull, B., 1998. Approximate is better than 'exact' for interval estimation of binomial proportions. Am. Stat. 52, 119–126.

Agresti, A., Min, Y., 2005. Simple improved confidence intervals for comparing matched proportions. Stat. Med. 24, 729–740.

Alreck, P.L., Settle, R.B., 1985. The Survey Research Handbook. Richard D. Irwin, Homewood, IL.

Bradley, J.V., 1976. Probability; Decision; Statistics. Prentice-Hall, Englewood Cliffs, NJ.

Brown, F.E., 1980. Marketing Research: A Structure for Decision Making. Addison-Wesley, Reading, MA.

Campbell, I., 2007. Chi-squared and Fisher–Irwin tests of two-by-two tables with small sample recommendations. Stat. Med. 26, 3661–3675.

Campbell, D.T., Stanley, J.C., 1963. Experimental and Quasi-Experimental Designs for Research. Rand McNally, Chicago, IL.

Churchill, Jr, G.A., 1991. Marketing Research: Methodological Foundations. Dryden Press, Fort Worth, TX.

Cohen, J., 1988. Statistical Power Analysis for the Behavioral Sciences, second ed. Lawrence Erlbaum, Hillsdale, NJ.

Cowles, M., 1989. Statistics in Psychology: An Historical Perspective. Lawrence Erlbaum, Hillsdale, NJ.

Diamond, W.J., 1981. Practical Experiment Designs for Engineers and Scientists. Lifetime Learning Publications, Belmont, CA.

Dumas, J.S., Salzman, M.C., 2006. Usability assessment methods. Williges, R.C. (Ed.), Reviews of Human Factors and Ergonomics, vol. 2, HFES, Santa Monica, CA, pp. 109–140.

Kirakowski, J., 2005. Summative usability testing: measurement and sample size. In: Bias, R.G., Mayhew, D.J. (Eds.), Cost-Justifying Usability: An Update for the Internet Age. Elsevier, Amsterdam, The Netherlands, pp. 519–554.

Kraemer, H.C., Thiemann, S., 1987. How Many Subjects? Statistical Power Analysis in Research. Sage Publications, Newbury Park, CA.

Landauer, T.K., 1997. Behavioral research methods in human–computer interaction. In: Helander, M., Landauer, T.K., Prabhu, P. (Eds.), Handbook of Human–Computer Interaction. second ed. Elsevier, Amsterdam, The Netherlands, pp. 203–227.

Lewis, J.R., 2012. Usability testing. In: Salvendy, G. (Ed.), Handbook of Human Factors and Ergonomics, fourth ed. John Wiley, New York, NY, pp. 1267–1312.

Mayer, R.E., 1997. From novice to expert. In: Helander, M.G., Landauer, T.K., Prabhu, P.V. (Eds.), Handbook of Human–Computer Interaction. second ed. Elsevier, Amsterdam, The Netherlands, pp. 781–795.

Minium, E.W., King, B.M., Bear, G., 1993. Statistical Reasoning in Psychology and Education, third ed. John Wiley, New York, NY.

Myers, J.L., 1979. Fundamentals of Experimental Design. Allyn & Bacon, Boston, MA.

Nielsen, J., 1997. Usability testing. In: Salvendy, G. (Ed.), Handbook of Human Factors and Ergonomics. second ed. John Wiley, New York, NY, pp. 1543–1568.

Parasuraman, A., 1986. Nonprobability sampling methods. Marketing ResearchAddison-Wesley, Reading, MA, pp. 498-516..

Salsburg, D., 2001. The Lady Tasting Tea: How Statistics Revolutionized Science in the Twentieth Century. Henry Holt, New York, NY.

Sauro, J., Lewis, J.R., 2010. Average task times in usability tests: what to report? In: Proceedings of CHI. ACM, Atlanta, GA, pp. 2347–2350.

Scriven, M., 1967. The methodology of evaluation. In: Tyler, R.W., Gagne, R.M., Scriven, M. (Eds.), Perspectives of Curriculum Evaluation. Rand McNally, Chicago, IL, pp. 39–83.

Stigler, S.M., 1986. The History of Statistics: The Measurement of Uncertainty Before 1900. The Belknap Press of Harvard University Press, Cambridge, MA.

Walpole, R.E., 1976. Elementary Statistical Concepts. Macmillan, New York, NY.

Wickens, C.D., 1998. Commonsense statistics. Ergon. Des. 6 (4), 18–22.

Winer, B.J., Brown, D.R., Michels, K.M., 1991. Statistical Principles in Experimental Design, third ed. McGraw-Hill, New York, NY.

CHAPTER

WHAT SAMPLE SIZES DO WE NEED? PART 2: FORMATIVE STUDIES

7

INTRODUCTION

Sample size estimation for summative usability studies (the topic of the previous chapter) draws upon techniques that are either the same as or closely related to methods taught in introductory statistics classes at the university level, with application to any user research in which the goal is to obtain measurements. In contrast to the measurements taken during summative user research, the goal of a formative usability study is to discover and enumerate the problems that users have when performing tasks with a product. It is possible, though, using methods not routinely taught in introductory statistics classes, to statistically model the discovery process and to use that model to inform sample size estimation for formative usability studies. These statistical methods for modeling the discovery of problems also have applicability for other types of user research, such as the discovery of requirements or interview themes (Guest et al., 2006).

USING A PROBABILISTIC MODEL OF PROBLEM DISCOVERY TO ESTIMATE SAMPLE SIZES FOR FORMATIVE USER RESEARCH

THE FAMOUS EQUATION $P(x \geq 1) = 1 - (1 - p)^n$

The most commonly used formula to model the discovery of usability problems as a function of sample size is:

$$P(x \geq 1) = 1 - (1 - p)^n$$

In this formula, p is the probability of an event (e.g., the probability of tossing a coin and getting heads), n is the number of opportunities for the event to occur (e.g., the number of coin tosses), and $P(x \geq 1)$ is the probability of the event occurring at least once in n tries.

For example, the probability of having heads come up at least once in five coin tosses (where x is the number of heads) is:

$$P(x \geq 1) = 1 - (1 - 0.5)^5 = 0.969$$

Even though the probability of heads is only 0.5, by the time you toss a coin five times you're almost certain to have seen at least one of the tosses come up heads—in fact, out of a series of tosses of five coins, you should see at least one head about 96.9% of the time. Fig. 7.1 shows how the value of $1 - (1 - p)^n$ changes as a function of sample size and value of p.

Quantifying the User Experience. http://dx.doi.org/10.1016/B978-0-12-802308-2.00007-2

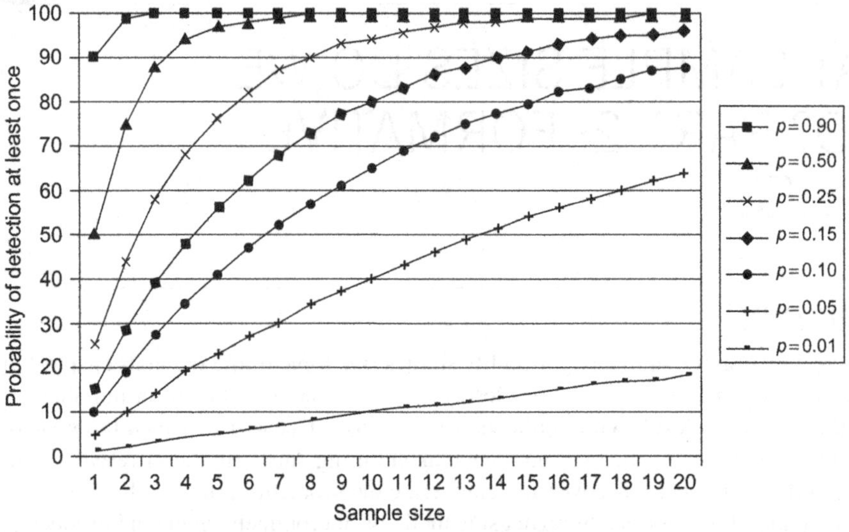

FIGURE 7.1 Probability of Discovery as a Function of *n* and *p*.

THE PROBABILITY OF AT LEAST ONE EQUALS ONE MINUS THE PROBABILITY OF NONE

A lesson from James V. Bradley—from the files of Jim Lewis

There are several ways to derive $1-(1-p)^n$. For example, Nielsen and Landauer (1993) derived it from a Poisson probability process. I first encountered it in college in a statistics class I had with James V. Bradley in the late 1970s at New Mexico State University.

Dr Bradley was an interesting professor, the author of numerous statistical papers and two books: *Probability; Decision; Statistics* and *Distribution-Free Statistical Tests*. He would leave the campus by 4:00 pm every afternoon to get to his trailer in the desert because if he didn't, he told me his neighbors would "steal everything that wasn't nailed down." He would teach *t*-tests, but would not teach analysis of variance because he didn't believe psychological data ever met its assumptions (a view not held by the authors of this book). I had to go to the College of Agriculture's stats classes to learn about ANOVA (see Chapter 10 for an introduction to ANOVA).

Despite these (and other) eccentricities, he was a remarkable and gifted teacher. When we were studying the binomial probability formula, one of the problems he posed to us was to figure out the probability of occurrence of at least one event of probability p given n trials. To work this out, you need to start with the binomial probability formula (Bradley, 1976), where $P(x)$ is the probability that an event with probability p will happen x times in n trials.

$$P(x)=\frac{n!}{(x!)(n-x)!}p^x(1-p)^{n-x}$$

The trick to solving Bradley's problem is the realization that the probability of an event happening at least once is one minus the probability that it won't happen at all (in other words 1 minus $P(x=0)$), which leads to:

$$P(x\geq 1)=1-\left(\frac{n!}{(0!)(n-0)!}p^0(1-p)^{n-0}\right)$$

Because the value of 0! is 1 and any number taken to the 0th power also equals 1, we get:

$$P(x \geq 1) = 1 - \left(\frac{n!}{1(n)!} 1(1-p)^n\right)$$

$$P(x \geq 1) = 1 - (1-p)^n$$

So, starting from the binomial probability formula and solving for the probability of an event occurring at least once, we derive $1 - (1 - p)^n$. I first applied this as a model of problem discovery to estimate sample size requirements for formative usability studies in the early 1980s (Lewis, 1982), and have always been grateful to Dr Bradley for giving us that problem to solve.

DERIVING A SAMPLE SIZE ESTIMATION EQUATION FROM $1 - (1 - p)^n$

To convert $P(x \geq 1) = 1 - (1 - p)^n$ to a sample-size formula, we need to solve for n. Because n is an exponent, it's necessary to take logs, which leads to:

$$(1-p)^n = 1 - P(x \geq 1)$$

$$n(\ln(1-p)) = \ln(1 - P(x \geq 1))$$

$$n = \frac{\ln(1 - P(x \geq 1))}{\ln(1-p)}$$

For these equations, we used natural logarithms (*ln*) to avoid having to specify the base, which simplifies the formulas. Excel provides functions for both the natural logarithm, *ln*, and for logarithms of specified base, *log*. When working with logarithms in Excel, use whichever function you prefer.

To use this equation to compute n, we need to have values for p and $P(x \geq 1)$. The most practical approach is to set p to the lowest value that you realistically expect to be able to find with the available resources (especially the time and money required to run participants in the formative usability study). Set $P(x \geq 1)$ to the desired goal of the study with respect to p.

For example, suppose you decide to run a formative usability study and, for the tasks you use and the types of participants you observe, you want to have an 80% chance of observing, at least once, problems that have a probability of occurrence of 0.15. To accomplish this goal, you'd need to run 10 participants.

$$n = \frac{\ln(1-0.80)}{\ln(1-0.15)}$$

$$n = \frac{\ln(0.20)}{\ln(0.85)}$$

$$n = 9.9$$

Table 7.1 Sample Size Requirements for Formative User Research

p	$P(x \geq 1) = 0.50$	$P(x \geq 1) = 0.75$	$P(x \geq 1) = 0.85$	$P(x \geq 1) = 0.90$	$P(x \geq 1) = 0.95$	$P(x \geq 1) = 0.99$
0.01	69 (168)	138 (269)	189 (337)	230 (388)	299 (473)	459 (662)
0.05	14 (34)	28 (53)	37 (67)	45 (77)	59 (93)	90 (130)
0.10	7 (17)	14 (27)	19 (33)	22 (38)	29 (46)	44 (64)
0.15	5 (11)	9 (18)	12 (22)	15 (25)	19 (30)	29 (42)
0.25	3 (7)	5 (10)	7 (13)	9 (15)	11 (18)	17 (24)
0.50	1 (3)	2 (5)	3 (6)	4 (7)	5 (8)	7 (11)
0.90	1 (2)	1 (2)	1 (3)	1 (3)	2 (3)	2 (4)

Note: The first number in each cell is the sample size required to detect the event of interest at least once; numbers in parentheses are the sample sizes required to observe the event of interest at least twice

Note that if you run 10 participants, then you will have a slightly better than 80% chance of observing (at least once) problems that have probabilities of occurrence greater than .15. In fact, using this formula, it's easy to set up tables to use when planning these types of studies that show this effect at a glance. Table 7.1 shows the sample size requirements as a function of the selected values of p (problem occurrence probability) and $P(x \geq 1)$ (likelihood of detecting the problem at least once). Table 7.1 also shows in parentheses the likelihood of detecting the problem at least twice. It isn't possible to derive a simple equation to compute the sample size for detecting a problem at least twice, but it is possible to use linear programming with the Excel Solver function to estimate the required sample sizes that appear in Table 7.1.

Table 7.2 shows similar information, but organized by sample size for $n = 1$ through 20 and for various values of p, with cells showing the likelihood of discovery—in other words, of occurring at least once in the study.

USING THE TABLES TO PLAN SAMPLE SIZES FOR FORMATIVE USER RESEARCH

Tables 7.1 and 7.2 are useful when planning formative user research. For example, suppose you want to conduct a formative usability study that has the following characteristics:

- Lowest probability of problem occurrence of interest: 0.25
- Minimum number of detections required: 1
- Cumulative likelihood of discovery (goal): 90%

For this study, Table 7.1 indicates that the appropriate sample size is nine participants.

If you kept the same criteria except you decided you would only pay attention to problems that occurred more than once, then you'd need 15 participants.

As an extreme example, suppose your test criteria were:

- Lowest probability of problem occurrence of interest: 0.01
- Minimum number of detections required: 1
- Cumulative likelihood of discovery (goal): 99%

Table 7.2 Likelihood of Discovery for Various Sample Sizes

p	*n* = 1	*n* = 2	*n* = 3	*n* = 4	*n* = 5
0.01	0.01	0.02	0.03	0.04	0.05
0.05	0.05	0.10	0.14	0.19	0.23
0.10	0.10	0.19	0.27	0.34	0.41
0.15	0.15	0.28	0.39	0.48	0.56
0.25	0.25	0.44	0.58	0.68	0.76
0.50	0.50	0.75	0.88	0.94	0.97
0.90	0.90	0.99	1.00	1.00	1.00
p	*n* = 6	*n* = 7	*n* = 8	*n* = 9	*n* = 10
0.01	0.06	0.07	0.08	0.09	0.10
0.05	0.26	0.30	0.34	0.37	0.40
0.10	0.47	0.52	0.57	0.61	0.65
0.15	0.62	0.68	0.73	0.77	0.80
0.25	0.82	0.87	0.90	0.92	0.94
0.50	0.98	0.99	1.00	1.00	1.00
0.90	1.00	1.00	1.00	1.00	1.00
p	*n* = 11	*n* = 12	*n* = 13	*n* = 14	*n* = 15
0.01	0.10	0.11	0.12	0.13	0.14
0.05	0.43	0.46	0.49	0.51	0.54
0.10	0.69	0.72	0.75	0.77	0.79
0.15	0.83	0.86	0.88	0.90	0.91
0.25	0.96	0.97	0.98	0.98	0.99
0.50	1.00	1.00	1.00	1.00	1.00
0.90	1.00	1.00	1.00	1.00	1.00
p	*n* = 16	*n* = 17	*n* = 18	*n* = 19	*n* = 20
0.01	0.15	0.16	0.17	0.17	0.18
0.05	0.56	0.58	0.60	0.62	0.64
0.10	0.81	0.83	0.85	0.86	0.88
0.15	0.93	0.94	0.95	0.95	0.96
0.25	0.99	0.99	0.99	1.00	1.00
0.50	1.00	1.00	1.00	1.00	1.00
0.90	1.00	1.00	1.00	1.00	1.00

For this study, the estimated sample size requirement is 459 participants—an unrealistic requirement for most moderated test settings. This type of exercise can help test planners and other stakeholders make the necessary adjustments to their expectations before running the study. Also, keep in mind that there is no requirement to run the entire planned sample through the usability study before reporting clear problems to development and getting those problems fixed before continuing. These sample size requirements are typically for total sample sizes, not sample sizes per iteration (Lewis, 2012).

Once you've settled on a sample size for the study, Table 7.2 is helpful for forming an idea about what you can expect to get from the sample size for a variety of problem probabilities. Continuing the first example in this section, suppose you've decided that you'll run nine participants in your study to ensure at least a 90% likelihood of detecting at least once problems that have a probability of occurrence of 0.25. From Table 7.2, what you can expect with nine participants is:

- For $p = 0.01$, P (at least one occurrence given $n = 9$): 9%
- For $p = 0.05$, P (at least one occurrence given $n = 9$): 37%
- For $p = 0.10$, P (at least one occurrence given $n = 9$): 61%
- For $p = 0.15$, P (at least one occurrence given $n = 9$): 77%
- For $p = 0.25$, P (at least one occurrence given $n = 9$): 92%
- For $p = 0.50$, P (at least one occurrence given $n = 9$): 100%
- For $p = 0.90$, P (at least one occurrence given $n = 9$): 100%

This means that with nine participants you can be reasonably confident that the study, within the limits of its tasks and population of participants (which establish what problems are available for discovery), is almost certain to reveal problems for which $p \geq 0.50$. As planned, the likelihood of discovery of problems for which $p = 0.25$ is 92% (>90%). For problems with $p < 0.25$, the rate of discovery will be lower, but will not be 0. For example, the expectation is that you will find 77% of problems for which $p = 0.15$, 61% of problems for which $p = 0.10$, and 37% (just over a third) of the problems available for discovery whose $p = 0.05$. You would even expect to detect 9% of the problems with $p = 0.01$. If you need estimates that the tables don't cover, you can use the general formula (where *ln* means to take the natural logarithm):

$$n = \frac{\ln(1 - P(x \geq 1))}{\ln(1 - p)}$$

ASSUMPTIONS OF THE BINOMIAL PROBABILITY MODEL

The preceding section provides a straightforward method for sample size estimation for formative user research that stays within the bounds of the assumptions of the binomial probability formula. Those assumptions are (Bradley, 1976):

- Random sampling
- The outcomes of individual observations are independent
- Every observation belongs to one of two mutually exclusive and exhaustive categories—for example, a coin toss is either heads or tails
- Observations come from an infinite population or from a finite population with replacement (so sampling does not deplete the population)

In formative user research, observations are the critical incidents of interest—for example, a usability problem observed in a usability test, a usability problem recorded during a heuristic evaluation, or a design requirement picked up during a user interview. In general, the occurrences of these incidents are consistent with the assumptions of the binomial probability model (Lewis, 1994).

- Ideally, usability practitioners should attempt to select participants randomly from the target population to ensure a representative sample. Although circumstances rarely allow true random sampling in user research, practitioners do not usually exert any influence on precisely who participates in a study, typically relying on employment agencies to draw from their pools to obtain participants who are consistent with the target population.
- Observations among participants are independent because the events of interest experienced by one participant cannot have an effect on those experienced by another participant. Note that the model does not require independence among the different types of events that can occur in the study.
- The two mutually exclusive and exhaustive event categories are (1) the event occurred during a session with a participant or (2) the event did not occur during the session.
- Finally, the sampled observations in a usability study do not deplete the source.

Another assumption of the model is that the value of p is constant from trial to trial (Ennis and Bi, 1998). It seems likely that this assumption does not strictly hold in user research due to differences in users' capabilities and experiences (Caulton, 2001; Woolrych and Cockton, 2001; Schmettow, 2008). The extent to which this can affect the use of the binomial formula in modeling problem discovery is an ongoing topic of research (Briand et al., 2000; Kanis, 2011; Lewis, 2001; Schmettow 2008, 2009)—a topic to which we will return later in this chapter. But note that the procedures provided earlier in this chapter are not affected by this assumption because they take as given (not as estimated) a specific value of p.

ADDITIONAL APPLICATIONS OF THE MODEL

There are other interesting, although somewhat controversial, things you can do with this model.

ESTIMATING THE COMPOSITE VALUE OF p FOR MULTIPLE PROBLEMS OR OTHER EVENTS

An alternative to selecting the lowest value of p for events that you want to have a good chance of discovering is to estimate a composite value of p, averaged across observed problems and study participants. For example, consider the hypothetical results shown in Table 7.3.

For this hypothetical usability study, the composite estimate of p is 0.5. There are a number of ways to compute the composite, all of which arrive at the same value. You can take the average of the proportions, either by problems or by participants, or you can divide the total number of cells in the table (100—10 participants by 10 discovered problems) by the number of cells filled with an "x" (50).

ADJUSTING SMALL-SAMPLE COMPOSITE ESTIMATES OF p

Composite estimates of p are the average likelihood of problem occurrence or, alternatively, the estimated problem-discovery rate. This estimate can come from previous studies using the same method

Table 7.3 Hypothetical Results for a Formative Usability Study

	Problem										
Participant	**1**	**2**	**3**	**4**	**5**	**6**	**7**	**8**	**9**	**10**	**Count**	**Proportion**
1	*x*	*x*		*x*		*x*	*x*	*x*			6	0.6
2	*x*	*x*		*x*		*x*		*x*			5	0.5
3	*x*	*x*		*x*	*x*	*x*					5	0.5
4	*x*	*x*		*x*			*x*				4	0.4
5	*x*	*x*	*x*	*x*		*x*			*x*		6	0.6
6	*x*	*x*	*x*					*x*			4	0.4
7	*x*	*x*	*x*		*x*						4	0.4
8	*x*	*x*	*x*		*x*		*x*				5	0.5
9	*x*		*x*		*x*		*x*		*x*		5	0.5
10	*x*		*x*		*x*		*x*		*x*	*x*	6	0.6
Count	10	8	6	5	5	4	5	3	3	1	**50**	
Proportion	1.0	0.8	0.6	0.5	0.5	0.4	0.5	0.3	0.3	0.1		**0.50**

Note: x = specified participant experienced specified problem.

and similar system under evaluation or can come from a pilot study. For standard scenario-based usability studies, the literature contains large-sample examples that show p ranging from 0.03 to 0.46 (Hwang and Salvendy, 2007, 2009, 2010; Lewis, 1994, 2001, 2012). For heuristic evaluations, the reported value of p from large-sample studies ranges from 0.08 to 0.60 (Hwang and Salvendy, 2007, 2009, 2010; Nielsen and Molich, 1990). The well-known (and often misused and maligned) guideline that five participants are enough to discover 85% of problems in a user interface is true only when p equals .315. As the reported ranges of p indicate, there will be many studies for which this guideline (or any similar guideline, regardless of its specific recommended sample size) will not apply (Schmettow, 2012), making it important for usability practitioners to obtain estimates of p for their usability studies.

If, however, estimates of p are not accurate, then other estimates based on p (for example, sample size requirements or estimates of the number of undiscovered events) will not be accurate. This is very important when estimating p from a small sample because small-sample estimates of p (from fewer than 20 participants) have a bias that can result in substantial overestimation of its value (Hertzum and Jacobsen, 2001). Fortunately, a series of Monte Carlo experiments (Lewis, 2001 – see the sidebar) demonstrated the efficacy of a formula that provides a reasonably accurate adjustment of initial estimates of p (p_{est}), even when the sample size for that initial estimate has as few as two participants (preferably four participants, though, because the variability of estimates of p is greater for smaller samples—Lewis, 2001; Faulkner, 2003). This formula for the adjustment of p is:

$$p_{adj} = \frac{1}{2}\left[\left(p_{est} - \frac{1}{n}\right)\left(1 - \frac{1}{n}\right)\right] + \frac{1}{2}\left[\frac{p_{est}}{\left(1 + GT_{adj}\right)}\right]$$

where GT_{adj} is the Good–Turing adjustment to probability space (which is the proportion of the number of problems that occurred once divided by the total number of different discovered problems—see the sidebar). The $p_{est}/(1 + GT_{adj})$ component in the equation produces the Good–Turing adjusted estimate of p by dividing the observed, unadjusted estimate of p (p_{est}) by the Good–Turing adjustment to probability space—a well-known discounting method (Jelinek, 1997). The $(p_{est} - 1/n)(1 - 1/n)$ component in the equation produces the deflated estimate of p from the observed, unadjusted estimate of p and n (the number of participants used to estimate p). The rationale for averaging these two different estimates (one based on the number of different discovered problems or other events of interest—the other based on the number of participants) is that the Good–Turing estimator tends to overestimate the true value (or at least, the large-sample estimate) of p, but the deflation procedure tends to underestimate it. The combined estimate is more accurate than either component alone (Lewis, 2001).

WHAT IS A MONTE CARLO EXPERIMENT?

It's really not gambling

Monte Carlo, part of the principality of Monaco, is home to one of the most famous casinos in the world. In statistics, a Monte Carlo experiment refers to a brute-force method of estimating population parameters (such as means, medians, and proportions) by repeatedly drawing random samples of cases from a larger database of cases. With the advent of cheap computing, Monte Carlo and other types of resampling methods (e.g., jackknifing and bootstrapping) are becoming more accessible and popular. Although the Monte Carlo method uses random sampling, because there are typically a large number of iterations (the default in some statistical packages is 1000), it can provide very accurate estimates.

One of the earliest uses of the Monte Carlo method in usability engineering was in Virzi's (1990, 1992) investigations of sample size requirements for usability evaluations. He reported three experiments in which he measured the rate at which trained usability experts identified problems as a function of the number of naive participants they had observed. For each experiment, he ran a Monte Carlo simulation to randomly create 500 different arrangements of the cases, where each case was the set of usability problems observed for each participant (similar to the data shown in Table 7.3). With the results of these Monte Carlo experiment, he measured the cumulative percentage of problems discovered for each sample size and determined empirically that the results matched the expected results for the cumulative binomial probability formula $[P(x \geq 1) = 1 - (1 - p)^n]$.

DISCOUNTING OBSERVED PROBABILITIES WITH GOOD–TURING

A way to reduce overestimated values of *p*

The Good-Turing adjustment is a discounting procedure. The goal of a discounting procedure is to attempt to allocate some amount of probability space to unseen events. The application of discounting is widely used in the field of statistical natural language processing, especially in the construction of language models (Manning and Schütze, 1999).

The oldest discounting method is LaPlace's law of succession (Jelinek, 1997; Lewis and Sauro, 2006; Wilson, 1927), sometimes referred to as the "add One" method because you add one to the count for each observation. Most statisticians do not use it for this purpose, however, because it has a tendency to assign too much probability to unseen events, underestimating the true value of p.

Because it is more accurate than the law of succession, the Good-Turing (GT) estimate is more common. There are many ways to derive the GT estimator, but the end result is that the total probability mass reserved for unseen events is $E(N_1)/N$, where $E(N_1)$ is the expected number of events that happen exactly once and N is the total number of events. For a given sample, the value used for $E(N_1)$ is the observed number of events that happened exactly once. In the context of a formative user study, the events are whatever the subject of the study is (e.g., in a usability study, they are the observed usability problems).

Table 7.4 Hypothetical Results for a Formative Usability Study: First Four Participants and all Problems

	Problem											
Participant	**1**	**2**	**3**	**4**	**5**	**6**	**7**	**8**	**9**	**10**	**Count**	**Proportion**
1	*x*	*x*		*x*		*x*	*x*	*x*			6	0.75
2	*x*	*x*		*x*		*x*		*x*			5	0.625
3	*x*	*x*		*x*	*x*	*x*					5	0.625
4	*x*	*x*		*x*			*x*				4	0.5
Count	4	4	0	4	1	3	2	2	0	0	**20**	
Proportion	1.0	1.0	0	1.0	0.25	0.75	0.5	0.5	0	0		**0.50**

Note: x = specified participant experienced specified problem.

For example, consider the hypothetical data for first four participants from Table 7.3, shown in Table 7.4.

The average value of p shown in Table 7.4 for these four participants, like that of the entire matrix shown in Table 7.3, is 0.5 (4 participants by 10 problems yields 40 cells, with 20 filled). However, after having run the first four participants, Problems 3, 9, and 10 have yet to be discovered. Removing the columns for those problems yields the matrix shown in Table 7.5.

In Table 7.5, there are still 20 filled cells, but only a total of 28 cells (4 participants by 7 problems). From that data, the estimated value of p is 0.71—much higher than the value of 0.5 from the table with data from ten participants. To adjust this initial small-sample estimate of p, you need the following information from Table 7.5:

- Initial estimate of p (p_{est}): 0.71
- Number of participants (n): 4

Table 7.5 Hypothetical Results for a Formative Usability Study: First Four Participants and Only Problems Observed with Those Participants

	Problem								
Participant	**1**	**2**	**4**	**5**	**6**	**7**	**8**	**Count**	**Proportion**
1	*x*	*x*	*x*		*x*	*x*	*x*	6	0.86
2	*x*	*x*	*x*		*x*		*x*	5	0.71
3	*x*	*x*	*x*	*x*	*x*			5	0.71
4	*x*	*x*	*x*			*x*		4	0.57
Count	4	4	4	1	3	2	2	**20**	
Proportion	1.0	1.0	1.0	0.25	0.75	0.5	0.5		**0.71**

Note: x = specified participant experienced specified problem.

- Number of known problems (N): 7
- Number of known problems that have occurred only once (N_{once}): 1

This first step is to compute the deflated adjustment.

$$p_{def} = \left[\left(p_{est} - \frac{1}{n}\right)\left(1 - \frac{1}{n}\right)\right]$$

$$p_{def} = \left[\left(0.71 - \frac{1}{4}\right)\left(1 - \frac{1}{4}\right)\right]$$

$$p_{def} = [(0.71 - 0.25)(1 - 0.25)]$$

$$p_{def} = (0.46)(0.75)$$

$$p_{def} = 0.345$$

The second step is to compute the Good–Turing adjustment (where GT_{adj} is the number of known problems that occurred only once (N_{once}) divided by the number of known problems (N)—in this example, 1/7, or 0.143).

$$p_{GT} = \frac{p_{est}}{\left(1 + \frac{N_{once}}{N}\right)}$$

$$p_{GT} = \frac{0.71}{\left(1 + \frac{1}{7}\right)}$$

$$p_{GT} = \frac{0.71}{1.143}$$

$$p_{GT} = 0.621$$

Finally, average the two adjustments to get the final adjusted estimate of p.

$$p_{adj} = \frac{0.345 + 0.621}{2}$$

$$p_{adj} = 0.48$$

With adjustment, the small sample estimate of p in this hypothetical example turned out to be very close to (and to slightly underestimate) the value of p in the table with ten participants. As is typical for small samples, the deflation adjustment was too conservative and the Good–Turing adjustment was too liberal, but their average was close to the value from the larger sample size. In a detailed study of

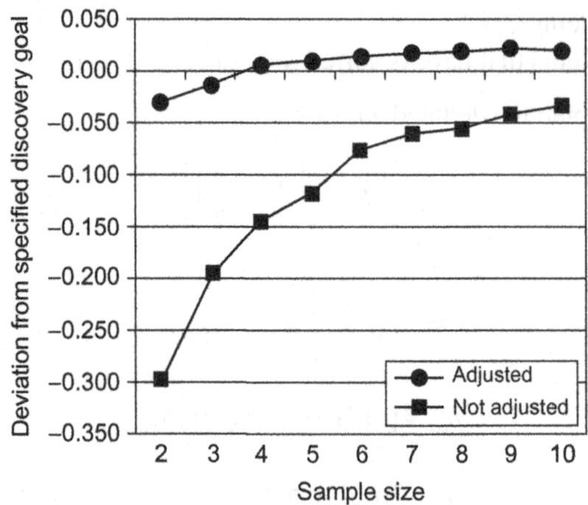

FIGURE 7.2 Accuracy of Adjustment Procedure.

the accuracy of this adjustment for four usability studies, where accuracy is the extent to which the procedure brought the unadjusted small-sample estimate of p closer to the value obtained with the full sample size, Lewis (2001) found:

- The overestimation of p from small samples is a real problem.
- It is possible to use the combination of deflation and Good–Turing adjustments to compensate for this overestimation bias.
- Practitioners can obtain accurate sample size estimates for discovery goals ranging from 70% to 95% (the range investigated by Lewis, 2001) by making an initial adjustment of the required sample size after running two participants, then adjusting the estimate after obtaining data from another four participants.

Figs. 7.2 and 7.3 show accuracy and variability results for this procedure from Lewis (2000, 2001). The accuracy results (Fig. 7.2) show, averaged across 1,000 Monte Carlo iterations for each of the four usability problem discovery databases at each sample size, that the adjustment procedure greatly reduces deviations from the specified discovery goal or 90% or 95%. For sample sizes from two through ten participants, the mean deviation from the specified discovery goal was between −0.03 and +0.02, on average just missing the goal for sample sizes of two or three, and slightly over-reaching the goal for sample sizes from five to ten, but all within a range of 0.05 around the goal.

Fig. 7.3 illustrates the variability of estimates of p, showing both the 50% range (commonly called the interquartile range) and the 90% range—where the ranges are the distances between the estimated values of p that contain, respectively, the central 50% or central 90% of the estimates from the Monte Carlo iterations. More variable estimates have greater ranges. As the sample size increases, the size of the ranges decreases—an expected outcome because in general increasing sample size leads to a decrease in the variability of an estimate.

A surprising result in Fig. 7.3 was that the variability of the deviation of adjusted estimates of p from small samples was fairly low. At the smallest possible sample size ($n = 2$), the central 50% of the distribution of adjusted values of p had a range of just ±0.05 around the median (a width of 0.10); the

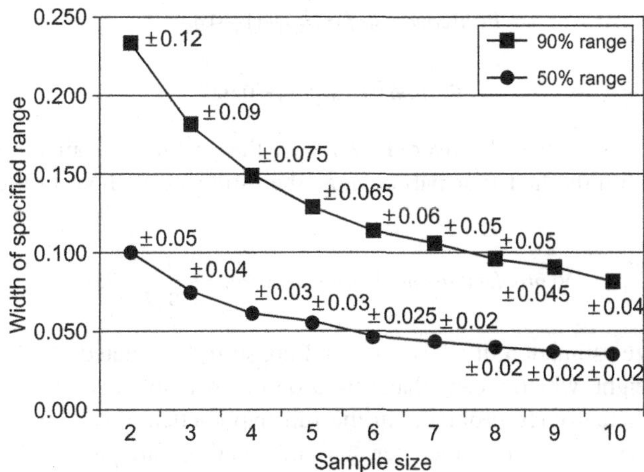

FIGURE 7.3 Variability of Adjustment Procedure.

central 90% were within 0.12 of the median. Increasing n to 6 led to about a 50% decrease in these measures of variability—±0.025 for the interquartile range and ±0.05 for the 90% range, and relatively little additional decline in variability as n increased to 10.

In Lewis (2001) the sample sizes of the tested usability problem databases ranged from 15 to 76, with large-sample estimates of p ranging from 0.16 to 0.38 for two usability tests and two heuristic evaluations. Given this variation among the tested databases, these results stand a good chance of generalizing to other problem-discovery (or similar types of) databases (Chapanis, 1988).

ESTIMATING THE NUMBER OF PROBLEMS AVAILABLE FOR DISCOVERY AND THE NUMBER OF UNDISCOVERED PROBLEMS

Once you have an adjusted estimate of p from the first few participants of a usability test, you can use it to estimate the number of problems available for discovery and from that, the number of undiscovered problems in the problem space of the study (defined by the participants, tasks, and environments included in the study). The steps are:

1. Use the adjusted estimate of p to estimate the proportion of problems discovered so far.
2. Divide the number of problems discovered so far by that proportion to estimate the number of problems available for discovery.
3. Subtract the number of problems discovered so far from the estimate of the number of problems available for discovery to estimate the number of undiscovered problems.

For example, let's return to the hypothetical data given in Table 7.5. Recall that the observed (initial) estimate of p was 0.71, with an adjusted estimate of 0.48. Having run four participants, use $1-(1-p)^n$ to estimate the proportion of problems discovered so far, using the adjusted estimate for p and the number of participants in the sample for n.

$$P(discovery\ so\ far) = 1-(1-p)^n$$

$$P(\textit{discovery so far}) = 1 - (1 - 0.48)^4$$

$$P(\textit{discovery so far}) = 0.927$$

Given this estimate of having discovered 92.7% of the problems available for discovery and 7 problems discovered with the first four participants, the estimated number of problems available for discovery is:

$$N(\textit{problems available for discovery}) = \frac{7}{0.927} = 7.6$$

As with sample size estimation, it's best to round up, so the estimated number of problems available for discovery is eight, which means that, based on the available data, there is one undiscovered problem. There were actually ten problems in the full hypothetical database (see Table 7.4), so the estimate in this example is a bit off. Remember that these methods are probabilistic, not deterministic, so there is always the possibility of a certain amount of error. From a practical perspective, the estimate of eight problems isn't too bad—especially given the small sample size used to estimate the adjusted value of p. The point of using statistical models is not to eliminate error, but to control risk—attempting to minimize error while still working within practical constraints, improving decisions in the long run while accepting the possibility of a mistake in any specific estimate.

Also, note the use of the phrase "problems available for discovery" in the title of this section. It is important to always keep in mind that a given set of tasks and participants (or heuristic evaluators) defines a pool of potentially discoverable usability problems from the set of all possible usability problems. Even within that restricted pool there will always be uncertainty regarding the "true" number of usability problems and the "true" value of p (Hornbæk, 2010; Kanis, 2011). The technique described in this section is a way to estimate, not to guarantee, the probable number of discoverable problems or, in the more general case of formative user studies, the probable number of discoverable events of interest.

TWO CASE STUDIES

Applying these methods in the real world—from the files of Jim Lewis

In 2006, I published two case studies describing the application of these methods to data from formative usability studies (Lewis, 2006a). The first study was of five tasks using a prototype speech recognition application with weather, news, and email/calendar functions. Participant 1 experienced no usability problems; Participant 2 had one problem in each of Tasks 2, 4, and 5; and Participant 3 had the same problem as Participant 2 in Task 2, and different problems in Tasks 1, 4, and 5. Thus, there were a total of 6 different problems in a problem-by-participant matrix with 18 cells (3 participants times 6 problems), for an initial estimate of $p = 7/18 = 0.39$. All but one of the problems occurred just once, so the adjusted estimate of p was 0.125 (less than half of the initial estimate). Solving for $1 - (1 - p)^n$ with $p = 0.125$ and $n = 3$ gives an estimated proportion of problem discovery of about 0.33. Dividing the number of different problems by this proportion (6/0.33) provided an estimate that there were about 19 problems available for discovery—so it would be reasonable to continue testing in this space (these types of participants and these tasks) for a while longer—there are still about 13 problems left to find.

A second round of usability testing of seven participants with a revised prototype of with the same functions but an expanded set of tasks revealed 33 different usability problems. The initial estimate of p was 0.27, with an adjusted estimate of 0.15. Given these values, a sample size of 7 should have uncovered about 68% of the problems available for discovery. With 33 observed problems, this suggests that for this set of testing conditions there were about 49 problems available for discovery, with 16 as yet undiscovered.

To practice with data from a third case study (Lewis, 2008), see Review Questions 4–6 at the end of this chapter.

WHAT AFFECTS THE VALUE OF *p*?

Because *p* is such an important factor in sample size estimation for formative user studies, it is important to understand the study variables that can affect its value. In general, to obtain higher values of *p*:

- Use highly skilled observers for usability studies.
- Use multiple observers rather than a single observer (Hertzum and Jacobsen, 2001).
- Focus evaluation on new products with newly designed interfaces rather than older, more refined interfaces.
- Study less-skilled participants in usability studies (as long as they are appropriate participants).
- Make the user sample as homogeneous as possible, within the bounds of the population to which you plan to generalize the results (to ensure a representative sample). Note that this will increase the value of *p* for the study, but will likely decrease the number of problems discovered, so if you have an interest in multiple user groups, you will need to test each group to ensure adequate problem discovery.
- Make the task sample as heterogeneous as possible, and include both simple and complex tasks (Lewis, 1994; Lewis et al., 1990; Lindgaard and Chattratichart, 2007).
- For heuristic evaluations, use examiners with usability and application-domain expertise (double experts) (Nielsen, 1992).
- For heuristic evaluations, if you must make a trade-off between having a single evaluator spend a lot of time examining an interface versus having more examiners spend less time each examining an interface, choose the latter option (Dumas et al., 1995; Virzi, 1997).

Note that some (but not all) of the tips for increasing *p* are the opposite of those that reduce measurement variability (see the previous chapter).

WHAT IS A REASONABLE PROBLEM DISCOVERY GOAL?

For historical reasons, it is common to set the cumulative problem discovery goal to 80–85%. In one of the earliest empirical studies of using $1 - (1 - p)^n$ to model the discovery of usability problems, Virzi (1990, 1992) observed that for the data from three usability studies "80% of the usability problems are detected with four or five subjects" (Virzi, 1992, p. 457). Similarly, Nielsen's "magic number five" comes from his observation that when $p = 0.31$ (an average over a set of usability studies and heuristic evaluations), a usability study with five participants should usually find about 85% of the problems available for discovery (Nielsen, 2000; Nielsen and Landauer, 1993).

As part of an effort to replicate the findings of Virzi (1990, 1992), Lewis (1994), in addition to studying problem discovery for an independent usability study, also collected data from economic simulations to estimate the return on investment (ROI) under a variety of settings. The analysis addressed the costs associated with running additional participants, fixing problems, and failing to discover problems. The simulation manipulated six variables (shown in Table 7.6) to determine their influence on:

- The sample size at maximum ROI
- The magnitude of maximum ROI
- The percentage of problems discovered at the maximum ROI

Table 7.6 Variables and Results of the Lewis (1994) ROI Simulations

Independent Variable	Value	Sample Size at Maximum ROI	Magnitude of Maximum ROI	Percentage of Problems Discovered at Maximum ROI
Average likelihood of problem discovery (p)	0.10	19.0	3.1	86
	0.25	14.6	22.7	97
	0.50	7.7	52.9	99
	Range:	11.3	49.8	13
Number of problems available for discovery	30	11.5	7.0	91
	150	14.4	26.0	95
	300	15.4	45.6	95
	Range:	3.9	38.6	4
Daily cost to run a study	500	14.3	33.4	94
	1000	13.2	19.0	93
	Range:	1.1	14.4	1
Cost to fix a discovered problem	100	11.9	7.0	92
	1000	15.6	45.4	96
	Range:	3.7	38.4	4
Cost of an undiscovered problem (low set)	200	10.2	1.9	89
	500	12.0	6.4	93
	1000	13.5	12.6	94
	Range:	3.3	10.7	5
Cost of an undiscovered problem (high set)	2000	14.7	12.3	95
	5000	15.7	41.7	96
	10000	16.4	82.3	96
	Range:	1.7	70.0	1

The definition of ROI was Savings/Costs, where:

- Savings was the cost of the discovered problems had they remained undiscovered minus the cost of fixing the discovered problems.
- Costs was the sum of the daily cost to run a usability study plus the costs associated with problems remaining undiscovered.

The simulations included problem discovery modeling for sample sizes from 1 to 20, for three values of p covering a range of likely values (0.10, 0.25, and 0.50), and for a range of likely numbers of problems available for discovery (30, 150, 300), estimating for each combination of variables the number of expected discovered and undiscovered problems. These estimates were crossed with a low set of costs ($100 to fix a discovered problem; $200, $500, and $1000 costs of undiscovered problems) and a high set of costs ($1000 to fix a discovered problem; $2000, $5000, and $10,000 costs of undiscovered problems) to calculate the ROIs. The ratios of the costs to fix discovered problems to the costs of undiscovered problems were congruent with software engineering indexes reported by Boehm (1981). Table 7.6 shows the average value of each dependent variable (last three columns) for each level of all the independent variables, and the range of the average values for each independent variable. Across the independent variables, the average percentage of discovered problems at the maximum ROI was 94%.

Although all of the independent variables influenced the sample size at the maximum ROI, the variable with the broadest influence (as indicated by the range) was the average likelihood of problem discovery (p), which also had the strongest influence on the percentage of problems discovered at the maximum ROI. This lends additional weight to the importance of estimating the parameter when conducting formative usability studies due to its influence on the determination of an appropriate sample size. According to the results of this simulation:

- If the expected value of p is small (e.g., 0.10), practitioners should plan to discover about 86% of the problems available for discovery.
- If the expected value of p is greater (e.g., 0.25 or 0.50), practitioners should set a goal of discovering about 98% of the problems available for discovery.
- For expected values of p between 0.10 and 0.25, practitioners should interpolate to estimate the appropriate discovery goal.

An unexpected result of the simulation was that variation in the cost of an undiscovered problem had a minor effect on the sample size at maximum ROI (although, like the other independent variables, it had a strong effect on the magnitude of the maximum ROI). Although the various costs associated with ROI are important to know when estimating the ROI of a study, it is not necessary to know these costs when planning sample sizes.

Note that the sample sizes associated with these levels of problem discovery are the total sample sizes. For studies that will involve multiple iterations, one simple way to determine the sample size per iteration is to divide the total sample size by the number of planned iterations. Although there is no research on how to systematically devise non-equal sample sizes for iterations, it seems logical to start with smaller samples, then move to larger ones. The rationale is that early iterations should reveal the very high-probability problems, so it's important to find and fix them quickly. Larger samples in later iterations can then pick up the lower-probability problems.

For example, suppose you want to be able to find 90% of the problems that have a probability of 0.15. Using Table 7.2, it would take 14 participants to achieve this goal. Also, assume that the development plan allows three iterations, so you decide to allocate 3 participants to the first iteration, 4 to the second, and 7 to the third. Again referring to Table 7.2, the first iteration ($n = 3$) should detect about 39% of problems with $p = 0.15$—a far cry from the ultimate goal of 90%. This first iteration should, however, detect 58% of problems with $p = 0.25$, 88% of problems with $p = 0.50$, and 100% of problems with $p = 0.90$, and fixing those problems should make life easier for the next iteration. At the end of the second iteration ($n = 4$), the total sample size is up to 7, so the expectation is the discovery of 68% of problems with $p = 0.15$ (and 87% of problems with $p = .25$). At the end of the third iteration ($n = 7$), the total sample size is 14, and the expectation is the target discovery of 90% of problems with $p = .15$ (and even discovery of 77% of problems with $p = 0.10$).

RECONCILING THE "MAGIC NUMBER FIVE" WITH "EIGHT IS NOT ENOUGH"

Some usability practitioners use the "Magic Number Five" as a rule-of-thumb for sample sizes for formative usability tests (Barnum et al., 2003; Nielsen, 2000), believing that this sample size will usually reveal about 85% of the problems available for discovery. Others (Perfetti and Landesman, 2001; Spool and Schroeder, 2001) have argued that "Eight is Not Enough"—in fact, that their experience showed that it could take over 50 participants to achieve this goal. Is there any way to reconcile these apparently opposing points of view?

SOME HISTORY—THE 1980s

Although strongly associated with Jakob Nielsen (e.g., Nielsen, 2000), the idea of running formative user studies with small-sample iterations goes back much further—to one of the fathers of modern human factors engineering, Alphonse Chapanis. In an award-winning paper for the IEEE Transactions on Professional Communication about developing tutorials for first-time computer users, Al-Awar et al. (1981, p. 34) wrote:

> Having collected data from a few test subjects – and initially a few are all you need – you are ready for a revision of the text. Revisions may involve nothing more than changing a word or a punctuation mark. On the other hand, they may require the insertion of new examples and the rewriting, or reformatting, of an entire frame. This cycle of test, evaluate, rewrite is repeated as often as is necessary.

Any iterative method must include a stopping rule to prevent infinite iterations. In the real world, resource constraints and deadlines often dictate the stopping rule. In the study by Al-Awar et al. (1981), their stopping rule was an iteration in which 95% of participants completed the tutorial without any serious problems.

Al-Awar et al. (1981) did not specify their sample sizes, but did refer to collecting data from "a few test subjects." The usual definition of "few" is a number that is greater than one, but indefinitely small. When there are two objects of interest, the typical expression is "a couple." When there are six, it's common to refer to "a half dozen." From this, it's reasonable to infer that the per-iteration sample sizes of Al-Awar et al. (1981) were in the range of three to five—at least, not dramatically larger than that.

The publication and promotion of this method by Chapanis and his students had an almost immediate influence on product development practices at IBM (Kennedy, 1982; Lewis, 1982) and other companies, notably Xerox (Smith et al., 1982) and Apple (Williams, 1983). Shortly thereafter, John Gould and his associates at the IBM T. J. Watson Research Center began publishing influential papers on usability testing and iterative design (Gould, 1988; Gould and Boies, 1983; Gould et al., 1987; Gould and Lewis, 1984), as did Whiteside et al. (1988) at DEC (Baecker, 2008; Dumas, 2007; Lewis, 2012).

SOME MORE HISTORY—THE 1990s

The 1990s began with three important Monte Carlo studies of usability problem discovery from databases with (fairly) large sample sizes. Nielsen and Molich (1990) collected data from four heuristic evaluations that had independent evaluations from 34 to 77 evaluators (p ranged from 0.20 to 0.51, averaging 0.34). Inspired by Nielsen and Molich, Virzi (1990) presented the first Monte Carlo evaluation of problem discovery using data from a formative usability study ($n = 20$—later expanded into a *Human Factors* paper in 1992—p ranged from 0.32 to 0.42, averaging 0.37). In a discussion of cost-effective usability evaluation, Wright and Monk (1991) published the first graph showing the problem discovery curves for $1 - (1 - p)^n$ for different values of p and n (similar to Fig. 7.1). In 1993, Nielsen and Landauer used Monte Carlo simulations to analyze problem detection for eleven studies (six heuristic evaluations and five formative usability tests) to see how well the results matched problem discovery prediction using $1 - (1 - p)^n$ (p ranged from 0.12 to 0.58, averaging 0.31).

The conclusions drawn from the Monte Carlo simulations were:

> The number of usability results found by aggregates of evaluators grows rapidly in the interval from one to five evaluators but reaches the point of diminishing returns around the point of ten evaluators. We recommend that heuristic evaluation is done with between three and five evaluators and that any additional resources are spent on alternative methods of evaluation (Nielsen and Molich, 1990, p. 255).

> The basic findings are that (a) 80% of the usability problems are detected with four or five subjects, (b) additional subjects are less and less likely to reveal new information, and (c) the most severe usability problems are likely to have been detected in the first few subjects (Virzi, 1992, p. 457).

> The benefits are much larger than the costs both for user testing and for heuristic evaluation. The highest ratio of benefits to costs is achieved for 3.2 test users and for 4.4 heuristic evaluators. These numbers can be taken as one rough estimate of the effort to be expended for usability evaluation for each version of a user interface subjected to iterative design (Nielsen and Landauer, 1993, p. 212).

Lewis (1994) attempted to replicate Virzi (1990, 1992) using data from a different formative usability study ($n = 15, p = 0.16$). The key conclusions from this study were:

> Problem discovery shows diminishing returns as a function of sample size. Observing four to five participants will uncover about 80% of a product's usability problems as long as the average likelihood of problem detection ranges between .32 and .42, as in Virzi. If the average likelihood of problem detection is lower, then a practitioner will need to observe more than five participants to discover 80% of the problems. Using behavioral categories for problem severity (or impact), these data showed no correlation between problem severity (impact) and rate of discovery (Lewis, 1994, p. 368).

One of the key differences between the findings of Virzi (1992) and Lewis (1994) was whether severe problems are likely to occur with the first few participants. Certainly, there is nothing in $1 - (1 - p)^n$ that would account for anything other than the probable frequency of occurrence as influencing early appearance of an event of interest in a user study. In a study similar to those of Virzi (1992) and Lewis (1994), Law and Hvannberg (2004) reported no significant correlation between problem severity and problem detection rate. Sauro (2014) studied the problem severity ratings of multiple evaluators across nine usability studies independently using their judgment, as opposed to data driven assessments and found that the average correlation across all nine studies was not significantly different from zero (only one study showed a significant positive correlation). Although a few studies have indicated a positive correlation between problem frequency and severity, the preponderance of the data indicates that there is no reliable relationship. Thus, the best policy is for practitioners to assume no relationship when planning usability studies.

THE DERIVATION OF THE "MAGIC NUMBER 5"

These studies of the early 1990s are the soil (or perhaps, euphemistically speaking, the fertilizer) that produced the "Magic Number 5" guideline for formative usability assessments (heuristic evaluations or usability studies). The average value of p from Nielsen and Landauer (1993) was 0.31. If you set n to 5 and compute the probability of seeing a problem at least once during a study, you get:

$$P(x \geq 1) = 1 - (1 - p)^n$$

$$P(x \geq 1) = 1 - (1 - 0.31)^5$$

$$P(x \geq 1) = 0.8436$$

In other words, considering the average results from published formative usability evaluations (but ignoring the variability), the first five participants should usually reveal about 85% of the problems available for discovery in that iteration (assuming a multiple-iteration study). Over time, in the minds of many usability practitioners, the guideline *mistakenly* became:

> *The Magic Number 5*: "All you need to do is watch five people to find 85% of a product's usability problems."

In 2000, Jakob Nielsen, in his influential Alert Box blog, published an article entitled "Why You Only Need to Test with 5 Users" (www.useit.com/alertbox/20000319.html). Citing the analysis from Nielsen and Landauer (1993), he wrote:

> The curve [$1 - (1 - .31)^n$] clearly shows that you need to test with at least 15 users to discover all the usability problems in the design. So why do I recommend testing with a much smaller number of users? The main reason is that it is better to distribute your budget for user testing across many small tests instead of blowing everything on a single, elaborate study. Let us say that you do have the funding to recruit 15 representative customers and have them test your design. Great. Spend this budget on three tests with 5 users each. You want to run multiple tests because the real goal of usability engineering is to improve the design and not just to document its weaknesses. After the first study with 5 users has found 85% of the usability problems, you will want to fix these problems in a redesign. After creating the new design, you need to test again.

GOING FISHING WITH JAKOB NIELSEN

It's all about iteration and changing test conditions—from the files of Jim Lewis

In 2002 I was part of a UPA panel discussion on sample sizes for formative usability studies. The other members of the panel were Carl Turner and Jakob Nielsen (for a write-up of the conclusions of the panel, see Turner et al., 2006). During his presentation, Nielsen provided addition explanation about his recommendation (Nielsen, 2000) to test with only five users, using the analogy of fishing (see Fig. 7.4).

Suppose you have several ponds in which you can fish. Some fish are easier to catch than others, so if you had ten hours to spend fishing, would you spend all ten fishing in one pond, or would you spend the first five in one pond and the second five in the other? To maximize your capture of fish, you should spend some time in both ponds to get the easy fish from each.

Applying that analogy to formative usability studies, Nielsen said that he never intended his recommendation of five participants to mean that practitioners should test with just five and then stop altogether. His recommendation of five participants is contingent on an iterative usability testing strategy with changes in the test conditions for each of the iterations (e.g., changes in tasks or the user group in addition to changes in design intended to fix the problems observed in the previous iteration). When you change the tasks or user groups and retest with the revised system, you are essentially fishing in a new pond, with a new set of (hopefully) easy fish to catch (usability problems to discover).

FIGURE 7.4 Imaginary Fishing with Jakob Nielsen.

EIGHT IS NOT ENOUGH—A RECONCILIATION

In 2001, Spool and Schroeder published the results of a large-scale usability evaluation from which they concluded that the "Magic Number 5" did not work when evaluating websites. In their study, five participants did not even get close to the discovery of 85% of the usability problems they found in the websites they were evaluating. Perfetti and Landesman (2001), discussing related research, stated:

> When we tested the site with 18 users, we identified 247 total obstacles-to-purchase. Contrary to our expectations, we saw new usability problems throughout the testing sessions. In fact, we saw more than five new obstacles for each user we tested. Equally important, we found many serious problems for the first time with some of our later users. What was even more surprising to us was that repeat usability problems did not increase as testing progressed. These findings clearly undermine the belief that five users will be enough to catch nearly 85 percent of the usability problems on a Web site. In our tests, we found only 35 percent of all usability problems after the first five users. We estimated over 600 total problems on this particular online music site. Based on this estimate, it would have taken us 90 tests to discover them all!

From this description, it's clear that the value of p for this study was very low. Given the estimate of 600 problems available for discovery using this study's method, then the percentage discovered with 18 users was 41%. Solving for p in the equation $1-(1-p)^{18}=0.41$ yields $p=0.029$. Given this estimate of p, the percentage of problem discovery expected when $n = 5$ is $1 - (1 - 0.41)^5 = 0.137$ (13.7%). Furthermore, 13.7% of 600 is 82 problems, which is about 35% of the total number of problems discovered in this study with 18 participants (35% of 247 is 86)—a finding consistent with the data reported by Perfetti and Landesman (2001). Their discovery of serious problems with later users is consistent with the findings of Lewis (1994) and Law and Hvannberg (2004), in which the discovery rate of serious problems was the same as that for other problems.

For this low rate of problem discovery and large number of problems, it is unsurprising to continue to find more than five new problems with each participant. As shown in Table 7.7, you wouldn't expect the number of new problems per participant to consistently fall below five until after the 47th participant. The low volume of repeat usability problems is also consistent with a low value of p. A high incidence of repeat problems is more likely with evaluations of early designs than those of more mature designs. Usability testing of products that have already had the common, easy-to-find problems removed is more likely to reveal problems that are relatively idiosyncratic. Also, as the authors reported, the tasks given to participants were relatively unstructured, which is likely to have increased the number of problems available for discovery by allowing a greater variety of paths from the participants' starting point to the task goal.

Even with a value of p this low—0.029—the expected percentage of discovery with eight participants is about 21%, which is better than not having run any participants at all. When p is this small, it would take 65 participants to reveal (at least once) 85% of the problems available for discovery, and 155 to discover almost all (99%) of the problems. Is this low value of p typical of website evaluation? Perhaps, but it could also be due to the type of testing (e.g., relatively unstructured tasks or the level of description of usability problems). In the initial publication of this analysis, Lewis (2006b, p. 33) concluded:

Table 7.7 Expected Problem Discovery When p = .029 and There are 600 Problems							
Sample Size	**Percent Discovered (%)**	**Total Number Discovered**	**New Problems**	**Sample Size**	**Percent Discovered (%)**	**Total Number Discovered**	**New Problems**
1	2.9	17	17	36	65.3	392	6
2	5.7	34	17	37	66.3	398	6
3	8.5	51	17	38	67.3	404	6
4	11.1	67	16	39	68.3	410	6
5	13.7	82	15	40	69.2	415	5
6	16.2	97	15	41	70.1	420	5
7	18.6	112	15	42	70.9	426	6
8	21.0	126	14	43	71.8	431	5
9	23.3	140	14	44	72.6	436	5
10	25.5	153	13	45	73.4	440	4
11	27.7	166	13	46	74.2	445	5
12	29.8	179	13	47	74.9	450	5
13	31.8	191	12	48	75.6	454	4
14	33.8	203	12	49	76.4	458	4
15	35.7	214	11	50	77.0	462	4
16	37.6	225	11	51	77.7	466	4
17	39.4	236	11	52	78.4	470	4
18	41.1	247	11	53	79.0	474	4
19	42.8	257	10	54	79.6	478	4
20	44.5	267	10	55	80.2	481	3
21	46.1	277	10	56	80.8	485	4
22	47.7	286	9	57	81.3	488	3
23	49.2	295	9	58	81.9	491	3
24	50.7	304	9	59	82.4	494	3
25	52.1	313	9	60	82.9	497	3
26	53.5	321	8	61	83.4	500	3
27	54.8	329	8	62	83.9	503	3
28	56.1	337	8	63	84.3	506	3
29	57.4	344	7	64	84.8	509	3
30	58.6	352	8	65	85.2	511	2
31	59.8	359	7	66	85.7	514	3
32	61.0	366	7	67	86.1	516	2
33	62.1	373	7	68	86.5	519	3
34	63.2	379	6	69	86.9	521	2
35	64.3	386	7	70	87.3	524	3

There will, of course, continue to be discussions about sample sizes for problem-discovery usability tests, but I hope they will be informed discussions. If a practitioner says that five participants are all you need to discover most of the problems that will occur in a usability test, it's likely that this practitioner is typically working in contexts that have a fairly high value of p and fairly low problem discovery goals. If another practitioner says that he's been running a study for three months, has observed 50 participants, and is continuing to discover new problems every few participants, then it's likely that he has a somewhat lower value of p, a higher problem discovery goal, and lots of cash (or a low-cost audience of participants). Neither practitioner is necessarily wrong – they're just working in different usability testing spaces. The formulas developed over the past 25 years provide a principled way to understand the relationship between those spaces, and a better way for practitioners to routinely estimate sample-size requirements for these types of tests.

HOW COMMON ARE USABILITY PROBLEMS?

Websites appear to have fewer usability problems than business or consumer software—from the files of Jeff Sauro

Just how common are usability problems in websites and software? Surprisingly there is very little out there on the frequency of usability problems. Part of the reason is that most usability testing happens early in the development phase and is at best documented for an internal audience. Furthermore, once a website is launched or product released, what little usability testing is done is typically more on benchmarking than on finding and fixing problems.

I recently reviewed usability publications and a collection of usability reports from various companies. I only included tests on completed applications and live websites, excluding those that were in the design phase and didn't have current users at the time of testing. My investigation turned up a wide range of products and websites from 24 usability tests. Examples included rental car websites, business applications (financial and HR) and consumer productivity software (calendars, spreadsheets and word-processors). I didn't include data from heuristic evaluations or cognitive walk-throughs because I wanted to focus just on problems that users actually experienced.

After adjusting the values of p for the various studies, I had data from 11 usability studies of business applications, 7 of consumer software, and 6 from websites. The mean values of p (and their 95% confidence intervals) for the three types were:

- Business applications: 0.37 (95% confidence interval ranged from 0.25 to 0.50)
- Consumer software: 0.23 (95% confidence interval ranged from 0.13 to 0.33)
- Websites: 0.04 (95% confidence interval ranged from 0.025 to 0.06)

The confidence intervals for business applications and consumer software overlapped, but not for websites, which showed substantially lower problem discovery rates than the other types. It is important to keep in mind that these applications and websites were not randomly drawn from the populations of all applications and websites, so these findings might not generalize. Despite that possibility, the results are reasonable.

Business applications are typically customized to integrate into enterprise systems, with users often receiving some training or having specialized skills. Business software typically contains a lot of complex functionality, so it makes sense that there are more things that can impede a good user experience.

Websites, on the other hand, are typically self-service and have a fraction of the functionality of large-scale business applications. Furthermore, switching costs for websites are low, so there is little tolerance for a poor user-experience. If users can't walk-up and use a website, they're gone.

(For more details, see www.measuringu.com/problem-frequency.php.)

MORE ABOUT THE BINOMIAL PROBABILITY FORMULA AND ITS SMALL-SAMPLE ADJUSTMENT

THE ORIGIN OF THE BINOMIAL PROBABILITY FORMULA

Many of the early studies of probability have their roots in the desire of gamblers to increase their odds of winning when playing games of chance, with much of this work taking place in the 17th century with contributions from Newton, Pascal, Fermat, Huygens, and Jacques Bernoulli (Cowles, 1989). Consider the simple game of betting on the outcome of tossing two coins and guessing how many heads will appear. An unsophisticated player might reason that there can be 0, 1, or 2 heads appearing, so each of these outcomes has a 1/3 (33.3%) chance of happening. There are, however, four different outcomes rather than three. Using T for tails and H for heads, they are:

- TT (0 heads)
- TH (1 head)
- HT (1 head)
- HH (2 heads)

Each of these outcomes has the same chance of 1/4 (25%), so the probability of getting 0 heads is 0.25, of getting 2 heads is 0.25, and of getting 1 head is 0.50. The reason each outcome has the same likelihood is because, given a fair coin, the probability of a head is the same at that of a tail—both equal to 0.5. When you have independent events like the tossing of two coins, you can compute the likelihood of a given pair by multiplying the probabilities of the events. In this case 0.5 × 0.5 = 0.25 for each outcome.

It's easy to list the outcomes when there are just two coin tosses, but as the number of tosses goes up, it gets very cumbersome to list them all. Fortunately, there are well-known formulas for computing the number of permutations or combinations of n things taken x at a time (Bradley, 1976). The difference between permutations and combinations is when counting permutations you care about the order in which the events occur (TH is different from HT), but when counting combinations, the order doesn't matter (you only care that you got one head, but you don't care whether it happened first or second). The formula for permutations is:

$$_{n}P_{x} = \frac{n!}{(n-x)!}$$

The number of combinations for a given set of n things taken x at a time will always be equal to or less than the number of permutations. In fact, the number of combinations is the number of permutations divided by $x!$—so when x is 0 or 1, the number of combinations will always equal the number of permutations. The formula for combinations is:

$$_{n}C_{x} = \frac{n!}{x!(n-x)!}$$

For the problem of tossing two coins ($n = 2$), the number of combinations for the number of heads (x) being 0, 1, or 2 is:

$$_2C_0 = \frac{2!}{0!(2-0)!} = \frac{2!}{0!2!} = 1$$

$$_2C_1 = \frac{2!}{1!(2-1)!} = \frac{2!}{1!1!} = 2$$

$$_2C_2 = \frac{2!}{2!(2-2)!} = \frac{2!}{2!0!} = 1$$

Having established the number of different ways to get 0, 1, or 2 heads, the next step is to compute the likelihood of the combination given the probability of tossing a head or tail. As mentioned earlier, the likelihood for any combination of two tosses of a fair coin is 0.5 × 0.5 = 0.25. Expressed more generally, the likelihood is:

$$p^x(1-p)^{n-x}$$

So, for the problem of tossing two coins where you're counting the number of heads (x) and the probability of a head is $p = 0.5$, the joint probabilities for $x = 0$, 1, or 2 are:

$$0.5^0(1-0.5)^{2-0} = 0.5^2 = 0.25$$

$$0.5^1(1-0.5)^{2-1} = 0.5(0.5) = 0.5^2 = 0.25$$

$$0.5^2(1-0.5)^{2-2} = 0.5^2 = 0.25$$

As noted earlier, however, there are two ways to get 1 head (HT or TH) but only one way to get HH or TT, so the formula for the probability of an outcome needs to include both the joint probabilities and the number of combinations of events that can lead to that outcome, which leads to the binomial probability formula:

$$P(x) = \frac{n!}{(x!)(n-x)!}p^x(1-p)^{n-x}$$

Applying this formula to the problem of tossing two coins, where x is the number of heads:

$$P(0) = \frac{2!}{(0!)(2-0)!}0.5^0(1-0.5)^{2-0} = 1(0.5^2) = 0.25$$

$$P(1) = \frac{2!}{(1!)(2-1)!}0.5^1(1-0.5)^{2-1} = 2(0.5^2) = 0.50$$

$$P(2) = \frac{2!}{(2!)(2-2)!}0.5^2(1-0.5)^{2-2} = 1(0.5^2) = 0.25$$

Table 7.8 Two Extreme Patterns of Three Participants Encountering Problems

Outcome A	**Problems**				
Participant	**1**	**2**	**3**	**Count**	**Proportion**
1	*x*	*x*	*x*	3	1.00
2	*x*	*x*	*x*	3	1.00
3	*x*	*x*	*x*	3	1.00
Count	3	3	3	**9**	
Proportion	1.00	1.00	1.00		1.00
Outcome B	**Problems**				
Participant	**1**	**2**	**3**	**Count**	**Proportion**
1	*x*			1	0.33
2		*x*		1	0.33
3			*x*	1	0.33
Count	1	1	1	**3**	
Proportion	0.33	0.33	0.33		0.33

HOW DOES THE DEFLATION ADJUSTMENT WORK?

The first researchers to identify a systematic bias in the estimation of p from small samples of participants were Hertzum and Jacobsen (2001—corrected paper published 2003). Specifically, they pointed out that, as expected, the largest possible value of p is 1, but the smallest possible value of p from a usability study is not 0—instead, it is $1/n$. As shown in Table 7.8, p equals 1 only when all participants encounter all observed problems (Outcome A); p equals $1/n$ when each observed problem occurs with only one participant (Outcome B). These are both very unlikely outcomes, but establish clear upper and lower boundaries on the values of p when calculated from this type of matrix. As the sample size increases, the magnitude of $1/n$ decreases, and as n approaches infinity, its magnitude approaches 0.

Having a lower boundary substantially greater than 0 strongly contributes to the overestimation of p that happens when estimating it from small-sample problem-discovery studies (Lewis, 2001). The deflation procedure reduces the overestimated value of p in two steps—(1) subtracting $1/n$ from the observed value of p, then (2) multiplying that result by $(1 - 1/n)$. The result is usually lower than the corresponding larger-sample estimate of p, but this works out well in practice as a counterbalance to the generally over-optimistic estimate obtained with the Good–Turing adjustment.

A FORTUITOUS MISTAKE

Unintentionally computing double-deflation rather than normalization—from the files of Jim Lewis

As described in Lewis (2001), when I first approached a solution to the problem posed by Hertzum and Jacobsen (2001), I wanted to normalize the initial estimate of p so the lowest possible value (Outcome B in Table 7.8) would have a value of 0 and the highest possible value (Outcome A in Table 7.8) would stay at 1. To do this, the first step is to subtract $1/n$ from the observed value of p in the matrix. The second step for normalization would be to divide, not multiply, the result of the first step by $(1 - 1/n)$. The result of applying this procedure would change the estimate of p for Outcome B from 0.33 to 0.

$$p_{\text{norm}} = \frac{p - \frac{1}{n}}{1 - \frac{1}{n}}$$

$$p_{\text{norm}} = \frac{\frac{1}{3} - \frac{1}{3}}{1 - \frac{1}{3}} = 0$$

And it would maintain the estimate of $p = 1$ for Outcome A.

$$p_{\text{norm}} = \frac{1 - \frac{1}{3}}{1 - \frac{1}{3}} = 1$$

Like normalization, the deflation equation reduces the estimate of p for Outcome B from 0.33 to 0.

$$p_{\text{def}} = \left(p - \frac{1}{n}\right)\left(1 - \frac{1}{n}\right)$$

$$p_{\text{def}} = \left(\frac{1}{3} - \frac{1}{3}\right)\left(1 - \frac{1}{3}\right) = 0$$

But for Outcome A, both elements of the procedure reduce the estimate of p.

$$p_{\text{def}} = \left(1 - \frac{1}{3}\right)\left(1 - \frac{1}{3}\right) = \left(\frac{2}{3}\right)\left(\frac{2}{3}\right) = \frac{4}{9} = 0.444$$

At some point, very early when I was working with this equation, I must have forgotten to write the division symbol between the two elements. Had I included it, the combination of normalization and Good–Turing adjustments would not have worked well as an adjustment method. Neither I nor any of the reviewers noticed this during the publication process of Lewis (2001), or in any of the following publications in which I have described the formula. It was only while I was first working through this chapter, 10 years after the publication of Lewis (2001), that I discovered this. For this reason, in this chapter, I've described that part of the equation as a deflation adjustment rather than my original term, "normalization." I believe I would have realized this error during the preparation of Lewis (2001) except for one thing—it worked so well that it escaped my attention. In practice, multiplication of these elements (which results in double-deflation rather than normalization) appears to provide the necessary magnitude of deflation of p to achieve the desired adjustment accuracy when used in association with the Good–Turing adjustment. This is not the formula I had originally intended, but it was a fortuitous mistake.

WHAT IF YOU DON'T HAVE THE PROBLEM-BY-PARTICIPANT MATRIX?

A quick way to approximate the adjustment of *p*—from the files of Jeff Sauro

To avoid the tedious computations, I wondered how good a regression equation might work to predict adjusted values of *p* from their initial estimates. I used data from 19 usability studies for which I had initial estimates of *p* and the problem discovery matrix to compute adjusted estimates of *p*, and got the following formula for predicting p_{adj} from *p*:

$$p_{adj} = 0.9p - 0.046$$

As shown in Fig. 7.5, the fit of this equation to the data was very good, explaining 98.4% of the variability in p_{adj}.

So, if you have an estimate of *p* for a completed usability study but don't have access to the problem-by-participant problem discovery matrix, you can use this regression equation to get a quick estimate of p_{adj}. Keep in mind, though, that it is just an estimate, and if the study conditions are outside the bounds of the studies used to create this model, that quick estimate could be off by an unknown amount. The parameters of the equation came from usability studies that had:

- A mean *p* of 0.33 (ranging from 0.05 to 0.79)
- A mean of about 13 participants (ranging from 6 to 26)
- A mean of about 27 problems (ranging from 6 to 145)

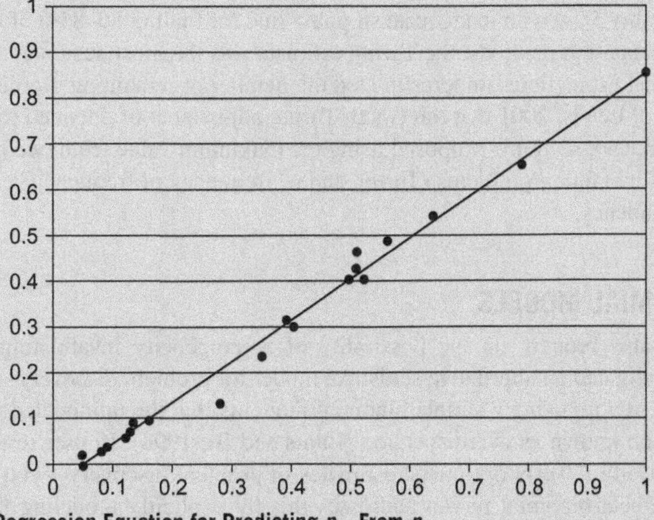

FIGURE 7.5 Fit of Regression Equation for Predicting p_{adj} From *p*.

OTHER STATISTICAL MODELS FOR PROBLEM DISCOVERY

CRITICISMS OF THE BINOMIAL MODEL FOR PROBLEM DISCOVERY

In the early 2000s, there were a number of published criticisms of the use of the binomial model for problem discovery. For example, Woolrych and Cockton (2001) pointed out that a simple point estimate of *p* might not be sufficient for estimating the sample size required for the discovery of a specified percentage of usability problems in an interface. They criticized the formula $1 - (1 - p)^n$ for failing to take into account individual differences among participants in problem discoverability and claimed that the typical values used for p (0.31) derived from Nielsen and Landauer (1993) tended to be too optimistic. Without citing a specific alternative distribution, they recommended the development of a formula that would replace a single value of p with a probability density function.

In the same year, Caulton (2001) also criticized simple estimates of p as only applying given a strict homogeneity assumption—that all types of users have the same probability of encountering all usability problems. To address this, Caulton added to the standard cumulative binomial probability formula a parameter for the number of heterogeneous groups. He also introduced and modeled the concept of problems that heterogeneous groups share and those that are unique to a particular subgroup. His primary claims were (1) the more subgroups, the lower will be the expected value of p; and (2) the more distinct the subgroups are, the lower will be the expected value of p.

Kanis (2011) recently evaluated four methods for estimating the number of usability problems from the results of initial participants in formative user research (usability studies and heuristic evaluations). The study did not include the combination deflation-discounting adjustment of Lewis (2001), but did include a Turing estimate related to the Good–Turing component of the combination adjustment. The key findings of the study were:

- The "Magic Number 5" was an inadequate stopping rule for finding 80–85% of usability problems.
- Of the studied estimation methods, the Turing estimate was the most accurate.
- The Turing estimate sometimes underestimated the number of remaining problems (consistent with the finding of Lewis, 2001 that the Good–Turing adjustment of p tended to be higher than the full-sample estimates), so Kanis proposed using the maximum value from two different estimates of the number of remaining problems (Turing and a "frequency of frequency" estimators) to overcome this tendency.

EXPANDED BINOMIAL MODELS

Schmettow (2008) also brought up the possibility of heterogeneity invalidating the usefulness of $1-(1-p)^n$. He investigated an alternative statistical model for problem discovery—the beta-binomial. The potential problem with using a simple binomial model is that the unmodeled variability of p can lead to a phenomenon known as overdispersion (Ennis and Bi, 1998). In user research, for example, overdispersion can lead to overly optimistic estimates of problem discovery—you think you're done, but you're not. The beta-binomial model addresses this by explicitly modeling the variability of p. According to Ennis and Bi (1998, p. 391–392):

> The beta-binomial distribution is a compound distribution of the beta and the binomial distributions. It is a natural extension of the binomial model. It is obtained with the parameter p in the binomial distribution is assumed to follow a beta distribution with parameters a and b. ... It is convenient to reparameterize to $\mu = a/(a+b)$, $\theta = 1/(a+b)$ because parameters μ and θ are more meaningful. μ is the mean of the binomial parameter p. θ is a scale parameter which measures the variation of p.

Schmettow (2008) conducted Monte Carlo studies to examine the relative effectiveness of the beta-binomial and the small-sample adjustment procedure of Lewis (2001), referred to by Schmettow as the $\hat{p}_{GT\text{-}Norm}$ procedure, for five problem-discovery databases. The results of the Monte Carlo simulations were mixed. For three of the five cases, the beta-binomial had a better fit to the empirical Monte Carlo problem-discovery curves (with the binomial overestimating the percentage of problem discovery), but in the other two cases the $\hat{p}_{GT-Norm}$ provided a slightly better fit. Schmettow (2008) concluded:

- For small studies or at the beginning of a larger study ($n < 6$) use the $\hat{p}_{GT-Norm}$ procedure.
- When the sample size reaches 10 or more, switch to the beta-binomial method.
- Due to possible unmodeled heterogeneity or other variability, have a generous safety margin when usability is mission-critical.

Schmettow (2009, 2012) has also studied the use of the logit-normal binomial model for problem discovery. Like the beta-binomial, the logit-normal binomial has parameters both for the mean value of p and its variability. Also like the beta-binomial, the logit-normal binomial (zero-truncated to account for unseen events) appeared to perform well for estimating the number of remaining defects.

Borsci and his colleagues (Borsci et al., 2011, 2013) have reported some success in using bootstrapping to fit the parameters of an expanded binomial model (their Bootstrap Discovery Behavior, or BDB model). This research culminated in the description of a grounded procedure for interaction evaluation which monitors discovery likelihoods from samples to allow for critical decisions during interaction testing that respect the goals of the study and its allotted budget.

CAPTURE-RECAPTURE MODELS

Capture-recapture models have their origin in biology for the task of estimating the size of unknown populations of animals (Dorazio and Royle, 2003; Walia et al., 2008). As the name implies, animals captured during a first (capture) phase are marked and released, then during a second (recapture) phase the percentage of marked animals is used to estimate the size of the population. One of the earliest examples is from Schnabel (1938), who described a method to estimate the total fish population of a lake (but only claiming an order of magnitude of precision). Similar to the concerns of usability researchers about the heterogeneity of the probability of individual usability problems, an area of ongoing research in biological capture-recapture analyses is to model heterogeneity among individual animals (not all animals are equally easy to capture) and among sampling occasions or locations (Agresti, 1994; Burnham and Overton, 1979; Coull and Agresti, 1999; Dorazio, 2009; Dorazio and Royle, 2003).

During the time that usability engineers were investigating the statistical properties of usability problem discovery, software engineers, confronted with the similar problem of determining when to stop searching for software defects (Dalal and Mallows, 1990), were borrowing capture-recapture methods from biology (Briand et al., 2000; Eick et al., 1993; Walia and Carver, 2008; Walia et al., 2008). It may be that some version of a capture-recapture model, like the beta-binomial and logit-normal binomial models studied by Schmettow (2008, 2009) may provide highly accurate, though complex, methods for estimating the number of remaining usability problems following a formative usability study (or, more generally, the number of remaining events of interest following a formative user study).

WHY NOT USE ONE OF THESE OTHER MODELS WHEN PLANNING FORMATIVE USER RESEARCH?

To answer this question for analyses that use the average value of p across problems or participants, we need to know how robust the binomial model is with regard to the violation of the assumption of homogeneity. In statistical hypothesis testing, the concept of robustness comes up when comparing the actual probability of a Type I error with its nominal (target) value (Bradley, 1978). Whether *t*-tests and analyses of variance are robust against violations of their assumptions has been an ongoing debate among statisticians for over 50 years, and shows no signs of abating. As discussed in our other chapters, we have found the *t*-test to be very useful for the analysis of continuous and rating-scale data. Part of the reason for the continuing debate is the lack of a quantitative definition of robustness and the great variety of distributions that statisticians have studied. We can probably anticipate similar discussions with regard to the various methods available for modeling discovery in formative user research.

The combination adjustment method of Lewis (2001) is reasonably accurate for reducing values of *p* estimated from small samples to match those obtained with larger samples. This does not, however, shed light on how well the binomial model performs relative to Monte Carlo simulations of problem discovery based on larger-sample studies. Virzi (1992) noted the tendency of the binomial model to be overly optimistic when sample sizes are small—a phenomenon also noted by critics of its use (Caulton, 2001; Kanis, 2011; Schmettow, 2008, 2009; Woolrych and Cockton, 2001). But just how misleading is this tendency?

Fig. 7.6 and Table 7.9 show comparisons of Monte Carlo simulations (1000 iterations) and binomial model projections of problem discovery for five user studies (using the program from Lewis, 1994). Lewis (2001) contains descriptions of four of the studies (MACERR, VIRZI90, SAVINGS, and MANTEL). KANIS appeared in Kanis (2011).

Table 7.9 shows, for this set of studies, the mean maximum deviation of the binomial from the Monte Carlo curve was 0.102 (10.2%—with 90% confidence interval ranging from 3.4% to 17.0%). Given the total number of problems discovered in the usability evaluations, the mean deviation of expected (binomial) versus observed (Monte Carlo) was 4.81 problems (with 90% confidence interval ranging from 2.3 to 7.4). The sample size at which the maximum deviation occurred ("At *n* =") was, on average, 5.4 (with 90% confidence interval ranging from 4.0 to 6.8, about 4 to 7). There was a strong relationship between the magnitude of the maximum deviation and the sample size of the study ($r = 0.97$, 90% confidence interval ranging from 0.73 to 1.00, $t(3) = 6.9$, $p = 0.006$). The key findings are:

- The binomial model tends to overestimate the magnitude of problem discovery early in an evaluation, especially for relatively large-sample studies.
- The average sample size at which the maximum deviation occurs (in other words, the typical point of maximum over-optimism) is at the "Magic Number 5."
- On average, however, that overestimation appears not to lead to very large discrepancies between the expected and observed numbers of problems.

To summarize, the data suggest that although violations of the assumptions of the binomial distribution do affect binomial problem-discovery models, the conclusions drawn from binomial models tend to be robust against those violations. Practitioners need to exercise care not to claim too much accuracy when using these methods, but, based on the available data, can use them with reasonable confidence.

It would be helpful to the field of usability engineering, however, to have more large-sample databases of usability problem discovery to include in analyses of problem discovery. The best model to use likely depends on different characteristics of the problem discovery databases (e.g., large or small sample size, user test or heuristic evaluation, etc.). To conduct generalizable usability research on this topic, we need more examples. Usability practitioners who have large-sample problem-discovery databases should include these matrices in their reports (using a format similar to those of Virzi, 1990,

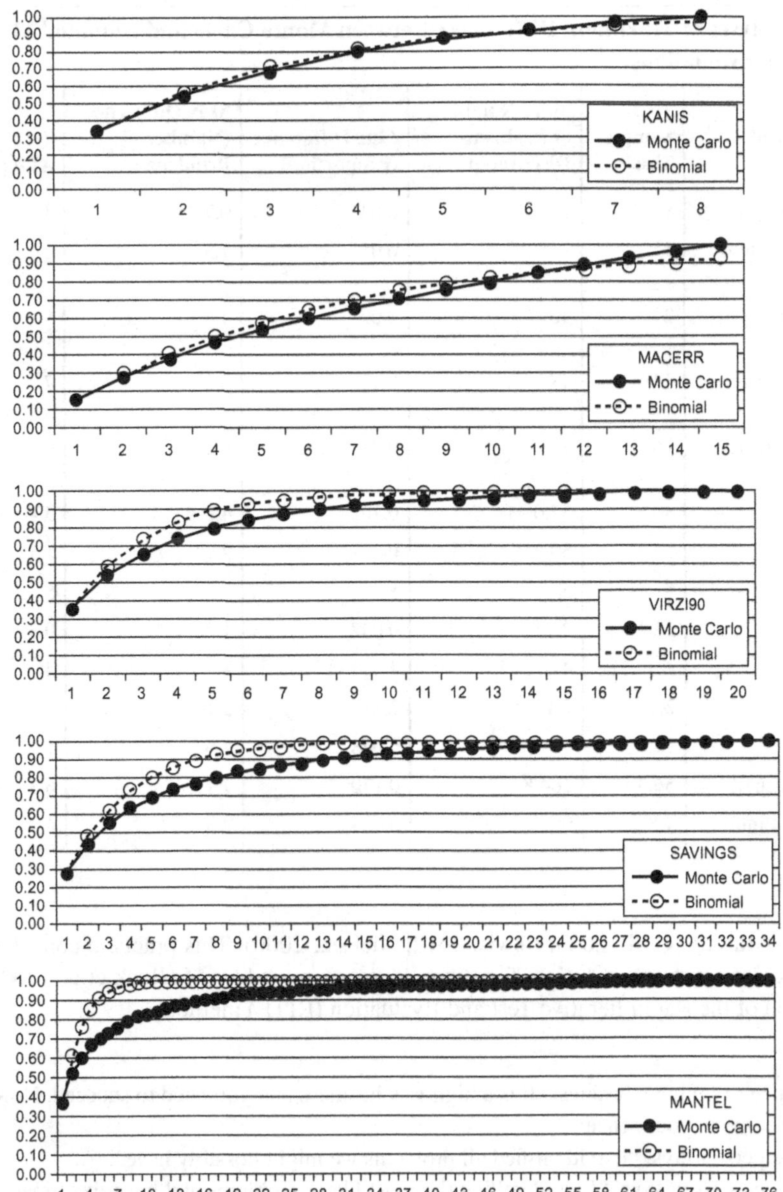

FIGURE 7.6 Monte Carlo and Binomial Problem Discovery Curves for Five Usability Evaluations.

Lewis, 2001, or Kanis, 2011), and should seek opportunities for external publication in venues such as the *Journal of Usability Studies*. Usability researchers should include any new problem discovery databases as appendices in their journal articles.

This type of research is interesting and important (at least, we think so), but it is also important not to lose sight of the practical aspects of formative user research, which is based on rapid iteration with

Table 7.9 Analyses of Maximum Differences Between Monte Carlo and Binomial Models for Five Usability Evaluations

Database/Type of Evaluation	Total Sample Size	Total Number of Problems Discovered	Max Difference (Proportion)	Max Difference (Number of Problems)	At n =	p
KANIS (Usability Test)	8	22	0.03	0.7	3	0.35
MACERR (Usability Test)	15	145	0.05	7.3	6	0.16
VIRZI90 (Usability Test)	20	40	0.09	3.6	5	0.36
SAVINGS (Heuristic Evaluation)	34	48	0.13	6.2	7	0.26
MANTEL (Heuristic Evaluation)	76	30	0.21	6.3	6	0.38
Mean	30.6	57.0	0.102	4.8	5.4	0.302
Std Dev	27.1	50.2	0.072	2.7	1.5	0.092
N Studies	5	5	5	5	5	5
sem	12.1	22.4	0.032	1.2	0.7	0.041
df	4	4	4	4	4	4
t-crit-90	2.13	2.13	2.13	2.13	2.13	2.13
d-crit-90	25.8	47.8	0.068	2.6	1.4	0.087
90% CI Upper Limit	56.4	104.8	0.170	7.4	6.8	0.389
90% CI Lower Limit	4.8	9.2	0.034	2.3	4.0	0.215

small samples (Barnum et al., 2003; Lewis, 2012; Nielsen, 2000). This practical consideration lies at the heart of iterative test and redesign, for example, as expressed by Medlock et al. (2005, p. 489) in their discussion of the Rapid Iterative Test and Evaluation (RITE) method:

> Pretend you are running a business. It is a high-risk business and you need to succeed. Now imagine two people come to your office:
>
> - The first person says, "I've identified all problems we might possibly have."
> - The second person says, "I've identified the most likely problems and have fixed many of them. The system is measurably better than it was."
>
> Which one would you reward? Which one would you want on your next project? In our experience, businesses are far more interested in getting solutions than in uncovering issues.

The beta-binomial, logit-normal binomial, and capture-recapture models may turn out to provide more accurate models than the simple binomial for the discovery of events of interest in user research.

This is an ongoing research topic in usability engineering, as well as in biology and software engineering. Time (and more Monte Carlo studies) will tell. For now, however, the most practical approach is to use the simple method taught at the beginning of this chapter unless it is mission critical to have a very precise estimate of the number of events available for discovery and the number of undiscovered events, in which case the usability testing team should include a statistician with a background in advanced discovery modeling.

Most usability practitioners do not need this level of precision in their day-to-day work. In fact, using the basic method (see Section "Using a Probabilistic Model of Problem Discovery to Estimate Sample Sizes for Formative User Research" at the beginning of this chapter), there is no need to attempt to compute any composite estimate of p or the number of undiscovered problems, thus avoiding the more complex issues discussed in the remainder of the chapter. This is analogous to the observation of Dorazio and Royle (2003) in their discussion of estimating the size of closed populations of animals (p. 357):

> Generally, we expect the MLE [maximum likelihood estimate] to perform better as the proportion of the population that is observed in a sample increases. The probability that a single individual detected with probability p is observed at least once in T capture occasions is $1 - (1 - p)^T$. Therefore, it is clear that increasing T is expected to increase the proportion of the population that is observed, even in situations where individual capture rates p are relatively small. In many practical problems T may be the only controllable feature of the survey, so it is important to consider the impact of T on the MLE's performance.

KEY POINTS

- The purpose of formative user research is to discover and enumerate the events of interest in the study (e.g., the problems that participants experience during a formative usability study).
- The most commonly used discovery model in user research is $P(x \geq 1) = 1 - (1 - p)^n$, derived from the binomial probability formula.
- The sample size formula based on this equation is $n = \ln(1 - P(x > 1))/\ln(1 - p)$, where $P(x > 1)$ is the discovery goal, p is the target probability of the events of interest under study (for example, the probability of a usability problem occurring during a formative usability test), and *ln* means to take the natural logarithm.
- Tables 7.1 and 7.2 are useful for planning formative user research.
- To avoid issues associated with estimates of p averaged across a set of problems or participants (which violates the homogeneity assumption of the binomial model), set p equal to the smallest level that you want to be able to discover (so you are setting rather than estimating the value of p).
- If you are willing to take some risk of overestimating the effectiveness of your research when n is small (especially in the range of $n = 4$–7), you can estimate p by averaging across a set of observed problems and participants.
- If this estimate comes from a small-sample study, then it is important to adjust the initial estimate of p (using the third formula in Table 7.10 below).
- For small values of p (around 0.10), a reasonable discovery goal is about 86%; for p between 0.25 and 0.50, the goal should be about 98%; for p between 0.10 and 0.25, interpolate.

Table 7.10 List of Sample Size Formulas for Formative Research

Name of Formula	Formula	Notes
The famous equation: $1-(1-p)^n$	$P(x \geq 1) = 1-(1-p)^n$	Computes the likelihood of seeing events of probability p at least once with a sample size of n—derived by subtracting the probability of 0 occurrences (binomial probability formula) from 1
Sample size for formative research	$n = \frac{\ln(1-P(x \geq 1))}{\ln(1-p)}$	The equation above, solved for n—to use, set $P(x > 1)$ to a discovery goal (for example, 0.85 for 85%) and p to the smallest probability of an event that you are interested in detecting in the study—*ln* stands for "natural logarithm"
Combined adjustment for small-sample estimates of p	$p_{adj} = \frac{1}{2}\left[\left(p_{est} - \frac{1}{n}\right)\left(1 - \frac{1}{n}\right)\right] + \frac{1}{2}\left[\frac{p_{est}}{(1+GT_{adj})}\right]$	From Lewis (2001)—two-component adjustment combining deflation and Good-Turing discounting: p_{est} is the estimate of p from the observed data; GT_{adj} is the number of problem types observed only once divided by the total number of problem types
Quick adjustment formula	$p_{adj} = 0.9(p) - 0.046$	Regression equation based on 19 usability studies—to use when problem-by-participant matrix not available
Binomial probability formula	$P(x) = \frac{n!}{(x!)(n-x)!} p^x (1-p)^{n-x}$	Probability of seeing exactly x events of probability p with n trials

- Note that the sample sizes for these goals are total sample sizes—the target sample size per iteration should be roughly equal to the total sample size divided by the planned number of iterations—if not equal, then use smaller sample sizes at the beginning of the study for more rapid iteration in the face of discovery of higher-probability events.
- You can use the adjusted estimate of p to roughly estimate the number of events of interest available for discovery and the number of undiscovered events.
- The limited data available indicates that even with the overestimation problem, the discrepancies between observed and expected numbers of problems are not large.
- Alternative models may provide more accurate estimation of problem discovery based on averages across problems or participants, but requires more complex modeling, so if a mission-critical study requires very high precision of these estimates, the team should include a statistician with a background in discovery modeling.
- Table 7.10 provides a list of the key formulas discussed in this chapter.

Table 7.11 Results from Lewis (2008) Formative Usability Study

	Problem												
Participant	**1**	**2**	**3**	**4**	**5**	**6**	**7**	**8**	**9**	**10**	**11**	**12**	**Count**	**Proportion**
1			X								X		2	0.17
2	X		X	X					X		X		5	0.42
3					X						X		2	0.17
4		X				X					X		3	0.25
5		X	X							X		X	4	0.33
6							X	X			X	X	4	0.33
Count	1	2	3	1	1	1	1	1	1	1	5	2	**20**	

Note: X = specified participant experienced specified problem

CHAPTER REVIEW QUESTIONS

1. Assume you need to conduct a single-shot (not iterative) formative usability study that can detect about 85% of the problems that have a probability of occurrence of 0.25 for the specific participants and tasks used in the study (in other words, not 85% of ALL possible usability problems, but 85% of the problems discoverable with your specific method). How many participants should you plan to run?
2. Suppose you decide that you will maintain your goal of 85% discovery, but need to set the target value of p to 0.20. Now how many participants do you need?
3. You just ran a formative usability study with 4 participants. What percentage of the problems of $p = 0.50$ are you likely to have discovered? What about $p = 0.01$; 0.90; 0.25?
4. Table 7.11 shows the results of a formative usability evaluation of an interactive voice response application (Lewis, 2008) in which six participants completed four tasks, with the discovery of twelve distinct usability problems. For this matrix, what is the observed value of p across these problems and participants?
5. Continuing with the data in Table 7.11, what is the adjusted value of p?
6. Using the adjusted value of p, what is the estimated total number of the problems available for discovery with these tasks and types of participants? What is the estimated number of undiscovered problems? How confident should you be in this estimate? Should you run more participants, or is it reasonable to stop?

ANSWERS TO CHAPTER REVIEW QUESTIONS

1. From Table 7.1, when $p = 0.25$, you need to run seven participants to achieve the discovery goal of 85% [$P(x \geq 1) = 0.85$]. Alternatively, you could search the row in Table 7.2 for $p = 0.25$ until you find the sample size at which the value in the cell first exceeds 0.85, which is at $n = 7$.

2. Tables 7.1 and 7.2 do not have entries for $p = 0.20$, so you need to use the formula below, which indicates a sample size requirement of 9 (8.5 rounded up).

$$n = \frac{\ln(1 - P(x \geq 1))}{\ln(1-p)} = \frac{\ln(1-0.85)}{\ln(1-0.20)} = \frac{\ln(0.15)}{\ln(0.80)} = \frac{-1.897}{-0.223} = 8.5$$

3. Table 7.2 shows that the expected percentage of discovery when $n = 4$ and $p = 0.50$ is 94%. For $p = 0.01$, it's 4% expected discovery; for $p = 0.90$, it's 100%; for $p = 0.25$, it's 68%.
4. For the results shown in Table 7.11, the observed average value of p is 0.28. You can get this by averaging the average values across the six participants (shown in the table), the average values across the twelve problems (not shown in the table), or dividing the number of filled cells by the total number of cells [20/(6 × 12) = 20/72 = 0.28].
5. To compute the adjusted value of p, use the formula below. The deflation component is (0.28 – 1/6)(1 – 1/6) = 0.11(0.83) = 0.09. Because there were 12 distinct problems, 8 of which occurred once, the Good-Turing component is 0.28/(1 + 8/12) = 0.28/1.67 = 0.17. The average of these two components—the adjusted value of p—is 0.13.

$$p_{adj} = \frac{1}{2}\left[\left(p_{est} - \frac{1}{n}\right)\left(1 - \frac{1}{n}\right)\right] + \frac{1}{2}\left[\frac{p_{est}}{(1 + GT_{adj})}\right].$$

6. The adjusted estimate of p (from Problem 5) is 0.13. We know from Table 7.11 that there were twelve problems discovered with six participants. To estimate the percentage of discovery so far, use $1 - (1 - p)^n$. Putting in the values of n and p, you get $1 - (1 - 0.13)^6 = 0.57$ (57% estimated discovery). If 57% discovery equals 12 problems, then the estimated number of problems available for discovery is 12/0.57 = 21.05 (rounds up to 22), so the estimated number of undiscovered problems is about 10. Because a sample size of 6 is in the range of over-optimism when using the binomial model, there are probably more than 10 problems remaining for discovery. Given the results shown in Table 7.9, it's reasonable to believe that there could be an additional two to seven undiscovered problems, so it's unlikely that there are more than 17 undiscovered problems. This low rate of problem discovery ($p_{adj} = .13$) is indicative of an interface in which there are few high-frequency problems to find. If there are resources to continue testing, it might be more productive to change the tasks in an attempt to create the conditions for discovering a different set of problems and, possibly, more frequently occurring problems.

REFERENCES

Agresti, A., 1994. Simple capture-recapture models permitting unequal catchability and variable sampling effort. Biometrics 50, 494–500.

Al-Awar, J., Chapanis, A., Ford, R., 1981. Tutorials for the first-time computer user. IEEE Trans. Prof. Commun. 24, 30–37.

Baecker, R.M., 2008. Themes in the early history of HCI—some unanswered questions. Interactions 15 (2), 22–27.

Barnum, C., Bevan, N., Cockton, G., Nielsen, J., Spool, J., Wixon, D., 2003. The "Magic Number 5": Is it enough for web testing? In: Proceedings of CHI 2003. Ft. Lauderdale, FL: ACM, pp. 698–699.

Boehm, B.W., 1981. Software Engineering Economics. Prentice-Hall, Englewood Cliffs, NJ.

Borsci, S., Londei, A., Federici, S., 2011. The bootstrap discovery behaviour (BDB): a new outlook on usability evaluation. Cogn. Process. 12, 23–31.

Borsci, S., MacRedie, R.D., Barnett, J., Martin, J., Kuljis, J., Young, T., 2013. Reviewing and extending the five-user assumption: A grounded procedure for interaction evaluation. ACM Trans. Comput. Hum. Interact. 20 (5), 1–23, Article 29.

Bradley, J.V., 1976. Probability; Decision; Statistics. Prentice-Hall, Englewood Cliffs, NJ.

Bradley, J.V., 1978. Robustness? Br. J. Math. Stat. Psychol. 31, 144–152.

Briand, L.C., El Emam, K., Freimut, B.G., Laitenberger, O., 2000. A comprehensive evaluation of capture-recapture models for estimating software defect content. IEEE Trans. Softw. Eng. 26 (6), 518–540.

Burnham, K.P., Overton, W.S., 1979. Estimation of the size of a closed population when capture probabilities vary among animals. Biometrika 65, 625–633.

Caulton, D.A., 2001. Relaxing the homogeneity assumption in usability testing. Behav. Inf. Technol. 20, 1–7.

Chapanis, A., 1988. Some generalizations about generalization. Hum. Factors 30, 253–267.

Coull, B.A., Agresti, A., 1999. The use of mixed logit models to reflect heterogeneity in capture-recapture studies. Biometrics 55, 294–301.

Cowles, M., 1989. Statistics in Psychology: An Historical Perspective. Lawrence Erlbaum, Hillsdale, NJ.

Dalal, S.R., Mallows, C.L., 1990. Some graphical aids for deciding when to stop testing software. IEEE J. Sel. Area. Comm. 8 (2), 169–175.

Dorazio, R.M., 2009. On selecting a prior for the precision parameter of Dirichlet process mixture models. J. Stat. Plan. Inference. 139, 3384–3390.

Dorazio, R.M., Royle, J.A., 2003. Mixture models for estimating the size of a closed population when capture rates vary among individuals. Biometrics 59, 351–364.

Dumas, J., 2007. The great leap forward: The birth of the usability profession (1988-1993). J. Usability Stud. 2 (2), 54–60.

Dumas, J., Sorce, J., Virzi, R., 1995. Expert reviews: How many experts is enough? In: Proceedings of the Human Factors and Ergonomics Society Thirty-Ninth Annual Meeting. Santa Monica, CA: Human Factors and Ergonomics Society, pp. 228–232.

Eick, S.G., Loader, C.R., Vander Wiel, S.A., Votta, L.G., 1993. How many errors remain in a software design document after inspection? In: Proceedings of the Twenty-Fifth Symposium on the Interface. Fairfax Station, V.A.: Interface Foundation of North America, pp. 195–202.

Ennis, D.M., Bi, J., 1998. The beta-binomial model: accounting for inter-trial variation in replicated difference and preference tests. J. Sens. Stud. 13, 389–412.

Faulkner, L., 2003. Beyond the five-user assumption: benefits of increased sample sizes in usability testing. Behav. Res. Methods Instrum. Comput. 35, 379–383.

Gould, J.D., 1988. How to design usable systems. In: Helander, M. (Ed.), Handbook of Human–Computer Interaction. North-Holland, Amsterdam, Netherlands, pp. 757–789.

Gould, J.D., Boies, S.J., 1983. Human factors challenges in creating a principal support office system: The Speech Filing System approach. ACM Trans. Inf. Syst. 1, 273–298.

Gould, J.D., Lewis, C., 1984. Designing for Usability: Key Principles and What Designers Think. IBM Corporation, Yorktown Heights, NY, (Tech. Report RC-10317).

Gould, J.D., Boies, S.J., Levy, S., Richards, J.T., Schoonard, J., 1987. The 1984 Olympic message system: a test of behavioral principles of system design. Commun. ACM 30, 758–769.

Guest, G., Bunce, A., Johnson, L., 2006. How many interviews are enough? An experiment with data saturation and variability. Field Methods 18 (1.), 59–82.

Hertzum, M., Jacobsen, N.J., 2001. The evaluator effect: A chilling fact about usability evaluation methods. Int. J. Hum. Comput. Interact. 13, 421–443.

Hornbæk, K., 2010. Dogmas in the assessment of usability evaluation methods. Behav. Inf. Technol. 29 (1), 97–111.

Hwang, W., Salvendy, G., 2007. What makes evaluators to find more usability problems?: A meta-analysis for individual detection rates. In: Jacko, J. (Ed.), Human-Computer Interaction, Part I, HCII 2007. Springer-Verlag, Heidelberg, Germany, pp. 499–507.

Hwang, W., Salvendy, G., 2009. Integration of usability evaluation studies via a novel meta-analytic approach: What are significant attributes for effective evaluation. Int. J. Hum. Comput. Interact. 25 (4), 282–306.

Hwang, W., Salvendy, G., 2010. Number of people required for usability evaluation: The 10 ± 2 rule. Commun. ACM 53 (5), 130–133.

Jelinek, F., 1997. Statistical Methods for Speech Recognition. MIT Press, Cambridge, MA.

Kanis, H., 2011. Estimating the number of usability problems. Appl. Ergon. 42, 337–347.

Kennedy, P. J., 1982. Development and testing of the operator training package for a small computer system. In: Proceedings of the Human Factors Society Twenty-Sixth Annual Meeting. Santa Monica, CA: Human Factors Society, pp. 715–717.

Law, E. L., Hvannberg, E. T., 2004. Analysis of combinatorial user effect in international usability tests. In: Proceedings of CHI 2004. Vienna, Austria: ACM, pp. 9–16.

Lewis, J. R., 1982. Testing small system customer set-up. In: Proceedings of the Human Factors Society Twenty-Sixth Annual Meeting. Santa Monica, CA: Human Factors Society.

Lewis, J.R., 1994. Sample sizes for usability studies: additional considerations. Hum. Factors 36, 368–378.

Lewis, J. R., 2000. Evaluation of problem discovery rate adjustment procedures for sample sizes from two to ten (Tech. Report 29.3362). Raleigh, NC: IBM Corp. Available from: http://drjim.0catch.com/pcarlo5-ral.pdf.

Lewis, J.R., 2001. Evaluation of procedures for adjusting problem-discovery rates estimated from small samples. Int. J. Hum. Comput. Interact. 13, 445–479.

Lewis, J. R., 2006a. Effect of level of problem description on problem discovery rates: Two case studies. In: Proceedings of the Human Factors, Ergonomics Fiftieth Annual Meeting. Santa Monica, C.A.: HFES, pp. 2567–2571.

Lewis, J.R., 2006b. Sample sizes for usability tests: mostly math, not magic. Interactions 13 (6), 29–33.

Lewis, J.R., 2008. Usability evaluation of a speech recognition IVR. In: Tullis, T., Albert, B. (Eds.), Measuring the User Experience, Chapter 10: Case Studies. Morgan-Kaufman, Amsterdam, Netherlands, pp. 244–252.

Lewis, J.R., 2012. Usability testing. In: Salvendy, G. (Ed.), Handbook of Human Factors and Ergonomics. 4th ed. John Wiley, New York, NY, pp. 1267–1312.

Lewis, J.R., Sauro, J., 2006. When 100% really isn't 100%: Improving the accuracy of small-sample estimates of completion rates. J. Usability Test. 3 (1), 136–150.

Lewis, J. R., Henry, S. C., Mack, R. L., 1990. Integrated office software benchmarks: a case study. In: Proceedings of the Third IFIP Conference on Human-Computer Interaction–INTERACT '90. Cambridge, UK: Elsevier Science Publishers, pp. 337–343.

Lindgaard, G., Chattratichart, J., 2007. Usability testing: What have we overlooked?" In: Proceedings of CHI 2007. San Jose, CA: ACM, pp. 1415–1424.

Manning, C.D., Schütze, H., 1999. Foundations of Statistical Natural Language Processing. MIT Press, Cambridge, MA.

Medlock, M.C., Wixon, D., McGee, M., Welsh, D., 2005. The rapid iterative test and evaluation method: Better products in less time. In: Bias, R.G., Mayhew, D.J. (Eds.), Cost-Justifying Usability: An Update for the Internet Age. Elsevier, Amsterdam, Netherlands, pp. 489–517.

Nielsen, J., 1992. Finding usability problems through heuristic evaluation. In: Proceedings of CHI '92. Monterey, CA: ACM, pp. 373–380.

Nielsen, J., 2000. Why you only need to test with 5 users. Alertbox, www.useit.com/alertbox/20000319.html. (Downloaded January 26, 2011.).

Nielsen, J., Landauer, T. K., 1993. A mathematical model of the finding of usability problems. In: Proceedings of INTERCHI'93. Amsterdam, Netherlands: ACM, pp. 206–213.

Nielsen, J., Molich, R., 1990. Heuristic evaluation of user interfaces. In: Proceedings of CHI '90. New York, NY: ACM, pp. 249–256.

Perfetti, C., Landesman, L., 2001. Eight is not enough. Available from: http://www.uie.com/articles/eight_is_not_enough/.

Sauro, J., 2014. The relationship between problem frequency and problem severity in usability evaluations. J. Usability Stud. 10 (1), 17–25.

Schmettow, M., 2008. Heterogeneity in the usability evaluation process. In: Proceedings of the Twenty-Second British HCI Group Annual Conference on HCI 2008: People and Computers XXII: Culture, Creativity, Interaction—Volume 1. Liverpool, UK: ACM, pp. 89–98.

Schmettow, M., 2009. Controlling the usability evaluation process under varying defect visibility. In: Proceedings of the 2009 British Computer Society Conference on Human-Computer Interaction. Cambridge, UK: ACM, pp. 188–197.

Schmettow, M., 2012. Sample size in usability tests. Commun. ACM 55 (4), 64–70.

Schnabel, Z.E., 1938. The estimation of the total fish population of a lake. Amer. Math. Monthly 45, 348–352.

Smith, D.C., Irby, C., Kimball, R., Verplank, B., Harlem, E., 1982. Designing the star user interface. Byte 7 (4), 242–282.

Spool, J., Schroeder, W., 2001. Testing websites: five users is nowhere near enough. In: CHI 2001 Extended Abstracts. New York, N.Y., AC.M., pp. 285–286.

Turner, C.W., Lewis, J.R., Nielsen, J., 2006. Determining usability test sample size. In: Karwowski, W. (Ed.), The International Encyclopedia of Ergonomics and Human Factors. CRC Press, Boca Raton, FL, pp. 3084–3088.

Virzi, R. A., 1990. Streamlining the design process: Running fewer subjects. In: Proceedings of the Human Factors Society Thirty-Fourth Annual Meeting. Santa Monica, CA: Human Factors Society, pp. 291–294.

Virzi, R.A., 1992. Refining the test phase of usability evaluation: how many subjects is enough? Hum. Factors 34, 457–468.

Virzi, R.A., 1997. Usability inspection methods. In: Helander, M.G., Landauer, T.K., Prabhu, P.V. (Eds.), Handbook of Human–Computer Interaction. second ed. Elsevier, Amsterdam, Netherlands, pp. 705–715.

Walia, G. S., Carver, J. C., 2008. Evaluation of capture-recapture models for estimating the abundance of naturally-occurring defects. In: Proceedings of ESEM '08. Kaiserslautern, Germany: ACM, pp. 158–167.

Walia, G. S., Carver, J. C., Nagappan, N., 2008. The effect of the number of inspectors on the defect estimates produced by capture-recapture models. In: Proceedings of ICSE '08. Leipzig, Germany: ACM, pp. 331–340.

Whiteside, J., Bennett, J., Holtzblatt, K., 1988. Usability engineering: Our experience and evolution. In: Helander, M. (Ed.), Handbook of Human–Computer Interaction. North-Holland, Amsterdam, Netherlands, pp. 791–817.

Williams, G., 1983. The Lisa computer system. Byte 8 (2), 33–50.

Wilson, E.B., 1927. Probable inference, the law of succession, and statistical inference. J. Am. Stat. Assoc. 22, 209–212.

Woolrych, A., Cockton, G., 2001. Why and when five test users aren't enough. In: Vanderdonckt, J., Blandford, A., Derycke, A. (Eds.), Proceedings of IHM–HCI 2001 Conference, vol. 2. Toulouse, France: Cépadèus Éditions, pp. 105–108.

Wright, P.C., Monk, A.F., 1991. A cost-effective evaluation method for use by designers. Int. J. Man Mach. Stud. 35, 891–912.

CHAPTER

STANDARDIZED USABILITY QUESTIONNAIRES

8

INTRODUCTION

WHAT IS A STANDARDIZED QUESTIONNAIRE?

A questionnaire is a form designed to obtain information from respondents. The items in a questionnaire can be open-ended questions, but are more typically multiple choice, with respondents selecting from a set of alternatives ("Please select the type of the car that you usually drive.") or points on a rating scale ("On a scale of 1–5, how satisfied were you with your recent stay at our hotel?"). This chapter does not provide comprehensive coverage of the techniques for designing ad hoc or special-purpose questionnaires. For information about those techniques, see references such as Parasuraman (1986), Kuniavsky (2003), Courage and Baxter (2005), Brace (2008), Tullis and Albert (2008), or Azzara (2010).

The primary focus of this chapter is to describe current standardized questionnaires designed to assess participants' satisfaction with the perceived usability of products or systems during or immediately after usability testing. A standardized questionnaire is a questionnaire designed for repeated use, typically with a specific set of questions presented in a specified order using a specified format, with specific rules for producing metrics based on the answers of respondents. As part of the development of standardized questionnaires, it is customary for the designer to report measurements of its reliability, validity, and sensitivity—in other words, for the questionnaire to have undergone psychometric qualification (Nunnally, 1978).

ADVANTAGES OF STANDARDIZED USABILITY QUESTIONNAIRES

Standardized measures offer many advantages to practitioners (Nunnally, 1978), specifically:

- *Objectivity*: A standardized measurement supports objectivity because it allows usability practitioners to independently verify the measurement statements of other practitioners.
- *Replicability*: It is easier to replicate the studies of others, or even one's own studies, when using standardized methods. For example, research on usability measurement has consistently shown that standardized usability questionnaires are more reliable than nonstandardized (ad hoc, homegrown) usability questionnaires (Hornbæk, 2006; Hornbæk and Law, 2007; Sauro and Lewis, 2009).
- *Quantification*: Standardized measurements allow practitioners to report results in finer detail than they could using only personal judgment. Standardization also permits practitioners to use powerful methods of mathematics and statistics to better understand their results (Nunnally, 1978). Although the application of statistical methods such as *t*-tests to multipoint scale data has a history of controversy (for details, see Chapter 9), our research and practice indicates that these methods work well with multipoint scale data.
- *Economy*: Developing standardized measures requires a substantial amount of work. However, once developed, they are very economical to reuse.

Quantifying the User Experience. http://dx.doi.org/10.1016/B978-0-12-802308-2.00008-4

- *Communication*: It is easier for practitioners to communicate effectively when standardized measures are available. Inadequate efficiency and fidelity of communication in any field impedes progress.
- *Scientific generalization*: Scientific generalization is at the heart of scientific work. Standardization is essential for assessing the generalization of results.

WHAT STANDARDIZED USABILITY QUESTIONNAIRES ARE AVAILABLE?

The earliest standardized questionnaires in this area focused on the measurement of computer satisfaction (e.g., the Gallagher Value of MIS Reports Scale and the Hatcher and Diebert Computer Acceptance Scale), but were not designed for the assessment of usability following participation in scenario-based usability tests. For a review of computer satisfaction questionnaires published between 1974 and 1988, see LaLomia and Sidowski (1990). The first standardized usability questionnaires appropriate for usability testing appeared in the late 1980s (Chin et al., 1988; Kirakowski and Dillon, 1988; Lewis, 1990a,b). Some standardized usability questionnaires are for administration at the end of a study. Others are for a quick, more contextual assessment at the end of each task or scenario.

Currently, the most widely used standardized usability questionnaires for assessment of the perception of usability at the end of a study (after completing a set of test scenarios) and those cited in national and international standards (ANSI, 2001; ISO, 1998) are:

- The Questionnaire for User Interaction Satisfaction (QUIS) (Chin et al., 1988)
- The Software Usability Measurement Inventory (SUMI) (Kirakowski and Corbett, 1993; McSweeney, 1992)
- The Post-Study System Usability Questionnaire (PSSUQ) (Lewis, 1990a, 1992, 1995)
- The System Usability Scale (SUS) (Brooke, 1996)

Questionnaires intended for administration immediately following the completion of a usability task or test scenario that is part of a larger overall study include:

- The After-Scenario Questionnaire (ASQ) (Lewis, 1990b, 1991)
- Expectation Ratings (ER) (Albert and Dixon, 2003)
- Usability Magnitude Estimation (UME) (McGee, 2003, 2004)
- The Single Ease Question (SEQ) (Sauro, 2010b; Tedesco and Tullis, 2006)
- The Subjective Mental Effort Question (SMEQ) (Sauro and Dumas, 2009)

RECOMMENDED QUESTIONNAIRES

For post-study, try the SUS; for post-task, the SEQ or SMEQ

If you've come to this chapter looking for a recommendation about what standardized usability questionnaires to use, here it is. For the reasons detailed in the body of the chapter, the SUS, originally developed to be a "quick and dirty" measure of satisfaction with usability, has become one of the most popular post-study standardized questionnaires with practitioners, and recent research indicates that although it is quick, it is far from "dirty."

Recent studies of post-task questionnaires generally support the use of single items, and the two best of those are the SEQ and the SMEQ. For pure simplicity and decent psychometric qualification, it's hard to beat the SEQ ("Overall, this task was Very Easy/Very Difficult.") If using the SEQ, however, we recommend using seven rather than five scale steps to increase its reliability of measurement (Lewis, 1993; Nunnally, 1978; Sauro and Dumas, 2009). For online questionnaires, consider using the SMEQ to take advantage of its slightly better sensitivity.

Keep in mind, however, that these are general recommendations. All of the standardized usability questionnaires have their strengths and weaknesses, and you might find that one of the others is a better fit for your specific situation.

ASSESSING THE QUALITY OF STANDARDIZED QUESTIONNAIRES: RELIABILITY, VALIDITY, AND SENSITIVITY

The primary measures of standardized questionnaire quality are reliability (consistency of measurement) and validity (measurement of the intended attribute) (Nunnally, 1978). There are several ways to assess reliability, including test–retest and split-half reliability. The most common method for the assessment of reliability is coefficient alpha (also known as Cronbach's alpha), a measurement of internal consistency (Cortina, 1993; Nunnally, 1978). Coefficient alpha can range from 0 (no reliability) to 1 (perfect reliability). Measures that can affect a person's future, such as IQ tests or college entrance exams, should have a minimum reliability of 0.90 (Nunnally, 1978). For other research or evaluation, measurement reliability in the range of 0.70–0.80 is acceptable (Landauer, 1997).

A questionnaire's validity is the extent to which it measures what it claims to measure. There are several distinct approaches to establishing validity.

Content validity depends on a rational (rather than empirical) assessment of where the items came from. Typically, content validity is assumed if the items were created by domain experts or selected from a literature review of existing questionnaires in the target or related domains.

Criterion-related validity refers to the relationship between the measure of interest and a different concurrent or predictive measure, typically assessed with the Pearson correlation coefficient (see Chapter 10 for information about correlations). These correlations do not have to be large to provide evidence of validity. For example, personnel selection instruments with validities as low as 0.30 or 0.40 can be large enough to justify their use (Nunnally, 1978).

Construct validity refers to the extent to which the items selected for a questionnaire align with the underlying constructs that the questionnaire was designed to assess. Questionnaire developers use statistical procedures (primarily factor analysis) to discover or confirm clusters of related items. When items cluster together in a reasonable (or expected) way, this is not only evidence of construct validity, but also is the basis for forming reasonable subscales. High correlations between measurements believed to tap into the same construct are evidence of convergent validity. Low correlations between variables that are not expected to measure the same construct are evidence of divergent validity (sometimes referred to as "discriminant validity").

If a questionnaire is reliable and valid, then it should also be sensitive to experimental manipulation. For example, responses from participants who experience difficulties working with Product A but find Product B easy to use should reflect Product B's relatively better usability through statistically significant differences. There is no direct measurement of sensitivity similar to those for reliability and validity. An indirect measure of sensitivity is the minimum sample size needed to achieve statistical significance when comparing products. Keeping everything else equal (i.e., the "true" difference in usability between Product A and Product B), the more sensitive a questionnaire, the smaller is the minimum required sample size.

OTHER ITEM CHARACTERISTICS

Number of scale steps

The question of the "right" number of scale steps often comes up when discussing questionnaire design. In general, more scale steps are better than fewer scale steps in standardized questionnaires, but with rapidly diminishing returns. For mathematical reasons (and confirmed by empirical studies), the reliability of individual items increases as a function of the number of steps (Nunnally, 1978). As the number of scale steps increases from 2 to 20, the increase in reliability is very rapid at first, tends to level off at about 7, and after 11 steps there is little gain in reliability from increasing the number. The number of steps in an item is very important for measurements based on a single item (thus our recommendation to use a 7-step version of the SEQ) but is less important when computing measurements over a number of items (as in the computation of an overall or subscale score from a multi-item questionnaire).

Availability of a neutral response

A question related to the number of scale steps is whether to provide a neutral response option. Neutral response options are a natural consequence of items with an odd number of steps—the neutral response is the option in the middle. Another way to allow a neutral response is with a Not Applicable (NA) choice on or off the scale. A neutral point allows respondents who honestly have no definite attitude with regard to the content of the item to indicate this. An even number of steps forces respondents to express a positive or negative attitude (although they always have the choice to refuse to respond to the item).

For questionnaire design in general, there is no simple recommendation for providing or withholding a neutral response option. Presser and Schuman (1980) found that offering a middle position increases the size of that category but "tends not to otherwise affect univariate distributions" (p. 70). As Parasuraman (1986, p. 399) puts it, "the choice between a forced or nonforced format must be made after carefully considering the characteristics unique to the situation."

The designers of most standardized usability questionnaires with items containing a relatively small number of steps have chosen an odd number of steps, implicitly indicating a belief that it is possible, perhaps even common, for respondents to have a neutral attitude when completing a usability questionnaire. An exception is earlier versions of the QUIS, which had ten steps ranging from 0 to 9. The current Version 7 has nine steps ranging from 1 to 9, with an NA choice (see http://lap.umd.edu/quis/).

Agreement versus bipolar scales

The two most common formats for standardized questionnaires designed to assess sentiments (such as satisfaction or perceived usability) are Likert-type agreement items and bipolar items. For a Likert-type agreement item, respondents indicate the extent to which they agree or disagree with a statement such as "I thought the system was easy to use" (e.g., Fig. 8.5). An analogous bipolar item would have respondents choose a number between opposing endpoints, for example, "Difficult to use" at one end and "Easy to use" on the other (e.g., Fig. 8.1). Both formats are in wide use, and both produce measurements that are amenable to similar psychometric analysis (e.g., factor analysis).

5.4 Messages which appear on screen:

	1	2	3	4	5	6	7	8	9		NA
Confusing	○	○	○	○	○	○	○	○	○	Clear	○

FIGURE 8.1 Sample QUIS item

DO ITEM FORMATS MATTER IN STANDARDIZED QUESTIONNAIRES?

Not really

There are many different ways to format the items in a standardized questionnaire—number of scale steps; availability of a neutral response; agreement versus bipolar structure; scale step labels (anchors) that are numeric only, text only, or a combination of numbers and text; vertical versus horizontal orientation, and so on. Regarding anchors, you can find advice to never show numbers and to limit the number of scale steps to five or fewer so you can anchor each step with verbal labels such as Strongly Disagree, Disagree, Neither Agree nor Disagree, Agree, and Strongly Agree (without numbers). Others advise anchoring just the endpoints and labeling each step with a number. Ultimately, however, none of these format differences matter when developing a standardized questionnaire. The important thing is to choose a format and use it consistently. The statistical mechanics of standardized questionnaire development don't care where the numbers came from. The proof of the psychometric quality of a questionnaire is in its measured reliability, validity (content, concurrent, and construct), and sensitivity—not the format of the items.

Norms

By itself a score, individual or average, anchored or unanchored, has no truly established meaning with regard to whether it is poor or good. Some sort of comparison is required. One way to provide meaning is through comparison using a statistical test, either with one set of data against a benchmark or comparison of two sets of data from, for example, different products or different user groups. Another is comparison with norms. The basis for norms is data collected from a representative group that has a sufficiently large sample size to establish percentiles. For a metric in which a low score is poorer than a high score, an observed score that is at the 5th percentile can be interpreted as markedly poorer than one that is at the 95th percentile. Thus, standardized questionnaires for which there is normative data are of greater value to practitioners than questionnaires that lack them. On the other hand, even when a questionnaire has norms, there is always a risk that the new sample doesn't match the normative sample, so it is important to understand where a questionnaire's norms came from. As Anastasi (1976, p. 89) stated, "Test norms are in no sense absolute, universal, or permanent."

POST-STUDY QUESTIONNAIRES

This section of the chapter contains information about a number of published post-study questionnaires, including the four "classic" standardized usability questionnaires (QUIS, SUMI, PSSUQ, and SUS) and two new short questionnaires (UMUX and UMUX-LITE).

QUIS (QUESTIONNAIRE FOR USER INTERACTION SATISFACTION)

Description of the QUIS

The QUIS was the first published of these four post-study questionnaires (Chin et al., 1988). According to the QUIS website (http://lap.umd.edu/QUIS/), a multidisciplinary team of researchers in the Human-Computer Interaction Lab (HCIL) at the University of Maryland at College Park created the QUIS to assess users' subjective satisfaction with specific aspects of the human–computer interface.

The current version of the QUIS (7.0) contains "a demographic questionnaire, a measure of overall system satisfaction along six scales, and hierarchically organized measures of nine specific interface factors (screen factors, terminology and system feedback, learning factors, system capabilities, technical manuals, online tutorials, multimedia, teleconferencing, and software installation)" (http://lap.umd.edu/QUIS/about.html, downloaded March 17, 2011). QUIS 7.0 is available in five languages (English, German, Italian, Brazilian Portuguese, and Spanish) and two lengths, short (41 items) and long (122 items), using 9-point bipolar scales for each item (Fig. 8.1). According to the QUIS website, most people use the short version, and only the sections that are applicable to the system or product.

To use the QUIS, it's necessary to license it from the University of Maryland's Office of Technology Commercialization. At the time of this writing, the fees are $50 for a student license, $200 for an academic or other nonprofit license, and $750 for a commercial license.

Psychometric evaluation of the QUIS

The primary source for information on the psychometric evaluation of the QUIS is Chin et al. (1988), which reported research on the QUIS Versions 3 through 5. The first long version of the QUIS had 90 items with:

- Bipolar scales numbered from 0 to 9
- All scales aligned with the negative response on the left
- An off-scale NA response option
- Five items for overall reaction to the system
- 85 component-related questions organized into 20 groups

The psychometric evaluation reported by Chin et al. (1988) was for a short form of Version 5 with 27 items covering overall reactions to the software, screen, terminology and system information, learning, and system capabilities. Data from 127 participants indicated an overall reliability of 0.94 (no information provided for the subscales). The participants completed four QUIS questionnaires each (one for a liked system, one for disliked, one for an MS-DOS command-line application, and one for any of several contemporary menu-driven applications). A factor analysis ($n = 96$) of the correlations among the items was, for the most part, consistent with expectation (an indication of construct validity), but with some notable exceptions—for example, the items hypothesized to be in a screen factor did not group as expected. Comparison of ratings for liked and disliked systems showed means for liked systems were higher (better) than those for disliked systems, providing some evidence of sensitivity.

Slaughter et al. (1994) compared responses from paper and online formats of the QUIS Version 5.5. Twenty participants used a word processor and then completed both questionnaires with one week between completions. Half of the participants completed the paper version first. Consistent with the findings of most research comparing paper and online questionnaire formats, there was no significant difference in user ratings.

SUMI (SOFTWARE USABILITY MEASUREMENT INVENTORY)

Description of the SUMI

The SUMI is a product of the Human Factors Research Group (HFRG) at University College Cork in Ireland, led by Jurek Kirakowski. Their first standardized questionnaire was the Computer Usability Satisfaction Inventory (CUSI—Kirakowski and Dillon, 1988). The CUSI was a 22-item questionnaire (overall reliability: 0.94) with two subscales, one for Affect (reliability of 0.91) and the other for Competence (reliability of 0.89).

Statements 1–10 of 50.	**Agree**	**Undecided**	**Disagree**
This software responds too slowly to inputs.	○	○	○

FIGURE 8.2 Sample SUMI item

In the early 1990s, the HFRG replaced the CUSI with the SUMI (Kirakowski, 1996). The SUMI is a 50-item questionnaire with a Global scale based on 25 of the items and five subscales for Efficiency, Affect, Helpfulness, Control, and Learnability (10 items each). As shown in the example in Fig. 8.2 (the first item of the SUMI), the items have three scale steps (Agree, Undecided, Disagree). The SUMI contains a mixture of positive and negative statements (e.g., "The instructions and prompts are helpful"; "I sometimes don't know what to do next with this system"). To view the entire SUMI, see http://sumi.ucc.ie/en/.

The SUMI is currently available in 14 languages (Dutch, English, Finnish, French, German, Greek, Italian, Norwegian, Polish, Portuguese, Slovenian, Spanish, Swedish, and Turkish). The use of the SUMI requires a license from the HFRG. At the time of writing this chapter, the HFRG offers three services with differing fees: offline (€1300), online (€650), and online student (no charge). For descriptions of the services and their requirements, see http://sumi.ucc.ie/pricing.html.

Psychometric evaluation of the SUMI

During its development, the SUMI underwent a considerable amount of psychometric development and evaluation (Kirakowski, 1996). The initial pool of SUMI items was 150. After content analysis by a group of ten HCI experts and software engineers, the remaining pool contained 75 items. A factor analysis of responses to these 75 items by 139 end users plus detailed item analysis led to the final 50 items and a decision to use a three-step agreement scale for the items. Factor analysis of an independent sample of 143 users who completed the 50-item version of the SUMI revealed five subscales:

- *Efficiency*: The degree to which the software helps users complete their work
- *Affect*: The general emotional reaction to the software
- *Helpfulness*: The degree to which the software is self-explanatory, plus the adequacy of help facilities and documentation
- *Control*: The extent to which the user feels in control of the software
- *Learnability*: The speed and facility with which users feel they mastered the system or learned to use new features

In addition to these subscales, there is a Global scale based on the 25 items that loaded most strongly on a general usability factor. After making a few minor changes to get to the final version of the SUMI, the researchers at HFRG collected over 1000 completed questionnaires from 150 systems, confirmed the preliminary factor structure, and used coefficient alpha to calculate the reliability of the SUMI scales. This large sample was also the start of one of the most powerful features of the SUMI—a normative database with which practitioners can compare their results to those of similar products and tasks, keeping in mind that variation in products and tasks can weaken the generalizability of norms (Cavallin et al., 2007). Table 8.1 shows the scales and their reliabilities.

Other psychometric features of the SUMI are scale standardization and sufficient data for item-level analysis. When analyzing raw SUMI scores (obtained by adding the responses for each item),

Table 8.1 Reliabilities of the SUMI Scales

SUMI Scale	Reliability	SUMI Scale	Reliability
Global	0.92	Helpfulness	0.83
Efficiency	0.81	Control	0.71
Affect	0.85	Learnability	0.82

HFRG uses proprietary formulas to convert raw scores to standard scores with a mean of 50 and standard deviation of 10. From the properties of the normal distribution, this means that about 68% of SUMI standard scores will fall between 40 and 60 and, by definition, those below 40 are below average and those above 60 are above average. Item-level analysis uses the standardization database to identify items that fall far away from the expected distribution of Agree, Undecided, and Disagree responses, which can sometimes provide more precise diagnostic information to use when interpreting the results.

The factor analyses conducted during the development and evaluation of the SUMI provide evidence of construct validity. There appear to be no published data on predictive or concurrent validity. A number of evaluations have demonstrated the sensitivity of the SUMI. For example, analysis of SUMI scores obtained from 94 users of word-processing systems showed significant differences in SUMI scale scores as a function of the system participants were using. There was also a significant interaction between the systems used and the different SUMI scale scores, which indicates that the various scales measured different aspects of user satisfaction with their systems (Kirakowski, 1996).

PSSUQ (POST-STUDY SYSTEM USABILITY QUESTIONNAIRE)

Description of the PSSUQ

The PSSUQ is a questionnaire designed to assess users' perceived satisfaction with computer systems or applications. The origin of the PSSUQ was an internal IBM project called SUMS (System Usability MetricS), headed by Suzanne Henry. The SUMS researchers created a large pool of items based on the contextual usability work of Whiteside et al. (1988). After content analysis by that group of human factors engineers and usability specialists, 18 items remained for the first version of the PSSUQ (Lewis, 1990a, 1992).

An independent IBM investigation into customer perception of usability of several different user groups indicated a common set of five usability characteristics (Doug Antonelli, personal communication, January 5, 1991). The 18-item version of the PSSUQ addressed four of those characteristics (quick completion of work, ease of learning, high-quality documentation and online information, and functional adequacy), but did not cover the fifth (rapid acquisition of productivity). The inclusion of an item to address this characteristic led to the second version of the PSSUQ, containing 19 items (Lewis, 1995). After several years' use of the PSSUQ Version 2, item analysis indicated that three questions in that version (3, 5, and 13) contributed relatively little to the reliability of the PSSUQ, resulting in a third version with 16 items (Lewis, 2002, 2012) after removing them (Fig. 8.3).

The Post-Study System Usability Questionnaire Version 3			Strongly agree 1	2	3	4	5	6	Strongly disagree 7		NA
1	Overall, I am satisfied with how easy it is to use this system.		O	O	O	O	O	O	O		O
2	It was simple to use this system.		O	O	O	O	O	O	O		O
3	I was able to complete the tasks and scenarios quickly using this system.		O	O	O	O	O	O	O		O
4	I felt comfortable using this system.		O	O	O	O	O	O	O		O
5	It was easy to learn to use this system.		O	O	O	O	O	O	O		O
6	I believe I could become productive quickly using this system.		O	O	O	O	O	O	O		O
7	The system gave error messages that clearly told me how to fix problems.		O	O	O	O	O	O	O		O
8	Whenever I made a mistake using the system, I could recover easily and quickly.		O	O	O	O	O	O	O		O
9	The information (such as online help, on-screen messages, and other documentation) provided with this system was clear.		O	O	O	O	O	O	O		O
10	It was easy to find the information I needed.		O	O	O	O	O	O	O		O
11	The information was effective in helping me complete the tasks and scenarios.		O	O	O	O	O	O	O		O
12	The organization of information on the system screens was clear.		O	O	O	O	O	O	O		O
13	The interface* of this system was pleasant.		O	O	O	O	O	O	O		O
14	I liked using the interface of this system.		O	O	O	O	O	O	O		O
15	This system has all the functions and capabilities I expect it to have.		O	O	O	O	O	O	O		O
16	Overall, I am satisfied with this system.		O	O	O	O	O	O	O		O

**The "interface" includes those items that you use to interact with the system. For example, some components of the interface are the keyboard, the mouse, the microphone, and the screens (including their graphics and language).*

FIGURE 8.3 The PSSUQ, Version 3

The instructions provided to participants in moderated usability tests before completing the PSSUQ are:

> This questionnaire gives you an opportunity to tell us your reactions to the system you used. Your responses will help us understand what aspects of the system you are particularly concerned about and the aspects that satisfy you. To as great an extent as possible, think about all the tasks that you have done with the system while you answer these questions. Please read each statement and indicate how strongly you agree or disagree with the statement. If a statement does not apply to you, select NA. Please write comments to elaborate on your answers. After you have completed this questionnaire, I'll go over your answers with you to make sure I understand all of your responses. Thank you! (Lewis, 1995, p. 77)

The PSSUQ items produce four scores—one overall and three subscales. The rules for computing them are:

- *Overall*: Average the responses for Items 1 through 16 (all the items)
- *System Quality (SysQual)*: Average Items 1 through 6
- *Information Quality (InfoQual)*: Average Items 7 through 12
- *Interface Quality (IntQual)*: Average Items 13 through 15

The resulting scores can take values between 1 and 7, with lower scores indicating a higher degree of satisfaction. Note that some practitioners prefer higher scores to indicate higher satisfaction, and switch the labels for "Strongly Agree" and "Strongly Disagree" (e.g., see Tullis and Albert, 2008, p. 140). From a strict interpretation of standardization, it's best to avoid this type of manipulation unless there is evidence that it does not affect the factor structure of the items. On the other hand, the various psychometric evaluations of the PSSUQ since its initial publication suggests that it should be robust against these types of minor manipulations (Lewis, 2002). If comparing across published studies, however, it is critical to know which item format was in use and, if necessary, to adjust one of the sets of scores. To reverse a 7-point PSSUQ score, subtract it from 7 and add 1. For example, that would change a 1 to a 7, a 7 to a 1, and would leave a 4 unchanged.

The PSSUQ does not require any license fee (Lewis, 2012—see p. 1303). Researchers who use it should cite their source (if using Version 3, please cite this book), and should make clear in their method sections which item format they used. Our experience has been that practitioners can add items to the questionnaires if there is a need, or, to a limited extent, can remove items that do not make sense in a specific context. Using the PSSUQ as the foundation for a special-purpose questionnaire, however, ensures that practitioners can score the overall PSSUQ scale and subscales, maintaining the advantages of standardized measurement.

Psychometric evaluation of the PSSUQ

The earliest versions of the PSSUQ showed very high scale and subscale reliability. For Version 3 (Lewis, 2002, 2012), the reliabilities are:

- Overall: 0.94
- SysQual: 0.90
- InfoQual: 0.91
- IntQual: 0.83

All of the reliabilities exceed 0.80, indicating sufficient reliability to be useful as standardized usability measurements (Anastasi, 1976; Landauer, 1997; Nunnally, 1978).

Factor analyses have been consistent across the various versions of the PSSUQ, indicating substantial construct validity (Lewis 1990a, 1992, 1995, 2002). In addition to construct validity, the PSSUQ has shown evidence of concurrent validity. For a sample of 22 participants who completed all PSSUQ (Version 1) and ASQ items in a usability study (Lewis et al., 1990), the overall PSSUQ score correlated highly with the sum of the ASQ ratings that participants gave after completing each scenario ($r(20) = 0.80$, $p = 0.0001$). The overall PSSUQ score correlated significantly with the percentage of successful scenario completions ($r(29) = -0.40$, $p = 0.026$). SysUse ($r(36) = -0.40$, $p = 0.006$) and IntQual ($r(35) = -0.29$, $p = 0.08$) also correlated with the percentage of successful scenario completions.

The PSSUQ has also proved to be sensitive to manipulation of variables that should affect it, and insensitive to other variables (Lewis, 1995, 2002). In the office applications study described by Lewis et al. (1990), three different user groups (secretaries without mouse experience, business professionals without mouse experience, and business professionals with mouse experience) completed a set of tasks with three different office systems in a between-subjects design. The overall scale and all three subscales indicated significant differences among the user groups, and InfoQual showed a significant system effect.

Analyses of variance conducted to investigate the sensitivity of PSSUQ measures using data collected from usability studies over five years (Lewis, 2002) indicated that the following variables significantly affected PSSUQ scores (as indicated by a main effect, an interaction with PSSUQ subscales, or both):

- Study (21 levels—the study during which the participant completed the PSSUQ)
- Developer (four levels—the company that developed the product under evaluation)
- Stage of development (two levels—product under development or available for purchase)
- Type of product (five levels—discrete dictation, continuous dictation, game, personal communicator, or pen product)
- Type of evaluation (two levels—speech dictation study or standard usability evaluation)

The following variables did not significantly affect PSSUQ scores:

- Gender (two levels—male or female)
- Completeness of responses to questionnaire (two levels—complete or incomplete)

For gender, neither the main effect nor the interaction was significant. The difference between the female and male questionnaire means for each of the PSSUQ scales was only 0.1. Although evidence of gender differences would not affect the usefulness of the PSSUQ, it's notable that the instrument does not appear to have an inherent gender bias.

Analysis of the distribution of incomplete questionnaires in the Lewis (2002) database showed that of 210 total questionnaires, 124 (59%) were complete and 86 (41%) were incomplete. Across the incomplete questionnaires, the completion rate for SysUse and IntQual items were, respectively, 95% and 97%; but the average completion rate for InfoQual items was only 60%. Thus, it appears that the primary cause of incomplete questionnaires was the failure to answer one or more InfoQual items. In most cases (78%), these incomplete questionnaires came from studies of speech dictation, which did not typically include documentation, or standard usability studies conducted on prototypes without documentation.

Unlike most attitude questionnaires with scales produced by summing the item scores, an early decision in the design of the PSSUQ was to average rather than sum item scores (Lewis, 1990a, 1992). The results of the analysis of completeness support this decision. As shown in Fig. 8.4, the completeness of responses to the questionnaire had neither a significant main effect nor a significant interaction. The difference between the complete and incomplete questionnaire means for each of the PSSUQ scales was only 0.1, and the changes cancelled out for the Overall score (means of 2.7 for both complete and incomplete questionnaires). This finding is important because it supports the practice of including rather than discarding partially completed PSSUQ questionnaires when averaging items to compute scale scores. The data do not provide information concerning how many items a participant might ignore and still produce reliable scores, but they do suggest that in practice participants typically complete enough items.

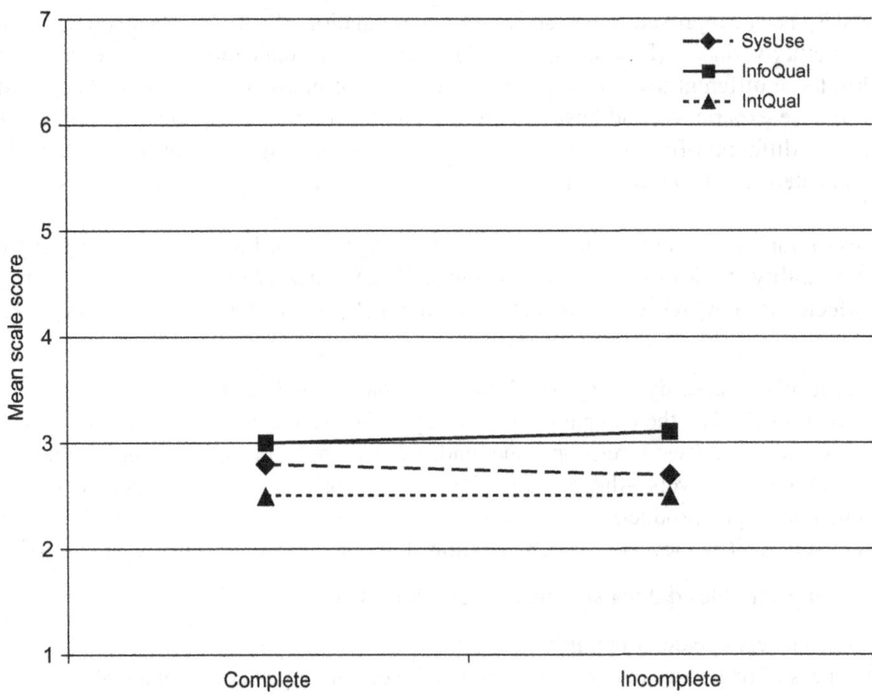

FIGURE 8.4 The PSSUQ completeness by factor interaction

PSSUQ norms and interpretation of normative patterns

PSSUQ item and scale norms correlate highly across versions. Table 8.2 shows the best available norms for Version 3 (means and 99% confidence intervals), using the original alignment such that lower scores are better than higher scores. Note that the means of all items and scales fall below the scale midpoint of 4 and, with the exception of Item 7 ("The system gave error messages that clearly told me how to fix problems"), the upper limits of the 99% confidence intervals are also below the scale midpoint. This demonstrates why for the PSSUQ (and probably for all similar questionnaires), practitioners should not use the scale midpoint exclusively as a reference from which to judge participants' perceptions of usability. The best reference is one's own data from similar evaluations with similar products, tasks, and users. If such data are not available, then the next best reference is the PSSUQ norms.

There are probably very few cases in which you could use these norms for direct assessment of a product under evaluation. These data came from a variety of sources that included different types of products at different stages of development and the performance of different types of tasks using systems that were available from the mid-1990s through the early 2000s. Despite this, there are some interesting and potentially useful patterns in the data, which have been consistent across the different versions of the questionnaire.

Ever since the introduction of the PSSUQ, the item that has received the poorest rating— averaging from 0.45 to 0.49 scale steps poorer than the next poorest rating—is Item 7 ("The system gave error messages that clearly told me how to fix problems"). Also, the mean ratings of InfoQual tend to be poorer than mean ratings of IntQual, with differences for the various versions ranging from 0.5 to 1.1.

Table 8.2 PSSUQ Version 3 Norms (Means and 99% Confidence Intervals)

Item	Item Text	Lower Limit	Mean	Upper Limit
1	Overall, I am satisfied with how easy it is to use this system.	2.60	2.85	3.09
2	It was simple to use this system.	2.45	2.69	2.93
3	I was able to complete the tasks and scenarios quickly using this system.	2.86	3.16	3.45
4	I felt comfortable using this system.	2.40	2.66	2.91
5	It was easy to learn to use this system.	2.07	2.27	2.48
6	I believe I could become productive quickly using this system.	2.54	2.86	3.17
7	The system gave error messages that clearly told me how to fix problems.	3.36	3.70	4.05
8	Whenever I made a mistake using the system, I could recover easily and quickly.	2.93	3.21	3.49
9	The information (such as online help, on-screen messages, and other documentation) provided with this system was clear.	2.65	2.96	3.27
10	It was easy to find the information I needed.	2.79	3.09	3.38
11	The information was effective in helping me complete the tasks and scenarios.	2.46	2.74	3.01
12	The organization of information on the system screens was clear.	2.41	2.66	2.92
13	The interface of this system was pleasant.	2.06	2.28	2.49
14	I liked using the interface of this system.	2.18	2.42	2.66
15	This system has all the functions and capabilities I expect it to have.	2.51	2.79	3.07
16	Overall, I am satisfied with this system.	2.55	2.82	3.09
Scale	**Scale Scoring Rule**			
SysUse	Average Items 1–6.	2.57	2.80	3.02
InfoQual	Average Items 7–12.	2.79	3.02	3.24
IntQual	Average Items 13–15.	2.28	2.49	2.71
Overall	Average Items 1–16.	2.62	2.82	3.02

These data are from 21 studies and 210 participants, analyzed at the participant level.

The consistently poor ratings for Item 7 suggest:

- If this happens in your data, it shouldn't surprise you.
- It really is difficult to provide usable error messages throughout a product.
- It will probably be worth the effort to focus on providing usable error messages.
- If you find the mean for this item to be equal to or less than the mean of the other items in InfoQual, you have probably achieved better-than-average error messages.

The consistent pattern of poor ratings for InfoQual relative to IntQual indicates that if you find this pattern in your data, you shouldn't conclude that you have terrible documentation or a great interface. If, however, this pattern appeared in the data for a first iteration of a usability study and the redesign focused on improving the quality of information, then any significant decline in the difference between InfoQual and IntQual would be suggestive of a successful intervention.

SUS (SYSTEM USABILITY SCALE)

Description of the SUS

Despite being a self-described "quick and dirty" usability scale, the SUS (Brooke, 1996), developed in the mid-1980s, has become a popular questionnaire for end-of-test subjective assessments of usability (Brooke, 2013; Lewis, 2012; Zviran et al., 2006). The SUS accounted for 43% of post-test questionnaire usage in a recent study of a collection of unpublished usability studies (Sauro and Lewis, 2009). Research conducted on the SUS (described later) has shown that although it is fairly quick, it is probably not all that dirty. The SUS (shown in Fig. 8.5) is a questionnaire with ten items, each with five scale steps. The odd-numbered items have a positive tone; the tone of the even-numbered items is negative.

According to Brooke (1996), participants should complete the SUS after having used the system under evaluation but before any debriefing or other discussion. Instructions to the participants should include asking them to record their immediate response to each item rather than thinking too much about them. The SUS scoring method requires participants to provide a response to all ten items. If for some reason participants can't respond to an item, they should select the center point of the scale.

The first step in scoring a SUS is to determine each item's score contribution, which will range from 0 to 4. For positively worded items (odd numbers), the score contribution is the scale position minus 1 ($x_i - 1$). For negatively worded items (even numbers), the score contribution is 5 minus the scale

The System Usability Scale
Standard Version

			Strongly disagree 1	2	3	4	Strongly agree 5
1	I think that I would like to use this system frequently.		O	O	O	O	O
2	I found the system unnecessarily complex.		O	O	O	O	O
3	I thought the system was easy to use.		O	O	O	O	O
4	I think that I would need the support of a technical person to be able to use this system.		O	O	O	O	O
5	I found the various functions in the system were well integrated.		O	O	O	O	O
6	I thought there was too much inconsistency in this system.		O	O	O	O	O
7	I would imagine that most people would learn to use this system very quickly.		O	O	O	O	O
8	I found the system very awkward to use.		O	O	O	O	O
9	I felt very confident using the system.		O	O	O	O	O
10	I needed to learn a lot of things before I could get going with this system.		O	O	O	O	O

FIGURE 8.5 The standard version of the SUS

Item 8 shown with "awkward" in place of the original "cumbersome."

position ($5 - x_i$). To get the overall SUS score, multiply the sum of the item score contributions by 2.5. Thus, overall SUS scores range from 0 to 100 in 2.5 point increments. A free spreadsheet for computing SUS scores is available at http://www.measuringux.com/SUS_Calculation.xls. A more comprehensive spreadsheet that scores the SUS, identifies unusual responses, and provides a normalized score and "grade" is available at www.measuringu.com/products/SUSpack.

The SUS does not require any license fee. "The only prerequisite for its use is that any published report should acknowledge the source of the measure" (Brooke, 1996, p. 194). See the References section of this chapter for the information needed to acknowledge Brooke (1996) as the source of the SUS.

Since its initial publication, some researchers have proposed minor changes to the wording of the items. For example, Finstad (2006) and Bangor et al. (2008) recommend replacing "cumbersome" with "awkward" in Item 8. The original SUS items refer to "system," but substituting the word "website" or "product," or using the actual website or product name seems to have no effect on the resulting scores (Lewis and Sauro, 2009). Of course, any of these types of minor substitutions should be consistent across the items.

Although there have been a number of translations of the SUS (Dutch, Finnish, French, Italian, German, Slovene, Spanish, Swedish), most have been ad hoc (Brooke, 2013), with only a few translations having undergone any psychometric evaluation. Sauro (2011a) described a Dutch translation that had internal reliability similar to the standard English version. Blažica and Lewis (2015) published a Slovene translation that had acceptable reliability, evidence of concurrent validity with likelihood-to-recommend ratings, and sensitivity to frequency of use.

Psychometric evaluation of the SUS

The ten SUS items were selected from a pool of 50 potential items, based on the responses of 20 people who used the full set of items to rate two software systems, one of which was relatively easy to use, and the other relatively difficult. The items selected for the SUS were those that provided the strongest discrimination between the systems. In the original paper by Brooke (1996), he reported strong correlations among the selected items (absolute values of r ranging from 0.7 to 0.9), but he did not report any measures of reliability or validity, referring to the SUS as a quick and dirty usability scale. For these reasons, he cautioned against assuming that the SUS was any more than a unidimensional measure of usability (p. 193): "SUS yields a single number representing a composite measure of the overall usability of the system being studied. Note that scores for individual items are not meaningful on their own." Given data from only 20 participants, this caution was appropriate at that time.

An early assessment of the SUS indicated a reliability of 0.85 (Lucey, 1991). More recent estimates using larger samples have consistently found its reliability to be at or just over 0.90 (Bangor et al., 2008; Lewis et al., 2015a,b; Lewis and Sauro, 2009).

A variety of studies have provided evidence of the validity and sensitivity of the SUS, including:

- Bangor et al. (2008) found the SUS to be sensitive to differences among types of interfaces and changes made to a product. They also found significant concurrent validity with a single 7-point rating of user friendliness ($r = 0.806$).
- Lewis and Sauro (2009) reported that the SUS was sensitive to the differences in a set of 19 usability tests.
- Kortum and Sorber (2015) found differences in the SUS ratings of mobile device operating systems (iOS and Android) and types of devices (phones and tablets).
- SUS scores are sensitive to successful task completion, with those completing tasks successfully providing higher scores (Kortum and Peres, 2014; Lewis et al., 2015a; Peres et al., 2013).
- Bangor et al. (2013) found a significant relationship between SUS scores and a composite metric based on business indicators of success in the marketplace.

- There is also evidence from multiple sources that the SUS is generally sensitive to differences in the magnitude of users' experience with a product such that users with more product experience tend to provide more favorable ratings (Borsci et al., 2015; Kortum and Johnson, 2013; Lewis et al., 2015b; McLellan et al., 2012).

In an ambitious investigation of the psychometric properties of the SUS, Bangor et al. (2008) conducted a factor analysis of 2324 SUS questionnaires and concluded there was only one significant factor, consistent with prevailing practitioner belief and practice. The method applied by Bangor et al., however, did not exclude the possibility of additional structure. Lewis and Sauro (2009) reanalyzed the data from Bangor et al. and an independent set of SUS cases from Sauro and Lewis (2009), and concluded that the factor structures of the two datasets converged at a two-factor solution. Later in the same year, Borsci et al. (2009), using a different measurement model and an independent set of data (196 Italian cases), arrived at the same conclusion—a two-factor solution with Items 1, 2, 3, 5, 6, 7, 8, and 9 on one factor and Items 4 and 10 on the other.

Based on the content of the items, Lewis and Sauro (2009) named the 8-item subscale "Usable" and the 2-item subscale "Learnable." Using the data from Sauro and Lewis, the subscale reliabilities (coefficient alpha) were 0.91 for Usable and 0.70 for Learnable. An analysis of variance on the data showed a significant study by scale interaction—evidence of scale sensitivity. To make the Usable and Learnable scores comparable with the Overall SUS score so they also range from 0 to 100, just multiply their summed score contributions by 3.125 for Usable and 12.5 for Learnable.

Analyses conducted since 2009 (Lewis et al., 2013, 2015b; Sauro and Lewis, 2011; and a number of unpublished analyses) have typically resulted in a two-factor structure but have not replicated the item-factor alignment that seemed apparent in 2009. The more recent analyses have been somewhat consistent with a general alignment of positive- and negative-tone items on separate factors—the type of unintentional structure that can occur with sets of mixed-tone items (Barnette, 2000; Blažica and Lewis, 2015; Cheung and Rensvold, 2000; Davis, 1989; Grimm and Church, 1999; Ibrahim, 2001; Kortum and Sorber, 2015; Nunnally, 1978; Quilty et al., 2006; van de Vijver and Leung, 2001).

Borsci et al. (2015) found that the structure of the SUS was unidimensional when administered to people who had less experience with an e-learning tool, but was bidimensional (with Usable and Learnable factors) when administered to users with more experience. Given the contradictory findings since 2009, we advise practitioners to be cautious when considering the use of the Usable and Learnable subscales, especially if the users in the study do not have significant experience using the product. There is a clear need for more research on the conditions under which the extraction of Usable and Learnable subscales would be reasonable.

WHERE DID THE 3.125 AND 12.5 MULTIPLIERS COME FROM?

Getting SUS subscales to range from 0 to 100

The standard SUS raw score contributions can range from 0 to 40 (ten items with five scale steps ranging from 0 to 4). To get the multiplier needed to increase the apparent range of the summed scale to 100, divide 100 by the maximum sum of 40, which equals 2.5 $\left(\frac{100}{40}=2.5\right)$. Because the Usable subscale has eight items, its range for summed score contributions is 0–32, so its multiplier is $\frac{100}{32}=3.125$. Following the same process for the Learnable subscale, you get a multiplier of 12.5 $\left(\frac{100}{8}=12.5\right)$.

SUS norms

The recent research on the psychometric properties of the SUS has also provided some normative data. For example, Table 8.3 shows some basic statistical information about the SUS from the data reported by Bangor et al. (2008) and Lewis and Sauro (2009).

Of particular interest is that the central tendencies of the Bangor et al. (2008) and the Lewis and Sauro (2009) Overall SUS distributions were not identical, with a mean difference of 8.0. The mean of the Bangor et al. distribution of Overall SUS scores was 70.1, with a 99.9% confidence interval ranging from 68.7 to 71.5. The mean of our Overall SUS data was 62.1, with a 99.9% confidence interval ranging from 58.3 to 65.9. Because the confidence intervals did not overlap, this difference in central tendency as measured by the mean was statistically significant ($p < 0.001$). There were similar differences (with the Bangor et al. scores consistently higher) for the first quartile (10 points), median (10 points), and third quartile (12.5 points). The distributions' measures of dispersion (variance, standard deviation, and interquartile range) were close in value. The difference in central tendency between the datasets is most likely due to the different types of users, products, and tasks included in the datasets.

Sauro (2011a) analyzed data from 3187 completed SUS questionnaires. Fig. 8.6 shows the distribution of the scores.

Table 8.3 SUS Statistics from Bangor et al. (2008) and Lewis and Sauro (2009)

	Bangor et al.	Lewis and Sauro		
Statistic	**Overall**	**Overall**	**Usable**	**Learnable**
N	2324	324	324	324
Minimum	0	7.5	0	0
Maximum	100	100	100	100
Mean	70.14	62.10	59.44	72.72
Variance	471.32	494.38	531.54	674.47
Standard Deviation	21.71	22.24	23.06	25.97
Standard error of the mean	0.45	1.24	1.28	1.44
Skewness	NA	−0.43	−0.38	−0.80
Kurtosis	NA	−0.61	−0.60	−0.17
First quartile	55.00	45.00	40.63	50.00
Median	75.00	65.00	62.50	75.00
Third quartile	87.50	75.00	78.13	100.00
Interquartile range	32.50	30.00	37.50	50.00
Critical z (99.9%)	3.09	3.09	3.09	3.09
Critical d (99.9%)	1.39	3.82	3.96	4.46
99.9% confidence interval upper limit	71.53	65.92	63.40	77.18
99.9% confidence interval lower limit	68.75	58.28	55.48	68.27

Note: *Add and subtract critical* d *(computed by multiplying the critical* z *and the standard error) from the mean to get the upper and lower bounds of the 99.9% confidence interval.*

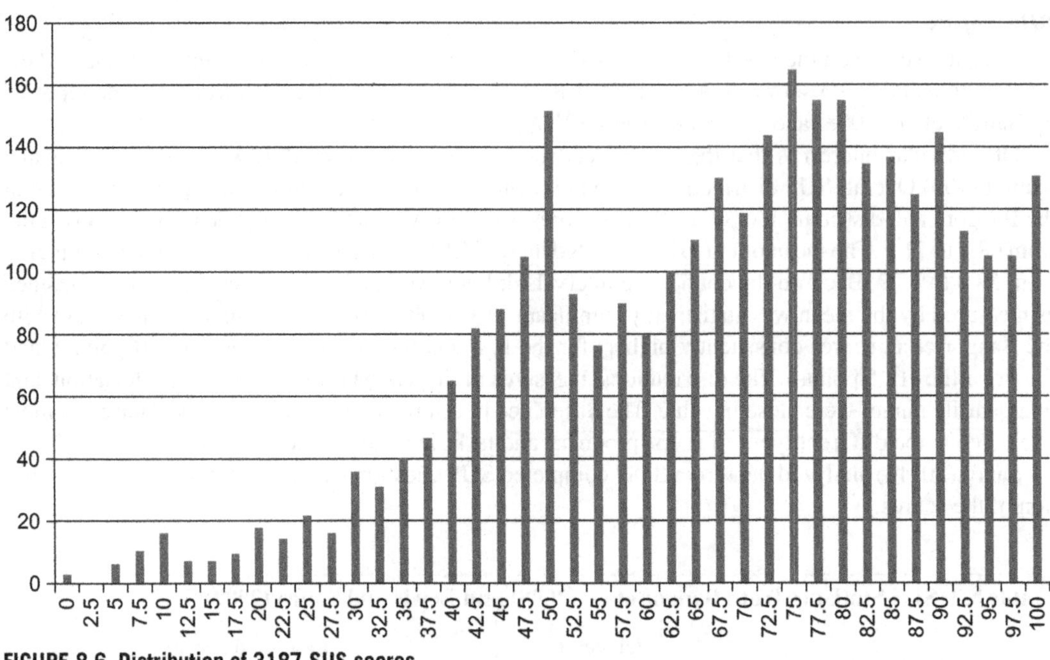

FIGURE 8.6 Distribution of 3187 SUS scores

The individual responses have a clear negative skew. There are also peaks in scores at 50, around 75, 90, and at 100. There are two important things to keep in mind when looking at this frequency distribution. First, although there are a finite number of possible responses, the combination of average SUS scores for a study is virtually infinite. For example, the frequency distribution in Fig. 8.6 has data from 112 different studies. Of these, only five pairs of studies, 10 in total (9%), have the same average SUS score. Note that due to the discrete nature of multipoint scale measures, the median is restricted to about 80 values—which is one of the key reasons to assess the central tendency of multipoint scale scores with the mean rather than the median (Lewis, 1993).

Second, the skew doesn't hurt the accuracy of statistical calculations or the computation of the mean. As discussed in previous chapters, even though the distribution of individual responses is skewed and not normally distributed, we typically base our statistical calculations on the distribution of the study means, not the individual scores. Normality does become an issue when we want to convert raw SUS scores into percentile ranks, but fortunately, a transformation procedure is available which adjusts SUS scores to a normal distribution (see the sidebar).

GETTING NORMAL

Converting SUS scores to percentile ranks—from the files of Jeff Sauro

Using data from 446 studies and over 5000 individual SUS responses, I've found the overall mean score of the SUS is 68 with a standard deviation of 12.5. To get a better sense of how to use that information to interpret a raw SUS score, you can use Table 8.4 to convert the raw score into a percentile rank. In essence, this percentile rank tells you how usable

Table 8.4 Percentile Ranks for Raw SUS Scores

Raw SUS Score	Percentile Rank (%)	Raw SUS Score	Percentile Rank (%)
5	0.3	69	53
10	0.4	70	56
15	0.7	71	60
20	1.0	72	63
25	1.5	73	67
30	2	74	70
35	4	75	73
40	6	76	77
45	8	77	80
50	13	78	83
55	19	79	86
60	29	80	88
65	41	85	97
66	44	90	99.80
67	47	95	99.9999
68	50	100	100

your application is relative to the other products in the total database. The distribution of SUS data is slightly negatively skewed, so the table entries were transformed prior to conversion (specifically, a logarithmic transformation on reflected scores—see Sauro, 2011a for details). To use the table, start in the "Raw SUS Score" column and find the score closest to the one for your study, then examine the percentile rank column to find the percentage of products that fall below your score. For example, a SUS score of 66 has a percentile rank of 44%. This means that a score of 66 is considered more usable than 44% of the products in the Sauro (2011a) database (and less usable than 56%). Anything with a percentile below 50% is, by definition, below average, and anything above 50% is above average.

With the advent of large-sample datasets of SUS scores, there have been a few attempts to provide a "grading scale" for their interpretation. For example, Bangor et al. (2009) added a 7-point scale user-friendliness item as an 11th question to nearly a thousand SUS questionnaires ("Overall, I would rate the user-friendliness of this product as:" (from left to right) "Worst Imaginable; Awful; Poor; OK; Good; Excellent; Best Imaginable"). They developed a grading scale in which SUS scores below 60 were an "F," between 60 and 69 were a "D," between 70 and 79 were a "C," between 80 and 89 were a "B," and 90 and above were an "A."

In the spirit of the relative (as opposed to an absolute) measurement of usability, we prefer to grade on a curve in which a SUS score of 68 is at the center of the range for a "C"—after all, from the data we have, that's the exact average, but in the Bangor et al. (2009) grading scheme, it's a "D." It's also virtually impossible to get an "A" following the grade assignment suggested by Bangor et al., reminding us of those feared college professors who never gave an "A." Although it does happen that individual participants give SUS scores of 100, in a review of 241 studies (Sauro, 2011a), only two—less than 1%—had mean SUS scores above 90. To provide a fairer grading assignment, we used percentiles like those calculated for Table 8.4 to develop the curved grading scale shown in Table 8.5 for mean SUS scores computed from a set of individual SUS scores for a study (keeping in mind the importance of computing confidence intervals to establish the range of likely mean SUS scores for any given sample of individual SUS scores—such a confidence interval might indicate a grade range rather than a single grade).

To get to a finer grain of analysis, Sauro (2011a) organized SUS data by the type of interface. To generate a global benchmark for SUS, he combined the Bangor et al. (2008), Sauro (2011a), and Tullis and Albert (2008) datasets. The Tullis data included 129 SUS surveys from the companion website for Tullis and Albert (2008), www.MeasuringUserExperience.com (which in turn was obtained from reviewing studies in the ACM portal and other publications for SUS). The means by interface type for the Bangor et al. data were provided by Philip Kortum (personal communication, 1/12/2011).

In total, this analysis included data from 446 surveys/usability studies. A survey/study has multiple respondents (most have been between 10 and 30 respondents and some have more than 300). Table 8.6 is a summary table of benchmarks by interface type created by weighting the means and standard deviations based on the sample size. As shown in the row labeled "Global," the weighted mean from all three sources was an average of 68 with a standard deviation of 12.5.

Kortum and Bangor (2013) published SUS ratings for a set of 14 everyday products from a survey of more than 1000 users. Respondents were asked to assess usability based not on a particular task, but on their overall integrated experience with the products (Grier et al., 2013) for the products with which they had some familiarity. The products included in the survey were either top products in their categories (e.g., Google search) or class-based categories (e.g., microwave ovens). Table 8.7 shows the mean SUS for each product along with 99% confidence intervals and associated grade ranges from

Table 8.5 Curved Grading Scale Interpretation of SUS Scores

SUS Score Range	Grade	Percentile Range
84.1–100	A+	96–100
80.8–84.0	A	90–95
78.9–80.7	A−	85–89
77.2–78.8	B+	80–84
74.1–77.1	B	70–79
72.6–74.0	B−	65–69
71.1–72.5	C+	60–64
65.0 –71.0	C	41–59
62.7–64.9	C−	35–40
51.7–62.6	D	15–34
0.0–51.6	F	0–14

Table 8.6 SUS Benchmarks by Interface Type

Category	Description	Mean	*SD*	*N*	99% Confidence Interval	
					Lower Limit	Upper Limit
Global	Data from the entire set of 446 surveys/studies	68.0	12.5	446	66.5	69.5
B2B	Enterprise software application such as accounting, HR, CRM, and order-management systems	67.6	9.2	30	63.0	72.2
B2C	Public facing mass-market consumer software such as office applications, graphics applications, and personal finance software	74.0	7.1	19	69.3	78.7
Web	Public facing large scale websites (airlines, rental cars, retailers, financial service) and intranets	67.0	13.4	174	64.4	69.6
Cell	Cell phone equipment	64.7	9.8	20	58.4	71.0
HW	Hardware such as phones, modems, and Ethernet-cards	71.3	11.1	26	65.2	77.4
Internal SW	Internal productivity software such as customer service and network operations applications	76.7	8.8	21	71.2	82.2
IVR	Interactive voice response (IVR) systems, both phone and speech based	79.9	7.6	22	75.3	84.5
Web/IVR	A combination of web-based and interactive voice response systems	59.2	5.5	4	43.1	75.3

Table 8.7 SUS Ratings for Everyday Products

Product	99% CI Lower Limit	Mean	99% CI Upper Limit	Sauro–Lewis Grade	Std Dev	*n*
Excel	55.3	56.5	57.7	D	18.6	866
GPS	68.5	70.8	73.1	B− to C	18.3	252
DVR	71.9	74.0	76.1	B+ to C+	17.8	276
PPT	73.5	74.6	75.7	B− to B	16.6	867
Word	75.3	76.2	77.1	B	15.0	968
Wii	75.2	76.9	78.6	B to B+	17.0	391
iPhone	76.4	78.5	80.6	B to A−	18.3	292
Amazon	80.8	81.8	82.8	A	14.8	801
ATM	81.1	82.3	83.5	A	16.1	731
Gmail	82.2	83.5	84.8	A to A+	15.9	605
Microwaves	86.0	86.9	87.8	A+	13.9	943
Landline	86.6	87.7	88.8	A+	12.4	529
Browser	87.3	88.1	88.9	A+	12.2	980
Google search	92.7	93.4	94.1	A+	10.5	948

our curved grading scale (Table 8.5). These data can be of value to practitioners who are working with these or similar products and need to set custom benchmarks rather than using the more general values provided in Table 8.5.

Does it hurt to be positive? evidence from an alternate form of the SUS

Consider the following statement (Travis, 2008):

> There are many issues to consider when designing a good questionnaire, and few usability questionnaires are up to scratch. For example, we've known for over 60 years that you need to avoid the "acquiescence bias": the fact that people are more likely to agree with a statement than disagree with it (Cronbach, 1946). This means that you need to balance positively-phrased statements (such as "I found this interface easy to use") with negative ones (such as "I found this interface difficult to navigate"). So it's surprising that two commonly used questionnaires in the field of usability—the Usefulness, Satisfaction, and Ease-of-Use (USE) questionnaire and the Computer System Usability Questionnaire (CSUQ)—suffer from just this problem: every question in both of these questionnaires is positively phrased, which means the results from them are biased towards positive responding.

Travis (2008) isn't alone in his criticism of usability questionnaires that have items with consistent positive tone—in other words, questionnaires that have all items express a positive thought with which respondents are to agree or disagree. However, the decision to vary or not to vary item tone is not simple. There are factors other than response biases that developers of standardized usability questionnaires must take into account.

THE DECISION TO USE A CONSISTENTLY POSITIVE TONE IN THE IBM QUESTIONNAIRES

Why not systematically vary the tone of items in usability questionnaires?—from the files of Jim Lewis

When I was working with the team that produced the PSSUQ and ASQ in 1988, we had quite a bit of discussion regarding whether to use a varied or consistent item tone. Ultimately, we decided to be consistently positive, even though that was not the prevailing practice in questionnaire development. In 1999, I wrote the following in response to criticisms of that decision (Lewis, 1999, pp. 1025–1026):

> *Probably the most common criticism I've seen of the IBM questionnaires is that they do not use the standard control for potential response bias. Our rationale in consistently aligning the items was to make it as easy as possible for participants to complete the questionnaire. With consistent item alignment, the proper way to mark responses on the scales is clearer and requires less interpretive effort on the part of the participant. Even if this results in some response bias, the typical use of usability questionnaires is to compare systems or experimental conditions. In this context of use, any systematic response bias will cancel out across comparisons.*
>
> *I have seen the caution expressed that a frustrated or lazy participant will simply choose one end point or the other and mark all items the same way. With all items aligned in the same way, this could lead to the erroneous conclusion that the participant held a strong belief (either positive or negative) regarding the usability of the system. With items constructed in the standard way, such a set of responses would indicate a neutral opinion. Although this characteristic of the standard approach is appealing, I have seen no evidence of such participant behavior, at least not in the hundreds of PSSUQs that I have personally scored. I am sure it is a valid concern in*

other areas of psychology—especially some areas of clinical or counseling psychology, where the emphasis is on the individual rather than group comparisons. It is possible that constructing a usability assessment questionnaire in the standard way could lead to more item-marking errors on the part of sincere participants than the approach of consistently aligning items (although I know of no research in this area).

Our primary concern was that varying the tone would make the questionnaires more difficult for users to complete, and as a consequence might increase the frequency of user error in marking items (Lewis, 1999, 2002). Until Jeff and I conducted our study of the all-positive version of the SUS (Sauro and Lewis, 2011), however, that was just a hypothesis—a hypothesis now confirmed 12 years after Lewis (1999) and over 20 years since the development of the PSSUQ, ASQ, and CSUQ.

On one hand, there are potential advantages to alternating the tone of questionnaire items. The major impetus for alternating item tone is to control response biases such as acquiescence (the tendency of respondents to agree with items) and extreme responses (the rare tendency of some respondents to provide the maximum or minimum response for all items). On the other hand, there are three major potential disadvantages of this practice (the three "Ms"):

1. *Misinterpret*: Users may respond differently to negatively worded items such that reversing responses from negative to positive doesn't account for the difference. For example, problems with misinterpreting negative items can include the creation of artificial two-factor structures and lowering internal reliability, especially in cross-cultural contexts (Barnette, 2000; Cheung and Rensvold, 2000; Davis, 1989; Grimm and Church, 1999; Ibrahim, 2001; Nunnally, 1978; Quilty et al., 2006; van de Vijver and Leung, 2001).
2. *Mistake*: Users might not intend to respond differently, but may forget to reverse their score, accidently agreeing with a negative statement when they meant to disagree. We have been with participants who acknowledged either forgetting to reverse their score or commenting that they had to correct some scores because they realized they had responded in the opposite of their intention.
3. *Miscode*: Researchers might forget to reverse the scales when scoring, and would consequently report incorrect data. Despite there being software to easily record user input, researchers still have to remember to reverse the scales. Forgetting to reverse the scales is not an obvious error. The improperly scaled scores are still acceptable values, especially when the system being tested is of moderate usability (in which case many responses will be neutral or close to neutral).

Regarding the prevalence of miscoding, there are two sources of data available. First, in 2009, eight of 15 teams used the SUS as part of the Comparative Usability Evaluation-8 (CUE-8) workshop at the Usability Professionals Association annual conference (Molich et al., 2009). Of the eight teams, one team improperly coded their SUS results. Second, as part of an earlier analysis of SUS, Sauro and Lewis (2009) examined 19 contributed SUS datasets; two were improperly coded and needed to be recoded prior to inclusion in the larger-scale analysis. Thus, three out of 27 SUS datasets (11.1%) had negative items that practitioners had failed to reverse, leading to incorrect SUS scores. Assuming this to be a reasonably representative selection of the larger population of SUS questionnaires, the associated 95% confidence interval suggests that miscoding affects somewhere between 3% and 28% of SUS datasets (most likely closer to 10%).

Despite published concerns about acquiescence bias, there is little evidence that the practice of including both positively and negatively worded items solves the problem. To our knowledge there is no research documenting the magnitude of acquiescence bias in general, or whether it specifically affects the measurement of attitudes toward usability. For that reason, in Sauro and Lewis (2011), we explored three questions:

1. Is there an acquiescence bias in responses to the SUS, and if so, how large is it?
2. Does the alternating wording of the SUS provide protection against acquiescence and extreme response biases?
3. Further, does its alternating item wording outweigh the negatives of misinterpreting, mistaking, and miscoding?

To explore those questions, we created an all-positive version of the SUS. As shown in Fig. 8.7, the even-numbered items, originally written in negative tone, maintain a similar content but are positive in this version. The odd-numbered items are the same as in the standard version. Given the planned tasks, both versions had the minor substitution of "website" for "system." Note that to get overall scores from 0 to 100, it is still necessary to recode responses, but the recoding rule is the same for all items—subtract 1 from the raw item score to get the recoded score, sum them, then multiply by 2.5.

In Aug and Sep of 2010, 213 users (recruited using Amazon's Mechanical Turk micro-tasking service, all from the United States) performed two representative tasks on one of seven websites (third party automotive or primary financial services websites: Cars.com, Autotrader.com, Edmunds.com, KBB.com, Vanguard.com, Fidelity.com, or TDAmeritrade.com). At the end of the study users completed

The System Usability Scale
Positive Version

			Strongly disagree 1	2	3	4	Strongly agree 5
1	I think that I would like to use the website frequently.		O	O	O	O	O
2	I found the website to be simple.		O	O	O	O	O
3	I thought the website was easy to use.		O	O	O	O	O
4	I think that I could use the website without the support of a technical person.		O	O	O	O	O
5	I found the various functions in the website were well integrated.		O	O	O	O	O
6	I thought there was a lot of consistency in the website.		O	O	O	O	O
7	I would imagine that most people would learn to use the website very quickly.		O	O	O	O	O
8	I found the website very intuitive.		O	O	O	O	O
9	I felt very confident using the website.		O	O	O	O	O
10	I could use the website without having to learn anything new.		O	O	O	O	O

FIGURE 8.7 The positive version of the SUS

either the standard or the positive version of the SUS. The assignment of questionnaires to participants was random. Between 15 and 17 users completed each version for each website.

Coefficient alpha was high for both versions, with 0.92 for the standard version and 0.96 for the positive version. There was no significant difference between the questionnaires for overall SUS score ($t(206) = 0.85, p > 0.39$), the average of the even items ($t(210) = 1.09, p > 0.27$), or the average of the odd items ($t(206) = 0.60, p > 0.54$). There was a difference in the means of the odd- and even-numbered items (Standard: $t(210) = 3.09, p < 0.01$; positive: $t(209) = 2.32, p < 0.03$), but that difference was consistent across the versions of the questionnaire, as indicated by the nonsignificant interaction ($F(1, 211) = 0.77, p > 0.38$), shown in Fig. 8.8.

In other words, carefully rewording the negative items to a positive tone appeared to have no significant effect on the resulting scores. Note that the means for the even- and odd-numbered items are the means after appropriate recoding for the items to shift the item scores from their raw form to a scale that runs from 0 to 4 for each item, where a 0 is a poor rating and 4 is the most favorable. Thus, the recoding rule for the even items in the positive version is different from the rule for even items in the standard version due to their difference in tone.

The measure of acquiescence bias was the number of agreement responses (4 or 5) to the odd-numbered (consistently positively worded) items in both questionnaires. The mean number of agreement responses was 1.64 per questionnaire for the standard SUS ($SD = 1.86, n = 107$) and 1.66 for the positive version ($SD = 1.87, n = 106$)—no significant difference ($t(210) = -0.06, p > 0.95$).

The measure of extreme response bias was the number of times respondents provided either the highest or lowest response option (1 or 5) for both questionnaire types for all items. The mean number of extreme responses was 1.68 for the standard SUS ($SD = 2.37, n = 107$) and 1.36 for the positive version ($SD = 2.23, n = 106$) – again, no significant difference ($t(210) = 1.03, p > 0.30$).

There were two potential indicators of mistakes, both based on consistency of response. One indicator was if there were at least three responses indicating agreement to positively and negatively worded items or three responses with disagreement to positively and negatively worded items. The second approach was to examine responses to the most highly correlated negative and positive item which, according to the large dataset of Bangor et al. (2008), were items 2 and 3 ($r = .593$). Examination of

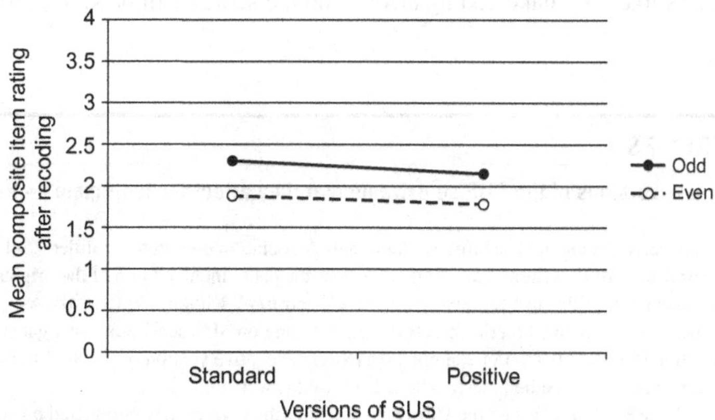

FIGURE 8.8 Nonsignificant interaction between odd and even items of standard and positive versions of the SUS

the responses to the standard SUS questionnaire found that 18 of the 107 original SUS questionnaires contained at least three internal inconsistencies (16.8%, 95% confidence interval ranged from 10.8% to 25.1%) and 53 questionnaires had inconsistent responses for items 2 and 3 (49.5%, 95% confidence interval ranged from 40.2% to 58.9%).

The final comparison was to use factor analysis to compare the two-factor structures of the data for the standard and positive versions of the SUS with the large-sample structure reported in Lewis and Sauro (2009). In that prior factor analytic work, the SUS items clustered into two factors, with one factor (Usable) containing items 1, 2, 3, 5, 6, 7, 8, and 9, and the other factor (Learnable) containing items 4 and 10. Neither of the resulting alignments of items with factors exactly duplicated the findings with the large samples of the SUS, and neither were they exactly consistent with each other, with discrepancies occurring on items 6, 8, and 9. Both the original and positive versions were consistent with the large-sample finding of including items 4 and 10 in the second factor. The original deviated slightly more than the positive from the large-sample factor structure (original items 6 and 8 aligned with the second rather than the first factor; positive item 9 aligned with the second rather than the first factor). The difference in the structure observed for this sample of standard SUS responses and the structure reported by Lewis and Sauro (2009) (and replicated by Borsci et al., 2009) could be due to its relatively small sample size. There is a need for further research to see if this pattern remains stable.

The major conclusions drawn from this study were:

- There is little evidence that the purported advantages of including negative and positive items in usability questionnaires outweigh the disadvantages.
- Researchers interested in designing new questionnaires for use in usability evaluations should avoid the inclusion of negative items.
- Researchers who use the standard SUS have no need to change to the all positive version provided that they verify the proper coding of scores. In moderated testing, researchers should include procedural steps (e.g., during debriefing) to ensure error-free completion.
- In unmoderated testing, it is more difficult to correct the mistakes respondents make, although these data suggest that the effect is unlikely to have a major impact on overall SUS scores.
- Researchers who do not have a current investment in the standard SUS can use the all positive version with confidence because respondents are less likely to make mistakes when responding, researchers are less likely to make coding errors, and the scores will be similar to the standard SUS.

GOING TO EXTREMES

Is it possible to create versions of the SUS so extreme that they affect measurement?—from the files of Jeff Sauro

In 2008 I was part of a panel at the annual Usability Professionals Association conference entitled "Subjective Ratings of Usability: Reliable or Ridiculous?" (Karn et al., 2008). Notably, the panel included two of the originators of two of the questionnaires discussed in this chapter: Kent Norman (QUIS) and Jurek Kirakowski (SUMI). As part of the panel presentation, we conducted an experiment on the effects of item wording on SUS scores to investigate two variables: item intensity and item direction (Sauro, 2010c). For example, the extreme negative version of the SUS Item 4 was "I think that I would need a permanent hot-line to the help desk to be able to use the website."

Participants were volunteers who reviewed the UPA website. After the review, they completed one of five SUS questionnaires—an all positive extreme, all negative extreme, one of two versions of an extreme mix (half positive and half negative extreme), or the standard SUS questionnaire (as a baseline). Sixty-two people participated in this between-subjects design, providing between 10 and 14 responses per questionnaire. Even with this relatively small sample size, the extreme positive and extreme negative items were significantly different from the original SUS ($F(4,57) = 6.90$, $p < 0.001$).

The results were consistent with prior research showing that people tend to agree with statements that are close to their attitude and to disagree with all other statements (Spector et al., 1997; Thurstone, 1928). By rephrasing items to extremes, only respondents who passionately favored the usability of the UPA website tended to agree with the extremely phrased positive statements—resulting in a significantly lower average score. Likewise, only respondents who passionately disfavored the usability agreed with the extremely negatively questions—resulting in a significant higher average score. Because intensity can affect item responses toward attitudes of usability, designers of usability questionnaires should avoid such extreme items.

UMUX (USABILITY METRIC FOR USER EXPERIENCE)

Description of the UMUX

The UMUX (Finstad, 2010b, 2013; Lewis, 2013b) is a relatively new addition to the set of standardized usability questionnaires. The primary goal of the UMUX was to get a measurement of perceived usability consistent with the SUS but using fewer items that more closely conformed to the ISO definition of usability (effective, efficient, satisfying). Although one might question the time savings of four versus 10 items in a standard usability evaluation, there are situations in which a shorter questionnaire might be useful. For example, "real estate" can be an issue when putting together a survey in which perceived usability is only one of many planned metrics.

UMUX items vary in tone and have seven scale steps from 1 (Strongly disagree) to 7 (Strongly agree). Starting with an initial pool of 12 items, the final UMUX had four items that included a general question similar to the SEQ ("[This system] is easy to use") and the best candidate item from each of the item sets associated with efficiency, effectiveness, and satisfaction, where "best" means the item with the highest correlation to concurrently collected SUS scores (Fig. 8.9). No license is required for its use.

Psychometric evaluation of the UMUX

To validate the UMUX, Finstad (2010b) had users of two systems, one with a reputation for poor usability (System 1, $n = 273$) and the other perceived as having good usability (System 2, $n = 285$), complete

	The Usability Metric for User Experience Version 1		Strongly agree 1	2	3	4	5	6	Strongly disagree 7
1	This system's capabilities meet my requirements.		O	O	O	O	O	O	O
2	Using this system is a frustrating experience.		O	O	O	O	O	O	O
3	This system is easy to use.		O	O	O	O	O	O	O
4	I have to spend too much time correcting things with this system.		O	O	O	O	O	O	O

FIGURE 8.9 The Usability Metric for User Experience (UMUX)

the UMUX and the SUS. Using a scheme similar to the SUS (recoding raw item scores to a 0–6 scale where 0 is poor and 6 is good, then multiplying the sum of the items by 100/24), UMUX scores can range from 0 to 100. As expected, the reliability of the SUS was high, with a coefficient alpha of 0.97. The reliability of the UMUX was also high, with coefficient alpha equaling 0.94. Finstad found a high correlation between the SUS and UMUX scores ($r = 0.96$, $p < 0.001$), providing evidence of concurrent validity. The UMUX was sensitive in the expected direction to the differences in usability for the two systems ($t(533) = 39.04$, $p < 0.01$). Finstad reported that the UMUX items aligned on a single factor, making it a unidimensional measurement.

Lewis et al. (2013) included the UMUX in two surveys ($n_1 = 402$, $n_2 = 389$), using the standard version of the SUS in one survey and the positive version in the other. The UMUX reliability estimates were 0.87 and 0.81, and the correlations with the SUS were 0.90 (standard) and 0.79 (positive). These estimates of reliability and concurrent validity were substantially lower than those in Finstad (2010b), but were still impressive. For both datasets there was no significant difference between the mean SUS and mean UMUX scores (extensive overlap of 99% confidence intervals). As predicted by Lewis (2013b), the factor structure of the UMUX had a clear bidimensional pattern with positive-tone items aligning with one factor and negative-tone items aligning with the other. Note that factor structure due to varying item tone is of little practical interest given the scale's reliability, validity, and sensitivity.

Borsci et al. (2015) conducted a study in which they used Italian translations of the SUS and UMUX (and UMUX-LITE—discussed in the next section) to obtain measurements of perceived usability from users who had relatively little experience with the website under study and users who had considerably more experience. Consistent with Lewis et al. (2013), estimates of UMUX reliability were between 0.80 and 0.90. As in Lewis et al. (2013), the correlations between the SUS and UMUX (Study 1: $r = 0.55$; Study 2: $r = 0.72$) were statistically significant, but lower than the correlations reported in Finstad (2010b). Unlike previous research, there were considerable differences between the means of the SUS and UMUX for the various studies and conditions in Borsci et al. (2015), with the UMUX scores consistently and significantly higher than the concurrently collected SUS scores.

In summary, the UMUX appears to be a reliable, valid, and sensitive questionnaire for the assessment of perceived usability. The jury is still out regarding the extent to which its scores closely correspond to those of concurrently collected SUS scores. The correspondence was close in Finstad (2010b) and Lewis et al. (2013), but was not close in Borsci et al. (2015). This might be due to differences in the English and Italian versions of the questionnaires, but it's too early yet to do anything other than speculate. Practitioners who would like to use the UMUX as a substitute for the SUS should start by using them concurrently to check for differences and, ideally, should publish their results.

UMUX-LITE

Description of the UMUX-LITE

Based on item analysis of the UMUX and after considering different candidate two-item versions, Lewis et al. (2013) derived the UMUX-LITE. As shown in Fig. 8.10, it consists of the two positive-tone items from the UMUX. This resulted in a parsimonious questionnaire that has a connection through the content of its items to the Technology Acceptance Model (Davis, 1989), a questionnaire from the market research literature that assesses the usefulness (Item 1) and ease-of-use (Item 2) of systems, and has an established relationship to likelihood of future use. No license is required for its use.

	The UMUX-LITE Version 1		Strongly agree 1	2	3	4	5	6	Strongly disagree 7
1	This system's capabilities meet my requirements.		O	O	O	O	O	O	O
2	This system is easy to use.		O	O	O	O	O	O	O

FIGURE 8.10 The UMUX-LITE

Psychometric evaluation of the UMUX-LITE

Lewis et al. (2013) computed UMUX-LITE scores from two surveys ($n = 402, 389$), using the standard version of the SUS in one survey and the positive version in the other. The UMUX-LITE reliability estimates were 0.83 and 0.82 (comparable to those found for the full UMUX in that study), and the correlations with the SUS were 0.81 (standard) and 0.85 (positive). It also correlated significantly ($r = 0.73$) with concurrently collected ratings of likelihood-to-use.

Applying a SUS-like scoring method for the UMUX-LITE entails converting each item score to a 0–6 point scale by subtracting one from the raw item score, summing the two resulting scores, then multiplying that sum by 100/12. Lewis et al. (2013) found a small but statistically significant difference between the overall SUS scores and UMUX-LITE scores computed in this way. To compensate for that difference, they used linear regression to achieve a closer correspondence between the SUS and UMUX-LITE scores, as shown in the following equation:

$$\text{UMUXLITE}_r = 0.65(\text{Item01} + \text{Item02} - 2)(100/12) + 22.9$$

Note that in this formula, you should use the raw item scores from the 1–7 point scale as shown in Fig. 8.10. Note also that when using this formula, the range of the metric is no longer 0–100, but is constrained to 22.9–87.9 (which still corresponds to a range from F to A+ on our curved grading scale for the SUS).

Lewis et al. (2015b) concurrently collected UMUX-LITE and SUS scores in a series of surveys of user evaluations of enterprise software ($n = 397$). The reliability of the UMUX-LITE was 0.86, and its correlations with the SUS, a rating of overall experience, and likelihood to recommend were all significant (respectively $r = 0.83$, 0.72, and 0.72). The overall mean difference between the SUS and the regression-adjusted UMUX-LITE was 1.1 (about 1% of the range of possible SUS scores). Strictly speaking, the difference was statistically significant ($t(396) = 2.2$, $p = 0.03$), but for any practical use (such as comparison to SUS norms like the curved grading scale in Table 8.5), it is essentially no difference. "When sample sizes are large, it is important not to confuse statistically significant differences with meaningful differences" (Lewis et al., 2015b, p. 501).

Using Italian versions of the questionnaires, Borsci et al. (2015) also found the regression-adjusted UMUX-LITE to have reasonably close correspondence to concurrently collected SUS scores. For their first study ($n = 186$), in which participants had relatively little experience with the website they were using, the mean difference was about three points, with 95% confidence intervals just failing to overlap. In their second study ($n = 93$), with more experienced participants, the mean difference was just 1.2 points—similar to the difference reported by Lewis et al. (2015b), with substantial overlap of the corresponding 95% confidence intervals. In addition to this second evaluation of the accuracy of the regression-adjusted UMUX-LITE metric, Borsci et al. also reported somewhat lower but still significant correlations between the UMUX-LITE and the SUS (Study 1: $r = 0.45$; Study 2: $r = 0.66$).

Thus, the UMUX-LITE appears to be an ultrashort reliable, valid, and sensitive metric that, after applying the regression adjustment, tracks closely with concurrently collected SUS scores. If using the UMUX-LITE, be sure to document its computation and, if using the regression-adjusted version, be sure to double check the scores and verify they fall in a range between 22.9 and 87.9. Finally, as Lewis et al. (2015b, p. 503) stated:

> Despite these encouraging results, it is important to note some limitations to generalizability. To date, the data we have used for psychometric evaluation of the UMUX-LITE have come from surveys. Indeed, this is the primary intended use of the UMUX-LITE when there is limited survey real estate available for the assessment of perceived usability. It would, however, be interesting to see if data collected in traditional usability studies would show a similar correspondence between the SUS and the UMUX-LITE. Until researchers have validated the UMUX-LITE across a wider variety of systems and research methods, we do not generally recommend its use independent of the SUS.

EXPERIMENTAL COMPARISON OF POST-STUDY USABILITY QUESTIONNAIRES

There are few direct comparisons of the various standardized usability questionnaires (making this a promising area of research for motivated graduate students). In addition to the traditional psychometric measures of reliability and validity, usability practitioners have a practical need for questionnaires that are sensitive to changes in usability. Going beyond the simple definition of sensitivity as the capability of a standardized usability questionnaire to indicate significant differences between systems, Tullis and Stetson (2004) examined differences in the sensitivity of five methods used to assess satisfaction with usability.

The five methods investigated by Tullis and Stetson (2004) were:

- *SUS*: The standard version of the SUS, as described earlier in this chapter.
- *QUIS*: A variant of the 27-item version of the QUIS described earlier in this chapter that used 10-point scales, with three items dropped that were not appropriate for assessing websites (e.g., "Remembering names and use of commands"), the term "system" replaced by "website," and the term "screen" generally replaced by "web page."
- *CSUQ*: As described later in this chapter, the CSUQ is a variant of the PSSUQ (previously described) with very similar psychometric properties—this study used the 19-item Version 2 (Lewis, 1995), replacing the term "system" with "website" and for consistency with the other methods, labeling the lower end of the scale with "Disagree" and the upper end with "Agree" so larger values indicate more satisfaction with usability.
- *Words*: Tullis and Stetson (2004) based this method on the 118 words used in Microsoft's Product Reaction Cards (Benedek and Miner, 2002)—participants chose the words that best described their interaction with the website, and were free to choose as many or as few words as they wished—satisfaction scores were the ratio of positive to total words selected.

- *Fidelity questionnaire*: Used at Fidelity for several years in usability tests of websites, composed of nine statements (e.g., "This website is visually appealing") to which users respond on a 7-point scale from "Strongly Disagree" to "Strongly Agree" with scale steps numbered −3, −2, −1, 0, 1, 2, 3 (obvious neutral point at 0).

A total of 123 Fidelity employees participated in the study, randomly assigned to one of the methods, which they used to evaluate their satisfaction after completing two tasks at two financial websites. The tasks were (a) find the highest price in the past year for a share of a specified company and (b) find the mutual fund with the highest three-year return. The order in which participants visited the sites was random.

Analysis of the overall results for all methods showed a significant preference for Site 1 over Site 2. In the more interesting analysis, Tullis and Stetson (2004) randomly selected subsamples of the data at sample sizes of 6, 8, 10, 12, and 14 for each method. They then investigated which methods most quickly converged on the "correct" conclusion regarding the usability of two websites as a function of sample size (a variable of practical importance to usability practitioners), where correct meant a significant *t*-test consistent with the decision reached using the total sample size—that Site 1 was more usable than Site 2.

As shown in Fig. 8.11, of the five methods assessed by Tullis and Stetson (2004), the SUS was the fastest to converge on the final (correct) conclusion, reaching 75% agreement at a sample size of 8 and 100% agreement when $n = 12$. The CSUQ (a variant of the PSSUQ, discussed later in this chapter) was the second fastest, reaching 75% agreement at a sample size of 10 and 90% agreement when $n = 12$. In contrast, even when $n = 14$, the other methods were in the low- to mid-70% of agreement with the correct decision. This is compelling evidence that practitioners should prefer the SUS as a method of assessing satisfaction with usability, especially when facing limited resources for sample size and having no need for multidimensional measurement. For studies that would benefit from multidimensional assessment of usability, practitioners should consider the CSUQ (or PSSUQ).

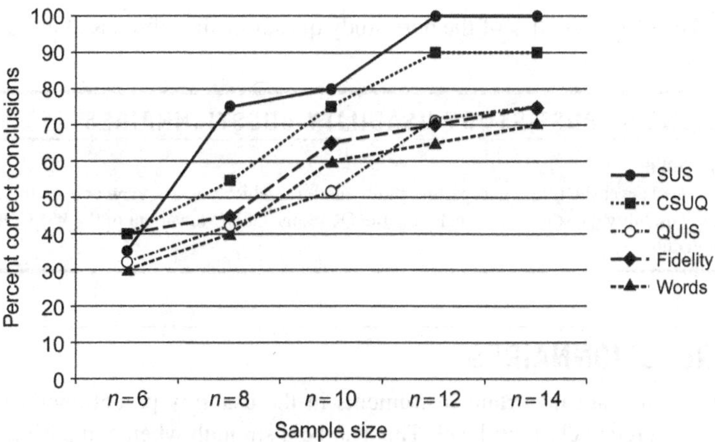

FIGURE 8.11 Relative sensitivities of five methods for assessing satisfaction with usability

ITEM RESPONSE THEORY AND STANDARDIZED USABILITY QUESTIONNAIRES

Is there a future for Item Response Theory (IRT) in the development of standardized usability questionnaires?

For most of the previous century, the basis for psychometric test development was a set of techniques collectively known as classical test theory (CTT) (Zickar, 1998). For a comprehensive treatment of basic CTT, see Nunnally (1978). Starting in the last quarter of the 20th century (and accelerating in its last two decades into the 21st century) was an alternative approach known as Item Response Theory (IRT) (Embretson and Reise, 2000; Reise et al., 2005). IRT had a major impact on educational testing, affecting, for example, the development and administration of the Scholastic Aptitude Test, Graduate Record Exam, and Armed Services Vocational Aptitude Battery. Given its success in these areas, some researchers have speculated that the application of IRT might improve the measurement of usability (Hollemans, 1999; Schmettow and Vietze, 2008).

It is beyond the scope of this chapter to go through all the differences between CTT and IRT (for details, refer to a source such as Embretson and Reise, 2000). A key difference is that CTT focuses on scale-level measurement whereas IRT focuses on modeling at the item level. This property of IRT makes it ideal for adaptive computerized testing (Zickar, 1998), which is one of the reasons it has become so popular in large-scale educational testing. Obtaining reliable estimates of the parameters of item response models, however, requires data collection from a very large sample of respondents (Embretson and Reise, 2000), which can make IRT unattractive to researchers with limited resources. Furthermore, it isn't clear whether the additional effort involved would be worthwhile. Embretson and Reise (2000) observed that raw (CTT) scores and trait level (IRT) scores based on the same data correlate highly, and "no one has shown that in real data a single psychological finding would be different if IRT scores were used rather than raw scale scores" (p. 324). For these reasons, most development of standardized usability questionnaires in the near future will likely continue to use CTT rather than IRT.

On the other hand, if the goal of the measurement of perceived usability is to create a yardstick of attitudes, then we want items that lie along the yardstick to separate poor from better applications. IRT has the potential to take advantage of additional information to create items that more effectively separate the objects of measurement (e.g., software products or user interfaces) than the means and methods of CTT. This isn't to say that measurements based on CTT are invalid, but IRT has the promise of producing measurements that are more elegant and theoretically sound. With IRT, the raw responses, which usually have ordinal properties, can be converted to interval data using a logit transformation (Andrich, 1978). We believe there is a future for IRT in the development of standardized usability questionnaires, but that potential has not yet been realized. For more information on applying IRT to questionnaires in general, see Bond and Fox (2001).

Table 8.8 lists key characteristics of the post-study questionnaires discussed in this chapter.

ONLINE VERSIONS OF POST-STUDY USABILITY QUESTIONNAIRES

Thanks to Gary Perlman

Gary Perlman has created a website (http://garyperlman.com/quest/) at which you can view or even use a variety of online versions of post-study usability questionnaires, including the QUIS, the CSUQ (a variant of the PSSUQ), and the SUS. See his website for details.

POST-TASK QUESTIONNAIRES

Post-study questionnaires are important instruments in the usability practitioner's toolbox, but they assess satisfaction at a relatively high level. This can be a strength when comparing general satisfaction with competitors or different versions of a product, but is a weakness when seeking more detailed diagnoses of problem areas in a user interface. To address this weakness, many practitioners perform a quick assessment of perceived usability immediately after participants complete each task or scenario

Table 8.8 Key Characteristics of the Post-Study Questionnaires

Questionnaire	Requires License Fee	Number of Items	Number of Subscales	Global Reliability	Validity Notes
QUIS	Yes ($50–750)	27	5	0.94	Construct validity; evidence of sensitivity
SUMI	Yes (€0–1000)	50	5	0.92	Construct validity; evidence of sensitivity; availability of norms
PSSUQ	No	16	3	0.94	Construct validity; concurrent validity; evidence of sensitivity; some normative information
SUS	No	10	2	> 0.89	Construct validity; evidence of sensitivity; emerging normative information
UMUX	No	4	1	> 0.80	Construct validity; concurrent validity; evidence of sensitivity
UMUX-LITE	No	2	1	> 0.82	Construct validity; concurrent validity; evidence of sensitivity; potential to apply SUS norms

in a usability study. Research indicates a substantial and significant correlation between post-study and post-task assessments of perceived usability (Sauro and Lewis, 2009), with $r = 0.64$ ($p < 0.0001$; $R^2 = 41\%$), showing that they tap into a common underlying construct, but do not perfectly align. In other words, they are similar but not identical, so it makes sense to take both types of measurements when conducting studies. This section of the chapter describes a variety of commonly used post-task questionnaires.

ASQ (AFTER-SCENARIO QUESTIONNAIRE)

Description of the ASQ

The development of the ASQ (Fig. 8.12) took place at the same time as the PSSUQ, described earlier in this chapter. It is a three-item questionnaire that uses the same format as the PSSUQ, probing overall

The After-Scenario Questionnaire Version 1

		Strongly agree 1	2	3	4	5	6	7 Strongly disagree	NA
1	Overall, I am satisfied with the ease of completing the tasks in this scenario.	O	O	O	O	O	O	O	O
2	Overall, I am satisfied with the amount of time it took to complete the tasks in this scenario.	O	O	O	O	O	O	O	O
3	Overall, I am satisfied with the support information (online help, messages, documentation) when completing the tasks.	O	O	O	O	O	O	O	O

FIGURE 8.12 The ASQ

ease of task completion, satisfaction with completion time, and satisfaction with support information. The overall ASQ score is the average of the responses to these items. Like the PSSUQ, the ASQ is available for free use by practitioners and researchers, but anyone using it should cite the source (e.g., Lewis, 1995; Lewis, 2012; or this book).

Psychometric evaluation of the ASQ

Measurements of ASQ reliability have ranged from 0.90 to 0.96 (Lewis, 1990b, 1991, 1995). Use of the ASQ in Lewis et al. (1990, analysis reported in Lewis, 1995) showed a significant correlation between ASQ scores and successful scenario completion ($r(46) = -0.40$, $p < 0.01$)—evidence of concurrent validity. A factor analysis of the ASQ scores from the eight tasks investigated in Lewis et al. (1990) showed a clear association of ASQ factors with associated tasks, with the eight factors explaining almost all (94%) of the total variance (Lewis, 1991). Of the 48 participants in Lewis et al. (1990), (27) completed all items on all ASQs. An analysis of variance on that data indicated a significant main effect of Scenario ($F(7,126) = 8.92$, $p < 0.0001$) and a significant Scenario by System interaction ($F(14,126) = 1.75$, $p = 0.05$), providing evidence of the sensitivity of the ASQ.

SEQ (SINGLE EASE QUESTION)

Description of the SEQ

As shown in Fig. 8.13, the SEQ simply asks participants to assess the overall ease of completing a task, similar to the ASQ Item 1. Some practitioners use a 5-point version of this scale. Given research on the relative reliability of and user preference for 5- and 7-point scales (Finstad, 2010a; Lewis, 1993; Nunnally, 1978; Preston and Colman, 2000), we recommend using the 7-point version.

Psychometric evaluation of the SEQ

Two studies have shown evidence of concurrent validity for the SEQ. Tedesco and Tullis (2006), using a 5-point version of the SEQ, reported a significant correlation with a metric of performance efficiency that combined task completion rates and times. Sauro and Dumas (2009) reported significant correlations of the SEQ (7-point version anchored on the left with "Very easy" and on the right with "Very difficult") with the SMEQ and the UME ($r > 0.94$) and with the SUS ($r = -0.6$, $p < 0.01$). (Note that as shown in Fig. 8.13, a higher number on the standard SEQ corresponds to an easier task—the scale was reversed for the Sauro and Dumas study to make it consistent with the direction of the SMEQ and UME metrics.) They also reported significant correlations with completion times ($r = -0.9$) and number of errors ($r = 0.84$).

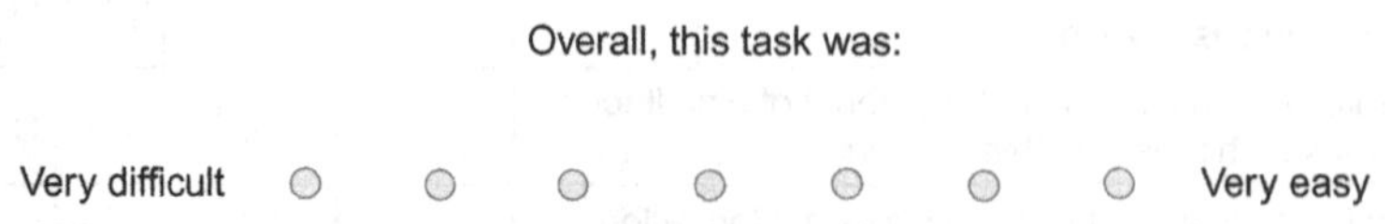

Overall, this task was:

Very difficult ○ ○ ○ ○ ○ ○ ○ Very easy

FIGURE 8.13 The SEQ

SMEQ (SUBJECTIVE MENTAL EFFORT QUESTION)

Description of the SMEQ

Zijlstra and van Doorn (1985) developed the SMEQ (also known as the Rating Scale for Mental Effort, or RSME). The SMEQ (Fig. 8.14) is a single item questionnaire with a rating scale from 0 to 150 with nine verbal labels ranging from "Not at all hard to do" (just above 0) to "Tremendously hard to do" (just above 110).

In the paper version of the SMEQ, participants draw a line through the scale (which is 150 mm in length) to indicate the perceived mental effort of completing a task, with the SMEQ score the number of millimeters the participant marked above the baseline of 0. In the online version developed by Sauro and Dumas (2009), participants use a slider control to indicate their ratings. The originators of the SMEQ claimed that it is reliable, easy to use, and that they placed the verbal labels (originally in Dutch) by calibrating them psychometrically against tasks (Sauro and Dumas, 2009).

Psychometric evaluation of the SMEQ

In Sauro and Dumas (2009), the SMEQ correlated significantly with the SEQ ($r = 0.94$, $p < 0.01$) and UME ($r = 0.845$, $p < 0.01$). Like the SEQ, the SMEQ had a significant correlation with SUS scores ($r = -0.6$, $p < 0.01$) as well as with completion time ($r = -0.82$), completion rates ($r = 0.88$), and errors ($r = -0.72$) collected during the experiment—all evidence of concurrent validity.

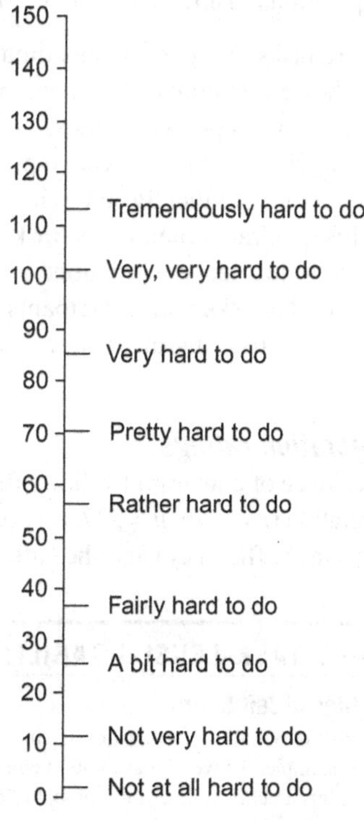

FIGURE 8.14 The SMEQ

ER (EXPECTATION RATINGS)

Description of expectation ratings

Albert and Dixon (2003) described the use of ERs in usability testing. Basically, ERs address the relationship between how easy or difficult a participant found a task to be after performing it relative to how they perceived it before beginning the task. The ER procedure uses a variation of the SEQ, getting participants to rate the expected difficulty of all of the tasks planned for a usability study before doing any of the tasks (the ERs), then collecting the post-task rating in the usual way after the completion of each task (the experience rating). For example, Tedesco and Tullis (2006) used the following two questions:

- Before doing all tasks (ER): "How difficult or easy do you expect this task to be?"
- After doing each task (experience rating): "How difficult or easy did you find this task to be?"

In the original study (Albert and Dixon, 2003), the rating scales for the two questions included seven steps with endpoints of "Very Easy" (1) and "Very Difficult" (7). Tedesco and Tullis (2006) used 5-point scales. As noted previously, given research on the relative reliability of and user preference for 5- and 7-point scales (Finstad, 2010a; Lewis, 1993; Nunnally, 1978; Preston and Colman, 2000), we recommend using seven points.

One advantage of having the before and after ratings is that practitioners can graph a scatterplot of the results and map them onto four quadrants (Tullis and Albert, 2008):

- Upper left ("Promote it"): These are tasks that participants thought would be difficult but turned out to be easier than expected, so they are features that an enterprise might reasonably promote.
- Lower left ("Big opportunity"): Participants perceived these tasks as difficult before and after performing them. There were no surprises, but these tasks represent potential opportunities for improvement, which would move them up to the "Promote it" category.
- Upper right ("Don't touch it"): This quadrant contains the tasks perceived as easy before and after task performance, so it's reasonable to just leave them alone.
- Lower right ("Fix it fast"): These are the tasks that participants thought would be easy but turned out to be difficult—a potential source of user dissatisfaction—making this the quadrant of primary focus for improvement.

Psychometric evaluation of expectation ratings

Tedesco and Tullis (2006) reported evidence of concurrent validity for the "after" question of an ER. Specifically, they found a significant correlation ($r = 0.46$, $n = 227$, $p < 0.0001$) between a combined measure of completion rates and times (performance efficiency) and the "after" rating for a set of six tasks.

HOW WELL CAN USERS PREDICT TASK-LEVEL USABILITY?

As it turns out, pretty well—from the files of Jeff Sauro

When you ask a user to attempt a task, it seems reasonable that they quickly interpret what they're asked to do and have some idea about how difficult it will be. For example, if I were to ask you to compute your adjusted gross income after accounting for deductions using some IRS forms and tax tables, you'd probably expect that to be more difficult than finding the hours of a local department store online. I wondered how much of the actual difficulty is revealed in the description of the task scenario. How accurate would ratings be if I just asked users how difficult they think a task is without actually testing them?

To find out, I had one group of users rate how difficult they'd think a set of tasks would be. I then had another set of users actually attempt the tasks then rate how difficult they thought they were. Using separate groups eliminates the possibility that users might have a bias to keep their before and after ratings consistent. I picked a mix of eight tasks with a range of difficulty and used some well-known websites (Craigslist.com, Apple.com, Amazon.com, eBay.com, and CrateandBarrel.com). I had between 30 and 40 people rate how difficult they thought each task would be, then I had separate groups of users (between 11 and 16 per task) attempt the tasks on the website. For example, one task expected to be fairly easy was to find out if a Crate and Barrel store in Denver (zip code 80210) is open on Sunday; a relatively difficult task was to estimate how much it would cost in commissions and fees to sell your iPhone 3GS on eBay.

In general users tended (on seven out of eight tasks) to overpredict how difficult tasks would be. The one task that was more difficult than expected was the "eBay Seller fees" task. While I think most people expect to pay fees to sell something on eBay, I think they expected the fee structure to be more straightforward. Part of the difficulty in the task is because there are multiple variables (such as total sale price, shipping costs, and the type of merchandise). The most notable miss was where users overpredicted the difficulty of the "Craigslist Find apt" task by 50%. For some reason people thought this would be rather difficult. I wondered if it had to do with people being less familiar with the SF rental market. In looking at the data, people outside of California did rate the task as more difficult, but even California residents thought finding an apartment on Craigslist would be more difficult than it was.

To understand how much the predicted score could explain the actual score I conducted a simple linear regression at the task level. Half of the variation in task difficulty can be explained by how a different set of users think the task will be (adjusted R^2 = 50.8%). The scatterplot in Fig. 8.15 shows this strong association, with the Craigslist "find apartment" and eBay "fees" tasks highlighted to show their departure from the trendline (for more information on this study, see www.measuringu.com/predicted-usability.php).

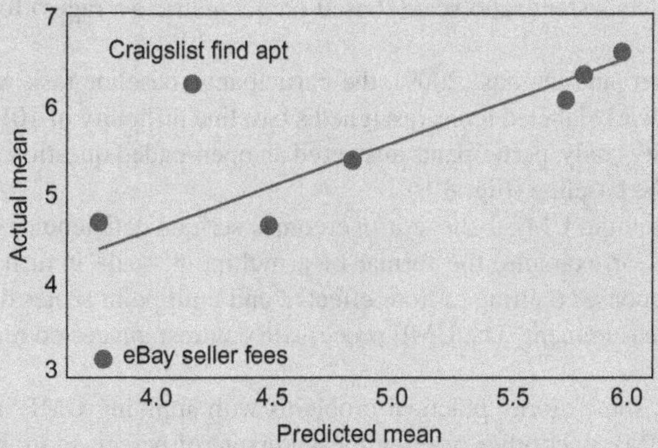

FIGURE 8.15 Relationship between predicted task-ease and actual task ease

UME (USABILITY MAGNITUDE ESTIMATION)

Description of UME

Magnitude estimation has a rich history in psychophysics, the branch of psychology that attempts to develop mathematical relationships between the physical dimensions of a stimulus and its perception. Psychophysics had its start in the early- to mid-19th century with the work of Weber (on just noticeable differences) and Fechner (sensory thresholds), culminating in Fechner's Law (Massaro, 1975): $S = k(\log_{10} I)$—that there is a logarithmic relationship between the intensity of a physical stimulus (I) and its perceived sensation (S), replaced in most psychophysics work about 100 years later by Stevens'

Power Law: $S = kI^n$, which provided a better fit for most relationships (Mussen et al., 1977). In his work, Fechner developed a variety of experimental methods, one of which was magnitude estimation. In magnitude estimation, participants judge the intensity of a stimulus against a baseline stimulus (e.g., how bright a stimulus light is as a ratio of the perceived brightness of a reference light—five times as bright, half as bright, etc.).

In a usability testing context, the goal of UME is to get a measurement of usability that enables ratio measurement, so a task (or product) with a perceived difficulty of 100 is perceived as twice as difficult as a task (or product) with a perceived difficulty of 50. There have been a few published attempts to apply magnitude estimation methods to the study of the perception of usability. Cordes (1984a,b) had participants draw lines to represent the relative ease of completing tasks in a usability study. About 20 years later, McGee (2003, 2004) published favorable papers describing his applications of UME to the measurement of usability.

It is customary to train participants in the magnitude estimation process before attempting to apply it to the evaluation of tasks in a usability study. The training stimuli are usually simple stimuli, such as judging the length of lines or the areas of circles against reference objects (McGee, 2003). One common approach to UME is to have participants experience and evaluate a baseline task, usually one that is very easy, before tackling the target tasks (Cordes, 1984a,b), although it is also possible to get estimates from an additional baseline, typically, a task that is relatively difficult, as in McGee (2004). After collecting all the data from a participant, the first step in analysis is to use log transformation to convert the data to a consistent ratio scale (based on geometric averages) for comparison purposes (McGee, 2003).

For example, in Sauro and Dumas (2009), the participants' baseline task was to select the Search icon from a set of five clearly labeled icons (assigned a baseline difficulty of 10). After completing each target task of the usability study, participants answered an open-ended question about relative difficulty of use that referenced the baseline (Fig. 8.16).

Researchers who promote UME believe it overcomes serious deficiencies of other measurements of perceived usability. For example, the format of a multipoint scale item has fixed endpoints that might overly restrict responses (ceiling or floor effects), and multipoint scales do not typically produce proven interval-level measurement. The UME process, in contrast, places no restrictions on the ratings that participants provide.

There are, however, some thorny practical problems with applying UME in usability testing. The claimed advantage of UME over other types of measurement of perceived usability is mired in a controversy that has gone on since the late 1940s. We won't cover it in this chapter, but you'll find a discussion of the controversy regarding levels of measurement (such as nominal, ordinal, interval, and ratio) and their interpretation in the next chapter.

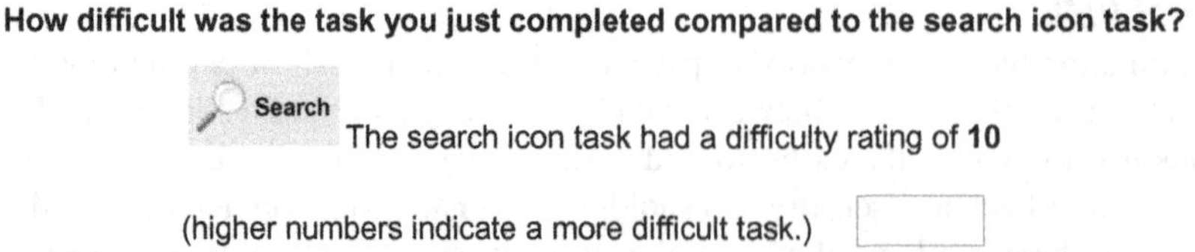

How difficult was the task you just completed compared to the search icon task?

Search

The search icon task had a difficulty rating of **10**

(higher numbers indicate a more difficult task.)

FIGURE 8.16 Sample UME item

Another problem with UME is that both practitioners and participants often find it difficult to do, especially in unmoderated testing. Tedesco and Tullis (2006) had planned to include it in their comparison of post-task subjective ratings, but:

> This condition was originally based on Usability Magnitude Estimation but was significantly modified through iterations in the study planning. In pilot testing using a more traditional version of Usability Magnitude Estimation, they found that participants had a very difficult time understanding the concepts and using the technique appropriately. As a result, they modified it to this simpler technique [using a 100-point bipolar scale]. This may mean that Usability Magnitude Estimation is better suited to use in a lab setting, or at least a moderated usability study, than in an online, unmoderated usability study. (Tullis and Albert, 2008, pp. 133–134)

In Sauro and Dumas (2009), participant training in UME was also an issue. "We found that users had some difficulty, especially early in the sessions, in grasping the ratio judgments" (p. 1601). "Concepts such as 'twice as difficult' and 'one half as difficult' take training and feedback to understand" (p. 1602). Given these issues in the usability of UME, it is likely to play a relatively minor role in the practical toolbox of most usability practitioners.

Psychometric evaluation of UME

There is no question regarding the effectiveness of magnitude scaling in psychophysics (Mussen et al., 1977). A variety of studies have provided evidence of the validity and sensitivity of UME. Cordes (1984a) reported significant improvements in his UME measurements across an iteration in the development of a complex software product in which developers fixed numerous usability problems between the two evaluations. He also fitted the relationship between perceived difficulty and task-completion time with a power function whose exponent (0.5) indicated that for every 100-fold increase in task-completion time there was a 10-fold increase in perceived difficulty.

McGee (2003) found significant correlation between UME and task completion time ($r = -0.244$, $p < 0.001$), number of clicks ($r = -0.387$, $p < 0.0001$), errors ($r = -0.195$, $p < 0.011$), and assists ($r = -0.193$, $p < 0.012$). Sauro and Dumas (2009) had 26 participants complete five travel expense reporting tasks with two products. UME had strong correlations with task completion time ($r = -0.91$, $p < 0.01$), the SMEQ ($r = 0.845$, $p < 0.01$), the average of the first two items of the ASQ ($r = 0.955$, $p < 0.01$), and also correlated significantly with overall SUS scores ($r = 0.316$, $p < 0.01$).

EXPERIMENTAL COMPARISONS OF POST-TASK QUESTIONNAIRES

The psychometric data support the use of all five post-task questionnaires: ASQ, SEQ, SMEQ, ER, and UME. Even though they all have acceptable psychometric properties, it would be useful for practitioners to know which tends to be the most sensitive—specifically, the one that most rapidly converges on large sample results when samples are small. Within the past 10 years, there have been two attempts to investigate this.

Tedesco and Tullis (2006) collected a set of data for five methods for eliciting post-task subjective ratings in usability testing, with 1131 Fidelity employees completing six tasks using an internal website. The methods tested were:

- SEQ-V1 ($n = 210$): A 5-point item from 1 (Very Difficult) to 5 (Very Easy), with the wording "Overall, this task was:"
- SEQ-V2 ($n = 230$): A 5-point item from 1 (Very Difficult) to 5 (Very Easy), with the wording "Please rate the usability of the site for *this* task:"
- ASQ ($n = 244$): The average of the first two items of the ASQ, using 5- rather than 7-point scales
- ER ($n = 227$): These were 5-point versions of the ER questions of Albert and Dixon (2003)—most analyses used only the second item, making it essentially another variant of the SEQ ("How difficult or easy did you find this task to be?")
- SEQ-V3 ($n = 221$): This was a 100-point scale from 1 (Not at all supportive and completely unusable) to 100 (Perfect, requiring absolutely no improvement), with the wording "Please assign a number between 1 and 100 to represent how well the Website *supported* you for this task."—the original intention was to do UME for this condition, but in the end, the item was more similar to a version of the SEQ with additional instructions to try to get participants to do ratio-level rating

Using a strategy similar to that of Tullis and Stetson (2004), Tedesco and Tullis (2006) conducted a subsampling analysis, taking 1000 random samples from the full data set with subsample sizes ranging from 3 to 29 in increments of 2, then computing the correlation between the average ratings for the six tasks at that sample size and the average ratings found with the full dataset. They found that all five methods worked well at the larger sample sizes, with all correlations exceeding 0.95 when $n \geq 23$. Even when $n = 3$ the correlations were reasonably high, ranging from about 0.72 for the ASQ to about 0.83 for the SEQ-V1. Across all the sample sizes from 3 to 29, the SEQ-V1 was consistently more sensitive, with its greatest advantage at the smaller sample sizes.

Sauro and Dumas (2009) compared the sensitivity of three post-task questionnaires:

- *SEQ:* The standard SEQ, as shown in Fig. 8.13, similar to the SEQ-V1 of Tedesco and Tullis (2006), but using a 7- rather than a 5-point scale
- *SMEQ:* An online version of the SMEQ, similar to that shown in Fig. 8.14, with a slider control for setting its value that started slightly above the top of the scale
- *UME:* An online version of the UME, similar to Fig. 8.16

In the study, 26 participants completed five travel expense reporting tasks using two released versions of a similar application. Half of the participants started with each application, and the assignment of rating types across tasks and products was also counterbalanced. To the extent that time allowed, participants attempted each task up to three times, for a maximum of up to 30 tasks per participant. In addition to completing the tasks and post-task ratings, participants also completed the standard SUS for both products.

The SUS scores for the two products indicated a significant difference in perceived usability, with no overlap between the products' 95% confidence intervals (one with a mean of just over 50, the other with a mean exceeding 75). Analyses at the task level indicated similar outcomes for SEQ and SMEQ, both of which picked up significant differences for four out of five tasks. In contrast, UME indicated significant differences between the products for only two of the five tasks. The results of a resampling exercise were consistent with these task-level results. Fig. 8.17 shows, for 1000 samples with replacement at sample sizes of 3, 5, 8, 10, 12, 15, 17, 19, and 20, the percentage of significant *t*-tests ($p < 0.05$) consistent with the findings from the entire sample.

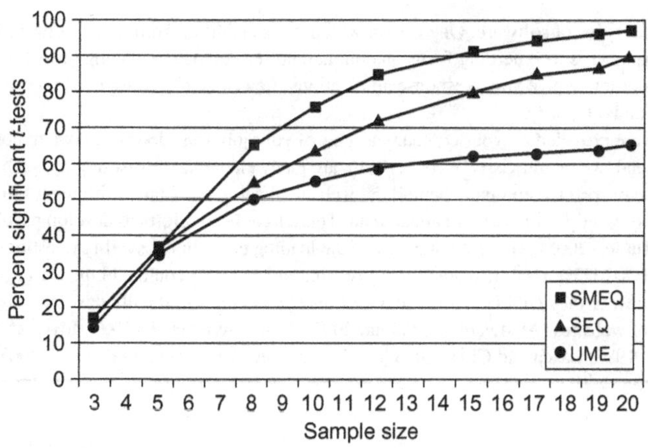

FIGURE 8.17 Sensitivity by sample size for SEQ, SMEQ, and UME

At very small samples sizes, there was little difference between the methods, all of which were insensitive (about 16% significant *t*-tests when $n = 3$; about 36% when $n = 5$). When $n = 8$ the methods began to diverge, with UME falling behind SEQ and SMEQ. As the sample size increased, UME continued to fall behind, never achieving higher than about 65% significant *t*-tests. For all sample sizes greater than 5, SMEQ had a higher percentage of significant *t*-tests than SEQ, but not significantly greater.

In both comparative studies (Sauro and Dumas, 2009; Tedesco and Tullis, 2006), UME fared poorly in comparison to the other post-task methods. Overall, the results support the use of the standard SEQ (as shown in Fig. 8.13) or, for online data collection, the SMEQ (Fig. 8.14) for practical post-task assessment of perceived task difficulty.

QUESTIONNAIRES FOR ASSESSING PERCEIVED USABILITY OF WEBSITES

The initial development of the major standardized usability questionnaires took place in the mid- to late-1980s, with publication in the early- to mid-1990s—before the widespread adoption of the Web. In fact, in 1988, during the studies that provided the initial data for the PSSUQ (Lewis et al., 1990), it was necessary to train many of the novice participants in how to use a mouse before they could start the key tasks of the studies. After the Web began to achieve its popularity as a means for conveying information and conducting commerce, questionnaires designed more specifically for the assessment of the perceived usability of websites appeared.

USING NON-WEB QUESTIONNAIRES TO ASSESS WEBSITE USABILITY

What's so special about the Web?

Because websites share many properties with other types of software, it is possible to evaluate some aspects of their usability with non-Web standardized usability questionnaires. This is especially true to the extent that the evaluation focuses on traditional usability attributes of effectiveness, efficiency, and satisfaction. There are, however, ways in which websites differ from other types of software. One way in which websites differ from other software is in the importance of effective browsing. Another is its emerging focus on commercial self-service, replacing tasks formerly performed by customer service agents or interactive voice response applications (Lewis, 2011). Associated with this are concerns about website responsiveness and reliability.

When you use software provided by your company as part of your job, trust doesn't play a major role in your decision to use it. On the other hand, when you visit a website, there are many elements of trust in play, such as whether you trust the information provided or trust the company behind the website to act in good faith with regard to purchases you might make or their treatment of your personal and financial data. There have been efforts to develop psychometrically qualified trust scales (Safar and Turner, 2005). Those are not part of the leading post-study usability questionnaires (QUIS, SUMI, PSSUQ, SUS, and UMUX-LITE). Usability practitioners evaluating websites could add the trust scales to one of the postwebsite questionnaires, or they could explore the use of questionnaires specifically developed for the evaluation of the perceived usability of websites (Aladwani and Palvia, 2002; Bargas-Avila et al., 2009; Joyce and Kirakowski, 2015; Kirakowski and Cierlik, 1998; Lascu and Clow, 2008, 2013; Sauro, 2011b; Wang and Senecal, 2007).

WAMMI (WEBSITE ANALYSIS AND MEASUREMENT INVENTORY)

Description of the WAMMI

One of the first research groups to recognize the need for an instrument specialized for the assessment of websites was the HFRG at University College Cork in Ireland (Kirakowski and Cierlik, 1998). In association with Nomos Management AB of Stockholm, they created the WAMMI. The source for its items were statements of opinion collected from a large number of designers, users, and Web masters about positive and negative experiences associated with websites. After content and factor analysis, the resulting questionnaire had the same factor structure as the SUMI, with 12 items for each of the factors (a total of 60 items). The current version of the WAMMI has a set of 20 5-point items, still covering five subscales (Attractiveness, Controllability, Efficiency, Helpfulness, and Learnability) and a global measure (www.wammi.com). Fig. 8.18 shows a sample WAMMI item. The entire questionnaire is available for review at www.wammi.com/samples/index.html (Fig. 6.17 of Tullis and Albert, 2008, p. 152).

Like the SUMI, standardized global WAMMI scores have a mean of 50 and a standard deviation of 10. Also like the SUMI, the instrument is available free of charge for educational use after receiving a letter of permission. There is a cost for commercial use, but the WAMMI website lists contact information rather than specific fees. The WAMMI is available in Danish, Dutch, English, Finnish, French, German, Italian, Norwegian, Polish, Portuguese (European), Spanish, and Swedish. Again using the SUMI strategy, one of the strengths of the WAMMI is the possibility of comparing a given set of results against a proprietary database of WAMMI scores: "The uniqueness of WAMMI is that visitor-satisfaction for the site being evaluated is compared with values from our reference database, which now contains data from over 300 surveys" (www.wammi.com/whatis.html, visited April 3, 2011).

Statements 1–10 of 20	Strongly agree	Strongly disagree
This website has much that is of interest to me.		

FIGURE 8.18 Sample WAMMI item

Psychometric evaluation of the WAMMI

Kirakowski and Cierlik (1998) reported the first version of the WAMMI to be reliable, valid, and sensitive. Coefficient alpha ranged from 0.70 to 0.90 for the subscales, and was 0.96 overall. A comparison of two websites showed correspondence between WAMMI scores and task-level measurements of SMEQ and RUE (relative user efficiency—the time on task of a test user divided by the time on task of an expert user), unfortunately, there were no data provided of statistical tests of validity or sensitivity.

In changing from 60 items in the original WAMMI to 20 items in the current version, you'd expect some decline in reliability. According to the WAMMI website (www.wammi.com/reliability.html), the current reliabilities (coefficient alpha) for the WAMMI global measurement and subscales are:

- Attractiveness: 0.64
- Controllability: 0.69
- Efficiency: 0.63
- Helpfulness: 0.70
- Learnability: 0.74
- Global: 0.90

With about four items per subscale, these values are a bit on the low side, but still indicative of a reasonable level of reliability, especially for large-sample studies. The WAMMI developers may well have decided to trade off some reliability to dramatically reduce the length of the questionnaire and the time required to complete it.

SUPR-Q (STANDARDIZED USER EXPERIENCE PERCENTILE RANK QUESTIONNAIRE)

Description of the SUPR-Q

The SUPR-Q (Sauro, 2011b, 2015) is a rating scale designed to measure perceptions of usability, credibility/trust, appearance, and loyalty for websites, now in its second version. Like the WAMMI, the SUPR-Q provides relative rankings expressed as percentages, so a SUPR-Q percentile score of 50 is average (roughly half the websites evaluated in the past with the SUPR-Q have received better scores and half received worse). In addition to this global comparison, the SUPR-Q normative database (with data from over 70 websites and over 2500 users across 18 industries) allows comparison of scores with a subset of up to 10 other websites or with an industry. At the time of this writing, the SUPR-Q prices were:

- $1999 for a commercial license with access to the normative database
- $499 for a standard individual license
- Discounted academic and student pricing are also available

As shown in Fig. 8.19, the second version of the SUPR-Q has eight items (derived from an initial pool of 33 items), with seven 5-point items (1 = "Strongly disagree"; 5 = "Strongly agree") and one 11-point item Likelihood to Recommend item (identical to the item used in the Net Promoter Score, described later in this chapter).

To score the SUPR-Q, add the responses for the first seven questions plus half the score for the eighth item (likelihood to recommend). These raw SUPR-Q scores can range from a low of 7 to a high of 45. Comparison of raw SUPR-Q scores with the SUPR-Q database allows conversion to percentile ranks for the global score, four subscales (Usability, Trust, Loyalty, Appearance), and each of the

	The SUPR-Q Version 2	Strongly disagree 1	2	3	4	Strongly agree 5
1	This website is easy to use.	O	O	O	O	O
2	It is easy to navigate within the website.	O	O	O	O	O
3	The information on the website is credible.	O	O	O	O	O
4	The information on the website is trustworthy.	O	O	O	O	O
5	I will likely return to this website in the future.	O	O	O	O	O
6	I find the website to be attractive.	O	O	O	O	O
7	The website has a clean and simple presentation.	O	O	O	O	O

		Not at all likely 0	1	2	3	4	Neutral 5	6	7	8	9	Extremely likely 10
8	How likely are you to recommend this website to a friend or colleague?	O	O	O	O	O	O	O	O	O	O	O

FIGURE 8.19 The SUPR-Q

individual questions. For example, a global SUPR-Q score of 75% means the global score for the tested website was higher than 75% of all websites in the SUPR-Q database.

Psychometric evaluation of the SUPR-Q

Based on surveys collected from website users (Sauro, 2015, n = 3891), the reliability of SUPR-Q global and subscale scores was:

- Usability (Items 1, 2): 0.88
- Trust (Items 3, 4): 0.85
- Loyalty (Items 5, 8): 0.64
- Appearance (Items 6, 7): 0.78
- Global (All items): 0.86

All the SUPR-Q scale reliabilities exceeded 0.70 except for Loyalty, which was 0.64. The global SUPR-Q scores correlated significantly with concurrently collected SUS scores (r = 0.75), as did all four subscales (Usability: 0.73; Trust: 0.39; Loyalty: 0.61; Appearance: 0.64). In a study of 40 websites (n = 2513), the global SUPR-Q and its subscales discriminated well between the poorest and highest quality websites, with about equal discriminating power as the SUS. The means and standard deviations from this study (which can provide the basis for interpreting SUPR-Q scores) were:

- SUPR-Q: M = 3.93, SD = 0.29
- Usability: M = 4.06, SD = 0.29
- Trust: M = 3.80; SD = 0.52
- Loyalty: M = 3.91; SD = 0.46
- Appearance: M = 3.88; SD = 0.25

The SUPR-Q exhibits generally acceptable levels of reliability, with the exception of the Loyalty subscale. Sauro (2015) suggested adding an item to that subscale in the future to improve its reliability. Across its development, item alignment with factors provided evidence of construct validity, and its correlations with concurrently collected SUS scores were evidence of convergent validity. Sauro (2015) provided means and standard deviations for the SUPR-Q and its subscales that provide initial normative information for the interpretation of relatively good and poor scores.

OTHER QUESTIONNAIRES FOR ASSESSING WEBSITES

Since the beginning of the 21st century, there have been a number of other publications of questionnaires designed for the assessment of websites. The focus of this research has ranged from assessment of perceived quality and satisfaction to perceived usability. None of these questionnaires are as well known in the user research community as the WAMMI and SUPR-Q, but may be of interest to practitioners specializing in the assessment of websites.

Aladwani and Palvia (2002) developed a questionnaire to capture key characteristics of Web quality from the user's perspective. Starting with a pool of 102 representative items, their 25-item questionnaire (7-point items from 1 = "Strongly disagree" to 7 = "Strongly agree," all positive tone) measured four dimensions of Web quality, all of which had coefficient alphas exceeding 0.85: specific content (0.94), content quality (0.88), appearance (0.88), and technical adequacy (0.92). The reliability of the overall scale was 0.91. A multitrait–multimethod matrix indicated significant convergent and divergent validity, and concurrent evaluation with a 3-point rating of overall Web quality resulted in significant correlations with their overall scale ($r = 0.73$, $p < 0.01$) and the subscales (r ranging from 0.30 to 0.73, all $p < 0.01$). For the 25-item user-perceived Web quality instrument, see their Table 5 (Aladwani and Palvia, 2002, p. 474).

The WEBQUAL questionnaire was developed by Loiacono et al. (2002) to capture key characteristics of Web quality from a user perspective. Starting with an initial pool of 142 representative items for 13 key constructs, the current version has 36 7-point Likert-type items (one negative tone)—three for each of the 12 remaining constructs. The questionnaire broadly covers Usefulness, Ease-of-Use, Entertainment, and Complimentary Relationship. The reliabilities of the subscales ranged from 0.72 to 0.90 (but note that there is considerable similarity among the items in some constructs, which tends to inflate coefficient alpha). Loiacono et al. reported significant convergent and discriminant validity and significant concurrent validities with overall Web quality ($r = 0.72$), intention to purchase ($r = 0.56$), and intention to revisit the website ($r = 0.53$).

Wang and Senecal (2007) sought to develop a short, reliable, and valid questionnaire for the assessment of perceived usability of a website for comparative benchmarking purposes. Based on their literature review, they conceptualized website usability as having three factors: ease of navigation, speed, and interactivity. From an initial pool of 12 items drawn from previous questionnaires, their final questionnaire contained eight items (three for navigation, three for speed, and two for interactivity—with coefficient alphas of 0.85, 0.91, and 0.77, respectively). A confirmatory factor analysis indicated an excellent fit of the data to their three-factor model. An assessment of concurrent validity showed a significant correlation between their overall usability scores and a measurement of user attitude toward the tested website ($r = 0.73$, $p < 0.001$).

Lascu and Clow (2008, 2013) developed and validated a questionnaire for the assessment of website interaction satisfaction, drawing on the market research literature on satisfaction and service quality and the information systems literature on user information satisfaction. From an initial pool of 132 items, the final questionnaire contained 15 items identified as important characteristics of excellent websites (see their Table 3, Lascu and Clow, 2008, p. 373). Each item had a positive tone, with five scale steps starting with 5 (strongly agree with the statement) on the left and ending with 1 (strongly disagree with the statement). Factor analysis indicated support for four subscales, all with coefficient alpha exceeding 0.6: customer centeredness (0.92), transaction reliability (0.80), problem-solving ability (0.77), and ease of navigation (0.6). Coefficient alpha for the overall scale was 0.898. The results of a confirmatory factor analysis and evaluation of discriminant validity supported the four-factor model.

The Intranet Satisfaction Questionnaire (ISQ) (Bargas-Avila et al., 2009; Lewis, 2013a; Orsini et al., 2013) is a questionnaire developed to measure user satisfaction with company intranets. After the initial evaluation of items, 18 items made the cut into the first large-sample evaluation of the intranet of an insurance company (n = 881). Item analysis from the initial dataset led to the deletion of five items, leaving 13 6-point items (all positive tone, 1 = "I strongly disagree," 6 = "I strongly agree") in the second version of the questionnaire (see their Table 6, p. 1247). The results of a second large-sample evaluation (n = 1350) revealed a mean ISQ score (averaging over items) of 4.5 (SD = 0.78). The overall coefficient alpha (based on items 1–12) was 0.89. Subscale reliabilities were 0.82 for Content Quality and 0.84 for Intranet Usability. Subscale correlations with the 13th item ("Overall, I am satisfied with the Intranet") were both significant (Content Quality: $r = 0.51$; Intranet Usability: $r = 0.68$), providing evidence of concurrent validity). An exploratory factor analysis indicated two factors: Content Quality and Intranet Usability, which explained about 57% of the variability in ISQ scores. The analyses used the original German version of the ISQ, which is also available in English, Chinese, French, Italian, Japanese, Portuguese, Russian, Spanish, and Slovenian. "In November 2006, the ISQ was offered via www.Intranetsatisfaction.com in various languages for free on the Internet. Since then, over 500 companies from around the world have downloaded the tool and dozens have already made use of it" (Bargas-Avila et al., 2009, p. 1250).

The most recent addition to the set of Internet questionnaires is Joyce and Kirakowski's (2015) General Internet Attitude Scale (GAIS). Unlike questionnaires designed to elicit information about a user's state (e.g., satisfaction or other sentiment) as a consequence of interacting with a website, the goal of the GAIS was "to explore the underlying components of the attitudes of individuals to the Internet, and to measure individuals on those attitude components" (Joyce and Kirakowski, 2015, p. 506). The method of initial item selection of 97 statements from existing questionnaires for the measurement of Internet attitudes supports the content validity of the GAIS. The theoretical basis for the structure of the questionnaire was a three-component psychological model of attitude (affect, behavior, and cognition). After several rounds of refinement, the final version of the GAIS contained 21 items with an overall reliability of 0.85. Factor analysis provided evidence for four subscales: Internet Affect (nine items, reliability of 0.87), Internet Exhilaration (three items, reliability of 0.76), Social Benefit of the Internet (six items, reliability of 0.79), and Internet Detriment (three items, reliability of 0.67). Although the factor structure of the GAIS did not explicitly replicate the three-component model of attitudes, those components tended to group together in the four factors that did emerge. Similar to the finding reported by Lewis (2002), males and females seemed to have similar attitudes toward the Internet. There were, however, statistically significant differences in attitude as a function of age group, with a steady decline in attitude scores observed as age increased beyond the 25–34 years age group. There was also a significant positive correlation between overall GAIS scores and a measure of Internet self-efficacy ($r(839) = 0.43, p < 0.001$).

OTHER QUESTIONNAIRES OF INTEREST

CSUQ (COMPUTER SYSTEM USABILITY QUESTIONNAIRE)

The CSUQ is a variant of the PSSUQ (Lewis, 1995), developed to permit the collection of a large number of completed questionnaires and to see if the factor structure found for the PSSUQ in a usability testing setting would stay the same in a mailed survey. The emergence of the same factors would demonstrate the potential usefulness of the questionnaire across different user groups and research settings. The CSUQ is identical to the PSSUQ, with slight changes to the wording due to the change to nonlab research. For example, Item 3 of the PSSUQ Version 3 states, "I was able to complete the tasks and scenarios quickly using this system," but Item 3 of the CSUQ Version 3 states, "I am able to complete my work quickly using this system." The computation of CSUQ scores is the same as that for PSSUQ scores (discussed earlier in this chapter). Fig. 8.20 shows the current version of the CSUQ (with items removed to match the current Version 3 of the PSSUQ).

	The Computer System Usability Questionnaire Version 3	1 (Strongly agree)	2	3	4	5	6	7 (Strongly disagree)	NA
1	Overall, I am satisfied with how easy it is to use this system.	O	O	O	O	O	O	O	O
2	It is simple to use this system.	O	O	O	O	O	O	O	O
3	I am able to complete my work quickly using this system.	O	O	O	O	O	O	O	O
4	I feel comfortable using this system.	O	O	O	O	O	O	O	O
5	It was easy to learn to use this system.	O	O	O	O	O	O	O	O
6	I believe I became productive quickly using this system.	O	O	O	O	O	O	O	O
7	The system gives error messages that clearly tell me how to fix problems.	O	O	O	O	O	O	O	O
8	Whenever I make a mistake using the system, I recover easily and quickly.	O	O	O	O	O	O	O	O
9	The information (such as online help, on-screen messages, and other documentation) provided with this system is clear.	O	O	O	O	O	O	O	O
10	It is easy to find the information I needed.	O	O	O	O	O	O	O	O
11	The information provided with the system is effective in helping me complete my work.	O	O	O	O	O	O	O	O
12	The organization of information on the system screens is clear.	O	O	O	O	O	O	O	O
13	The interface* of this system is pleasant.	O	O	O	O	O	O	O	O
14	I like using the interface of this system.	O	O	O	O	O	O	O	O
15	This system has all the functions and capabilities I expect it to have.	O	O	O	O	O	O	O	O
16	Overall, I am satisfied with this system.	O	O	O	O	O	O	O	O

**The "interface" includes those items that you use to interact with the system. For example, some components of the interface are the keyboard, the mouse, the microphone, and the screens (including their graphics and language).*

FIGURE 8.20 The CSUQ

Out of 825 randomly selected IBM employees in the early 1990s, 325 returned the questionnaire (CSUQ Version 2, which had 19 items). A maximum likelihood confirmatory factor analysis indicated that the factor structure of the CSUQ was virtually identical to that of Version 1 of the PSSUQ (which had 18 items—see Lewis, 1992, 1995), with a coefficient alpha of 0.95 for the Overall score, 0.93 for SysUse, 0.91 for InfoQual, and 0.89 for IntQual. The values of coefficient alpha for the CSUQ scales were within 0.03 of those for the earlier evaluation of PSSUQ scales (Lewis, 1992). The CSUQ was sensitive to differences in a number of variables, including:

- Number of years of experience with the computer system (Overall: $F(4,294) = 3.12$, $p = 0.02$; InfoQual: $F(4,311) = 2.59$, $p = 0.04$; IntQual: $F(4,322) = 2.47$, $p = 0.04$)
- Type of computer used (InfoQual: $F(5,311) = 2.14$, $p = 0.06$)
- Range of experience with different computers (Overall: $F(3,322) = 2.77$, $p = 0.04$; InfoQual: $F(3,311) = 2.60$, $p = 0.05$)

These results demonstrated that the factor structure of the PSSUQ held in a nonusability lab setting, so the CSUQ scales are comparable to their corresponding PSSUQ scales. The results also show (as noted for the SUS in Sauro and Lewis, 2011) that minor changes in the wording of items for these standardized usability questionnaires do not appear to dramatically change the factor structure. The CSUQ is also available in a Turkish version (Erdinç and Lewis, 2013).

USE (USEFULNESS, SATISFACTION, AND EASE-OF-USE)

Lund (1998, 2001) published a preliminary report on the USE, a 30-item questionnaire designed to capture information about Usefulness, Ease-of-Use, Ease of Learning, and Satisfaction. The USE is available at Gary Perlman's website (http://hcibib.org/perlman/question.cgi?form=USE, or see http://usesurvey.com/ExampleQuestionnaire.html). All items have a positive tone, with scale steps that go from 1 (strongly disagree) to 7 (strongly agree). Lund used standard psychometric methods in the development of the USE (large initial item pool, factor analysis, computation of coefficient alpha, iterative development), but to date the psychometric details have not been published.

HQ (HEDONIC QUALITY)

To support research into nontask-related aspects of user experience, Hassenzahl et al. (2000) developed a questionnaire for assessing hedonic quality (HQ). The HQ has seven 7-point bipolar items. Originally in German, translated into English (Hassenzahl, 2001; Hassenzahl et al., 2000), the HQ bipolar scale anchors are:

- HQ1: interesting–boring
- HQ2: costly–cheap
- HQ3: exciting–dull
- HQ4: exclusive–standard
- HQ5: impressive–nondescript
- HQ6: original–ordinary
- HQ7: innovative–conservative

The initial study by Hassenzahl et al. (2000) included questionnaires for assessing ergonomic quality (EQ—attributes of standard definitions of usability, such as simple/complex and clear/confusing) and judgment of a product's appeal (APPEAL—attributes such as pleasant/unpleasant and desirable/undesirable). Twenty participants used seven software prototypes of varying designs to complete a task (switching off a pump in a hypothetical industrial plant). Factor analysis of the resulting data showed distinct groupings for the hypothesized HQ and EQ items into separate factors. Regression analysis showed about equal contribution of HQ and EQ to the prediction of APPEAL.

In a replication and elaboration of the previous study, Hassenzahl (2001) had 15 users rate their experience using three different types of displays (CRT, LCD, and VS—a virtual screen projected on the user's desk) using HQ, EQ, APPEAL, and the SMEQ (a measure of mental effort, described earlier in this chapter). The factor structure discriminating HQ and EQ was reasonably stable and again, regression analysis showed about equal impact of HQ and EQ on the prediction of APPEAL. As evidence of discriminant validity, EQ correlated significantly with SMEQ ($r = -0.61$, $p < 0.01$), but did not correlate with HQ ($r = 0.01$).

Hassenzahl (2004) developed related instruments exploring the measurement of hedonics, including the following:

- Stimulation hedonics (novelty, challenge)
- Identification hedonics (self-expression)
- Evocation hedonics (memory provoking)

He has also differentiated between EQ and pragmatic quality (PQ) as different aspects of standard usability (efficiency and effectiveness). The reliabilities of these various questionnaires tend to be high, usually exceeding coefficient alpha of 0.85, with reasonable patterns of relationship among them and assessments of perceived beauty and goodness.

Further application of this research has led to the development and use of the AttrakDiff questionnaire (see attrakdiff.de/index-en.html) and has influenced the development of the User Experience Questionnaire (UEQ, Rauschenberger et al., 2013). These questionnaires differ from more traditional assessments of perceived usability by virtue of their more direct focus on the perceived user experience (e.g., hedonic plus ergonomic/pragmatic quality). For example, Hassenzahl et al. (2015) recently used a version of AttrakDiff to explore aspects of experience-oriented and product-oriented evaluation.

EMO (EMOTIONAL METRIC OUTCOMES)

The EMO (Lewis and Mayes, 2014) is a standardized questionnaire designed to assess the emotional outcomes of interaction, especially the interaction of customers with service-provider personnel or software. It is a concise multifactor instrument that provides an assessment of transaction-driven personal and relationship emotional outcomes, both positive and negative. A primary goal of the EMO is to move beyond traditional assessment of satisfaction to more effectively measure customers' emotional responses to products and processes. The EMO development took place over several stages, starting with a survey that included 52 items drawing upon a variety of sources from psychology, human–computer interaction, machine learning, and market research (supporting content validity). The full version of the EMO (EMO16, shown in Fig. 8.21) has 16 items that support the computation of four subscales: Positive Relationship Affect (PRA04: Items 1–4), Negative Relationship Affect (NRA04: Items 5–8), Positive Personal Affect (PPA04: Items 9–12), and Negative Personal Affect (NPA04: Items 13–16). It is also possible to use a short (8-item) version of the EMO (EMO08) which has two rather than four items per subscale (PRA02: Items 1–2; NRA02: Items 5–6; PPA02: Items 9–10; NPA02: Items 13–14).

	The EMO Version 1	Strongly disagree 0	1	2	3	4	5	6	7	8	9	Strongly agree 10
1	This company values and appreciates my business.	O	O	O	O	O	O	O	O	O	O	O
2	This company looks out for my best interests.	O	O	O	O	O	O	O	O	O	O	O
3	This company provides personalized service.	O	O	O	O	O	O	O	O	O	O	O
4	This company responds to my questions and requests quickly.	O	O	O	O	O	O	O	O	O	O	O
5	This company finds it necessary to stretch the truth when communicating with me.	O	O	O	O	O	O	O	O	O	O	O
6	I'm apprehensive about this company's intent, actions, or outputs.	O	O	O	O	O	O	O	O	O	O	O
7	This company cares more about selling to me than about satisfying me.	O	O	O	O	O	O	O	O	O	O	O
8	Other people have told me they do not trust this company.	O	O	O	O	O	O	O	O	O	O	O
9	I felt confident.	O	O	O	O	O	O	O	O	O	O	O
10	I was content.	O	O	O	O	O	O	O	O	O	O	O
11	I felt satisfied.	O	O	O	O	O	O	O	O	O	O	O
12	I was pleased.	O	O	O	O	O	O	O	O	O	O	O
13	I felt irritated.	O	O	O	O	O	O	O	O	O	O	O
14	I was tense.	O	O	O	O	O	O	O	O	O	O	O
15	I was annoyed.	O	O	O	O	O	O	O	O	O	O	O
16	I felt frustrated.	O	O	O	O	O	O	O	O	O	O	O

FIGURE 8.21 The EMO questionnaire

To compute EMO scores, it is necessary to first reverse the scoring of the negative-tone items (NRA and NPA) using the formula $10 - x_i$, where x_i is the item score. The score for each subscale is the average of its items, and the overall EMO is the average of the four subscales. Because the EMO items use 11-point scales from 0–10, all subscale and overall means can range from 0 to 10.

Data from three surveys ($n = 3029$, 1041, and 1943—see Lewis and Mayes, 2014, for details) and from a large-sample unmoderated usability study ($n = 471$—see Lewis et al., 2015a, for details) provided substantial evidence for the psychometric quality of the EMO. Factor analysis and regression analysis generally support the designed four-factor structure, with the strongest evidence for construct validity appearing in the data from the usability study. Overall reliability estimates were high (around 0.94), with subscale reliabilities (including the two-item scales) ranging from 0.76 to 0.94. Evidence of concurrent validity comes from significant correlations with ratings of likelihood-to-recommend (ranging from 0.41 for NRA02 to 0.79 for PRA04) and overall experience (ranging from 0.44 for NRA02 to 0.83 for EMO16). The EMO has been shown to be sensitive to industry differences (insurance vs. banking), auto insurance website experience, and successful vs. unsuccessful task completion.

ACSI (AMERICAN CUSTOMER SATISFACTION INDEX)

Claes Fornell of the Stephen M. Ross Business School at the University of Michigan developed the ACSI. Based on annual national satisfaction surveys, ACSI uses a 0–100 scale for its indexes for 10 economic sectors, 45 industries, over 225 companies, and over 200 federal or local government services (www.theasci.org). The ACSI model includes perceived quality, perceived value, and customer expectations driving customer satisfaction, which in turn affects customer loyalty and complaints. The ACSI is particularly popular for its assessments of US government and commercial websites (Tullis and Albert, 2008). Their questionnaire for websites (see Tullis and Albert, 2008, Fig. 6.19, p. 154) has a core set of 14–20 questions using 10-point scales and covering attributes such as the quality of information, freshness of information, clarity of site organization, overall satisfaction, and loyalty (likelihood to return and/or recommend to others). We do not know of any published data on the psychometric properties of the ACSI, but it is a commonly used industrial metric for tracking changes in customer satisfaction.

NPS (NET PROMOTER SCORE)

Introduced in 2003 by Fred Reichheld, the NPS has become a popular metric of customer loyalty in industry (Reichheld, 2003, 2006—see www.netpromoter.com). The NPS uses a single Likelihood to Recommend (LTR) question ("How likely is it that you would recommend our company to a friend or colleague?") with 11 scale steps from 0 (Not at all likely) to 10 (Extremely likely) (Fig. 8.19, Item 13). In NPS terminology, respondents who select a 9 or 10 are "Promoters," those selecting 0 through 6 are "Detractors," and all others are "Passives." The NPS from a survey is the percentage of Promoters minus the percentage of Detractors, making the NPS a type of top-box-minus-bottom-box metric (actually, top two minus bottom seven boxes)—thus, the "net" in Net Promoter. The developers of the NPS hold that this metric is easy for managers to understand and to use to track improvements over time, and improvements in NPS have a strong relationship to company growth.

Since its introduction, the NPS has generated controversy. For example, Keiningham et al. (2007) challenged the claim of a strong relationship between NPS and company growth. In general, top-box and top-box-minus-bottom-box metrics lose information during the process of collapsing measurements from a multipoint scale to percentages of a smaller number of categories (Sauro, 2010d), and thus lose sensitivity (although increasing sample sizes can make up for lack of sensitivity in a metric).

Also, there is no well-defined method for computing confidence intervals around the NPS. When you have access to the raw LTR ratings, you can convert the LTR data to −1 for Detractors, 0 for Passives, and +1 for Promoters. The mean of this converted data will be the NPS expressed as a proportion, and you can compute a confidence interval using the methods presented in Chapter 3 for rating scales. As far as we know, there has been no systematic research on the accuracy of this approach, but at least it provides some indication of the plausible range of a given NPS.

RELATIONSHIP BETWEEN THE SUS AND NPS

Perceived usability significantly affects customer loyalty—from the files of Jeff Sauro

Even practitioners and researchers who promote the use of the NPS point out that the metric, by itself, is of limited value. You also need to understand why respondents provide the rating they do. We all want higher customer loyalty, so knowing what "levers" move the loyalty needle is important. If you can make changes that will increase loyalty, then increased revenue should follow. So, do improvements in usability increase customer loyalty?

To find out, we performed regression analyses of SUS against Net Promoter Scores (Lewis, 2012a; Sauro, 2010a)—more specifically, against responses to the NPS LTR question. In total, we examined LTR data from 2201 users from over 80 products such as rental car companies, financial applications, and websites like Amazon.com. The data came from both lab-based usability tests and surveys of recent product purchases where the same users answered both the SUS and the LTR questions. Responses to the LTR and SUS had a strong positive correlation of 0.623, meaning SUS scores explained about 39% of the variability in responses to the LTR question. A simplified yet effective regression equation for predicting LTR from SUS scores is LTR = SUS/10, so a SUS score of 70 predicts an approximate response to the LTR question of about 7. A slightly more accurate (but harder to remember) regression equation is LTR = 1.33 + 0.08(SUS).

Another way to look at the data is to see what the SUS scores are for Promoters and Detractors. As shown in Fig. 8.22, Promoters have an average SUS score of 81 whereas Detractors have an average score of 52.5. If you're looking for a benchmark SUS score based on these data, it looks like anything above an 80 will usually put you in the Promoter range.

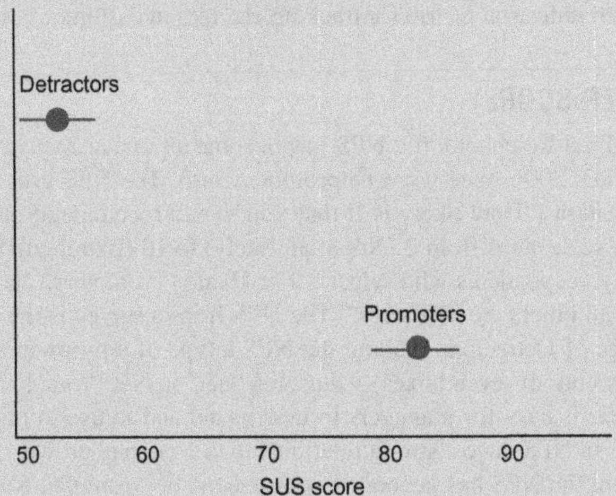

FIGURE 8.22 Mean and 99.9% confidence intervals for SUS scores for NPS Detractors and Promoters

CxPi (FORRESTER CUSTOMER EXPERIENCE INDEX)

Forrester (www.forrester.com) is a market research company with considerable focus on customer experience. Since 2007 they have produced an annual Customer Experience Index report. For their 2011 report (using data collected in 4Q 2010), they asked over 7000 US consumers about their interactions with airlines, banks, credit card providers, health insurance plans, hotels, insurance providers, ISPs, investment firms, parcel shipping firms, PC manufacturers, retailers, TV service providers, and wireless service providers.

For each of these industries and companies within industries, they provide a Customer Experience (CxPi) score. The CxPi uses responses to three questions designed to address perceived usefulness, usability, and enjoyability ("Thinking of your interactions with these firms over the past 90 days: (1) how well did they meet your needs?, (2) how easy were they to do business with?, (3) how enjoyable were they to do business with?"). For each question, respondents make choices along a 5-point scale (1 = a very negative experience; 5 = a very positive experience). Similar to the NPS, the score for each of the three indexes is a top-box-minus-bottom-box net percentage score (actually, top-two minus bottom-two). The CxPi is the average of the three index scores. We do not know of any published data on the psychometric properties of the CxPi, but it is a commonly used industrial metric for tracking annual changes in customer experience.

TAM (TECHNOLOGY ACCEPTANCE MODEL)

At roughly the same time that usability researchers were producing the first standardized usability questionnaires, market researchers were tackling similar issues. Of these, one of the most influential has been the Technology Acceptance Model, or TAM (Davis, 1989). According to the TAM, the primary factors that affect a user's intention to use a technology are its perceived usefulness and perceived ease of use. Actual use of technologies is affected by the intention to use, which is itself affected by the perceived usefulness and usability of the technology. In the TAM, perceived usefulness is the extent to which a person believes a technology will enhance job performance, and perceived ease of use is the extent to which a person believes that using the technology will be effortless. A number of studies support the validity of the TAM and its satisfactory explanation of end-user system usage (Wu et al., 2007).

There are two six-item questionnaires used in the TAM, one for Perceived Usefulness and one for Perceived Ease-of-Use (starting from initial pools of 14 items for each construct—mixed positive and negative tone). As shown in Fig. 8.23, the items for these questionnaires have seven steps from "likely" to "unlikely," each with a verbal rather than numeric label.

An initial study with 112 participants provided the data needed to refine the scales (Davis, 1989). The results of this initial study indicated that mixing the tone of the items was causing problems in the factor structure for the intended constructs. "These 'reversed' items tended to correlate more with the same item used to measure a different trait than they did with other items of the same trait, suggesting the presence of common method variance. This is ironic, since reversed scales are typically used in an effort to reduce common method variance" (Davis, 1989, p. 327). Consequently, Davis eliminated the items with negative tone, converting a few of them to positive tone to ensure enough items in the scales for high reliability, and ending with six items per construct. The final versions of the Perceived Usefulness and Perceived Ease-of-Use items appear in Table 8.9.

Davis (1989) conducted a lab study in which 40 participants evaluated (in counterbalanced order) two graphics applications with different user interfaces. Coefficient alpha was 0.98 for Perceived Usefulness and 0.94 for Perceived Ease-of-Use, and multitrait–multimethod analyses indicated appropriate convergent and divergent validity. A factor analysis of the data had the expected pattern of association of items with factors. Both Perceived Usefulness and Perceived Ease-of-Use (pooled data) correlated significantly with self-predictions of likelihood of use if the product were available at the participants' place of work (respectively, $r = 0.85$ and 0.59, both $p < 0.001$). Since its original publication, there have been some attempts to add perceived enjoyment to the model (e.g., Sun and Zhang, 2011; Teo and Noyes, 2011).

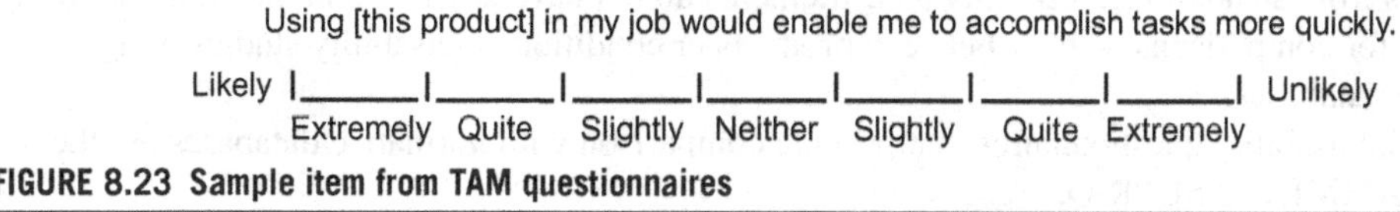

FIGURE 8.23 Sample item from TAM questionnaires

Table 8.9 The TAM Perceived Usefulness and Perceived Ease-of-Use Items

Perceived Usefulness	Perceived Ease-of-Use
Using [this product] in my job would enable me to accomplish tasks more quickly.	Learning to operate [this product] would be easy for me.
Using [this product] would improve my job performance.	I would find it easy to get [this product] to do what I want it to do.
Using [this product] in my job would increase my productivity.	My interaction with [this product] would be clear and understandable.
Using [this product] would enhance my effectiveness on the job.	I would find [this product] to be flexible to interact with.
Using [this product] would make it easier to do my job.	It would be easy for me to become skillful at using [this product].
I would find [this product] useful in my job.	I would find [this product] easy to use.

KEY POINTS

- This chapter contains descriptions of 24 standardized questionnaires designed to assess perceptions of usability or related constructs (e.g., satisfaction or usefulness).
- Those questionnaires fall into four broad categories: post-study, post-task, website, and other.
- Standardized post-study questionnaires include the QUIS, SUMI, PSSUQ, SUS, USE, and UMUX.
- Standardized post-task questionnaires include the ASQ, ER, SEQ, SMEQ, and UME.
- All of these post-study and post-task questionnaires are of potential value to usability practitioners due to psychometric qualification indicating significant reliability, validity, and sensitivity.
- Head-to-head comparisons of the methods indicate that the most sensitive post-study questionnaire is the SUS, followed by the PSSUQ; the most sensitive post-task questionnaire is the SMEQ, followed by the SEQ.
- Unless there is a compelling reason to use one of the other questionnaires, our recommendation is to use the SUS for post-study and SEQ or SMEQ for post-task assessments.
- Due to their growing use for commercial transactions, standardized usability questionnaires for websites include items focused on the assessment of attributes such as trust and service quality.
- Recent research indicates that the common practice of mixing the tone (positive and negative) of items in standardized usability questionnaires is more likely to harm rather than benefit the quality of measurement.
- Recent research also indicates that minor adjustments to the wording of items in standardized usability questionnaires do not appear to have an effect on the resulting scores (but extreme changes can affect the resulting metrics).
- The scores from standardized usability measurements do not have any inherent meaning, but they are useful for comparisons—either between products or conditions in usability studies or against normative databases.
- Commercial usability questionnaires that provide comparison with normative databases are the SUMI, WAMMI, and SUPR-Q.

- For noncommercial usability questionnaires, some normative information in the public domain is available for the PSSUQ and CSUQ (Lewis, 2002) and researchers have recently published norms for the SUS (Bangor et al., 2008, 2009; Sauro, 2011a).
- Questionnaires from the market research literature that may be of interest to usability practitioners are the ASCI, NPS, CxPi, and TAM scales (Perceived Usefulness and Perceived Ease-of-Use).

CHAPTER REVIEW QUESTIONS

1. You've run a study using the PSSUQ (standard Version 3), with the results shown in Table 8.10. What are each participant's overall and subscale scores, and what are the mean overall and subscale scores for the study?
2. Given the published information about normative patterns in responses to the PSSUQ, are you surprised by the mean score of Item 7 relative to the other items for the data in Table 8.10? What about the relative values of InfoQual and IntQual? Based on the typical values for the PSSUQ, does this product seem to be above or below average in perceived usability?

Table 8.10 Sample PSSUQ Data for Review Question 1

	Participant					
	1	2	3	4	5	6
Item 1	1	2	2	2	5	1
Item 2	1	2	2	1	5	1
Item 3	1	2	3	1	4	1
Item 4	1	1	2	1	4	1
Item 5	1	1	2	1	5	1
Item 6	1	1	4	1	4	3
Item 7	1	2	.	1	6	1
Item 8	3	1	.	1	6	1
Item 9	3	1	1	1	5	1
Item 10	1	3	2	1	4	1
Item 11	2	2	2	1	4	1
Item 12	1	1	2	1	4	1
Item 13	1	1	2	2	4	1
Item 14	1	1	2	3	4	1
Item 15	1	1	3	1	4	1
Item 16	1	1	2	1	4	1

Table 8.11 Sample SUS Data for Review Question 3

	Participant				
	1	2	3	4	5
Item 1	3	2	5	4	5
Item 2	1	1	2	2	1
Item 3	4	4	4	5	5
Item 4	1	3	1	1	1
Item 5	3	4	4	4	5
Item 6	1	2	2	2	1
Item 7	4	3	4	3	5
Item 8	1	2	1	1	1
Item 9	4	4	5	3	5
Item 10	2	1	2	3	1

3. Suppose you've run a study using the standard version of the SUS, with the following results (Table 8.11). What are the SUS scores for each participant and their average for the product?
4. Given the published information about typical SUS scores, is the average SUS for the data in Table 8.11 generally above or below average? What grade would it receive using the Sauro-Lewis SUS grading curve? If you computed a 90% confidence interval, what would the grade range be? If these participants also responded to the NPS Likelihood to Recommend item, are any of them likely to be Promoters? Using those estimated Likelihood to Recommend ratings, what is the estimated NPS?

ANSWERS TO CHAPTER REVIEW QUESTIONS

1. Table 8.12 shows the overall and subscale PSSUQ scores for each participant and the mean overall and subscale scores for the study (averaged across participants). Even though there is some missing data, only two cells in the table are empty, so it's OK to just average the available data.
2. To answer these questions, refer to Table 8.2 (PSSUQ Version 3 norms). Regarding Item 7, generally, its scores tend to be higher (poorer) than those for other items, but in this set of data, the mean item scores are fairly uniform, ranging from 1.67 to 2.40, with 2.20 for Item 7, making it one of the higher scoring items but not as much higher as is usual, which is a bit surprising. The same is true for the relative pattern of the subscales. Typically, InfoQual is about half a point higher than IntQual, but for these data the difference is only about 0.15. Based on the typical values for the PSSUQ, the mean Overall score is usually about 2.82, so with an Overall score of 1.98, this product seems to be above average in perceived usability—at least, in reference to the products evaluated to produce the norms in Table 8.2. To determine if it is significantly better than average, you'd need to compute a confidence interval on the data from the study to see if

Table 8.12 Answers for Review Question 1

	Participant						
	1	2	3	4	5	6	Mean
Item 1	1	2	2	2	5	1	2.17
Item 2	1	2	2	1	5	1	2.00
Item 3	1	2	3	1	4	1	2.00
Item 4	1	1	2	1	4	1	1.67
Item 5	1	1	2	1	5	1	1.83
Item 6	1	1	4	1	4	3	2.33
Item 7	1	2	.	1	6	1	2.20
Item 8	3	1	.	1	6	1	2.40
Item 9	3	1	1	1	5	1	2.00
Item 10	1	3	2	1	4	1	2.00
Item 11	2	2	2	1	4	1	2.00
Item 12	1	1	2	1	4	1	1.67
Item 13	1	1	2	2	4	1	1.83
Item 14	1	1	2	3	4	1	2.00
Item 15	1	1	3	1	4	1	1.83
Item 16	1	1	2	1	4	1	1.67
Overall	1.31	1.44	2.21	1.25	4.50	1.13	1.97
SysUse	1.00	1.50	2.50	1.17	4.50	1.33	2.00
InfoQual	1.83	1.67	1.75	1.00	4.83	1.00	2.01
IntQual	1.00	1.00	2.33	2.00	4.00	1.00	1.89

the interval included or excluded the benchmark. It turns out that the 95% confidence interval for Overall ranges from 0.622 to 3.33—a fairly wide interval due to the small sample size and relatively high variability—so even though the mean is lower than the norm, the interval is consistent with the norm. This Overall score is not statistically significantly different from the norm of 2.82.

3. Table 8.13 shows the *recoded* item values and SUS scores for each participant and the mean SUS score for the study averaged across participants.
4. Based on the data collected by Sauro (2011a), the mean SUS score across a large number of usability studies is 68, so the mean from this study is above average. On the Sauro-Lewis SUS grading curve, scores between 80.8 and 84.0 get an A (Table 8.5). A 90% confidence interval on these data ranges from about 71 to 93, so the corresponding grade range is from C to A+ (at least you know it's probably not a D), and because the confidence interval does not include 68, the result is significantly above average ($p < 0.10$). If these participants also responded to the

Table 8.13 Answers for Review Question 3

	Participants					
	1	2	3	4	5	
Item 1	2	1	4	3	4	
Item 2	4	4	3	3	4	
Item 3	3	3	3	4	4	
Item 4	4	2	4	4	4	
Item 5	2	3	3	3	4	
Item 6	4	3	3	3	4	
Item 7	3	2	3	2	4	
Item 8	4	3	4	4	4	
Item 9	3	3	4	2	4	
Item 10	3	4	3	2	4	
						Mean
Overall	80	70	85	75	100	82.00
Pred-LTR	8	7	8	7	10	Grade: A

NPS Likelihood to Recommend item, only one of them is likely to be a Promoter (responding with a 9 or 10 to the Likelihood to Recommend question). The simplified regression equation for estimating Likelihood to Recommend from SUS is LTR = SUS/10, so the predicted Likelihood to Recommend responses for these five participants are, respectively, 8, 7, 8, 7, and 10. Given these LTR scores, there are 0% Detractors and 20% (1/5) Promoters, for an estimated NPS of 20% (%Promoters minus %Detractors).

REFERENCES

Aladwani, A.M., Palvia, P.C., 2002. Developing and validating an instrument for measuring user perceived Web quality. Inform. Manag. 39, 467–476.

Albert, W., Dixon, E., 2003. Is this what you expected? The use of expectation measures in usability testing. Paper presented at the Usability Professionals Association Annual Conference, UPA, Scottsdale, AZ.

Anastasi, A., 1976. Psychological Testing. Macmillan, New York, NY.

Andrich, D., 1978. Application of a psychometric rating model to ordered categories which are scored with successive integers. Appl. Psychol. Meas. 2 (4), 581–594.

ANSI, 2001. Common Industry Format for Usability Test Reports (ANSI-NCITS 354-2001). Washington, DC: Author.

Azzara, C.V., 2010. Questionnaire Design for Business Research. Tate Publishing, Mustang, OK.

Bangor, A., Kortum, P.T., Miller, J.T., 2008. An empirical evaluation of the System Usability Scale. Int. J. Hum.-Comput. Interact. 24, 574–594.

Bangor, A., Kortum, P.T., Miller, J.T., 2009. Determining what individual SUS scores mean: adding an adjective rating scale. J. Usability Stud. 4 (3), 114–123.

Bangor, A., Joseph, K., Sweeney-Dillon, M., Stettler, G., Pratt, J., 2013. Using the SUS to help demonstrate usability's value to business goals. In: Proceedings of the Human Factors Society and Ergonomics Society Annual Meeting, HFES, Santa Monica, CA, pp. 202–205.

Bargas-Avila, J.A., Lötscher, J., Orsini, S., Opwis, K., 2009. Intranet Satisfaction Questionnaire: development and validation of a questionnaire to measure user satisfaction with the Intranet. Comput. Hum. Behav. 25, 1241–1250.

Barnette, J.J., 2000. Effects of stem and Likert response option reversals on survey internal consistency: if you feel the need, there is a better alternative to using those negatively worded stems. Educ. Psychol. Meas. 60, 361–370.

Benedek, J., Miner, T., 2002. Measuring desirability: new methods for evaluating desirability in a usability lab setting. Paper presented at the Usability Professionals Association Annual Conference, UPA, Orlando, FL.

Blažica, B., Lewis, J.R., 2015. A Slovene translation of the System Usability Scale (SUS). Int. J. Hum.-Comput. Interact. 31, 112–117.

Bond, T.G., Fox, C.M., 2001. Applying the Rasch Model: Fundamental Measurement in the Human Sciences. Lawrence Erlbaum, Mahwah, NJ.

Borsci, S., Federici, S., Lauriola, M., 2009. On the dimensionality of the System Usability Scale: a test of alternative measurement models. Cogn. Process. 10, 193–197.

Borsci, S., Federici, S., Bacci, S., Gnaldi, M., Bartolucci, F., 2015. Assessing user satisfaction in the era of user experience: comparison of the SUS, UMUX and UMUX-LITE as a function of product experience. Int. J. Hum.-Comput. Interact. 31, 484–495.

Brace, I., 2008. Questionnaire Design: How to Plan, Structure, and Write Survey Material for Effective Market Research, second ed. Kogan Page Limited, London, UK.

Brooke, J., 1996. SUS: A 'quick and dirty' usability scale. In: Jordan, P., Thomas, B., Weerdmeester, B. (Eds.), Usability Evaluation in Industry. Taylor & Francis, London, UK, pp. 189–194.

Brooke, J., 2013. SUS: a retrospective. J. Usability Stud. 8 (2), 29–40.

Cavallin, H., Martin, W.M., Heylighen, A., 2007. How relative absolute can be: SUMI and the impact of the nature of the task in measuring perceived software usability. Artif. Intell. Soc. 22, 227–235.

Cheung, G.W., Rensvold, R.B., 2000. Assessing extreme and acquiescence response sets in cross-cultural research using structural equations modeling. J. Cross-Cult. Psychol. 31, 187–212.

Chin, J.P., Diehl, V.A., Norman, K.L., 1988. Development of an instrument measuring user satisfaction of the human–computer interface. In: Proceedings of CHI 1988, ACM, Washington, DC, pp. 213–218.

Cordes, R.E., 1984a. Software ease of use evaluation using magnitude estimation. In: Proceedings of the Human Factors Society, HFS, Santa Monica, CA, pp. 157–160.

Cordes, R.E., 1984b. Use of magnitude estimation for evaluating product ease of use (Tech. Report 82.0135), IBM, Tucson, AZ.

Cortina, J.M., 1993. What is coefficient alpha? An examination of theory and applications. J. Exp. Psychol. 78 (1), 98–104.

Courage, C., Baxter, K., 2005. Understanding Your Users: A Practical Guide to User Requirements. Morgan Kaufmann, San Francisco, CA.

Cronbach, L.J., 1946. Response sets and test validity. Educ. Psychol. Meas. 6, 475–494.

Davis, D., 1989. Perceived usefulness, perceived ease of use, and user acceptance of information technology. MIS Quart. 13 (3), 319–339.

Embretson, S.E., Reise, S.P., 2000. Item Response Theory for Psychologists. Lawrence Erlbaum Associates, Inc, Mahwah, NJ.

Erdinç, O., Lewis, J.R., 2013. Psychometric evaluation of the T-CSUQ: the Turkish version of the Computer System Usability Questionnaire. Int. J. Hum.-Comput. Interact. 29, 319–323.

Finstad, K., 2006. The System Usability Scale and non-native English speakers. J. Usability Stud. 1 (4), 185–188.

Finstad, K., 2010a. Response interpolation and scale sensitivity: evidence against 5-point scales. J. Usability Stud. 5 (3), 104–110.

Finstad, K., 2010b. The usability metric for user experience. Interact. Comput. 22, 323–327.

Finstad, K., 2013. Response to commentaries on "The Usability Metric for User Experience". Interact. Comput. 25, 327–330.

Grier, R.A., Bangor, A., Kortum, P., Peres, S.C., 2013. The System Usability Scale: beyond standard usability testing. In: Proceedings of the Human Factors Society and Ergonomics Society Annual Meeting, HFES, Santa Monica, CA, pp. 187–191.

Grimm, S.D., Church, A.T., 1999. A cross-cultural study of response biases in personality measures. J. Res. Pers. 33, 415–441.

Hassenzahl, M., 2001. The effect of perceived hedonic quality on product appealingness. Int. J. Hum.-Comput. Interact. 13 (4), 481–499.

Hassenzahl, M., 2004. The interplay of beauty, goodness, and usability in interactive products. Hum.-Comput. Interact. 19, 319–349.

Hassenzahl, M., Platz, A., Burmester, M., Lehner, K., 2000. Hedonic and ergonomic quality aspects determine a software's appeal. In: Proceedings of CHI 2000, ACM, The Hague, Amsterdam, pp. 201–208.

Hassenzahl, M., Wiklund-Engblom, A., Bengs, A., Hägglund, S., Diefenbach, S., 2015. Experience-oriented and product-oriented evaluation: psychological need fulfillment, positive affect, and product perception. Int. J. Hum.-Comput. Interact. 31, 530–544.

Hollemans, G., 1999. User satisfaction measurement methodologies: extending the user satisfaction questionnaire. In: Proceedings of HCI International 1999, Lawrence Erlbaum, Mahwah, NJ, pp. 1008–1012.

Hornbæk, K., 2006. Current practice in measuring usability: challenges to usability studies and research. Int. J. Hum.-Comput. Stud. 64 (2), 79–102.

Hornbæk, K., Law, E.L., 2007. Meta-analysis of correlations among usability measures. In: Proceedings of CHI 2007, ACM, San Jose, CA, pp. 617–626.

Ibrahim, A.M., 2001. Differential responding to positive and negative items: the case of a negative item in a questionnaire for course and faculty evaluation. Psychol. Rep. 88, 497–500.

ISO. (1998). Ergonomic requirements for office work with visual display terminals (VDTs), Part 11, Guidance on usability (ISO 9241-11:1998E). Geneva, Switzerland: Author.

Joyce, M., Kirakowski, J., 2015. Measuring attitudes towards the Internet: the General Internet Attitude Scale. Int. J. Hum.-Comput. Interact. 31, 506–517.

Karn, K., Little, A., Nelson, G., Sauro, J., Kirakowski, J., Albert, W., Norman, K., 2008. Subjective ratings of usability: reliable or ridiculous? Panel Presentation at the Usability Professionals Association Annual Conference, UPA, Baltimore, MD.

Keiningham, T.L., Cooil, B., Andreassen, T.W., Aksoy, L., 2007. A longitudinal examination of Net Promoter and firm revenue growth. J. Market. 71, 39–51.

Kirakowski, J., 1996. The software usability measurement inventory: background and usage. In: Jordan, P., Thomas, B., Weerdmeester, B. (Eds.), Usability Evaluation in Industry. Taylor & Francis, London, UK, pp. 169–178, Available from: www.ucc.ie/hfrg/questionnaires/sumi/index.html.

Kirakowski, J., Cierlik, B., 1998. Measuring the usability of websites. In: Proceedings of the Human Factors and Ergonomics Society 42nd Annual Meeting, HFES, Santa Monica, CA, pp. 424–428. Available from: www.wammi.com

Kirakowski, J., Corbett, M., 1993. SUMI: the Software Usability Measurement Inventory. Br. J. Educ. Technol. 24, 210–212.

Kirakowski, J., Dillon, A., 1988. The Computer User Satisfaction Inventory (CUSI): Manual and Scoring Key. Human Factors Research Group, University College of Cork, Cork, Ireland.

Kortum, P., Bangor, A., 2013. Usability ratings for everyday products measured with the System Usability Scale. Int. J. Hum.-Comput. Interact. 29, 67–76.

Kortum, P., Johnson, M., 2013. The relationship between levels of user experience with a product and perceived system usability. In: Proceedings of the Human Factors Society and Ergonomics Society Annual Meeting, HFES, Santa Monica, CA, pp. 197–201.

Kortum, P., Peres, S.C., 2014. The relationship between system effectiveness and subjective usability scores using the System Usability Scale. Int. J. Hum.-Comput. Interact. 30, 575–584.

Kortum, P., Sorber, M., 2015. Measuring the usability of mobile applications for phones and tablets. Int. J. Hum.-Comput. Interact. 31, 518–529.

Kuniavsky, M., 2003. Observing the User Experience: A Practitioner's Guide to User Research. Morgan Kaufmann, San Francisco, CA.

LaLomia, M.J., Sidowski, J.B., 1990. Measurements of computer satisfaction, literacy, and aptitudes: a review. Int. J. Hum.–Comput. Interact. 2, 231–253.

Landauer, T.K., 1997. Behavioral research methods in human–computer interaction. In: Helander, M., Landauer, T.K., Prabhu, P. (Eds.), Handbook of Human–Computer Interaction. second ed. Elsevier, Amsterdam, Netherlands, pp. 203–227.

Lascu, D., Clow, K.E., 2008. Web site interaction satisfaction: scale development consideration. J. Internet Commer. 7 (3), 359–378.

Lascu, D., Clow, K.E., 2013. Website interaction satisfaction: a reassessment. Interact. Comput. 25, 307–311.

Lewis, J.R., 1990a. Psychometric evaluation of a post-study system usability questionnaire: The PSSUQ (Tech. Report 54.535), International Business Machines Corp, Boca Raton, FL.

Lewis, J. R., 1990b. Psychometric evaluation of an after-scenario questionnaire for computer usability studies: The ASQ (Tech. Report 54.541), International Business Machines Corp., Boca Raton, FL .

Lewis, J.R., 1991. Psychometric evaluation of an after-scenario questionnaire for computer usability studies: the ASQ. SIGCHI Bull. 23, 78–81.

Lewis, J.R., 1992. Psychometric evaluation of the Post-Study System Usability Questionnaire: the PSSUQ. In: Proceedings of the Human Factors Society 36th Annual Meeting, Human Factors Society, Santa Monica, CA, pp. 1259–1263.

Lewis, J.R., 1993. Multipoint scales: mean and median differences and observed significance levels. Int. J. Hum.-Comput. Interact. 5, 382–392.

Lewis, J.R., 1995. IBM computer usability satisfaction questionnaires: psychometric evaluation and instructions for use. Int. J. Hum.-Comput. Interact. 7, 57–78.

Lewis, J.R., 1999. Tradeoffs in the design of the IBM computer usability satisfaction questionnaires. In: Proceedings of HCI International 1999, Lawrence Erlbaum, Mahwah, NJ , pp. 1023–1027.

Lewis, J.R., 2002. Psychometric evaluation of the PSSUQ using data from five years of usability studies. Int. J. Hum.–Comput. Interact. 14, 463–488.

Lewis, J.R., 2011. Practical Speech User Interface Design. Taylor & Francis, Boca Raton, FL.

Lewis, J.R., 2012a. Predicting net promoter scores from system usability scale scores. Available from: www.measuringu.com/blog/nps-sus.php.

Lewis, J.R., 2012b. Usability testing. In: Salvendy, G. (Ed.), Handbook of Human Factors and Ergonomics. fourth ed. John Wiley, New York, NY, pp. 1267–1312.

Lewis, J.R., 2013a. Critical review of "Intranet Satisfaction Questionnaire: development and validation of a questionnaire to measure user satisfaction with the intranet". Interact. Comput. 25, 299–301.

Lewis, J.R., 2013b. Critical review of "The Usability Metric for User Experience". Interact. Comput. 25, 320–324.

Lewis, J.R., Mayes, D.K., 2014. Development and psychometric evaluation of the Emotional Metric Outcomes (EMO) questionnaire. Int. J. Hum.-Comput. Interact. 30, 685–702.

Lewis, J.R., Sauro, J., 2009. The factor structure of the System Usability Scale. In: Kurosu, M. (Ed.), Human Centered Design, HCII 2009. Springer-Verlag, Heidelberg, Germany, pp. 94–103.

Lewis, J.R., Henry, S.C., Mack, R.L., 1990. Integrated office software benchmarks: a case study. In: Diaper, D. et al.,(Ed.), In: Proceedings of the 3rd IFIP Conference on Human–Computer Interaction, INTERACT '90. Elsevier Science, Cambridge, UK, pp. 337–343.

Lewis, J.R., Utesch, B.S., Maher, D.E., 2013. UMUX-LITE—when there's no time for the SUS. In: Proceedings of CHI 2013, Association for Computing Machinery, Paris, France, pp. 2099–2102.

Lewis, J.R., Brown, J., Mayes, D.K., 2015a. Psychometric evaluation of the EMO and the SUS in the context of a large-sample unmoderated usability study. Int. J. Hum.-Comput. Interact. 31, 545–553.

Lewis, J.R., Utesch, B.S., Maher, D.E., 2015b. Measuring perceived usability: the SUS, UMUX-LITE, and AltUsability. Int. J. Hum.-Comput. Int. 31, 496–505.

Loiacono, E.T., Watson, R.T., Goodhue, D.L., 2002. WEBQUAL: a measure of website quality. Market. Theory Appl. 13 (3), 432–438.

Lucey, N.M., 1991. More than meets the I: User-satisfaction of computer systems (Unpublished thesis for Diploma in Applied Psychology). University College Cork, Cork, Ireland.

Lund, A., 1998. USE Questionnaire Resource Page, Available from: http://usesurvey.com.

Lund, A., 2001. Measuring usability with the USE questionnaire. Usability User Exp. Newslett. STC Usability SIG 8 (2), 1–4, Available from: www.stcsig.org/usability/newsletter/0110_measuring_with_use.html.

Massaro, D.W., 1975. Experimental Psychology and Information Processing. Rand McNally College Publishing Company, Chicago, IL.

McGee, M., 2003. Usability magnitude estimation. In: Proceedings of the Human Factors and Ergonomics Society 47th Annual Meeting, HFES, Santa Monica, CA, pp. 691–695.

McGee, M., 2004. Master usability scaling: magnitude estimation and master scaling applied to usability measurement. In: Proceedings of CHI 2004, ACM, Vienna, Austria, pp. 335–342.

McLellan, S., Muddimer, A., Peres, S.C., 2012. The effect of experience on System Usability Scale ratings. J. Usability Stud. 7 (2), 56–67.

McSweeney, R., 1992. SUMI: A psychometric approach to software evaluation (unpublished M.A. (Qual.) thesis in applied psychology). University College of Cork, Cork, Ireland. Available from: http://sumi.ucc.ie/sumipapp.html.

Molich, R., Kirakowski, J, Sauro, J., Tullis, T., 2009. Comparative usability task measurement workshop (CUE-8). Workshop conducted at the UPA 2009 Conference in Portland, OR.

Mussen, P., Rosenzweig, M.R., Aronson, E., Elkind, D., Feshbach, S., Geiwitz, J., Glickman, S.E., Murdock, B.B., Wertheimer, M., Harvey, L.O., 1977. Psychology: An Introduction, second ed. D.C. Heath and Company, Lexington, MA.

Nunnally, J.C., 1978. Psychometric Theory. McGraw-Hill, New York, NY.

Orsini, S., Opwis, K., Bargas-Avila, J.A., 2013. Response to the reviews on Bargas-Avila et al (2009) 'Intranet Satisfaction Questionnaire: Development and validation of a questionnaire to measure user satisfaction with the intranet'. Interact. Comput. 25, 304–306.

Parasuraman, A., 1986. Marketing Research. Addison-Wesley, Reading, MA.

Peres, S.C., Pham, T., Phillips, R., 2013. Validation of the System Usability Scale (SUS): SUS in the wild. In: Proceedings of the Human Factors and Ergonomics Society Annual Meeting, HFES, Santa Monica, CA, pp. 192–196.

Presser, S., Schuman, H., 1980. The measurement of a middle position in attitude surveys. Pub. Opin. Quart. 44 (1), 70–85.

Preston, C.C., Colman, A.M., 2000. Optimal number of response categories in rating scales: reliability, validity, discriminating power, and respondent preferences. Acta Psychol. 104, 1–15.

Quilty, L.C., Oakman, J.M., Risko, E., 2006. Correlates of the Rosenberg Self-Esteem Scale method effects. Struct. Eq. Model. 13 (1), 99–117.

Rauschenberger, M., Schrepp, M., Cota, M.P., Olschner, S., Thomaschewski, J., 2013. Efficient measurement of the user experience of interactive products: How to use the User Experience Questionnaire (UEQ). Int. J. Artif. Intell. Interact. Multimed. 2 (1), 39–45.

Reichheld, F.F., 2003. The one number you need to grow. Harvard Bus. Rev. 81, 46–54.

Reichheld, F., 2006. The Ultimate Question: Driving Good Profits and True Growth. Harvard Business School Press, Boston MA.

Reise, S.P., Ainsworth, A.T., Haviland, M.G., 2005. Item response theory: fundamentals, applications, and promise in psychological research. Curr. Dir. Psychol. Sci. 14 (2), 95–101.

Safar, J.A., Turner, C.W.,2005. Validation of a two factor structure of system trust. In: Proceedings of the Human Factors and Ergonomics Society 49th Annual Meeting, HFES, Santa Monica, CA, pp. 497–501.

Sauro, J., 2010a. Does better usability increase customer loyalty? Available from: www.measuringu.com/usability-loyalty.php.

Sauro, J., 2010b. If you could only ask one question, use this one. Available from: www.measuringu.com/blog/single-question.php.

Sauro, J., 2010c. That's the worst website ever! Effects of extreme survey items. Available from: www.measuringu.com/blog/extreme-items.php.

Sauro, J., 2010d. Top-box scoring of rating scale data. Available from: www.measuringu.com/blog/top-box.php.

Sauro, J., 2011a. A Practical Guide to the System Usability Scale (SUS): Background, Benchmarks & Best Practices. Measuring Usability LLC, Denver, CO.

Sauro, J., 2011b. The Standardized User Experience Percentile Rank Questionnaire (SUPR-Q). Available from: www.suprq.com/

Sauro, J., 2015. SUPR-Q: A comprehensive measure of the quality of the website user experience. J. Usability Stud. 10 (2), 68–86.

Sauro, J., Dumas, J.S., 2009. Comparison of three one-question, post-task usability questionnaires. In: Proceedings of CHI 2009, ACM, Boston, MA, pp. 1599–1608.

Sauro, J., Lewis, J.R., 2009. Correlations among prototypical usability metrics: evidence for the construct of usability. In: Proceedings of CHI 2009, ACM, Boston, MA, pp. 1609–1618.

Sauro, J., Lewis, J.R., 2011. When designing usability questionnaires, does it hurt to be positive? In: Proceedings of CHI 2011, ACM, Vancouver, Canada, pp. 2215–2223.

Schmettow, M., Vietze, W., 2008. Introducing item response theory for measuring usability inspection processes. In: Proceedings of CHI 2008, ACM, Florence, Italy, pp. 893–902.

Slaughter, L., Harper, B., Norman, K., 1994. Assessing the equivalence of the paper and on-line formats of the QUIS 5.5. In: Proceedings of the 2nd Annual Mid-Atlantic Human Factors Conference, HFES, Washington, DC, pp. 87–91.

Spector, P., Van Katwyk, P., Brannick, M., Chen, P., 1997. When two factors don't reflect two constructs: how item characteristics can produce artifactual factors. J. Manag. 23 (5), 659–677.

Sun, H., Zhang, P., 2011. Causal relationships between perceived enjoyment and perceived ease of use: an alternative approach. J. Assoc. Inform. Syst. 7 (9), 618–645.

Tedesco, D.P., Tullis, T.S., 2006. A comparison of methods for eliciting post-task subjective ratings in usability testing. Paper presented at the Usability Professionals Association Annual Conference, UPA, Broomfield, CO.

Teo, T., Noyes, J., 2011. An assessment of the influence of perceived enjoyment and attitude on the intention to use technology among pre-service teachers: a structural equation modeling approach. Comput. Educ. 57 (2), 1645–1653.

Thurstone, L.L., 1928. Attitudes can be measured. Am. J. Sociol. 33, 529–554.

Travis, D. (2008). Measuring satisfaction: beyond the usability questionnaire. Available from: www.userfocus.co.uk/articles/satisfaction.html

Tullis, T., Albert, B., 2008. Measuring the User Experience: Collecting, Analyzing, and Presenting Usability Metrics. Morgan Kaufmann, Burlington, MA.

Tullis, T.S., Stetson, J.N., 2004. A comparison of questionnaires for assessing website usability. Paper presented at the Usability Professionals Association Annual Conference, UPA, Minneapolis, MN(home.comcast.net/~tomtullis/publications/UPA2004TullisStetson.pdf).

van de Vijver, F.J.R., Leung, K., 2001. Personality in cultural context: methodological issues. J. Pers. 69, 1007–1031.

Wang, J., Senecal, S., 2007. Measuring perceived website usability. J. Internet Commer. 6 (4), 97–112.

Whiteside, J., Bennett, J., Holtzblatt, K., 1988. Usability engineering: Our experience and evolution. In: Helander, M. (Ed.), Handbook of Human–Computer Interaction. North-Holland, Amsterdam, Amsterdam, Netherlands, pp. 791–817.

Wu, J., Chen, Y., Lin, L., 2007. Empirical evaluation of the revised end user computing acceptance model. Comput. Hum. Behav. 23, 162–174.

Zickar, M.J., 1998. Modeling item-level data with item response theory. Curr. Dir. Psychol. Sci. 7, 104–109.

Zijlstra, R., van Doorn, L., 1985. The construction of a scale to measure subjective effort (Tech. Rep.). Delft, Netherlands: Delft University of Technology, Department of Philosophy and Social Sciences.

Zviran, M., Glezer, C., Avni, I., 2006. User satisfaction from commercial web sites: the effect of design and use. Inform. Manag. 43, 157–178.

CHAPTER

SIX ENDURING CONTROVERSIES IN MEASUREMENT AND STATISTICS

9

INTRODUCTION

> "There is, of course, nothing strange or scandalous about divisions of opinion among scientists. This is a condition for scientific progress." (Grove, 1989, p. 133)

> "Criticism is the mother of methodology." (Abelson's 8th law, 1995)

Controversy is one of the engines of scientific progress. Proponents of one point of view debate those who hold a different point of view, ideally using empirical (data-based) and rational (logic-based) arguments. When there is no clear winner, these debates can carry on over decades, or even centuries. The fields of measurement and statistics are no strangers to such debates (Abelson, 1995; Cowles, 1989; Stigler, 1986, 1999).

Because many usability practitioners deeply depend on the use of measurement and statistics to guide their design recommendations, they inherit these controversies. In earlier chapters of this book, we've already addressed a number of controversies, including:

- Can you use statistical analysis when samples are small? (see Chapters 3–7 for numerous examples of using statistics with small sample sizes)
- What is the best average to report when estimating task completion times? (Chapter 3, "The Geometric Mean")
- What is the best choice for estimating binomial confidence intervals? (Chapter 3, "Adjusted-Wald: Add Two Successes and Two Failures")
- Is it legitimate to use mid-probabilities rather than exact tests? (Chapter 4, "Mid-probabilities")
- When are *t*-tests robust (insensitive) to violations of the assumptions of normality and equal variance? (Chapter 5, "Normality assumption of the paired *t*-test" and "Assumptions of the *t*-tests")
- What is the best choice for analyzing 2 × 2 contingency tables? (Chapter 5, "Comparing Completion Rates, Conversion Rates, and A/B Testing")
- Does observing five users enable the discovery of 85% of usability problems (Chapter 7, "Reconciling the 'Magic Number Five' with 'Eight is Not Enough')
- Is it possible to estimate the total number of problems available for discovery (and thus the number of still undiscovered problems) in a formative usability study? (Chapter 7, "Estimating the number of problems available for discovery and the number of undiscovered problems")

Quantifying the User Experience. http://dx.doi.org/10.1016/B978-0-12-802308-2.00009-6

- Should usability practitioners use methods based on the binomial probability formula when planning and analyzing the results of formative user research? (Chapter 7, "Other Statistical Models for Problem Discovery")
- How many scale steps should there be in the items used in standardized usability questionnaires? (Chapter 8, "Number of scale steps")
- Is it necessary to balance positive and negative tone of the items in standardized usability questionnaires? (Chapter 8, "Does it hurt to be positive? Evidence from an alternate form of the SUS")

In this chapter we discuss in a little more detail six enduring controversies, summarizing both sides of each issue and what we, as pragmatic user researchers, recommend. Whether you ultimately agree or disagree with our analyses and recommendations, always keep in mind Abelson's third law (Abelson, 1995, xv): "Never flout a convention just once." In other words, within a single study or group of related studies, you should consistently apply whatever decision you've made, controversial or not. Ideally, you should make and document these decisions before collecting any data to reduce the temptation to pick and choose among the alternatives to make the findings favorable to your point of view (capitalizing on chance effects). The main goal of this chapter is to provide the information needed to make those decisions. Several of the controversies involve discussions of Type I and Type II errors, so if you don't remember what they are, be sure to review Chapter 6 ("Example 7: Where's the Power?", especially Fig. 6.3).

IS IT OK TO AVERAGE DATA FROM MULTIPOINT SCALES?

ON ONE HAND

In 1946, S. S. Stevens declared that all numbers are not created equal. Specifically, he defined four levels of measurement:

- **Nominal**: Numbers that are simply labels, such as the numbering of football players or model numbers.
- **Ordinal**: Numbers that have an order, but where the differences between numbers do not necessarily correspond to the differences in the underlying attribute, such as levels of multipoint rating scales or rank order of baseball teams based on percentage of wins.
- **Interval**: Numbers that are not only ordinal, but for which equal differences in the numbers correspond to equal differences in the underlying attribute, such as Fahrenheit or Celsius temperature scales.
- **Ratio**: Numbers that are not only interval, but for which there is a true 0 point so equal ratios in the numbers correspond to equal ratios in the underlying attribute, such as time intervals (reaction time, task completion times) or the Kelvin temperature scale.

From these four classes of measurements, Stevens developed a rational argument that certain types of arithmetic operations were not reasonable to apply to certain types of data. Based on his "principle of invariance," he argued against doing anything more than counting nominal and ordinal data, and restricted addition, subtraction, multiplication, and division to interval and ratio data. For example, because you need to add and divide data to compute an arithmetic mean, he stated (Stevens, 1959, pp. 26–28):

> Depending upon what type of scale we have constructed, some statistics are appropriate, others not. … The criterion for the appropriateness of a statistic is invariance under the transformations permitted by the scale. … Thus, the mean is appropriate to an interval scale and also to a ratio scale (but not, of course, to an ordinal or a nominal scale).

From this perspective, strictly speaking, the multipoint scales commonly used for rating attitudes are ordinal measurements, so it would not be permissible to even compute their arithmetic means. If it's illogical to compute means of rating scale data, then it follows that it is incorrect when analyzing ordinal or nominal data to use statistical procedures such as *t*-tests that depend on computing the mean. Stevens' levels of measurement have been very influential, appearing in numerous statistics textbooks and used to guide recommendations given to users of some statistical analysis programs (Velleman and Wilkinson, 1993).

ON THE OTHER HAND

After the publication of Stevens' levels of measurement, arguments against their relationship to permissible arithmetic operations and associated statistical procedures appeared. For example:

> That I do not accept Stevens' position on the relationship between strength of measurement and "permissible" statistical procedures should be evident from the kinds of data used as examples throughout this Primer: level of agreement with a questionnaire item, as measured on a 5-point scale having attached verbal labels … This is not to say, however, that the researcher may simply ignore the level of measurement provided by his or her data. It is indeed crucial for the investigator to take this factor into account in considering the kinds of theoretical statements and generalizations he or she makes on the basis of significance tests. (Harris, 1985, pp. 326–328)

> Even if one believes that there is a "real" scale for each attribute, which is either mirrored directly in a particular measure or mirrored as some monotonic transformation, an important question is, "What difference does it make if the measure does not have the same zero point or proportionally equal intervals as the 'real' scale?" If the scientist assumes, for example, that the scale is an interval scale when it "really" is not, something should go wrong in the daily work of the scientist. What would really go wrong? All that could go wrong would be that the scientist would make misstatements about the specific form of the relationship between the attribute and other variables. … How seriously are such misassumptions about scale properties likely to influence the reported results of scientific experiments? In psychology at the present time, the answer in most cases is "very little." (Nunnally, 1978, p. 28)

For analyzing ordinal data, some researchers have recommended the use of statistical methods that are similar to the well-known *t*- and *F*-tests, but which replace the original data with ranks before analysis (Bradley, 1976). These methods (e.g., the Mann–Whitney *U*-test, the Friedman test, or the Kruskal–Wallis test), however, involve taking the means and standard deviations of the ranks, which are ordinal—not interval or ratio—data. Despite these violations of permissible manipulation of the data from Stevens' point-of-view, those methods work perfectly well.

FIGURE 9.1 Example of assignment of football numbers.

Source: Gabe Clogston (2009), used with permission.

Probably the most famous counterargument was by Lord (1953) with his parable of a retired professor who had a machine used to randomly assign football numbers to the jerseys of freshmen and sophomore football players at his university—a clear use of numbers as labels (nominal data). After assigning numbers, the freshmen complained that the assignment wasn't random—they claimed to have received generally smaller numbers than the sophomores, and that the sophomores must have tampered with the machine. "The sophomore team was laughing at them because they had such low numbers (Fig. 9.1). The freshmen were all for routing the sophomores out of their beds one by one and throwing them in the river" (pp. 750–751).

In a panic and to avoid the impending violence, the professor consulted with a statistician to investigate how likely it was that the freshmen got their low numbers by chance. Over the professor's objections, the statistician determined the population mean and standard deviation of the football numbers—54.3 and 16.0, respectively. He found that the mean of the freshmen's numbers was too low to have happened by chance, strongly indicating that the sophomores had tampered with the football number machine to get larger numbers. The famous fictional dialog between the professor and the statistician was (Lord, 1953, p. 751)

> "But these numbers are not cardinal numbers," the professor expostulated. "You can't add them."
>
> "Oh, can't I?" said the statistician. "I just did. Furthermore, after squaring each number, adding the squares, and proceeding in the usual fashion, I find the population standard deviation to be exactly 16.0."
>
> "But you can't multiply 'football numbers,' the professor wailed. "Why, they aren't even ordinal numbers, like test scores."

> "The numbers don't know that," said the statistician. "Since the numbers don't remember where they came from, they always behave just the same way, regardless."

And so it went on for decades, with measurement theorists generally supporting the idea that levels of measurement should influence the choice of statistical analysis methods and applied statisticians arguing against the practice. In their recap of the controversy, Velleman and Wilkinson (1993, p. 68) wrote, "At times, the debate has been less than cordial. Gaito (1980) aimed sarcastic barbs at the measurement theory camp and Townsend and Ashby (1984) fired back. Unfortunately, as Mitchell (1986) noted, they often shot past each other." The debate continues into the 21st century (Scholten and Borsboom, 2009).

In Stevens' original paper (1946, p. 679), he actually took a more moderate stance on this topic than most people realize.

> On the other hand, for this 'illegal' statisticizing there can be invoked a kind of pragmatic sanction: In numerous instances it leads to fruitful results. While the outlawing of this procedure would probably serve no good purpose, it is proper to point out that means and standard deviations computed on an ordinal scale are in error to the extent that the successive intervals on the scale are unequal in size. When only the rank-order of data is known, we should proceed cautiously with our statistics, and especially with the conclusions we draw from them.

Responding to criticisms of the implications of his 1953 paper, Lord (1954, pp. 264–265) stated, "nominal and ordinal numbers (including test scores) may be treated by the usual arithmetic operations so as to obtain means, standard deviations, and other similar statistics from which (in certain restricted situations) correct conclusions may usefully be deduced with complete logical rigor." He then suggested that critics of his logic agree to participate in a game based on the "football numbers" story, with the statistician paying the critic one dollar every time the statistician incorrectly designates a sample as being drawn from one of two populations of nominal two-digit numbers and the critic paying the statistician one dollar when he is right. As far as we know, no critic ever took Lord up on his offer to play this game.

OUR RECOMMENDATION

So, which is it—all numbers are not equal (Stevens, 1946), or the numbers don't remember where they came from (Lord, 1953)? Given our backgrounds in applied statistics (and personal experiences attempting to act in accordance with Stevens' reasoning that didn't work out very well—see the sidebar), we fall firmly in the camp that supports the use of statistical techniques (such as the *t*-test, analysis of variance, and factor analysis) on ordinal data such as multipoint rating scales. However, you can't just ignore the level of measurement of your data.

When you make claims about the meaning of the outcomes of your statistical tests, you do have to be careful not to act as if rating scale data are interval rather than ordinal data. An average rating of 4 might be better than an average rating of 2, and a *t*-test might indicate that across a group of participants, the difference is consistent enough to be statistically significant. Even so, you can't claim that it is twice as good (a ratio claim), nor can you claim that the difference between 4 and 2 is equal to the difference between 4 and 6 (an interval claim). You can only claim that there is a consistent difference. Fortunately, even if you made the mistake of thinking one product is twice as good as another when the scale doesn't justify it, it would be a mistake that often would not affect the practical decision of which product is better. You would still have identified the better of the two products even if the actual difference in satisfaction was more modest.

MEANS WORK BETTER THAN MEDIANS WHEN ANALYZING ORDINAL MULTIPOINT DATA

How acting in accordance with Stevens' levels of measurement nearly tripped me up—from the files of Jim Lewis

In the late 1980s I was involved in a high-profile project at IBM in which we were comparing performance and satisfaction across a set of common tasks for three competitive office application suites (Lewis et al., 1990). Based on what I had learned in my college statistics classes about Stevens' levels of measurement, I pronounced that the multipoint rating scale data we were dealing with did not meet the assumptions required to take the mean of the data for the rating scales because they were ordinal rather than interval or ratio, so we should present their central tendencies using medians rather than means. I also advised against the use of *t*-tests for individual comparisons of the rating scale results, promoting instead its nonparametric analog, the Mann–Whitney *U*-test.

The folks who started running the statistics and putting the presentation together (which would have been given to a group that included high-level IBM executives) called me in a panic after they started following my advice. In the analyses, there were cases where the medians were identical, but the *U*-test detected a statistically significant difference. It turns out that the *U*-test is sensitive not only to central tendency, but also to the shape of the distribution, and in these cases the distributions had opposite skew but overlapping medians. As a follow-up, I systematically investigated the relationship among mean and median differences for multipoint scales and the observed significance levels of *t*- and *U*-tests conducted on the same data, all taken from our fairly large-scale usability test. It turned out that the mean difference correlated more than the median difference with the observed significance levels (both parametric and nonparametric) for discrete multipoint scale data.

Consequently, I no longer promote the concepts of Steven's levels of measurement with regard to permissible statistical analysis, although I believe this distinction is critical when interpreting and applying results. It appears that *t*-tests have sufficient robustness for most usability work—especially when you can create a set of difference scores to use for the analysis. For details, see Lewis (1993).

DO YOU NEED TO TEST AT LEAST 30 USERS?

ON ONE HAND

Probably most of us who have taken an introductory statistics class (or know someone who took such a class) have heard the rule of thumb that to estimate or compare means, your sample size should be at least 30. According to the central limit theorem, as the sample size increases, the distribution of the mean becomes more and more normal, regardless of the normality of the underlying distribution. Some simulation studies have shown that for a wide variety of distributions (but not all—see Bradley, 1978), the distribution of the mean becomes near normal when $n = 30$.

Another consideration is that it is slightly simpler to use *z*-scores rather than *t*-scores because *z*-scores do not require the use of degrees of freedom. As shown in Table 9.1 and Fig. 9.2, by the time you have about 30 degrees of freedom the value of *t* gets pretty close to the value of *z*. Consequently, there can be a feeling that you don't have to deal with small samples that require small-sample statistics (Cohen, 1990).

Table 9.1 Comparison of *t* With 30 Degrees of Freedom to *z*

	$\alpha = 0.10$	$\alpha = 0.05$	$\alpha = 0.01$
$t(30)$	1.697	2.042	2.750
z	1.645	1.960	2.576
Difference	0.052	0.082	0.174
Percent	3.2%	4.2%	6.8%

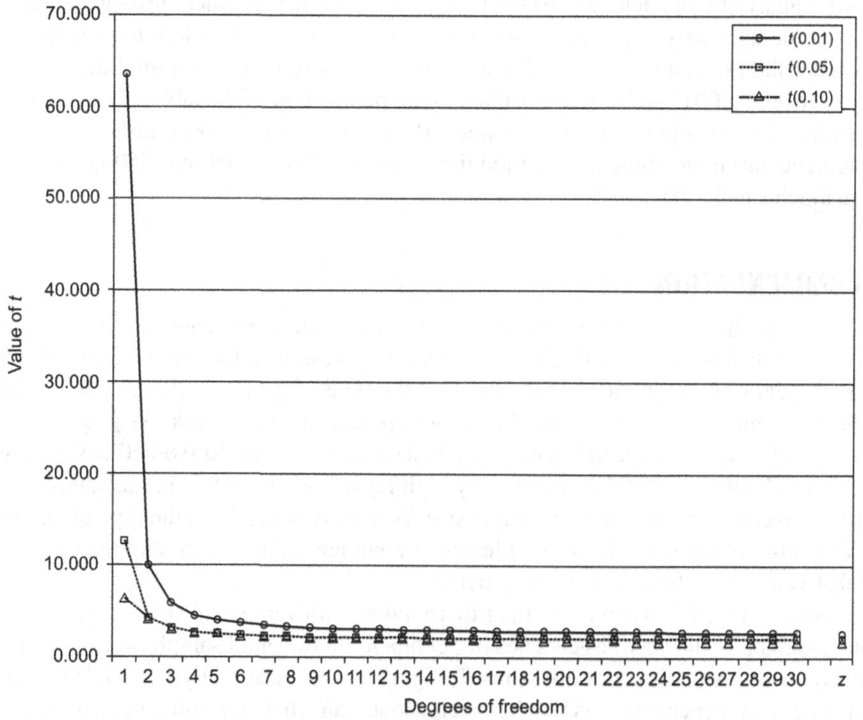

FIGURE 9.2 Approach of *t* to *z* as a function of α and degrees of freedom.

ON THE OTHER HAND

When the cost of a sample is expensive, as it typically is in many types of user research (e.g., moderated usability testing), it is important to estimate the needed sample size as accurately as possible, with the understanding that it is an estimate. The likelihood that 30 is exactly the right sample for a given set of circumstances is very low. As shown in our chapters on sample size estimation, a more appropriate approach is to take the formulas for computing the significance levels of a statistical test and, using algebra to solve for *n*, convert them to sample size estimation formulas. Those formulas then provide specific guidance on what you have to know or estimate for a given situation to estimate the required sample size.

The idea that even with the *t*-distribution (as opposed to the *z*-distribution) you need to have a sample size of at least 30 is inconsistent with the history of the development of the distribution. In 1899, William S. Gossett, a recent graduate of New College in Oxford with degrees in chemistry and mathematics, became one of the first scientists to join the Guinness brewery. "Compared with the giants of his day, he published very little, but his contribution is of critical importance. … The nature of the process of brewing, with its variability in temperature and ingredients, means that it is not possible to take large samples over a long run" (Cowles, 1989, p. 108–109).

This meant that Gossett could not use *z*-scores in his work—they just don't work well with small samples. After analyzing the deficiencies of the *z*-distribution for statistical tests with small samples, he worked out the necessary adjustments as a function of degrees of freedom to produce his *t* tables, published under the pseudonym "Student" due to the policies of Guinness prohibiting publication by employees (Salsburg, 2001). In the work that led to the publication of the tables, Gossett performed an early version of Monte Carlo simulations (Stigler, 1999). He prepared 3000 cards labeled with physical measurements taken on criminals, shuffled them, then dealt them out into 750 groups of size 4—a sample size much smaller than 30.

OUR RECOMMENDATION

This controversy is similar to the "five is enough" versus "eight is not enough" argument covered in Chapter 7, but applied to summative rather than formative research. For any research, the number of users to test depends on the purpose of the test and the type of data you plan to collect. The "magic number" 30 has some empirical rationale, but in our opinion, it's very weak. As you can see from the numerous examples in this book that have sample sizes not equal to 30 (sometimes less, sometimes more), we do not hold this rule of thumb in very high regard. As described in our sample size chapter for summative research, the appropriate sample size for a study depends on the type of distribution, the expected variability of the data, the desired levels of confidence and power, and the minimum size of the effect that you need to be able to reliably detect.

As illustrated in Fig. 9.2, when using the *t*-distribution with very small samples (e.g., with degrees of freedom less than 5), the very large values of *t* compensate for small sample sizes with regard to the control of Type I errors (claiming a difference is significant when it really is not). With sample sizes these small, your confidence intervals will be much wider than what you would get with larger samples. But once you're dealing with more than 5 degrees of freedom, there is very little absolute difference between the value of *z* and the value of *t*. From the perspective of the approach of *t* to *z*, there is very little gain past 10 degrees of freedom.

It isn't much more complicated to use the *t*-distribution than the *z*-distribution (you just need to be sure to use the right value for the degrees of freedom), and the reason for the development of the *t*-distribution was to enable the analysis of small samples. This is just one of the less obvious ways in which usability practitioners benefit from the science and practice of beer brewing. Historians of statistics widely regard Gossett's publication of Student's *t*-test as a landmark event (Box, 1984; Cowles, 1989; Stigler, 1999). In a letter to Ronald A. Fisher (one of the fathers of modern statistics) containing an early copy of the *t* tables, Gossett wrote, "You are probably the only man who will ever use them" (Box, 1978). Gossett got a lot of things right, but he certainly got that wrong.

SHOULD YOU ALWAYS CONDUCT A TWO-TAILED TEST?

ON ONE HAND

The controversy over the legitimate use of one-tailed tests began in the early 1950s (Cowles, 1989). Before then, the standard practice was to run two-tailed tests with equal rejection regions in each tail. For example, a researcher setting α to 0.05 would use $z \pm 1.96$ as the critical value for a *z*-test, which corresponds to a rejection region of 0.025 in each tail (Fig. 9.3, two-tailed test). The rationale for two-sided tests was that in advance of data collection, the researcher could not be sure of the direction the results would take, so the unbiased approach was to put an equal amount of rejection region in each

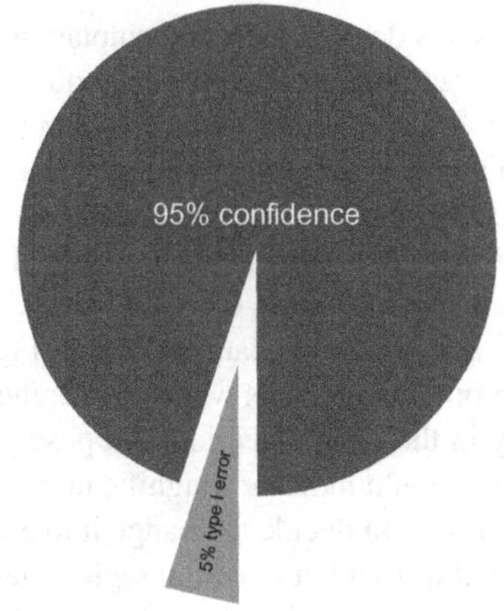

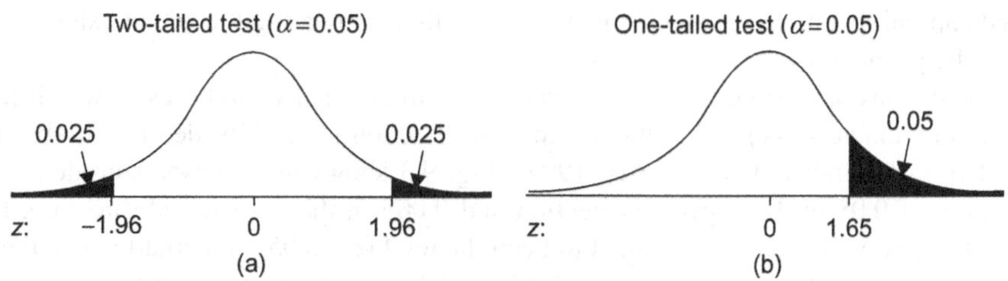

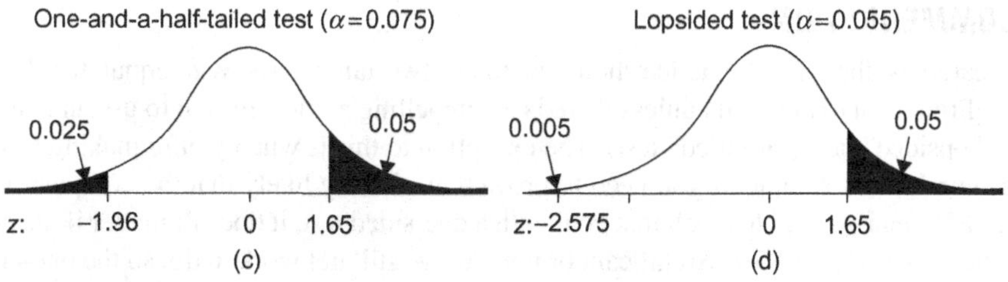

FIGURE 9.3 Different ways to allocate probability to rejection regions.

tail (where the rejection region is the set of test outcomes that indicate sufficient evidence to reject the null hypothesis).

The controversy began with the realization that many experimental hypotheses are not pure null hypotheses of no difference. Instead, there can be a directional component to the hypothesis, for example, after having fixed a number of usability problems in an early version of a product, participants should do better with the next version—higher completion rate, faster completion times, and greater satisfaction. For that test context, it seems reasonable to put all of the rejection probability in the same tail—a one-tailed test (Fig. 9.3, one-tailed test).

ON THE OTHER HAND

One concern over using one-tailed tests is dealing with the temptation to convert what started as a two-tailed test to a one-tailed test after the fact. Suppose you're really not sure which product will better support users' tasks, so you decide to run a two-tailed test with 0.025 in each tail ($\alpha = 0.05$). Also, suppose your sample size is large enough that you can use a z-test, and the value of z that you get is 1.8. If you had run a one-tailed test in the right direction, you'd have a statistically significant result. If, after having run the test, you decide to treat the result like a one-tailed test, then instead of it really being a one-tailed test with $a = 0.05$, it's a one-and-a-half-tailed test with $\alpha = 0.075$ (Abelson, 1995)—you can't make the 0.025 in the left tail disappear just by wishing it gone after data collection (Fig. 9.3, one-and-a-half-tailed test).

Another of the concerns with the one-tailed test is what a researcher should do if, against all expectation, the test result points strongly in the other direction. Suppose you originally set up a one-tailed test so any value of z greater than 1.65 would indicate a significant result but the result you actually get is $z = -2.12$. If, after having run the test, you decide to change it to a two-tailed test, you actually have another case of a one-and-a-half-tailed test with a rejection region that turns out to be 0.075 instead of the planned 0.05. Note that we're not saying that there's anything wrong with deciding to set $\alpha = 0.075$ or even higher before running the test. The problem is that changing your mind after you've got the data in hand capitalizes on chance (which is not a good thing), inflating the actual value of α by 50% compared to the planned α.

A few statisticians have suggested a test strategy for directional hypotheses in which just a little bit of rejection region gets assigned to the unexpected direction—the "lopsided test" (Abelson, 1995) or "split-tailed test" (Braver, 1975; Harris, 1997). Fig. 9.3 shows the Abelson lopsided test, with a rejection region of 0.05 in the expected direction and 0.005 in the unexpected direction, for a total $\alpha = 0.055$. By the way, if you really wanted to keep the total $\alpha = 0.05$, you could adjust the rejection region on the right to 0.045 ($z = 1.7$ instead of 1.65, a relatively minor adjustment).

OUR RECOMMENDATION

For user researchers, the typical practice should be to use two-tailed tests, with equal distribution of the probability of rejection to both tails unless there is a compelling a priori reason to use an unequal distribution (the "lopsided" or "split-tailed" test). The exception to this is when you're making a comparison with a benchmark. For example, if you need to prove that it's very likely that the completion rate for a task exceeds 85% and you fail to reach that goal with a one-sided test, it doesn't matter if the completion rate is significantly less than 85%. Significant or not, you've still got work to do, so the one-tailed test is appropriate for this situation (which is more of a usability engineering than a usability research context).

CAN YOU REJECT THE NULL HYPOTHESIS WHEN $p > 0.05$?

ON ONE HAND

Setting $\alpha = 0.05$ provides significant control over the likelihood of a Type I error (rejecting the null hypothesis when there is actually no difference). With this test criterion, any result with $p < 0.05$ is, by definition, statistically significant; all others are not. Over the long run, you should only make a Type I error once out of every 20 tests.

In the late 19th century, Francis Edgeworth, one of the first statisticians to routinely conduct tests of significance, used a very conservative $\alpha = 0.005$ (Stigler, 1999). The first formal statement of judging significance with $p < 0.05$ dates back to Fisher in the early 20th century, although there is evidence that it had been conventional for some time (Cowles, 1989).

ON THE OTHER HAND

> "Surely, God loves the .06 nearly as much as the .05" (Rosnow and Rosenthal, 1989, p. 1277).

> "Use common sense to extract the meaning from your data. Let the science of human factors and psychology drive the statistics; do not let statistics drive the science" (Wickens, 1998, p. 22).

The history of setting $\alpha = 0.05$ shows that it is a convention that has some empirical basis, but is still just a convention, not the result of some law of nature. The problem with a narrow focus on just the Type I error is that it takes attention away from the Type II error—emphasizing confidence over power (Baguley, 2004). For scientific publication, the $p < 0.05$ convention and an emphasis on the Type I error is reasonable because it's generally less damaging to commit a Type II error (delaying the introduction of a real effect into the scientific database due to low power) than to commit a Type I error (introducing false findings into the scientific discourse). This might also be true for certain kinds of user research, but for other kinds of user research, it is possible that Type II errors might be more damaging than Type I errors, which would indicate using a different strategy for balancing the two types of error.

Wickens (1998) discussed the importance of balancing Type I and Type II errors in system development. Suppose you've conducted a usability study of two systems (one old, the other new), with the null hypothesis being that the new system is no better than the old. If you make a Type I error, the likely decision will be to adopt the new system when it's really no better than the old (but also very likely no worse). If you make a Type II error, the likely decision will be to keep the old system when the new one is really better. Wickens (1998, p. 19) concluded:

> From this viewpoint, the cost of each type of error to user performance and possibly to user safety should be regarded as equivalent, and not as in the classical statistics of the 0.05 level, weighted heavily to avoiding Type I errors (a 1-in-20 chance of observing the effect, given that there is no difference between the old and new system). Indeed, it seems irresponsible to do otherwise than treat the two errors equivalently. Thus, there seems no possible reason why the decision criterion should be locked at 0.05 when, with applied studies that often are destined to have relatively low statistical power, the probability of a Type II error may be considerably higher than 0.05. Instead, designers should be at the liberty to adjust their own decision criteria (trading off between the two types of statistical errors) based on the consequences of the errors to user performance.

As discussed in Chapter 6, when you're planning a study you should have some idea of what sample size you're going to need to provide adequate control over Type I and Type II errors for your specific situation. To estimate the sample size for a within-subjects *t*-test, for example, you start with the formula:

$$n = \frac{(z_\alpha + z_\beta)^2 s^2}{d^2}$$

The z_α and z_β in the numerator correspond to the planned values for the Type I and Type II errors, respectively; *s* is the expected standard deviation, and *d* is the minimum size of the effect that you want to be able to detect in the study. The value for z_α depends on the desired level of confidence and whether the test will be one- or two-tailed. The value for z_β depends on the desired amount of power, and is always one-tailed (Diamond, 1981). Once you add z_α and z_β together, though, to paraphrase Lord (1953), that sum doesn't remember where it came from.

For example, suppose you take Wicken's (1998) advice and decide to relax the Type I error to $\alpha = 0.10$ and to also set the Type II error to $\beta = 0.10$ (so you have 90% confidence and 90% power). For *z*-scores corresponding to 0.10, the two-tailed *z* is about 1.65 (z_α) and the one-tailed *z* is about 1.28 (z_β), so ($z_\alpha + z_\beta$) equals 2.93. Table 9.2 shows some of the possible combinations of z_α and z_β (in addition to 1.65 + 1.28) that equal 2.93.

The same *z* of 2.93 could mean that you've set α to 0.003, so you're almost certain not to make a Type I error—in the long run, only about 3/1000 tests conducted when the null hypothesis is true would

Table 9.2 Different Combinations of z_α and z_β Summing to 2.93

z_α	z_β	α	β
2.93	0.00	0.003	0.500
2.68	0.25	0.007	0.401
2.43	0.50	0.015	0.309
2.18	0.75	0.029	0.227
1.93	1.00	0.054	0.159
1.65	**1.28**	**0.100**	**0.100**
1.25	1.68	0.211	0.046
1.00	1.93	0.317	0.027
0.75	2.18	0.453	0.015
0.50	2.43	0.617	0.008
0.25	2.68	0.803	0.004
0.00	2.93	1.000	0.002

Note: Bold indicates the values for which alpha = beta.

produce a false alarm. Unfortunately, you only have a 50–50 chance of proving that real differences exist because when $\alpha = 0.003$, then $\beta = 0.50$. If you take the opposite approach of setting α to 1.0 and β to 0.002, then you'll almost never make a Type II error (missing a real effect only 2/1000 times), but you're guaranteed to make many, many Type I errors (false alarms). If you set α to 0.054 and β to 0.159, then you will have results that are close to the convention of setting α to 0.05 and β to 0.20 (95% confidence and 80% power—more precisely for these z-scores of 1.93 and 1.00, 94.6% confidence and 84.1% power).

FISHER ON THE CONVENTION OF USING $\alpha = 0.05$

How Fisher recommended using *p*-values

When Karl Pearson was the grand old man of statistics and Ronald Fisher was a relative newcomer, Pearson, apparently threatened by Fisher's ideas and mathematical ability, used his influence to prevent Fisher from publishing in the major statistical journals of the time, Biometrika and the Journal of the Royal Statistical Society. Consequently, Fisher published his ideas in a variety of other venues such as agricultural and meteorological journals, including several papers for the Proceedings of the Society for Psychical Research. It was in one of the papers for this latter journal that he mentioned the convention of setting what we now call the acceptable Type I error (alpha) to 0.05 (Fisher, 1929, p. 191) and, critically, also mentioned the importance of reproducibility when encountering an unexpected significant result.

> *An observation is judged to be significant, if it would rarely have been produced, in the absence of a real cause of the kind we are seeking. It is a common practice to judge a result significant, if it is of such a magnitude that it would have been produced by chance not more frequently than once in twenty trials. This is an arbitrary, but convenient, level of significance for the practical investigator, but it does not mean that he allows himself to be deceived once in every twenty experiments. The test of significance only tells him what to ignore, namely, all experiments in which significant results are not obtained. He should only claim that a phenomenon is experimentally demonstrable when he knows how to design an experiment so that it will rarely fail to give a significant result. Consequently, isolated significant results which he does not know how to reproduce are left in suspense pending further investigation.*

OUR RECOMMENDATION

Unless you're planning to submit your results to an academic journal for publication, we recommend not worrying excessively about trying to control your Type I error to 0.05. The goal of statistics is not to make the correct decision every time—that just isn't possible. The purpose of using statistics is to help you make better decisions in the long run. In an industrial setting, that could well mean setting α to 0.10 or in some cases, even to 0.20 (in which case you'll make a Type I error in about one out of every five tests).

The important thing is to make these decisions before you run the test. Spend some time thinking about the relative consequences of making Type I and Type II errors in your specific context, carefully choosing appropriate criteria for α and β. Then use your analysis along with the expected standard deviation (s) and critical difference (d) to estimate the sample size you'll need to achieve the statistical goals of your study. If the sample size turns out to be unfeasible, then revisit your decisions about α, β, and d until you find a combination that will work for you (as discussed in more detail in Chapter 6).

ESTIMATING THE SAMPLE SIZE INCREASE NEEDED TO ACHIEVE SIGNIFICANCE

You need to consider both confidence and power—from the files of Jeff Sauro

I was working with an Internet retailer who wanted to determine which of two changes to an item-detail page would help users make better decisions about a product and ultimately lead to more purchases. We had participants attempt to understand information about a product and answer a series of 11-point scales about the experience. We recruited participants using a customer list and launched the unmoderated study. We estimated we'd need approximately 700 participants for each of the two designs (1400 total) to detect a difference of at least 0.3 of a point (a 3% difference), using an alpha of 0.05 and power of 0.80. After one week of data collection though, we had fewer than 200 responses (92 in each group)—a fraction of the number we were planning for! Collecting more data costs money and time, so we needed to know how many more samples we absolutely needed to find statistical differences—if they existed. I ran a *t*-test on one of the items for the 184 participants who saw either Design A or B (Table 9.3). Design A was currently leading by 0.46 of a point. The *p*-value of 0.15 indicated it wasn't statistically significant (at $\alpha < 0.05$), but the lower limit of the confidence interval suggested it was getting close.

With this information, at what sample size would we expect a 0.46 point difference to be statistically significant at the designated level of alpha? If we ran the sample size calculation using the formula in Chapter 6 for two independent means, we'd find that to detect a 0.46 difference (using an alpha of 0.05, power of 0.80, and standard deviation of 2.135—the average of 2.04 and 2.23—we would need a sample size of 340 in each group (680 in total). That's more than three times the sample size at which we were getting close to a statistically significant difference. Furthermore, if everything stayed as it was except for increasing the sample size to 680, the *p*-value would not be close to 0.05—it would be a much smaller 0.005. What's going on here?

The information in Table 9.2 provides a clue. When you do sample size estimation from scratch, you make a decision about your acceptable Type I and Type II error rates (associated with confidence and power, respectively), and then put the appropriate *z*-scores in the numerator of the formula $n = \frac{(z_\alpha + z_\beta)^2 s^2}{d^2}$ where they are summed into a single composite value of *z*. Using a value higher than 0 for z_β means that you are essentially purchasing additional power. Think of it as an insurance policy that protects you in case the actual variability is greater than you expected, or the mean difference is smaller than expected. Once you have data and you're trying to determine the **minimum** sample size you need to declare a statistically significant outcome exactly at the specified level of α, you need to set power to 50% because the question you're trying to answer has changed, and "purchasing" additional power will cause you to overestimate the minimum required sample size for these conditions. With this adjustment (setting power to 50%), the recalculated sample size estimate is $n = 334$ (167 in each group) and, if everything stayed as it was except for increasing the sample size, the *p*-value would be exactly 0.05. This is a much more manageable sample size increase—one that's achievable from sending out reminders rather than needing to pull a whole new list of customers.

Table 9.3 Findings With $n = 184$

Design	Mean	*s*	*n*
A	8.21	2.04	92
B	7.75	2.23	92
Difference	0.46		
p-value	0.15		
95% Confidence interval around the difference			
Upper limit	1.08		
Lower limit	−0.16		

CAN YOU COMBINE USABILITY METRICS INTO SINGLE SCORES?

ON ONE HAND

Throughout the history of statistics, there has been an initial reluctance to combine measurements in any way, typically followed by empirical and theoretical work that supports the combination. For example, before the mid-17th century, astronomers would not average their observations—"the idea that accuracy could be increased by combining measurements made under different conditions was slow to come" (Stigler, 1986, p. 4).

We are now so used to the arithmetic mean that we often don't give a second thought to computing it (and in some situations we really should). But what about combining similar measurements from different sources into a composite metric? That's exactly what we do when we compute a stock index such as the Dow-Jones Industrial Average. We are comfortable with this type of combined score, especially given its successful use for over 100 years, but that level of comfort was not always in place. When William Stanley Jevons published analyses in which he combined the prices of different commodities into an index to study the global variation in the price of gold in the mid-19th century, he met with significant criticism (Stigler, 1986, 1999).

Stock and commodity indices at least have the common metric of price. What about the combination of different metrics—for example, the standard usability metrics of successful completion rates, completion times, and satisfaction? The statistical methods for accomplishing this task, based on the concepts of correlation and regression, appeared in the early 20th century and underwent an explosion of development in its first half (Cowles, 1989), producing principal components analysis, factor analysis, discriminant analysis, and multivariate analysis of variance (MANOVA).

Lewis (1991) used nonparametric rank-based methods to combine and analyze time-on-task, number of errors, and task-level satisfaction in summative usability tests. Conversion to ranks puts the different usability metrics on a common ordinal scale, allowing their combination through rank averaging. An important limitation of a rank-based approach is that it can only represent a relative comparison between like-products with similar tasks—it does not result in a measure of usability comparable across products or different sets of tasks. More recently, Sauro and Kindlund (2005) described methods for converting different usability metrics (task completion, error counts, task times, and satisfaction scores) to *z*-scores—another way to get different metrics to a common scale (their Single Usability Metric, or SUM).

Sauro and Kindlund (2005) reported significant correlations among the metrics they studied. Advanced analysis (specifically, a principal components analysis) indicated that the four usability metrics contributed about equally to the composite SUM score. In 2009, Sauro and Lewis also found substantial correlations among prototypical usability metrics such as task times, completion rates, errors, post-task satisfaction, and post-study satisfaction collected during a large number of unpublished summative usability tests. According to psychometric theory, an advantage of any composite score is an increase in the reliability of measurement, with the magnitude of the increase depending on correlations among the component scores (Nunnally, 1978).

SUM: THE SINGLE USABILITY METRIC

Calculating SUM scores—from the files of Jeff Sauro

SUM is a standardized, summated, and single usability metric, developed to represent the majority of variation in four common usability metrics used in summative usability tests: task completion rates, task time, error counts, and satisfaction. To standardize each of the usability metrics Erika Kindlund and I created a *z*-score type value or *z*-equivalent.

For the continuous data (time and average satisfaction), we subtracted the mean value from a specification limit and divided by the standard deviation. For discrete data (completion rates and errors) we divided the unacceptable conditions (defects) by all opportunities for defects—a method of standardization adapted from the process sigma metric used in Six Sigma. For more details on how to standardize and combine these scores, see Sauro and Kindlund (2005).

To make it easier to work with SUM, I've provided free Web (Usability Scorecard) and Excel (SUM Calculator) tools (see www.measuringu.com/sum). The Usability Scorecard application takes raw usability metrics (completion, time, satisfaction, errors, and clicks) and automatically calculates confidence intervals and graphs. You can also work with any combination of the metrics into a 2-, 3- or 4-measure score. The SUM calculator takes raw usability metrics and converts them into a SUM score with confidence intervals.

You need to provide the raw metrics on a task-by-task basis and know the opportunity for errors. SUM will automatically calculate the maximum acceptable task time, or you can provide it. This calculator is an Excel-based version of the Usability Scorecard, with the limitation that it can only combine four measures (time, errors, sat, and completion) rather than any combination, and it does not graph the results. Once you have a set of SUM scores, you can treat them statistically as you would any raw score, computing confidence intervals, comparing them against benchmarks, or comparing SUM scores from different products or tasks.

ON THE OTHER HAND

If the component scores do not correlate, the reliability of the composite score will not increase relative to the component scores. Hornbæk and Law (2007), based on correlational analyses of a wide range of metrics and tasks gathered from published human–computer–interaction (HCI) literature, argued that attempts to reduce usability to one measure are bound to lose important information because there is no strong correlation among usability aspects (a finding that appears to be true for the broad range of HCI metrics studied by Hornbæk & Law, but not for prototypical usability metrics—see Sauro and Lewis, 2009). Indeed, loss of information occurs whenever you combine measurements. This is one of the reasons why it is important to provide additional information such as the standard deviation or a confidence interval when reporting a mean.

The combination of data can be particularly misleading if you blindly use statistical procedures such as MANOVA or discriminant analysis to combine different types of dependent measures. These methods automatically determine how to weight the different component metrics into a combined measure in a way that maximizes the differences between levels of independent variables. This increases the likelihood of getting a statistically significant result, but runs the risk of creating composite measures that are uninterpretable with regard to any real world attribute such as usability (Lewis, 1991). More generally in psychological experimentation, Abelson has warned against the blind use of these methods (1995, pp. 127–128):

> In such cases [multiple dependent variables] the investigator faces a choice of whether to present the results for each variable separately, to aggregate them in some way before analysis, or to use multivariate analysis of variance. … One of these alternatives—MANOVA—stands at the bottom of my list of options. … Technical discussion of MANOVA would carry us too far afield, but my experience with the method is that it is effortful to articulate the results. … Furthermore, when MANOVA comes out with simple results, there is almost always a way to present the same outcome with one of the simpler analytical alternatives. *Manova mania* is my name for the urge to use this technique.

As true as this might be for psychological research, it is even truer for usability research intended to affect the design of products or systems. If you run a test with a composite measure and find a significant difference between products, then what do you really know? You will have to follow up that test with separate tests of the component metrics, so one could reasonably argue against running the test with the composite metric, instead starting with the tests of the component metrics.

OUR RECOMMENDATION

Both of us, at various times in our careers, have worked on methods for combining different usability metrics into single scores (Lewis, 1991; Sauro and Kindlund, 2005)—clearly, we are on the side of combining usability metrics when it is appropriate, but using a method that produces an interpretable composite such as SUM rather than MANOVA. There are situations in the real world in which practitioners must choose only one product from a summative competitive usability test of multiple products and, in so doing, must either rely on a single measurement (a very limiting approach), must try to rationally justify some priority of the dependent measures, or must use a composite score. Composite usability scores can also be useful on executive management dashboards. Even without an increase in reliability it can still be advantageous to combine the scores for these situations, but the factor analysis of Sauro and Lewis (2009) lends statistical support to the practice of combining component usability metrics into a single score.

Any summary score (median, mean, index, or other composite) must lose important information (just as an abstract does not contain all of the information in a full paper)—it is the price paid for summarizing data. It is certainly not appropriate to rely exclusively on summary data, but it is important to keep in mind that the data that contribute to a summary score remain available as component scores for any analyses and decisions that require more detailed information (such as providing guidance about how a product or system should change in a subsequent design iteration). You don't lose anything permanently when you combine scores—you just gain an additional view.

WHAT IF YOU NEED TO RUN MORE THAN ONE TEST?

What if you have collected data from three groups instead of two, and want to compare Group A with B, A with C, and B with C? You'll need to perform multiple comparisons. As Cowles (1989, p. 171) pointed out, this has been a controversial topic in statistics for decades.

> In 1972 Maurice Kendall commented on how regrettable it was that during the 1940s mathematics had begun to 'spoil' statistics. Nowhere is this shift in emphasis from practice, with its room for intuition and pragmatism, to theory and abstraction, more evident than in the area of multiple comparison procedures. The rules for making such comparisons have been discussed ad nauseam and they continue to be discussed.

ON ONE HAND

When the null hypothesis of no difference is true, you can think of a single test with $\alpha = 0.05$ as the flip of a single coin that has a 95% chance of heads (correctly failing to reject the null hypothesis) and a 5% chance of tails (falsely concluding there is a difference when there really isn't one—a false alarm, a

Type I error). These are the probabilities for a single toss of the coin (a single test), but what if you run more than one test? Statisticians sometimes make a distinction between the error rate per comparison (EC) and the error rate per family (EF, or family-wise error rate) (Myers, 1979).

For example, if you ran 20 *t*-tests after collecting data in a usability study and there was really no difference in the tested products, you'd expect one Type I error, falsely concluding that there was a difference when that outcome happened just by chance. Unfortunately, other possible outcomes, such as seeing two or three Type I errors, also have a reasonable likelihood of happening by chance. The technical term for this is *alpha inflation*. For this series of tests, the actual value of α (defining α as the likelihood of getting one or more Type I errors) is much higher than 0.05. Table 9.4 shows, as expected, that the most likely number of Type I errors in a set of 20 independent tests with $\alpha = 0.05$ is one, with a point probability of 0.37735. The likelihood of at least one Type I error, however, is higher—as shown in Table 9.4, it's 0.64151. So, rather than having a 5% chance of encountering a Type I error when there is no real difference, α has inflated to about 64%.

A quick way to compute the inflation of α (defining inflation as the probability of one or more Type I errors) is to use the same formula we used in Chapter 7 to model the discovery of problems in formative user research:

$$p(\text{at least one Type I error}) = 1-(1-\alpha)^n$$

where n is the number of independent tests (Winer et al., 1991). For the previous example (20 tests conducted with $\alpha = 0.05$), that would be:

$$p(\text{at least one Type I error}) = 1-(1-0.05)^{20} = 1-0.95^{20} = 1-0.35849 = 0.64151$$

In other words, the probability of at least one Type I error equals one minus the probability of none (see the entries for $p(0)$ and $p(\text{at least } 1)$ in Table 9.4).

Since the middle of the 20th century, there have been many strategies and techniques published to guide the analysis of multiple comparisons (Abelson, 1995; Cliff, 1987; Myers, 1979; Winer et al., 1991), such as omnibus tests (e.g., ANOVA and MANOVA) and procedures for the comparison of pairs of means (e.g., Tukey's WSD and HSD procedures, the Student–Newman–Keuls test, Dunnett's test, the Duncan procedure, the Scheffé procedure, the Bonferroni adjustment, and the Benjamini–Hochberg adjustment). A detailed discussion of all these techniques for reducing the effect of alpha inflation on statistical decision-making is beyond the scope of this book.

A popular and conceptually simple approach to controlling alpha inflation is the Bonferroni adjustment (Cliff, 1987; Myers, 1979; Winer et al., 1991). To apply the Bonferroni adjustment, divide the desired overall level of alpha by the number of tests you plan to run. For example, to run 10 tests for a family-wise error rate of 0.05, you would set $\alpha = 0.005$ for each individual test. For 20 tests, it would be 0.0025 (0.05/20). Setting $\alpha = 0.0025$ and running 20 independent tests would result in alpha inflation bringing the family-wise error rate to just under 0.05:

$$p(\text{at least one Type I error}) = 1-(1-0.0025)^{20} = 1-0.9975^{20} = 1-0.9512 = 0.0488$$

A relatively new method called the Benjamini–Hochberg adjustment (Benjamini and Hochberg, 1995) offers a good balance between making the Bonferroni adjustment and no adjustment at all.

Table 9.4 Illustration of Alpha Inflation for 20 Tests Conducted With $\alpha = 0.05$

x	$p(x)$	p(at least x)
0	0.35849	1.00000
1	0.37735	0.64151
2	0.18868	0.26416
3	0.05958	0.07548
4	0.01333	0.01590
5	0.00224	0.00257
6	0.00030	0.00033
7	0.00003	0.00003
8	0.00000	0.00000
9	0.00000	0.00000
10	0.00000	0.00000
11	0.00000	0.00000
12	0.00000	0.00000
13	0.00000	0.00000
14	0.00000	0.00000
15	0.00000	0.00000
16	0.00000	0.00000
17	0.00000	0.00000
18	0.00000	0.00000
19	0.00000	0.00000
20	0.00000	0.00000

Rather than using a significance threshold of α/k (where k is the number of comparisons) for all multiple comparisons (the Bonferroni approach), the Benjamini–Hochberg method produces a graduated series of significance thresholds. To use the method, take the p-values from all the comparisons and rank them from lowest to highest. Then create a new threshold for statistical significance by dividing the rank by the number of comparisons and then multiplying this by the initial significance threshold (alpha). The first threshold will always be the same as the Bonferroni threshold, and the last threshold will always be the same as the unadjusted value of α. The thresholds in between the first and last comparisons rise in equal steps from the Bonferroni to the unadjusted threshold. For a detailed example of applying the Bonferroni and Benjamini–Hochberg adjustments to multiple comparisons, see Chapter 10 ("Comparing More than Two Means").

Problem solved—or is it?

ON THE OTHER HAND

When the null hypothesis is not true, applying techniques such as Bonferroni or Benjamini–Hochberg adjustments can increase the number of Type II errors—the failure to detect differences that are really there (misses as opposed to the false alarms of Type I errors) (Abelson, 1995; Myers, 1979; Perneger, 1998; Winer et al., 1991). As illustrated in Table 9.2, an overemphasis on the prevention of Type I errors leads to the proliferation of Type II errors. Unless, for your situation, the cost of a Type I error is much greater than the cost of a Type II error, you should avoid applying any of the techniques designed to suppress alpha inflation, including Bonferroni or Benjamini–Hochberg adjustments. "Simply describing what tests of significance have been performed, and why, is generally the best way of dealing with multiple comparisons" (Perneger, 1998, p. 1236).

ABELSON'S STYLES OF RHETORIC

Brash, stuffy, liberal, and conservative styles

In Chapter 4 of his highly regarded book *Statistics as Principled Argument*, Robert Abelson (1995) noted that researchers using statistics to support their claims can adopt different styles of rhetoric, of which he defined four:

- **Brash (unreasonable)**: Overstates every statistical result, specifically, always uses one-tailed tests, runs different statistical tests on the same data and selects the one that produces the most significant result, when running multiple comparisons focuses on the significant results without regard to the number of comparisons, states actual value of *p* but talks around it to include results not quite significant according to preselected value of alpha
- **Stuffy (unreasonable)**: Determined to never be brash under any circumstances—excessively cautious
- **Liberal (reasonable)**: Less extreme version of brash—willing to explore and speculate about data
- **Conservative (reasonable)**: Less extreme version of stuffy—more codified and cautious approach to data analysis than the liberal style

From our experience, we encourage a liberal style for most user research, but we acknowledge Abelson (1995, p. 57): "Debatable cases arise when null hypotheses are rejected according to liberal test procedures, but accepted by conservative tests. In these circumstances, reasonable people may disagree. The investigator faces an apparent dilemma: 'Should I pronounce my results significant according to liberal criteria, risking skepticism by critical readers, or should I play it safe with conservative procedures and have nothing much to say?' Throughout this chapter, we've tried to provide guidance to help user researchers resolve this apparent dilemma logically and pragmatically for their specific research situations.

OUR RECOMMENDATION

Abelson (1995, p. 70) stated:

> When there are multiple tests within the same study or series of studies, a stylistic issue is unavoidable. As Diaconis (1985) put it, "Multiplicity is one of the most prominent difficulties with data-analytic procedures. Roughly speaking, if enough different statistics are computed, some of them will be sure to show structure" (p. 9). In other words, random patterns will seem to contain something systematic when scrutinized in many particular ways. If you look at enough boulders, there is bound to be one that looks like a sculpted human face. Knowing this, if you apply extremely strict criteria for what is to be recognized as an intentionally carved face, you might miss the whole show on Easter Island.

As discussed throughout this chapter, user researchers need to balance confidence and power in their studies, avoiding excessive attention to Type I errors over Type II errors unless the relative cost of a Type I error (thinking an effect is real when it isn't) is much greater than that of a Type II error (failing to find and act upon real effects). This general strategy applies to the treatment of multiple comparisons just as it did in the previous discussions of one- versus two-tailed testing and the legitimacy of setting $\alpha > 0.05$.

For most situations, we encourage user researchers to follow Perneger's (1998) advice to run multiple comparisons at the designated level of alpha, making sure to report what tests have been done and why. For example, in summative usability tests, most practitioners use a fairly small set of well-defined and conventional measurements (success rates, completion times, user satisfaction) collected in a carefully constructed set of test scenarios, either for purposes of estimation or comparison with benchmarks or a fairly small and carefully selected set of products/systems. This practice helps to legitimize multiple testing at a specified and not overly conservative level of alpha because the researchers have clear a priori hypotheses under test.

Researchers engaging in this practice should, however, keep in mind the likely number of Type I errors for the number of tests they conduct. For example, Table 9.5 shows the likelihoods of different numbers of Type I errors when the null hypothesis is true and $\alpha = 0.05$. When $n = 10$ tests, the most likely number of Type I errors is 0 ($p = 0.60$), the likelihood of getting at least one Type I error is 0.40, and the likelihood of getting two Type I errors is less than 10% ($p = 0.086$). When $n = 100$, the most likely number of Type I errors is 5 ($p = 0.18$), the likelihood of getting at least one Type I error is 0.994 (virtually certain), and the likelihood of getting 9 Type I errors is less than 10% ($p = 0.06$).

So, if you ran 100 tests (e.g., tests of your product against five competitive products with five tasks and four measurements per task) and had only five statistically significant results with $p < 0.05$, then you're seeing exactly the number of expected Type I errors. You could go ahead and consider what those findings mean for your product, but you should be relatively cautious in their interpretation. On the other hand, if you had ten statistically significant results, the likelihood of that happening if there really was no difference is just 2.8%, so you could be stronger in your interpretation of those results and what they mean for your product.

This alleviates a potential problem with the Bonferroni adjustment strategy, which addresses the likelihood of getting one or more Type I errors when the null hypothesis is true. A researcher who conducts 100 tests (e.g., from a summative usability study with multiple products, measures, and tasks) and who has set $\alpha = 0.05$ is not expecting one Type I error if the null hypothesis is true, the expectation is five Type I errors. Adjusting the EC to hold the expected number of Type I errors to one in this situation does not seem like a logically consistent strategy. In fact, the Benjamini–Hochberg method was developed to address this logical inconsistency. Rather than controlling the family-wise error rate to a specified level, the Benjamini–Hochberg method controls the false discovery rate—the proportion of rejected null hypotheses that are incorrect rejections (false discoveries)—rather than allowing only one Type I error. For this reason, if there is a need to adjust thresholds of significance, we recommend the Benjamini—Hochberg procedure due to its placement between liberal (unadjusted) and conservative (Bonferroni) approaches.

Using the method illustrated in Table 9.5, but covering a broader range of number of tests and values of alpha, Table 9.6 shows for $\alpha = 0.05$ and $\alpha = 0.10$ how many Type I errors would be unexpected (less than or equal to a 10% cumulative likelihood for that number or more) given the number of tests if the null hypothesis of no difference is true.

Table 9.5 Likelihoods of Number of Type I Errors When the Null Hypothesis Is True Given 10, 20, and 100 Tests When $\alpha = 0.05$

	$n = 10$	$\alpha = 0.05$	$n = 20$	$\alpha = 0.05$	$n = 100$	$\alpha = 0.05$
x	$p(x)$	p(at least x)	$p(x)$	p(at least x)	$p(x)$	p(at least x)
0	0.59874	1.00000	0.35849	1.00000	0.00592	1.00000
1	0.31512	0.40126	0.37735	0.64151	0.03116	0.99408
2	**0.07463**	**0.08614**	0.18868	0.26416	0.08118	0.96292
3	0.01048	0.01150	**0.05958**	**0.07548**	0.13958	0.88174
4	0.00096	0.00103	0.01333	0.01590	0.17814	0.74216
5	0.00006	0.00006	0.00224	0.00257	0.18002	0.56402
6	0.00000	0.00000	0.00030	0.00033	0.15001	0.38400
7	0.00000	0.00000	0.00003	0.00003	0.10603	0.23399
8	0.00000	0.00000	0.00000	0.00000	0.06487	0.12796
9	0.00000	0.00000	0.00000	0.00000	**0.03490**	**0.06309**
10	0.00000	0.00000	0.00000	0.00000	0.01672	0.02819

Table 9.6 Critical Values of Number of Type I Errors (x) Given 5–100 Tests Conducted With $\alpha = 0.05$ or 0.10

$\alpha = 0.05$		$\alpha = 0.10$	
Number of Tests	**Critical x (p(x or more) $\leq$ 0.10)**	**Number of Tests**	**Critical x (p(x or more) $\leq$ 0.10)**
5–11	2	5	2
12–22	3	6–11	3
23–36	4	12–18	4
37–50	5	19–25	5
51–64	6	26–32	6
65–79	7	33–40	7
80–95	8	41–48	8
96–111	9	49–56	9
		57–64	10
		65–72	11
		73–80	12
		81–88	13
		89–97	14
		98–105	15

For example, suppose you've conducted 25 tests of significance using $\alpha = 0.10$, and got four significant results. For $\alpha = 0.10$ and 25 tests, the critical value of x is 5. Because 4 is less than 5, you should be relatively cautious in how you interpret and act upon the significant findings. Alternatively, suppose you had found seven significant results. Because this is greater than the critical value of 5, you can act upon these results with more confidence.

One quick note—these computations assume that the multiple tests are independent, which will rarely be the case, especially when conducting within-subjects studies or doing multiple comparisons of all pairs of products in a multiproduct study. Fortunately, according to Winer et al. (1991), dependence among tests reduces the extent of alpha inflation as a function of the degree of dependence. This means that acting as if the data are independent even when they are not is consistent with a relatively conservative approach to this aspect of data analysis. The potential complexities of accounting for dependencies among data are beyond the scope of this book, and are not necessary for most practical user research.

MULTIPLE COMPARISONS IN THE REAL WORLD

A test of multiple medical devices—from the files of Jeff Sauro

I recently assisted in the comparison of competing medical devices related to diabetes. A company wanted to know if they could claim that their product was easier to use than their three competitors. They conducted a usability test in which over 90 people used each device in a counterbalanced order, then ranked the products from most to least preferred and answered multiple questions to assess the perceived ease of use and learning. Was there any evidence that their product was better?

There were three competing products requiring three within-subjects t-tests (see Chapter 5) for each of the three measures of interest, for a total of nine comparisons. Although I tend to be cautious when assessing medical devices, I recommended against using a Bonferroni or other adjustment strategy because the comparisons were both planned and sensible. The company's only interest was in how their product's scores compared to the competition, and really didn't care if competitor B was better than competitor C. What's more, the metrics were all correlated (in general, products that are more usable are also more learnable and preferred).

The company commissioning the study paid a lot of money to have the test done. Had we included an adjustment to correct for alpha inflation we'd have increased the chance of a Type II error, concluding there was no difference in the products when there really was. In the end there were five significant differences using $\alpha = 0.05$. One of the differences showed the product of interest was the most difficult to learn—good thing we used two-tailed tests! The other four significant findings showed the product as easier to use and ranked more highly than some of the competitors. Using Table 9.6 for alpha = 0.05 the critical value of x for nine tests is 2, making it very likely that the five observed significant differences were due to real differences rather than alpha inflation.

KEY POINTS

- There are quite a few enduring controversies in measurement and statistics that can affect user researchers and usability practitioners. They endure because there is at least a grain of truth on each side, so there is no absolute right or wrong position to take on these controversies.
- It's OK to average data from multipoint scales, but be sure to take into account their ordinal level of measurement when interpreting the results.
- Rather than relying on a rule-of-thumb to set the sample size for a study, take the time to use the methods described in this book to determine the appropriate sample size. "Magic numbers,"

whether for formative ("5 is enough") or summative ("you need at least 30") are rarely going to be exactly right for a given study.

- You should use two-tailed testing for most user research. The exception is when testing against a benchmark, in which case you should use a one-tailed test.
- Just like other aspects of statistical testing, there is nothing magic about setting your Type I error (α) to 0.05 unless you plan to publish your results. For many industrial testing contexts, it will be just as important (if not more so) to control the Type II error. Before you run a study, give careful thought to the relative costs of Type I and Type II errors for that specific study then make decisions about confidence and power accordingly. Use the methods described in this book to estimate the necessary sample size and, if the sample size turns out to be unfeasible, continue trying different combinations of α, β, and d until you find one that will accomplish your goals without exceeding your resources.
- Single-score (combined) usability metrics can be useful for executive dashboards or when considering multiple dependent measurements simultaneously to make a high-level go/no-go decision. They tend to be ineffective when providing specific direction about how to improve a product or system. Fortunately, the act of combining components into a single score does not result in the loss of the components—they are still available for analysis if necessary.
- When running more than one test on a set of data, go ahead and conduct multiple tests with α set to whatever value you've deemed appropriate given your criteria for Type II errors and your sample size. If the number of significant tests is close to what you'd expect for the number of false alarms (Type I errors) if the null hypothesis is true, then proceed with caution in interpreting the findings. Otherwise, if the number of significant tests is greater than the expected number of false alarms under the null hypothesis, you can take a stronger stand, interpreting the findings as indicating real differences and using them to guide your decisions.
- The proper use of statistics is to guide your judgment—not to replace it.

CHAPTER REVIEW QUESTIONS

1. Refer back to Fig. 9.1. Assume the coach of that football team has decided to assign numbers in sequence to players as a function of chest width to ensure that players with smaller chests get single-digit numbers. The smallest player (chest width of 275 mm) got the number 1; the next smallest (chest width 287 mm) got the 2; the next (chest width 288 mm) got the 3, and so on. What is the level of measurement of those football numbers—nominal, ordinal, interval, or ratio?
2. Suppose you're planning a within-subjects comparison of the accuracy of two dictation products, with the following criteria (similar to Example 5 in Chapter 6):
   - Difference score variability from a previous evaluation = 10.0
   - Critical difference (d) = 3.0
   - Desired level of confidence (two-tailed): 90% (so the initial value of z_α is 1.65)
   - Desired power (one-tailed): 90% (so the initial value of z_β is 1.28)
   - Sum of desired confidence and power: $z_\alpha + z_\beta = 2.93$

   What sample size should you plan for the test? If it turns out to be less than 30 (and it will), what should you say to someone who criticizes your plan by claiming "you have to have a sample size of at least 30 to be statistically significant?"

3. For the planned study in Review Question 2—would it be OK to run that as a one-tailed rather a two-tailed test? Why?
4. Once more referring to the study described in Review Question 2, how would you respond to the criticism that you have to set $\alpha = 0.05$ (95% confidence) to be able to claim statistical significance?
5. If you use SUM to combine a set of usability measurements that include successful completion rates, successful completion times, and task-level satisfaction, will that SUM score be less reliable, more reliable, or have the same reliability as its component scores?
6. Suppose you've run a formative usability study comparing your product against five competitive products with four measures and five tasks, for a total of 100 tests, using $\alpha = 0.05$, with the results shown in Table 9.7 (an asterisk indicates a significant result). Are you likely to have seen this many significant results out of 100 tests by chance if the null hypothesis is true? How would you interpret the findings by product?

Table 9.7 Significant Findings for 100 Tests Conducted With $\alpha = 0.05$

Task	Measure	Product A	Product B	Product C	Product D	Product E
1	1	*	*	*	*	*
1	2					
1	3					
1	4				*	*
2	1			*	*	*
2	2					
2	3					
2	4				*	*
3	1		*			*
3	2					
3	3					
3	4					*
4	1				*	*
4	2			*		
4	3					
4	4					
5	1				*	*
5	2					
5	3					
5	4					*
# Sig?		1	2	3	6	9

Table 9.8 Sample Size Estimation for Review Question 2

	Initial	1	2
t_α	1.65	1.83	1.80
t_β	1.28	1.38	1.36
$t_{\alpha+\beta}$	2.93	3.22	3.16
$t_{\alpha+\beta}^2$	8.58	10.34	9.98
s^2	10	10	10
d	3	3	3
d^2	9	9	9
df	9	11	11
Unrounded	9.5	11.5	11.1
Rounded up	**10**	**12**	**12**

ANSWERS TO CHAPTER REVIEW QUESTIONS

1. This is an ordinal assignment of numbers to football players. The player with the smallest chest will have the lowest number and the player with the largest chest will have the largest number, but there is no guarantee that the difference in chest size between the smallest and next-to-smallest player will be the same as the difference in chest size between the largest and next-to-largest player, and so on.
2. As shown in Table 9.8, you should plan for a sample size of 12. If challenged because this is less than 30, your response should acknowledge the general rule of thumb (no need to get into a fight), but point out that you've used a statistical process to get a more accurate estimate based on the needs of the study, the details of which you'd be happy to share with the critic. After all, no matter how good a rule of thumb might (or might not) be, when it states a single specific number, it's very unlikely to be exactly right.
3. You can do anything that you want to do, but we would advise against a one-tailed test when you're comparing competitive products because you really do not know in advance which one (if either) will be better. For most user research, the only time you'd use a one-tailed test is when you're making a comparison to a benchmark.
4. You could respond to the criticism by pointing out that you've determined that the relative costs of Type I and Type II errors to your company are about equal, and you have no plans to publish the results in a scientific journal. Consequently, you've made the Type I and Type II errors equal rather than focusing primarily on the Type I error. The result is that you can be 90% confident that you will not claim a difference where one does not exist, and the test will also have 90% power to detect differences of at least 3% in the accuracy of the two products. If you hold the sample size to 12 and change α to 0.05 (increasing confidence to 95%), then the power of the test will drop from 90% to about 84% (Table 9.2).
5. It should be more reliable. Based on data we published a few years ago (Sauro and Lewis, 2009), these data are usually correlated in industrial usability studies. Composite metrics derived from correlated components, according to psychometric theory, will be more reliable than the components.

Table 9.9 Probabilities for Number of Significant Results Given 20 Tests and $\alpha = 0.05$

Product	x (# sig)	P(x or more)
A	1	0.642
B	2	0.264
C	3	0.075
D	6	0.0003
E	9	0.0000002

6. For the full set of 100 tests, there were 21 significant results ($\alpha = 0.05$). From Table 9.6, the critical value of *x* (number of significant tests) for 100 tests if the null hypothesis is true is 9, so it seems very unlikely that the overall null hypothesis is true (in fact, the probability is just 0.00000002). For a study like this, the main purpose is usually to understand where a control product is in its competitive usability space, so the focus is on differences in products rather than differences in measures or tasks. For the subsets of 20 tests by product, the critical value of *x* is 3, so you should be relatively cautious in how you use the significant results for Products A and B, but can make stronger claims with regard to the statistically significant differences between the control product and Products C, D, and E (slightly stronger for C, much stronger for D and E). Table 9.9 shows the probabilities for these hypothetical product results.

REFERENCES

Abelson, R.P., 1995. Statistics as Principled Argument. Lawrence Erlbaum, Hillsdale, NJ.

Baguley, T., 2004. Understanding statistical power in the context of applied research. Appl. Ergon. 35, 73–80.

Benjamini, Y., Hochberg, Y., 1995. Controlling the false discovery rate: a practical and powerful approach to multiple testing. J. R. Soc. Ser. B 57 (1), 289–300.

Box, J.F., 1978. Fisher, the Life of a Scientist. John Wiley, New York, NY.

Box, G.E.P., 1984. The importance of practice in the development of statistics. Technometrics 26 (1), 1–8.

Bradley, J.V., 1976. Probability; Decision; Statistics. Prentice-Hall, Englewood Cliffs, NJ.

Bradley, J.V., 1978. Robustness? Br. J. Math. Stat. Psychol. 31, 144–152.

Braver, S.L., 1975. On splitting the tails unequally: a new perspective on one- versus two-tailed tests. Educ. Psychol. Meas. 35, 283–301.

Cliff, N., 1987. Analyzing Multivariate Data. Harcourt, Brace, Jovanovich, San Diego, CA.

Cohen, J., 1990. Things I have learned (so far). Am. Psychol. 45 (12), 1304–1312.

Cowles, M., 1989. Statistics in Psychology: An Historical Perspective. Lawrence Erlbaum, Hillsdale, NJ.

Diaconis, P., 1985. Theories of data analysis: from magical thinking through classical statistics. In: Hoaglin, D.C., Mosteller, F., Tukey, J.W. (Eds.), Exploring Data Tables, Trends, and Shapes. John Wiley, New York, pp. 1–36.

Diamond, W.J., 1981. Practical Experiment Designs for Engineers and Scientists. Lifetime Learning Publications, Belmont, CA.

Fisher, R.A., 1929. The statistical method in psychical research. Proc. Soc. Psychical Res. 39, 189–192.

Gaito, J., 1980. Measurement scales and statistics: resurgence of an old misconception. Psychol. Bull. 87 (3), 564–567.

Grove, J.W., 1989. In Defence of Science: Science, Technology, and Politics in Modern Society. University of Toronto Press, Toronto, Canada.

Harris, R.J., 1985. A Primer of Multivariate Statistics. Academic Press, Orlando, FL.

Harris, R.J., 1997. Significance tests have their place. Psychol. Sci. 8 (1), 8–11.

Hornbæk, K., Law, E., 2007. Meta-analysis of correlations among usability measures. In: Proceedings of CHI 2007, ACM, San Jose, CA pp. 617–626.

Lewis, J.R., 1991. A rank-based method for the usability comparison of competing products. In: Proceedings of the Human Factors Society 35th Annual Meeting, HFS, Santa Monica pp. 1312–1316.

Lewis, J.R., 1993. Multipoint scales: mean and median differences and observed significance levels. Int. J. Hum.-Comput. Interact. 5 (4), 383–392.

Lewis, J.R., Henry, S.C., Mack, R.L., 1990. Integrated office software benchmarks: a case study. In: Diaper, D., et al. (Eds.), Proceedings of the third IFIP Conference on Human–Computer Interaction, INTERACT'90, Elsevier Science, Cambridge, UK, pp. 337–343.

Lord, F.M., 1953. On the statistical treatment of football numbers. Am. Psychol. 8, 750–751.

Lord, F.M., 1954. Further comment on "football numbers.". Am. Psychol. 9 (6), 264–265.

Mitchell, J., 1986. Measurement scales and statistics: a clash of paradigms. Psychol. Bull. 100, 398–407.

Myers, J.L., 1979. Fundamentals of Experimental Design, third ed. Allyn and Bacon, Boston, MA.

Nunnally, J.C., 1978. Psychometric Theory. McGraw-Hill, New York, NY.

Perneger, T.V., 1998. What's wrong with Bonferroni adjustments? Br. Med. J. 316, 1236–1238.

Rosnow, R.L., Rosenthal, R., 1989. Statistical procedures and the justification of knowledge in psychological science. Am. Psychol. 44, 1276–1284.

Salsburg, D., 2001. The Lady Tasting Tea: How Statistics Revolutionized Science in the Twentieth Century. W. H. Freeman, New York, NY.

Sauro, J., Kindlund, E., 2005. A method to standardize usability metrics into a single score. In: Proceedings of CHI 2005, ACM, Portland, OR, pp. 401–409.

Sauro, J., Lewis, J.R., 2009. Correlations among prototypical usability metrics: evidence for the construct of usability. In: Proceedings of CHI 2009, ACM, Boston, MA, pp. 1609–1618.

Scholten, A.Z., Borsboom, D., 2009. A reanalysis of Lord's statistical treatment of football numbers. J. Math. Psychol. 53 (2), 69–75.

Stevens, S.S., 1946. On the theory of scales of measurement. Science 103 (2684), 677–680.

Stevens, S.S., 1959. Measurement, psychophysics, and utility. In: Churchman, C.W., Ratoosh, P. (Eds.), Measurement: Definitions and Theories. John Wiley, New York, NY, pp. 18–82.

Stigler, S.M., 1986. The History of Statistics: The Measurement of Uncertainty Before 1900. Harvard University Press, Cambridge, MA.

Stigler, S.M., 1999. Statistics on the Table: The History of Statistical Concepts and Methods. Harvard University Press, Cambridge, MA.

Townsend, J.T., Ashby, F.G., 1984. Measurement scales and statistics: the misconception misconceived. Psychol. Bull. 96 (2), 394–401.

Velleman, P.F., Wilkinson, L., 1993. Nominal, ordinal, interval, and ratio typologies are misleading. Am. Stat. 47 (1), 65–72.

Wickens, C.D., 1998. Commonsense statistics. Ergon. Des. 6 (4), 18–22.

Winer, B.J., Brown, D.R., Michels, K.M., 1991. Statistical Principles in Experimental Design, third ed. McGraw-Hill, New York, NY.

CHAPTER

AN INTRODUCTION TO CORRELATION, REGRESSION, AND ANOVA

10

INTRODUCTION

The previous chapters have covered the fundamentals that practitioners need to conduct usability testing and other user research. There is a world of more advanced statistical methods that can inform user research. In this chapter we provide an introduction to three related methods: correlation, regression, and analysis of variance (ANOVA)—methods that allow user researchers to answer some common questions such as:

- **Correlation**: Are two measurements associated or independent? For example, is there a significant correlation between perceived usability and likelihood-to-recommend?
- **Regression**: Can I use one variable to predict the other with reasonable accuracy? For example, if I know the perceived usability as measured with the System Usability Scale (SUS), can I accurately predict likelihood-to-recommend? (For the answer, see Chapter 8, "Relationship between the SUS and NPS"?)
- **ANOVA**: Are the mean SUS scores for five websites all the same, or is at least one of them different?

These methods were primarily developed in the late 18th and early 19th centuries (Cowles, 1989). Francis Galton, Charles Darwin's cousin, sought to establish a mathematical basis for the covariations observed in heredity. In 1896 Karl Pearson, a student of Galton, developed his product–moment correlation coefficient, a single unitless numerical index for assessing the extent to which two variables have a linear relationship. Galton himself had graphed linear relationships between correlated variables using the method now known as linear regression (e.g., Fig. 10.4). In 1929 Sir Ronald Fisher used intraclass correlation to develop ANOVA.

Decades later statisticians worked out the mathematics that showed that all three analytical methods were variations of the general linear model (GLM; Rutherford, 2011). You might recall from high school math that the equation for a straight line is $y = mx + b$, where y is the dependent variable, x is the independent variable, m is the slope of the line, and b is the y intercept (the point where the line crosses the y axis). This equation describes the relationship between x and y. When your data do not all fall precisely on a straight line, it is possible to use linear regression to estimate the slope and intercept of the best-fitting line. Once you start estimating, you introduce error into the process, which is why this involves inferential statistics.

The GLM method insures that the estimated values provide the best possible linear fit to the data, minimizing the error with the method of least squares. The Pearson correlation coefficient (r) is a measure of how well the regression line fits the data when both x and y are continuous variables. When independent variables are dichotomous (binary 0/1) instead of continuous, the GLM becomes equivalent to ANOVA. The GLM can also be extended from the simple case of one dependent variable and one independent variable to matrices of variables and errors—topics that we will only touch on in

Quantifying the User Experience. http://dx.doi.org/10.1016/B978-0-12-802308-2.00010-2

this chapter. For more information on these complex multivariate methods, consult a textbook such as Tabachnick and Fidell (2012).

The irony of the mathematical equivalence among these methods is that personality conflicts between Pearson and Fisher led to a division among statisticians (and psychologists adopting their methods) who either focused on correlational analysis of uncontrolled data or ANOVA of data from controlled experiments. "Had they been collaborators and friends, rather than adversaries and enemies, statistics might have had a quite different history" (Cowles, 1989, p. 5).

CORRELATION

Correlation addresses the fundamental question of whether two variables are related or independent. Correlations can range from −1 to +1, where −1 means a perfect negative correlation (as one variable goes up the other goes down), 0 means no correlation (the variables are independent with no pattern of relationship), and +1 means a perfect (error-free) positive correlation between two variables (both go up and down at the same time)—Fig. 10.1.

WHY CORRELATE?

It's a very flexible tool—from the files of Jeff Sauro

Want to know what customers are likely to do? You're not alone. Most organizations would love to predict their customers' next action or attitude. Unfortunately, there isn't an analytics crystal ball that provides a clear and accurate picture of the future. Instead, we have to rely on the much murkier reality of past data to predict the future. And while the past is no guarantee of the future, it's often all we have to make decisions. More specifically, we look for correlations between various types of customer analytics to uncover patterns. For example, you might ask correlation-revealing questions like these:

- Does a longer time on a website result in more purchases?
- Do customers rate tasks as easier if they take less time?
- For customers who purchase product A, what other products do they purchase?
- Will coupons increase same-store sales?
- Will a reduced price mean higher sales?
- Is customer loyalty tied to future company growth?

If you want to make predictions based on customer analytics, you need to know how to evaluate relationships between variables—including assessing the strength of the correlations. For more details about correlations for customer analytics, see Sauro (2015).

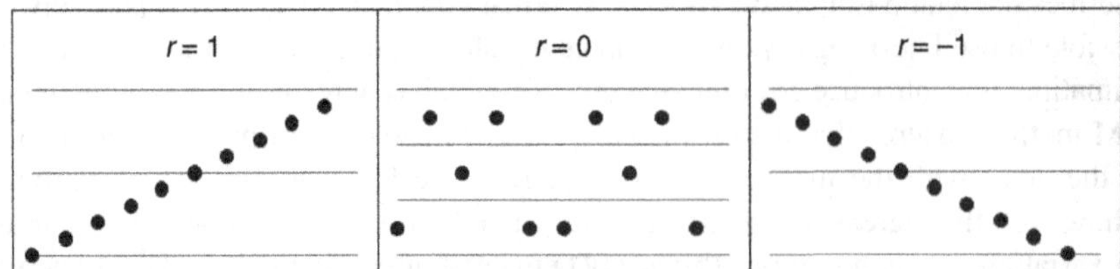

FIGURE 10.1 Scatterplots of various relationships between variables

From left to right: perfect positive correlation, no correlation, and perfect negative correlation.

HOW TO COMPUTE A CORRELATION

To compute a correlation, you have to have two variables, usually referred to as x and y, where each x–y pair came from the same source. In user research, that source will usually (but not necessarily) be a person. The formula for the Pearson correlation is:

$$r = \frac{SS_{xy}}{\sqrt{(SS_{xx})(SS_{yy})}}$$

where:

$$SS_{xx} = \Sigma(x_i - \bar{x})^2$$

$$SS_{yy} = \Sigma(y_i - \bar{y})^2$$

$$SS_{xy} = \Sigma(x_i - \bar{x})(y_i - \bar{y})$$

So, the correlation coefficient is the ratio of the sum of the crossproducts of x and y (the signal) and the square root after multiplying their sums of squares (the noise), illustrated in Table 10.1. The pairs of UMUX-LITE and SUS data in the table are a portion of the data adapted from a larger-sample survey conducted to explore the relationship between these two questionnaires which were designed to assess perceived usability (from Lewis et al., 2013—for details about the questionnaires, see their descriptions in Chapter 8).

For these data, the value of r is 0.80. In Excel, you can use the =CORREL function to compute a correlation, so you don't need to set up a table like this each time you want to find out how two variables correlate. However, examining a table like this can help you understand how the correlation coefficient works.

For example, note that the denominator of the ratio will always be positive because SS_{xx} and SS_{yy} are sums of squares (and squares are always positive). The numerator, however, can be positive or negative depending on whether there is a tendency for the deviations of x and y from their means to be

Table 10.1 Example of Computing *r*

Participant	UMUX-LITE (x)	SUS (y)	$x_i - \bar{x}$	$y_i - \bar{y}$	$(x_i - \bar{x}^2)$	$(y_i - \bar{y})^2$	$(x_i - \bar{x})((y_i - \bar{y})$
1	55.4	72.5	−2.3	11.8	5.39	138.90	−27.36
2	87.9	82.5	30.2	21.8	910.75	474.62	657.46
3	66.2	50.0	8.5	−10.7	72.45	114.80	−91.20
4	82.5	82.5	24.8	21.8	613.15	474.62	539.46
5	22.9	10.0	−34.8	−50.7	1212.53	2571.94	1765.94
6	44.6	65.0	−13.2	4.3	173.05	18.37	−56.38
7	44.6	62.5	−13.2	1.8	173.05	3.19	−23.49
Mean	57.7	60.7					
St Dev	23.0	25.2		*Sum*	3160.37	3796.43	2764.43
						r	**0.80**

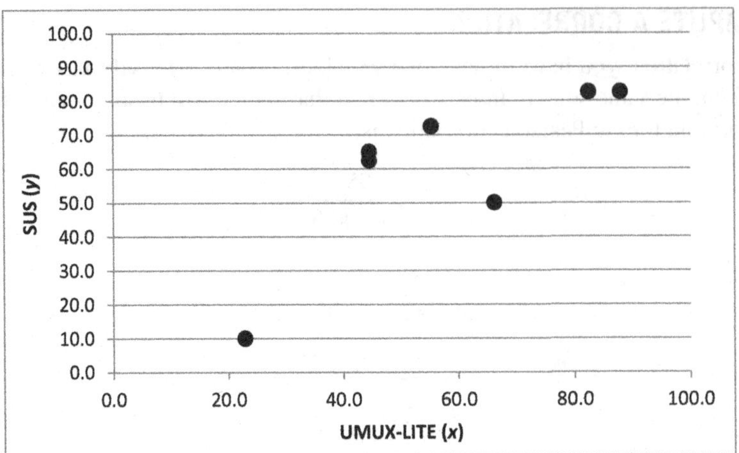

FIGURE 10.2 Scatterplot of data from Table 10.1

in the same or opposite directions. If there is no general tendency for the deviations of x and y from their means to be in the same (positive correlation) or opposite (negative correlation) directions, then they will tend to cancel out and indicate no correlation. As shown in Fig. 10.2, the values of x and y in Table 10.1 have a strong tendency to increase and decrease together.

ALWAYS CHECK FOR NONLINEARITY

Most, but not all, paired data will have a linear component

A fundamental assumption of correlation and regression is that the relationship between the variables is linear (straight line). It is always a good idea to graph your data as a scatterplot when considering correlation or regression analysis to look for a linear relationship. Even though the four graphs in Fig. 10.3 are all nonlinear, it would be possible to

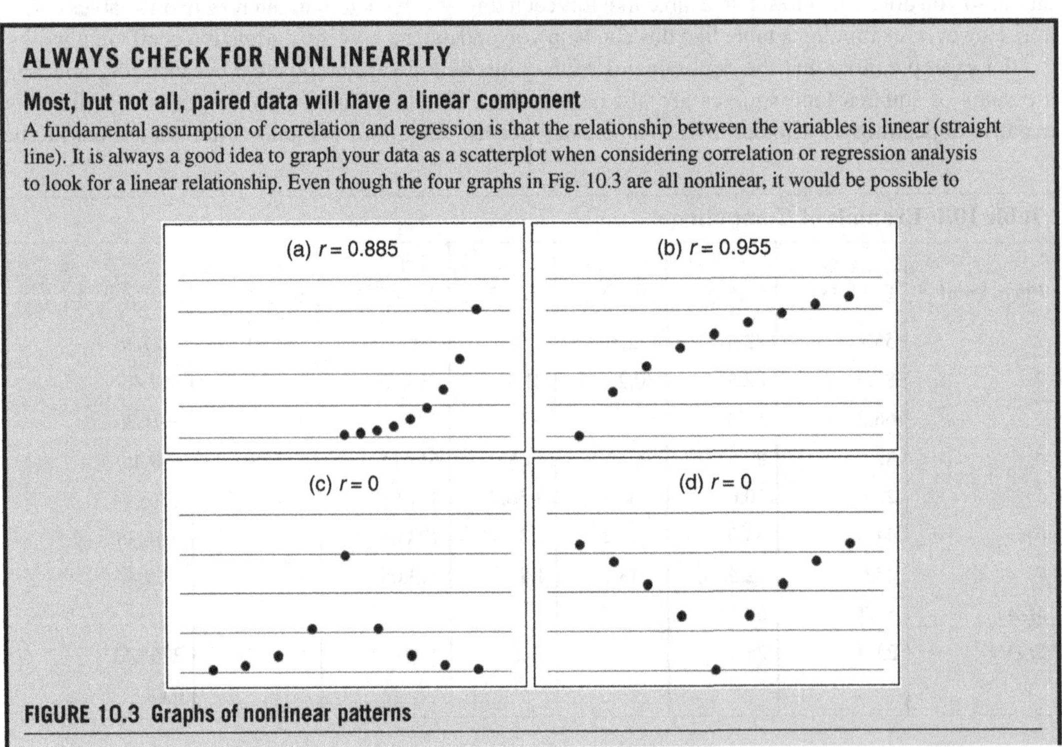

FIGURE 10.3 Graphs of nonlinear patterns

approximate the first two (a and b) with straight lines (although prediction would be better using the appropriate nonlinear equation or data transformation—topics that are outside the scope of this book). The second two (c and d), however, have linear correlations of 0 because there is no linearity at all in their patterns. Graphing the data before you start computing linear correlations and regressions could prevent you from concluding there are no relationships among the data when there really are—it's just that they're nonlinear rather than linear.

STATISTICAL SIGNIFICANCE OF *r*

As we've seen throughout this book, whenever we select a sample of users we need to take into account sampling error. Like completion rates and task times, correlations computed from a sample will fluctuate and what we may think is a solid relationship between two variables may change if we sample more users. To declare a correlation as statistically significant, we are saying the correlation is different from 0 (similar to comparing differences to 0 as was done in Chapters 4 and 5). Table 10.2 shows the smallest correlations you can detect as statistically significant based on various sample sizes and significance levels. Note that when reporting a correlation, its degrees of freedom are the sample size minus two ($n - 2$).

For example, if you have a correlation of 0.80 with a sample size of 7, you would report the result as $r(5) = 0.80$, $p < 0.05$. For values not in the table, you can convert r to t, then use the Excel function =TDIST to get the significance level (p).

$$t = \frac{r}{\sqrt{\frac{1-r^2}{n-2}}}$$

Table 10.2 Some Critical Values of |*r*|

df	$p < 0.10$	$p < 0.05$	$p < 0.02$	$p < 0.01$
1	0.988	0.997	0.9995	0.9999
2	0.900	0.950	0.980	0.990
3	0.805	0.878	0.934	0.959
4	0.729	0.811	0.882	0.917
5	0.669	0.754	0.833	0.874
10	0.497	0.576	0.658	0.708
15	0.412	0.482	0.558	0.606
20	0.360	0.423	0.492	0.537
25	0.323	0.381	0.445	0.487
50	0.231	0.273	0.322	0.354
100	0.164	0.195	0.230	0.254

$df = n - 2$

Continuing with the example:

$$t = \frac{0.80}{\sqrt{\frac{1-0.80^2}{7-2}}} = 2.98$$

$$= \text{TDIST}(2.98, 5, 2) = 0.031$$

As expected, $p < 0.05$, meaning a correlation of 0.80 from a sample size of 7 is statistically significant. If you did the same calculation with $r = 0.754$, you'd find $p = 0.05$, as shown in Table 10.2.

One important take-away from the table is that you need a reasonably large sample size to detect modest, but potentially important relationships between variables. That is, if you're hoping to confidently detect a correlation of $r = 0.3$ or less, you should plan on a sample size of around 50. If you're limited to using only a small sample size (e.g., 10) you can still look for correlations in your data, you'll just be limited to finding stronger associations (above $r = 0.575$).

CONFIDENCE INTERVALS FOR *r*

Throughout this book we've emphasized the importance of supplementing tests of significance with confidence intervals. Essentially, a test of significance of r tells you whether the confidence interval (range of plausibility) contains 0—in other words, whether 0 (no correlation at all) is or is not a plausible value for r given the data. To compute the confidence interval, you first need to transform r into z'. This is necessary because the distribution of r is skewed and this procedure normalizes the distribution.

$$z' = 0.5 \ln[(1+r)/(1-r)]$$

This establishes the center of the confidence interval. The margin of error (d) is:

$$d = \frac{z(1-\alpha)}{\sqrt{n-3}}$$

The confidence interval around z' is $z' \pm d$.

After you compute the endpoints of the interval, you need to convert them back to r.

$$r = \frac{\exp(2z')-1}{\exp(2z')+1}$$

Applying these formulas to the previous example (and showing the Excel method for computing them using the ln and exp functions—see Chapter 3), you get a 95% confidence interval that ranges from 0.12 to 0.97:

$$z' = 0.5 * \ln((1+0.80)/(1-0.80)) = 1.0986$$

$$d = 1.96 * (1/\text{sqrt}(7-3)) = 0.98$$

$$\text{Upper bound: } 1.0986 + 0.98 = 2.0786$$

$$\text{Lower bound: } 1.0986 - 0.98 = 0.1186$$

$$r_{\text{upper}} = ((\exp(2*2.0786)-1)/((\exp(2*2.0786)+1))) = 0.97$$

$$r_{\text{lower}} = ((\exp(2*0.1186)-1)/((\exp(2*0.1186)+1))) = 0.12$$

Given such a small sample size, the 95% confidence interval is very wide (from 0.12 to 0.97), but you now know that not only is 0 implausible given the data, 0.10 is also implausible (but 0.15 is plausible). It is important to note that the resulting confidence interval will not be symmetrical around the value of *r* unless the observed correlation is equal to 0.

HOW TO AVERAGE CORRELATIONS

Another use for the z' transformation

In addition to its use when computing confidence intervals, you also need to use the z' transformation when averaging correlations either within studies or across multiple studies. For example, in Sauro and Lewis (2009), we were exploring different ways to compute the correlations among prototypical usability metrics like task time and errors. To summarize those results, we needed to average correlations, and to do that properly, we had to (1) transform each correlation to its corresponding z', (2) compute the average z', and (3) transform the average z' to *r*. Averaging without transformation tends to underestimate the true mean of the correlations.

INTERPRETING THE MAGNITUDE OF *r*

Although the interpretation of correlations can depend on the context, it can help to have some guidance on how to interpret their magnitudes. Like statistical confidence, what's considered a "strong" relationship depends on how much error you can tolerate and the consequences of being wrong. Cohen (1988) examined correlations in the behavioral sciences and provided the following interpretative guidelines based on how commonly the correlations appeared in the peer-reviewed literature:

- $r = 0.10$ small
- $r = 0.30$ medium
- $r = 0.50$ large

Although the correlation of 0.80 in the previous example is very large, the 95% confidence interval shows that the plausible range could go from small to almost perfect (0.12–0.97). If all we need to know is whether the correlation is statistically significant, we're done. But if we need a more precise estimate of the correlation, then we clearly need more data.

Keep in mind that "small" does not necessarily mean "unimportant." Small significant correlations can have large impacts. For example, on ecommerce websites that receive millions of visitors a month, paying attention to a "small" correlation between attitudes toward a new design and number of sales could increase sales by millions of dollars. Always consider the context when interpreting the strength of a correlation.

SAMPLE SIZE ESTIMATION FOR *r*

There are a number of approaches to estimating sample sizes for the correlation coefficient. Moinester and Gottfried (2014) recently surveyed the methods based on prespecification of the desired width of the resulting confidence interval. The formula they recommended is:

$$n = \frac{z^2(1-r^2)^2}{d^2} + 1 + 6r^2$$

To use the formula, you need to decide the level of confidence (for 95% confidence $z = 1.96$), the size of the critical difference (also known as the margin of error, d in the equation), and the expected value of r. If you have no idea what value of r to expect, set it to 0 to maximize the estimated sample size. As described in Chapter 6 ("Basic Principles of Summative Sample Size Estimation"), if you're not sure what value to use for d, try the "what if" approach, exploring a range of values to either (1) settle on a feasible sample size that meets your needs or (2) determine that it is not possible to address the question at hand with the resources available.

As you may recall, in the example from the previous section $n = 7$ and the resulting 95% confidence interval was very wide, ranging from 0.12 to 0.97. Keeping the level of confidence at 95%, assuming that the true correlation is close to the observed correlation ($r = 0.80$), and setting d to 0.20, the estimated sample size is:

$$n = \frac{1.96^2(1-0.8^2)^2}{0.2^2} + 1 + 6(0.8)^2 = 17.3 \text{ (round up to 18)}$$

Recalculating the confidence interval while keeping everything the same but setting n to 18 results in a 95% confidence interval ranging from 0.52 to 0.92. The slight increase in the sample size had little effect on the upper bound, but a dramatic effect on the lower bound. Given the data, a correlation of 0.90 is still plausible, but a correlation of 0.50 is no longer plausible. The width of the interval of 0.40 (0.92−0.52) is equal to two times the value of d used in the sample size formula. The observed value of r is not in the center of the interval. As mentioned previously, r will be in the center of the interval only when it is equal to 0.

COEFFICIENT OF DETERMINATION (R^2)

Multiplying r by itself (squaring it) produces a metric known as the coefficient of determination. It's represented as R^2—usually expressed as a percentage—and provides another way of interpreting the strength of a relationship. For the correlation of 0.80 between the SUS and the UMUX-LITE in our running example, R^2 is 64%: the SUS explains 64% of the variation in the UMUX-LITE, and the UMUX-LITE explains 64% of the variation in the SUS. Even a strong correlation such as $r = 0.5$ only explains a minority (25%) of the variation between variables.

It is important to be careful with the word "explains" in this context, which should not be taken to imply causation (see the sidebar, "Correlation Is Not Causation"). Height, for example, explains around 64% of the variation in weight. Knowing people's heights explains most, but not all, of why they are a certain weight. Other factors—perhaps exercise, diet, and genetics—may account for the other 36% of the variation.

CORRELATION IS NOT CAUSATION

You've probably heard it before, but it bears repeating

Correlation does not prove causation. High SAT scores don't cause better university grades. Higher Net Promoter Scores don't create higher revenue. Association? Yes. Causation? No. Establishing causation requires three ingredients:

- You have to have an association (a correlation significantly different from 0).
- You need to establish a temporal relationship (*a* precedes *b*).
- You need to rule out other explanations for the cause of the relationship. This is best done using a randomized controlled experiment.

It seems like the warning that correlation does not equal causation always applies to someone else's research. But even well-trained researchers and scientists get so vested in their ideas that they get caught in the correlation is causation trap. You should always look for alternative explanations when you think there's a causal relationship. For example:

- A new design might have caused the increased website conversion rates or perhaps it was because a main competitor stopped selling a product around the time the design was released.
- Does having been born around 1955 make you more likely to be a software millionaire due to the timing of the emergence of technologies (Gladwell, 2008), or is this effect better explained by the baby-boom (Sauro, 2010)?
- Customer coupons might have caused the uptick in same-store sales, or maybe same-store sales were already increasing because of an improving economy or industry.
- Is lower pay for women due to gender bias, years of experience, or some combination of both (Sauro, 2011)?

This type of critical thinking isn't natural, but is an important skill for user researchers.

CORRELATION WITH BINARY DATA

When working with binary data (such as task-completion rates) the association is based on the same principle of correlation used between continuous variables, but the computations are different.

To start, arrange your data in rows and columns. The example shown in Table 10.3 covers 15 customer transactions involving any of four books (Books A, B, C, and D). For example, Customer 1 purchased Book A and Book B, and not Book C or Book D. Customer 2 purchased Book B and none of the others. These could just as easily be software products, groceries, songs in a playlist, TV shows, or any other products or services.

One way to use these data would be to guide recommendations for future purchases. When building the list of recommendations, it would be reasonable to arrange the list based on the strength of association, highest first. Keep in mind that in this matrix, all 15 customers were exposed to all four books, so a 0 means that the customer made a deliberate decision not to purchase. Considering a book and not purchasing it is different from not ever seeing the book.

COMPUTING THE PHI CORRELATION

An association between binary variables is called a phi correlation, represented with the Greek symbol φ. You can compute phi by hand or by using the Excel function =CORREL().

To calculate phi by hand:

1. Arrange your data into a contingency table as shown in Table 10.4 for each pair of books. Each cell is labeled from *a* to *d*. Six customers purchased both Book A and Book B, two purchased Book A but not Book B, and so forth.

Table 10.3 Purchases Per Customer (1 = Purchased; 0 = Did Not Purchase)

Customer	Book A	Book B	Book C	Book D
1	1	1	0	0
2	0	1	0	0
3	1	1	0	0
4	1	0	0	1
5	0	0	0	0
6	1	1	0	0
7	1	0	1	0
8	0	0	1	0
9	1	1	0	0
10	1	1	0	0
11	0	1	0	0
12	0	1	0	0
13	1	1	0	0
14	0	0	0	0
15	0	0	0	0

Table 10.4 Contingency Table for Purchases of Books A and B

	Book B	
Book A	**Y**	**N**
Y	6 (*a*)	2 (*b*)
N	3 (*c*)	4 (*d*)

2. Compute the phi correlation using the following formula:

$$\varphi = \frac{ad - bc}{\sqrt{(a+b)(c+d)(a+c)(b+d)}}$$

3. Inserting the data for Book A and B into the formula shows that their phi correlation is 0.327.

$$\varphi = \frac{6(4) - 2(3)}{\sqrt{(6+2)(3+4)(6+3)(2+4)}}$$

$$\varphi = \frac{18}{\sqrt{3024}} = 0.327$$

Table 10.5 Phi Correlation Matrix of Each Book Combination

	Phi Correlations			
	A	B	C	D
A				
B	0.33			
C	−0.03	−0.48		
D	0.25	−0.33	−0.10	

The phi correlations of all the pairs of books purchased are shown in Table 10.5 (rounded to two decimal places). For example, the phi correlation between Book A and Book B is 0.33; the correlation between Book A and Book D is 0.25. You don't need to correlate a book with itself (so cells A:A, B:B, C:C, and D:D are blank) and the top-half of the matrix is blank because it's a duplication of the data on the bottom.

You can interpret the strength of phi similarly to the way we interpret the Pearson correlation *r*, so the correlation between Book A and Book B (0.33) is of medium strength. In our scenario, if a customer were viewing Book A, it would make sense to recommend (and possibly offer that customer an incentive to also purchase) Book B and Book D because Book A has a positive correlation with both those books. Note that phi correlations can be artificially restricted based on the proportions, in which case they underestimate the actual association. That is, unlike the correlation of continuous variables that can range between −1 and 1, under certain circumstances phi correlations can have maximum values less than 0.20 (see Bobko, 2001 for further explanation).

To assess the significance of phi, you can convert it to a chi-squared value (with one degree of freedom) using $\chi^2 = n\varphi^2$ (Cohen et al., 2011). For 0.33, $\chi^2(1) = 15(0.33^2) = 1.63$ ($p = 0.20$). You can assess the probability of chi-squared using the =CHIDIST() function in Excel which, for this example, is =CHIDIST(1.63,1).

With a sample size of 15, a phi of 0.33 isn't large enough to provide convincing evidence of a relationship. Using the formula for the confidence interval of *r*, the estimated 95% confidence interval for a phi of 0.33 ranges from −0.22 to 0.72. Applying the formula for sample size estimation of *r* to find the smallest sample size for which a phi of 0.33 would be significant (lower limit greater than 0) results in an estimate of 36. The revised confidence interval with $n = 36$ ranges from 0.002 to 0.594 (just excluding 0). This suggests that user researchers can, with caution, use the confidence interval and sample size estimation formulas for *r* when working with phi.

WATCH OUT FOR RANGE RESTRICTION

When you don't find an expected correlation, this might be the reason

Two variables might have a low correlation because you're only measuring in a narrow range. For example, height and weight have a strong positive correlation but if you measure only National Basketball Association (NBA) players, the correlation would mostly go away. For a user research example, this could happen if you were looking at the correlation between income and likelihood to purchase, but the customers in your sample had a narrow range of income (e.g., customers with annual incomes over a million dollars).

REGRESSION

To predict one variable from another requires the use of an extension of linear correlation called linear regression. Regression analysis is a "workhorse" in applied statistics. The math isn't too complicated and most software packages support regression analysis. Linear regression extends the idea of the scatterplot used in correlation and adds a line that best "fits" the data. Because it is an extension of linear correlation, linear regression models the linear component of the relationship between variables. If the relationship has no linear component, then the correlation will be close to 0 and the linear regression will have little to no predictive accuracy.

Although there are many ways to draw lines through the data, least-squares analysis is a mathematical approach that minimizes the squared distance between the line and each dot in the scatterplot. This analysis can be done by hand or using software such as Minitab, SPSS, SAS, R, or Excel (e.g., see the Excel calculator documented in Lewis and Sauro, 2016, available at measuringu.com/products/expandedStats). Fig. 10.4 adds the least-squares regression line to the scatterplot of SUS and UMUX-LITE scores from Fig. 10.2. In addition to showing the line, the figure also shows the regression equation and value of R^2.

The regression equation takes the general form of:

$$\hat{y} = b_0 + b_1 x + e$$

- $\hat{y}$ (pronounced *y*-hat): Represents the predicted value of the dependent variable (in this example, the predicted value of the SUS score).
- b_0: Called the *y*-intercept, this is where the line would cross (or intercept) the *y*-axis (in other words, this is the predicted value of y when $x = 0$).
- b_1: The slope of the predicted line (how steep it is).
- x: Represents a particular value of the independent variable (in this example, the UMUX-LITE score).
- e: Represents the inevitable error the prediction will contain.

So in this example the regression equation indicates the predicted SUS score is 10.22 (the *y*-intercept) plus 0.874 (the slope) multiplied by the UMUX-LITE score (x).

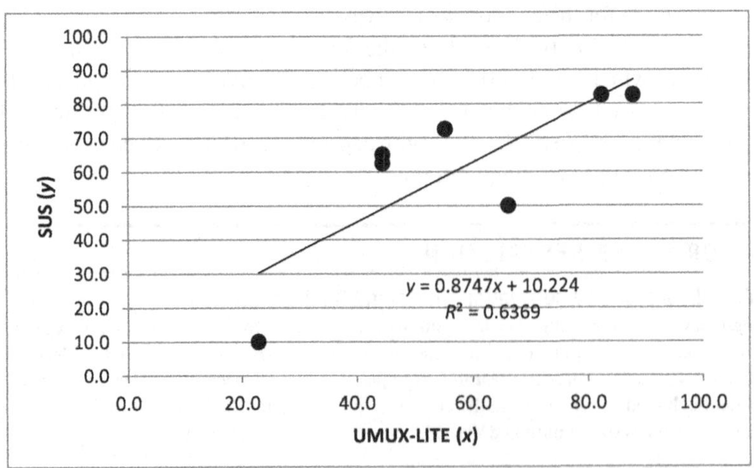

FIGURE 10.4 A least-squares regression line

ESTIMATING SLOPES AND INTERCEPTS

The formula for computing the slope of the best-fitting line is:

$$b_1 = r\frac{s_y}{s_x}$$

where r is the correlation between x and y
s_x and s_y are the standard deviations of the x- and y-values.

The formula for the intercept is:

$$b_0 = \bar{y} - b_1\bar{x}$$

where $\bar{x}$ and $\bar{y}$ are the means of the x- and y-values and
b_1 is the slope.

For example, using the data from Table 10.1, the slope of the best fitting line is 0.80(23.0/25.2) ≈ 0.874 and the intercept is 60.7−0.874(57.7) ≈ 10.22, matching the equation shown in Fig. 10.4 (the values are only approximately equal due to round off error).

CONFIDENCE INTERVALS FOR SLOPES AND PREDICTED VALUES

Any time you estimate, there will be error and uncertainty. In linear regression you estimate slopes, intercepts, and predicted values. To establish the plausible values for your estimates, compute confidence intervals. Note that computing the confidence interval of the intercept is a special case of computing the confidence interval for a predicted value ($\hat{y}$) when $x = 0$.

Confidence interval for the slope

First, compute the standard error (SE) using the following equation:

$$\text{SE} = \frac{\sqrt{\frac{\Sigma(y_i - \hat{y}_i)^2}{(n-2)}}}{\sqrt{\Sigma(x_i - \bar{x})^2}}$$

where y_i is the value of the dependent variable for observation i,
$\hat{y}_i$ is the estimated value of the dependent variable for observation i,
x_i is the observed value of the independent variable for observation i,
$\bar{x}$ is the mean of the independent variable, and
n is the sample size.

Next, determine the value of t for your desired level of confidence, using $n - 2$ degrees of freedom.

Then compute the margin of error by multiplying SE by t.

Finally, add and subtract the margin of error from the slope.

For example, Table 10.6 shows the SUS/UMUX-LITE data we've been using throughout the chapter with these new calculations.

Substituting the values from the table into the equation for the standard error, you get:

$$\text{SE} = \frac{\sqrt{\frac{1378.34}{(7-2)}}}{\sqrt{3160.37}}$$

Table 10.6 Example of Computing the Standard Error of the Slope

Participant	UMUX-LITE (x)	SUS (y)	xi–x	ŷ	y–ŷ	(xi–x)²	(y–ŷ)²
1	55.4	72.5	−2.3	58.6	13.9	5.39	192.11
2	87.9	82.5	30.2	87.0	−4.5	910.75	20.65
3	66.2	50.0	8.5	68.1	−18.1	72.45	327.90
4	82.5	82.5	24.8	82.3	0.2	613.15	0.04
5	22.9	10.0	−34.8	30.2	−20.2	1212.53	409.44
6	44.6	65.0	−13.2	49.2	15.8	173.05	250.55
7	44.6	62.5	−13.2	49.2	13.3	173.05	177.66
Mean	57.7	60.7					
Std Dev	23.0	25.2			*Sum*	3160.37	1378.34
df	5					*SE*	**0.2953**

The standard error is 0.2953. With $n = 7$, there are 5 degrees of freedom for this procedure. The corresponding value of t for a 95% confidence interval is 2.57, so the margin of error is 0.2953(2.57) = 0.76. Thus, the 95% confidence interval for the slope of 0.874 ranges from 0.12 to 1.63.

Confidence interval for predicted values (including the intercept)

The process for computing the confidence interval around a predicted value is similar, using the following equation for the standard error:

$$\text{SE} = \sqrt{\frac{\Sigma(y_i - \hat{y}_i)^2}{(n-2)}}\sqrt{\frac{1}{n} + \frac{(x-\bar{x})^2}{\Sigma(x_i - \bar{x})^2}}$$

Note that the intercept is the special case where $x = 0$, so in that case, $(x-\bar{x})^2$ becomes $(\bar{x})^2$.

Continuing with the sample data in Table 10.6, suppose we have set UMUX-LITE to 68 and predicted the corresponding value of SUS (69.65). To compute the confidence interval around that prediction, start with the standard error:

$$\text{SE} = \sqrt{\frac{1378.34}{5}}\sqrt{\frac{1}{7} + \frac{(68-57.7)^2}{3160.37}}$$

The standard error is 6.97. With $n = 7$, there are 5 degrees of freedom for this procedure. The corresponding value of t for a 95% confidence interval is 2.57, so the margin of error is 6.97(2.57) = 17.92. Thus, the 95% confidence interval for the predicted value of 69.65 ranges from 51.73 to 87.57. That's a pretty wide interval, but keep in mind that the sample size in this example is **very** small. For practical regression, you'll usually be dealing with much larger sample sizes, and the statistics program that you use (e.g., SPSS) will likely provide the standard errors that you'll need to compute your confidence intervals. However, in general, there is much more uncertainty around predicting a data point compared to predicting the slope of a regression line.

Finally, let's look at the special case of the intercept. For this example, compute the standard error using:

$$SE = \sqrt{\frac{1378.34}{5}}\sqrt{\frac{1}{7}+\frac{(57.7)^2}{3160.37}}$$

The standard error is 18.17. With $n = 7$, there are 5 degrees of freedom for this procedure. The corresponding value of t for a 95% confidence interval is 2.57, so the margin of error is $18.17(2.57) = 46.7$. The 95% confidence interval for the estimated intercept of 10.22 ranges from −36.48 to 56.92. That interval is even wider than the one for the estimated value of 69.65. It is a property of linear regression models that predictions are more accurate when x is closer to $\bar{x}$ because when they are equal $x - \bar{x} = 0$, so the standard error is the smallest it can be.

EXTRAPOLATE WITH CAUTION

It's much riskier than interpolation

When using linear regression, interpolation (estimating values that are between observed data points) is much less risky than extrapolation (estimating beyond the ends of the observed values). As shown in the formula for the standard error of an estimated value, the further x is from the mean of the x's the less precise the estimate will be. Even more importantly, there's no guarantee that the regression line will continue to be linear as it extends before and after the observed data points. For a practical, real-world example, Fig. 10.5 shows the population of Japan after WWII from 1945 till 1990.

The simple linear-regression equation fits the data well ($R^2 = 97\%$). The regression equation is Population = −2,120,000,000 + 1,126,540 (Year). Using the regression equation, we can then predict what the population of Japan would be in the future (beyond the 1990 dataset). Fig. 10.6 shows the predicted population (squares) against the actual population (triangles) from 1995 to 2014.

Despite the good fit of a line to the earlier data, going beyond the bounds of the dataset to predict values is risky. In this case, using simple linear regression to predict the future population of Japan during the 1990s overpredicted the

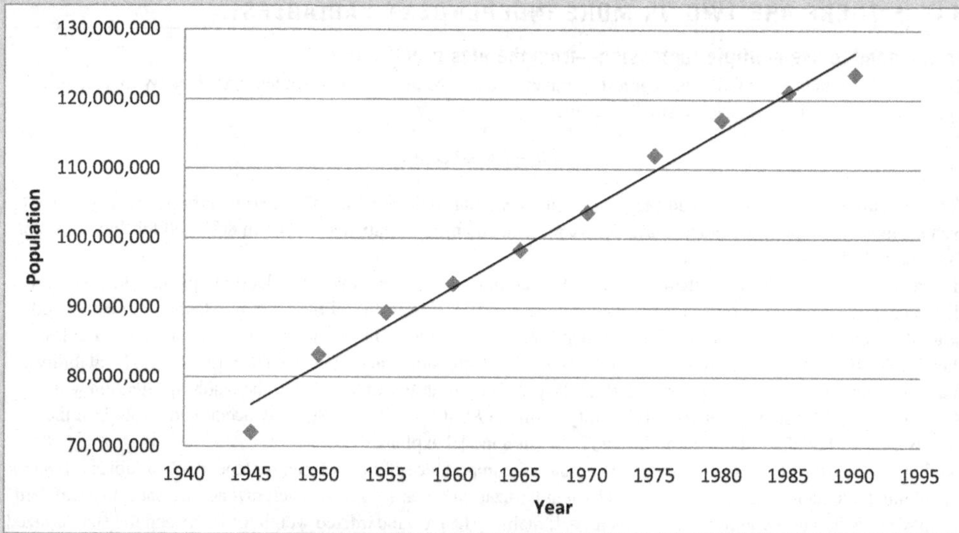

FIGURE 10.5 Population of Japan from 1945 through 1990

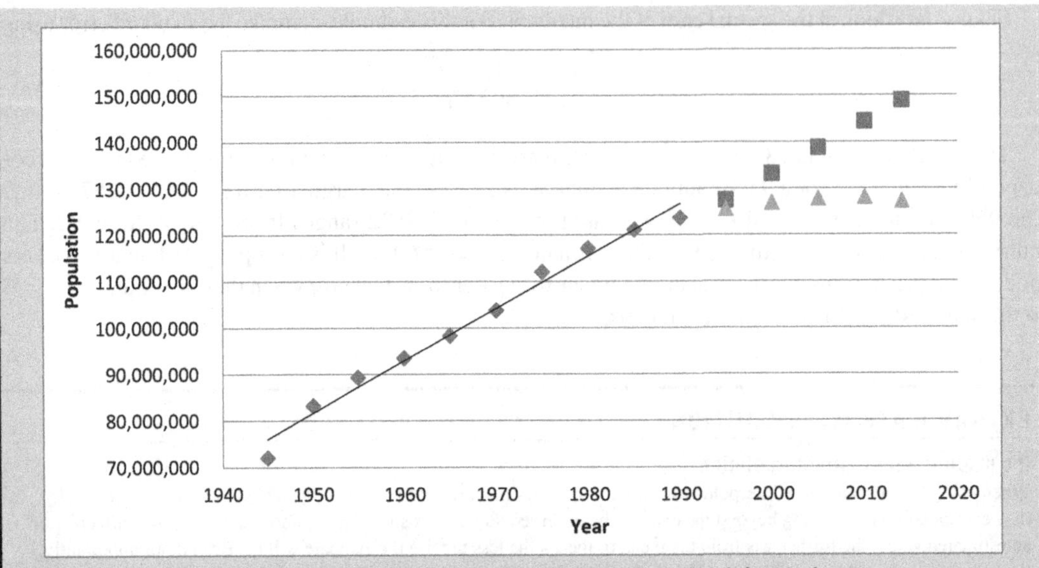

FIGURE 10.6 Predicted population of Japan (squares) and actual population (triangles)

actual population substantially. In fact, Japan's population has actually begun to shrink and is over 20 million less than we predicted! Although you're unlikely to be predicting future populations of countries, you may find yourself predicting page views or purchases—both of which often increase linearly with positive customer attitudes, but not indefinitely!

WHAT IF THERE ARE TWO OR MORE INDEPENDENT VARIABLES?

Then you need to use multiple regression—from the files of Jeff Sauro

With multiple regression, you build the regression equation with two or more independent variables. With another independent variable, the regression formula becomes:

$$\hat{y} = b_0 + b_1x_1 + b_2x_2 + e$$

The computational methods of multiple regression are similar to those of simple linear regression, but if you need to evaluate more than one independent variable, we recommend using a statistical program designed for these types of analyses (e.g., SPSS, SAS, R, Minitab).

I once had 2584 customers rate their likelihood to recommend (LTR) a university's learning management system (LTR is a common measure of customer loyalty). They also rated the stability of the system (whether it crashed) and its usability (using a four-item questionnaire). I then used regression to evaluate the extent to which these variables predicted LTR. For the independent variable of Stability, the regression equation was LTR = 1.950 + 1.423(Stability), with a correlation of 0.49 and corresponding R^2 of 24%. Adding usability to the model, the resulting equation was LTR = −0.937 + 0.541(Stability) + 0.419(Usability), with an R^2 of 56%. Alone, Stability accounted for 24% of the variability in LTR, but after adding Usability the regression model explained 56%.

Multiple regression also provides a way to compare the importance of the different independent variables (predictors) by examining their standardized coefficients. The standardization process converts each raw coefficient into a standard score, making their values comparable. In this model, Stability had a standardized weight of 0.188 and the standardized weight for Usability was 0.641. In other words, Usability appeared to be more than three times as important as Stability in predicting customer loyalty.

SAMPLE SIZE ESTIMATION FOR LINEAR REGRESSION

The first step in determining a sample size for linear regression is to decide which aspect is of primary interest. The correlation is the best metric of overall quality, but depending on the situation, you might be more focused on the slope or the intercept. Earlier in this chapter we provided a sample size formula for correlation. Following are formulas for estimating sample sizes when focused on estimating the slope or the intercept.

Slope

To simplify the formula, instead of working with the sums of squares (as shown in Table 10.6), we're going to work with the formula for population variances—the sums of squares divided by the sample size n (rather than dividing by $n - 1$). Starting with the equation of the standard error of the slope, substituting the population variabilities of x and e for their sums of squares (their denominators of n cancel out), using the fact that $d = t(\text{SE})$, and solving for n, you get:

$$n = \frac{t^2 s_e^2}{d^2 s_x^2} + 2$$

For the detailed derivation of this formula, see the Appendix. To estimate n you need:

- An estimate of the population variability of x (s_x^2)
- An estimate of the population variability of e (s_e^2)
- The desired level of confidence (used to determine the value of t)
- The smallest difference between the obtained and true value that you want to be able to detect (d)

For the example we've been using in this chapter, the 95% confidence interval for the slope of 0.874 ranges from 0.12 to 1.63 (±0.76). Suppose there was a need to have an estimate that controlled the accuracy to ±0.25 (so $d^2 = 0.0625$). From the data in Table 10.6, we have estimates of s_x^2 and s_e^2 which are, respectively, 451.48 (3160.37/7) and 196.91 (1378.34/7). As discussed in Chapter 6, use the value of z in place of t for an initial sample size estimate (with $df = n - 2$), then iterate until the sample size doesn't change. For 95% confidence, $z = 1.96$ (so $z^2 = 3.84$). Table 10.7 shows the iterations, which result in a sample size estimate of 32.

Let's see if increasing n from 7 to 32 has the desired effect, keeping everything else equal.

$$\text{SE} = \frac{\sqrt{\frac{196.91}{(32-2)}}}{\sqrt{451.48}}$$

The new standard error is 0.12, the value of t given 95% confidence and 30 degrees of freedom is 2.04, so the critical difference (d, aka, margin of error) is 0.12(2.04) = 0.25—exactly the desired value.

Intercept

The formula for the intercept also uses the population variance for e and x. Starting with the equation of the standard error of the intercept, using the fact that $d = t(\text{SE})$, and solving for n, you get:

$$n = \frac{t^2 s_e^2 \left(1 + \frac{\bar{x}^2}{s_x^2}\right)}{d^2} + 2$$

Table 10.7 Example Sample Size Estimation for Regression Slope

Iteration	d	d^2	t	df	t^2	s_x^2	s_e^2	n	Round up
1	0.25	0.0625	1.96	na	3.84	451.48	196.91	28.81	29
2	0.25	0.0625	2.05	27	4.21	451.48	196.91	31.38	32
3	0.25	0.0625	2.04	30	4.17	451.48	196.91	31.10	32

For the detailed derivation of this formula, see the Appendix. To estimate n you need:

- An estimate of the population variability of x (s_x^2)—the sum of the squared deviations of x from the mean of x, with that sum divided by n
- An estimate of the population variability of e (s_e^2)—the sum of the squared deviations of each y from its estimated value, with that sum divided by n
- The desired level of confidence (used to determine the value of t)
- The smallest difference between the obtained and true value that you want to be able to detect (d)
- An estimate of the mean value of x ($\bar{x}$).

Continuing with the chapter example, the 95% confidence interval of the intercept of 10.22 ranged from −36.48 to 56.92. Because the accuracy of our estimate of the intercept has a large effect on the accuracy of our predictions, suppose we've decided that we need a more precise estimate and have determined that constraining it within a range of ±5 will be accurate enough for our purposes (so $d^2 = 25$). From the data in Table 10.6, we have estimates of s_x^2 and s_e^2 which are, respectively, 451.48 (3160.37/7) and 196.91 (1378.34/7). Again, we use the value of z in place of t for an initial sample size estimate (with $df = n-2$), then iterate until the sample size doesn't change. For 95% confidence, $z = 1.96$ (so $z^2 = 3.84$). Table 10.8 shows the iterations for a sample size estimate of 258.

Keeping everything else the same, the new estimate of the standard error is:

$$\mathrm{SE} = \sqrt{\frac{ns_e^2}{n-2}}\sqrt{\frac{1}{n}+\frac{(\bar{x})^2}{ns_x^2}}$$

$$\mathrm{SE} = \sqrt{\frac{258(196.91)}{258-2}}\sqrt{\frac{1}{258}+\frac{3331.76}{258(451.48)}}$$

The new standard error is 2.54, the value of t given 95% confidence and 256 degrees of freedom is 1.97, so the critical difference (d, aka, margin of error) is the desired value of 5 (2.54(1.97) = 5.00).

Table 10.8 Example Sample Size Estimation for Regression Intercept

Iteration	d	d^2	t	df	t^2	$\bar{x}$	$\bar{x}^2$	s_x^2	s_e^2	n	Round up
1	5	25	1.96	na	3.84	57.7	3331.76	451.48	196.91	255.55	256
2	5	25	1.97	254	3.88	57.7	3331.76	451.48	196.91	257.97	258
3	5	25	1.97	256	3.88	57.7	3331.76	451.48	196.91	257.95	258

To estimate a specific value of x other than the y-intercept, replace $\bar{x}^2$ with $(x-\bar{x})^2$. When $x=\bar{x}$ the equation simplifies to:

$$n = \frac{t^2 s_e^2}{d^2} + 2$$

ANALYSIS OF VARIANCE

The ANOVA has its roots in agriculture, just a little less than a century ago. In 1919, Ronald Fisher began working at the Rothamsted Experimental Station to reanalyze agricultural data collected since 1843 and to improve their methods for future agricultural research (Cowles, 1989). It was in this latter effort that he began working out the methods of ANOVA and modern methods of experimental design, of which random assignment to treatment conditions is the hallmark. From this seed (pun intended), ANOVA became ubiquitous in the 20th century, supporting the analysis of experimental designs of varying complexities. The *F*-test—the test used to assess the statistical significance of ANOVA results—was named in honor of Fisher (Cowles, 1989).

It can take years of graduate classes and training to become proficient in the use of ANOVA. In this chapter, we're going to focus on two of its simpler (and very common) applications. One is the extension of the *t*-test to the comparison of more than two means—in other words, when there are more than two levels of an independent variable. The other is the assessment of factorial designs, which involve the manipulation of multiple independent variables and permit the assessment of main effects (the significance of each of the independent variables) and their interaction (the extent to which the effects of one variable are dependent on the levels of the other variables in the experiment). Also, these applications of ANOVA in this chapter are only for between-subjects experiments. The underlying models become more complicated for within-subjects (repeated measures) experiments.

COMPARING MORE THAN TWO MEANS

In Chapter 5 we introduced the two-sample *t*-test for use when comparing a continuous dependent variable and a categorical variable with two levels (e.g., Design A and Design B). When there are more than two levels of a variable, however, you can use ANOVA.

WHY NOT JUST USE MULTIPLE *t*-TESTS?

This is an option, but ...

We touched on this topic at the end of Chapter 9 in the section entitled, "What if You Need to Run More than One Test?" For most practical work with variables that have more than two levels, you'll usually need to drill down to comparisons of pairs of means, so ultimately you'll be using multiple *t*-tests or some other approach to multiple comparisons. What ANOVA offers to researchers is an additional initial level of protection against Type I errors when the researcher has made no predictions or decisions in advance about specific pairs of means to compare. This additional level of protection against alpha inflation (described in Chapter 9) is known as an omnibus test. Conventional (although not universal) practice is to conduct an omnibus *F*-test to first determine if the group of means and their variances indicate a statistically significant difference, which means that at least one of the means is significantly different from the others, but without indicating which they are. A significant omnibus test gives the green light to continue with multiple comparisons to explore which means are different. As discussed in Chapter 9, there is some controversy regarding the practical value of omnibus tests, especially if the control of Type I errors is less important than the control of Type II errors, but it is a common practice that researchers should be aware of, especially if there are plans to publish the study in a refereed journal or conference proceedings.

How the omnibus test works

The technical term for an ANOVA with one independent variable is "one-way ANOVA" (think "one-variable ANOVA"). The null hypothesis for this test is that all means are equal. The alternative hypothesis is that at least one of the means is different from at least one of the others. The primary assumptions of this test are essentially the same as those for the two-sample *t*-test discussed in Chapter 5.

- *Representativeness:* The samples are representative of the populations to which the researcher intends to generalize the results.
- *Independence:* Data collected from each participant should not affect the scores of other participants.
- *Homogeneity of Variance:* Each group should have roughly equal standard deviations.
- *Normality:* The sampling distributions of the means for each group should be normal.

As with the *t*-test, the ANOVA is considered generally robust to violations of normality and homogeneity of variance. If you have very unequal sample sizes and vastly different variances, you may have to investigate nonparametric alternatives to ANOVA, data transformations, adjustments to the degrees of freedom used for the *F*-tests (such as the Welch–Satterthwaite procedure described in Chapter 5), or consult with a professional statistician. As with the *t*-test, the assumptions of representativeness and independence are the most important—you should be sure one participant's metrics don't affect other participants' metrics in some way and that participants are representative of the populations of interest, ideally by the structure of the study (the experimental design).

Recall that a *t*-test is essentially an assessment of a signal-to-noise ratio, with the difference between means in the numerator (the signal) and a standard error in the denominator (the noise). The test of a one-way ANOVA is similar, but when there are more than two means it gets more complicated to compute the estimates of signal and noise. One way to approach this conceptually is through the partitioning of sums of squares (SS), then comparing the mean squares (sums of squares divided by the appropriate degrees of freedom) for variability between groups (signal, denoted $MS_{Between}$) divided by variability within groups (noise, denoted MS_{Within}). When you see mean squares, think of these as variances. The ANOVA is telling you if the variance *between* groups is sufficiently greater than the variance *within* groups. A large enough ratio indicates a statistical difference involving at least one of the group means.

To compute the ratio by hand, start by calculating the total sums of squares:

$$SS_{Total} = \Sigma x^2 - \frac{(\Sigma x)^2}{n}$$

Then compute $SS_{Between}$:

$$SS_{Between} = \left(\sum_{i=1 \text{ to } k} \frac{(\Sigma x_i)^2}{n_i} \right) - \frac{(\Sigma x)^2}{n}$$

where the subscript *i* refers to the groups,
k is the number of groups, and
n without a subscript is the total sample size. Finally:

$$SS_{Within} = SS_{Total} - SS_{Between}$$

You assess the significance of the ANOVA with an *F*-test. An *F*-test is similar to a *t*-test, but because you're dealing with more than two means, the numerator and denominator both have degrees of

Table 10.9 Some Critical Values of F for $\alpha = 0.05$

	Numerator *df*									
Denominator *df*	**1**	**2**	**3**	**4**	**5**	**6**	**7**	**8**	**9**	**10**
1	161.4	199.5	215.7	224.6	230.2	234.0	236.8	238.9	240.5	241.9
2	18.51	19.00	19.16	19.25	19.30	19.33	19.35	19.37	19.38	19.40
3	10.13	9.552	9.277	9.117	9.013	8.941	8.887	8.845	8.812	8.786
4	7.709	6.944	6.591	6.388	6.256	6.163	6.094	6.041	5.999	5.964
5	6.608	5.786	5.409	5.192	5.050	4.950	4.876	4.818	4.772	4.735
10	4.965	4.103	3.708	3.478	3.326	3.217	3.135	3.072	3.020	2.978
20	4.351	3.493	3.098	2.866	2.711	2.599	2.514	2.447	2.393	2.348
30	4.171	3.316	2.922	2.690	2.534	2.421	2.334	2.266	2.211	2.165
40	4.085	3.232	2.839	2.606	2.449	2.336	2.249	2.180	2.124	2.077
50	4.034	3.183	2.790	2.557	2.400	2.286	2.199	2.130	2.073	2.026
100	3.936	3.087	2.696	2.463	2.305	2.191	2.103	2.032	1.975	1.927

freedom. The *df* for the numerator (also referred to as df_1) is $k-1$, and for the denominator (also referred to as df_2) is $n-k$. To calculate the mean squares divide $SS_{Between}$ by df_1 to get $MS_{Between}$ and SS_{Within} by df_2 to get MS_{Within}. Then compute F by calculating the ratio of $MS_{Between}/MS_{Within}$.

Table 10.9 shows some critical values of F for $\alpha = 0.05$ and various *df* with denominator *df* listed in the first column and numerator *df* listed as the remaining row headers. More extensive tables are available in statistics books or online, or you can use the Excel functions FDIST (which produces a p-value to evaluate the results of an F-test) and FINV (which provides critical values of F). If the observed value of F for a given α, df_1, and df_2 is greater than the critical value, this only indicates that **at least one** of the means is significantly different from **at least one** of the others. When reporting the results of F-tests, provide both *df*—numerator first, then denominator (error) *df* using the standard format, for example: $F(2, 5) = 6.5$, $p < 0.05$.

RELATIONSHIP BETWEEN CRITICAL VALUES OF *F* AND *t*

When the numerator *df* = 1 ...

When the numerator has one degree of freedom, the critical value of F is the square of the critical value of t for the same error (denominator) degrees of freedom and value of α. For example, the critical two-tailed value of t given $\alpha = 0.05$ and 10 *df* is 2.228. The critical value of F given $\alpha = 0.05$, one *df* in the numerator (comparison of two means), and 10 *df* in the denominator is 4.965, which is 2.228^2.

Consider the findings shown in Table 10.10, from an unpublished study in which four groups of participants rated the quality of four artificial voices using the revised version of the Mean Opinion Scale (MOS-R; Polkosky and Lewis, 2003). The MOS-R is a standardized questionnaire with 10 bipolar items (7-point scales). The overall MOS-R score is the average of responses to those 10 items and can range

Table 10.10 MOS-R Ratings of Four Artificial Voices

		Voice A	Voice B	Voice C	Voice D
		4.2	3.9	3.4	4.9
		5.7	2.1	4.0	5.9
		5.3	4.3	2.6	6.0
		5.7	3.3	3.8	6.8
Computed	**Combined**				
Mean	4.49	5.23	3.40	3.45	5.90
Sum(x)	71.9	20.9	13.6	13.8	23.6
$(\text{Sum}(x))^2$	5169.6	436.8	185.0	190.4	557.0
$((\text{Sum}(x))^2)/n$	323.10	109.20	46.24	47.61	139.24
Sum(x^2)	349.5	110.7	49.0	48.8	141.1
n	16	4	4	4	4

from 1 to 7, with 7 being the best possible score. Table 10.10 shows the calculations needed to compute an omnibus *F*-test to assess the overall significance of participants' reaction to the artificial voices.

Using the values from Table 10.10 (note that there are some small discrepancies due to round off error):

- $SS_{Total} = 349.5 - 5169.6/16 = 26.43$
- $SS_{Between} = 109.20 + 46.24 + 47.61 + 139.24 - 323.10 = 19.19$
- $SS_{Within} = 26.43 - 19.19 = 7.24$
- $MS_{Between} = 19.19/3 = 6.40$
- $MS_{Within} = 7.24/12 = 0.60$
- $F = 6.40/0.60 = 10.6$

Table 10.11 shows the ANOVA results presented in a traditional summary table. Note that the Total SS (strictly speaking, the adjusted total) equals the sum of Between SS and Within SS, and the *df* for Total SS equals the sum of the *df* for Between SS and Within SS. The results indicate that at least one of the means is significantly different from at least one of the others ($F(3, 12) = 10.6$, $p = 0.001$).

Multiple comparisons

Now we're pretty sure at least one pair of means is different, but which one(s)? Voice D got the best mean rating, Voice A the second best, then Voice C, and finally, Voice B. It is beyond the scope of this chapter to provide a comprehensive review of the multitude of post hoc multiple comparison

Table 10.11 ANOVA Summary Table for Study of Four Artificial Voices

Source	SS	*df*	MS	*F*	Sig
Total	26.43	15			
Between	19.19	3	6.40	10.6	0.001
Within	7.24	12	0.60		

procedures. One way in which multiple comparison procedures differ is with regard to which they are conservative or liberal. Now would be a good time to review "What if You Need to Run More than One Test?" in Chapter 9, especially the sidebar on Abelson's styles of rhetoric.

PLANNED VERSUS POST HOC COMPARISONS

Are you exploring or confirming?

An important distinction in research is that of exploration versus confirmation. When you conduct a study because you suspect there might be interesting effects but you can't predict them in advance, you're exploring. Confirmation, on the other hand, requires up-front prediction. When comparisons are planned in advance, they are a priori (confirmatory); otherwise they are post hoc (exploratory). As previously discussed, when conducting post hoc multiple comparisons, picking and choosing among the various effects available for investigation (or looking at them all) increases the possibility that you are capitalizing on chance (mathematically modeled as alpha inflation), so it is common to control for that using adjustment procedures like the Bonferroni or Benjamini–Hochberg methods.

When you're confirming a small number of expected results in a confirmation study, however, it is common to conduct those comparisons without adjustment. Note that some statisticians think this is overly liberal, and encourage researchers to apply adjustment procedures regardless of whether the comparisons are a priori or post hoc (e.g., see graphpad.com/support/faqid/1092/). If you are making only two or three planned comparisons, the adjusted values of alpha will be much higher than if you were making 20 post hoc comparisons, but will still be more stringent than no adjustment at all.

This leads us back to Abelson's (1995) styles of rhetoric (discussed in Chapter 9). As a researcher, you need to know in your research context which type of error is potentially more damaging—Type I or Type II. If controlling Type I errors is more important, then your research strategies should be more conservative. If it's more important to control Type II errors, then your research strategies should be more liberal. A common research strategy is to start with exploration, then to conduct additional studies to independently confirm the findings discovered during exploration.

Running an omnibus test in the first place indicates a conservative style, so maintaining that style for this section, we'll start with the Bonferroni correction, which is a conservative method. Despite being conservative (fewer differences identified as statistically significant but fewer false positives), it remains popular because it's easy to understand and easy to compute by hand. With four means to compare, there are six possible pairs of means. The basis of the Bonferroni correction is to divide α by the number of comparisons, which for this example would be 0.05/6 = 0.008. The results of the six t-tests are:

- Voice A versus Voice B: $t(6) = 3.06$, $p = 0.022$
- Voice A versus Voice C: $t(6) = 3.77$, $p = 0.009$
- Voice A versus Voice D: $t(6) = -1.28$, $p = 0.25$
- Voice B versus Voice C: $t(6) = -0.09$, $p = 0.93$
- Voice B versus Voice D: $t(6) = -4.05$, $p = 0.007$
- Voice C versus Voice D: $t(6) = -4.93$, $p = 0.003$

Using the conservative Bonferroni adjustment to guide the interpretation of the results, only two comparisons (B vs. D and C vs. D) were significant. If instead we took the most liberal approach (simply running multiple t-tests at $\alpha = 0.05$ for each test), we would deem four of the comparisons to be significant (A vs. B, A vs. C, B vs. D, and C vs. D).

A relatively new approach to balancing the conservative and liberal styles is the control of the false discovery rate (FDR—see Chapter 9) using the Benjamini–Hochberg method (Benjamini and Hochberg, 1995). To use the Benjamini–Hochberg method, take the p-values from all the comparisons

Table 10.12 Benjamini–Hochberg Comparisons of Four Artificial Voices

Comparison	*p*	Rank	New Threshold	Outcome
Voice C versus Voice D	0.003	1	0.008	Sig.
Voice B versus Voice D	0.007	2	0.017	Sig.
Voice A versus Voice C	0.009	3	0.025	Sig.
Voice A versus Voice B	0.022	4	0.033	Sig.
Voice A versus Voice D	0.25	5	0.042	
Voice A versus Voice C	0.93	6	0.050	

and rank them from lowest to highest. Then create a new threshold for statistical significance for each comparison by dividing the rank by the number of comparisons and then multiplying this by the initial significance threshold (alpha). For six comparisons, the lowest *p*-value, with a rank of 1, is compared against a new threshold of (1/6)*0.05 = 0.008, the second is compared against (2/6)*0.05 = 0.017, and so on, with the last one being (6/6)*0.05 = 0.05. If the observed *p*-value is less than or equal to the new threshold, it's considered statistically significant. Table 10.12 shows the *p*-values in order and the new significance thresholds obtained from the Benjamini–Hochberg method. In this case, the Benjamini–Hochberg method designates the same paired comparisons to be significant as the multiple *t*-tests without adjustment. This will not always happen (see the sidebar, "A Large-Sample Real-World Example of Multiple Pairwise Comparisons").

As shown in Table 10.12, the Benjamini–Hochberg method positions itself between unadjusted testing and the Bonferroni method by adopting a sliding scale for the threshold of statistical significance. The first threshold will always be the same as the Bonferroni threshold, and the last threshold will always be the same as the unadjusted value of α. The thresholds in between the first and last comparisons rise in equal steps from the Bonferroni to the unadjusted threshold. Note that the approach we described in Chapter 9 ("What if You Need to Run More than One Test?)" has a similar goal—focusing on the rate of false discovery rather than minimizing the Type I error. When there are a larger-than-expected number of significant comparisons, the Benjamini–Hochberg method provides additional guidance to researchers.

It may sometimes happen that the omnibus *F*-test is statistically significant, but using even a liberal approach, none of the paired comparisons are significant. This is unusual, but can happen because the omnibus *F*-test and multiple pairwise comparisons do not address exactly the same null hypotheses (Rutherford, 2011). Don't panic. Just accept the ambiguity of the outcome, draw the best conclusions you can, and move on.

A LARGE-SAMPLE REAL-WORLD EXAMPLE OF MULTIPLE PAIRWISE COMPARISONS

Investigating the user experience of popular retail websites—from the files of Jeff Sauro

In 2013, I measured the quality of the user experience with ten popular US-based retail websites using the SUPR-Q (Sauro, 2013). SUPR-Q scores are derived by taking the average of the eight items in the questionnaire, with higher scores indicating better perceived experiences (for details, see the section on SUPR-Q in Chapter 8). Fig. 10.7 shows the mean scores along with 90% confidence intervals (I used $\alpha = 0.10$ for this research).

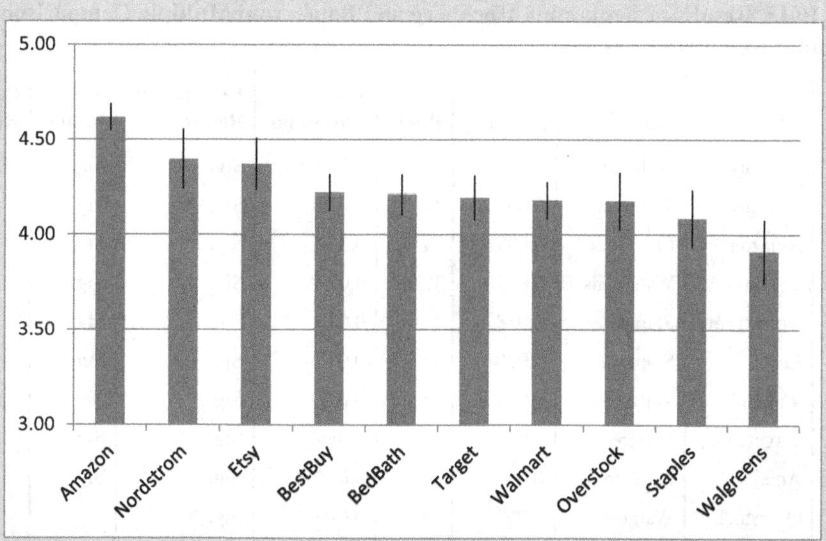

FIGURE 10.7 Mean SUPR-Q scores of popular retail websites

Amazon had the highest SUPR-Q score and Walgreens the lowest, but which websites were statistically different from each other? With 10 websites, there are 45 total paired comparisons and plenty of opportunity to falsely identify a difference. All pairwise comparisons were made and the *p*-values were ranked from lowest to highest as shown in Table 10.13. Without any adjustments, 22 of the 45 comparisons were statistically significant at $p < 0.10$ (the column labeled "Unadjusted Result" in the table). Using the Benjamini–Hochberg method, 17 were statistically significant (the column labeled "BH Result"). The threshold for the Bonferroni method was $p \leq 0.002$ (0.10/45), which flagged just nine comparisons as statistically significant (the column labeled "Bonferroni Result"). This illustrates how the Benjamini–Hochberg method strikes a good balance between the more liberal unadjusted *p*-values and the more conservative Bonferroni method.

Table 10.13 Results of Benjamini–Hochberg and Bonferroni Multiple Comparisons of Popular Retail Websites

Pair	Site 1	Site 2	*p*-value	Rank	BH Threshold	Unadjusted Result	BH Result	Bonferroni Result
1	Walmart	Amazon	0.000	1	0.002	Sig.	Sig.	Sig.
2	BestBuy	Amazon	0.000	2	0.004	Sig.	Sig.	Sig.
3	Amazon	Target	0.000	3	0.007	Sig.	Sig.	Sig.
4	Amazon	BedBath	0.000	4	0.009	Sig.	Sig.	Sig.
5	Amazon	Overstock	0.000	5	0.011	Sig.	Sig.	Sig.
6	Amazon	Staples	0.000	6	0.013	Sig.	Sig.	Sig.
7	Amazon	Walgreens	0.000	7	0.016	Sig.	Sig.	Sig.
8	Etsy	Walgreens	0.001	8	0.018	Sig.	Sig.	Sig.

(Continued)

Table 10.13 Results of Benjamini–Hochberg and Bonferroni Multiple Comparisons of Popular Retail Websites (*cont.*)

Pair	Site 1	Site 2	*p*-value	Rank	BH Threshold	Unadjusted Result	BH Result	Bonferroni Result
9	Nordstrom	Walgreens	0.001	9	0.020	Sig.	Sig.	Sig.
10	BestBuy	Walgreens	0.009	10	0.022	Sig.	Sig.	
11	Amazon	Etsy	0.009	11	0.024	Sig.	Sig.	
12	BedBath	Walgreens	0.013	12	0.027	Sig.	Sig.	
13	Nordstrom	Staples	0.018	13	0.029	Sig.	Sig.	
14	Etsy	Staples	0.020	14	0.031	Sig.	Sig.	
15	Walmart	Walgreens	0.023	15	0.033	Sig.	Sig.	
16	Target	Walgreens	0.024	16	0.036	Sig.	Sig.	
17	Amazon	Nordstrom	0.037	17	0.038	Sig.	Sig.	
18	Overstock	Walgreens	0.051	18	0.040	Sig.		
19	Walmart	Nordstrom	0.054	19	0.042	Sig.		
20	Walmart	Etsy	0.060	20	0.044	Sig.		
21	Target	Nordstrom	0.090	21	0.047	Sig.		
22	Nordstrom	Overstock	0.095	22	0.049	Sig.		
23	Target	Etsy	0.105	23	0.051			
24	BedBath	Nordstrom	0.108	24	0.053			
25	Etsy	Overstock	0.114	25	0.056			
26	BestBuy	Nordstrom	0.117	26	0.058			
27	BedBath	Etsy	0.127	27	0.060			
28	BestBuy	Etsy	0.138	28	0.062			
29	Staples	Walgreens	0.200	29	0.064			
30	BestBuy	Staples	0.207	30	0.067			
31	BedBath	Staples	0.255	31	0.069			
32	Target	Staples	0.345	32	0.071			
33	Walmart	Staples	0.381	33	0.073			
34	Overstock	Staples	0.471	34	0.076			
35	Walmart	BestBuy	0.616	35	0.078			
36	BestBuy	Overstock	0.682	36	0.080			
37	Walmart	BedBath	0.716	37	0.082			
38	BedBath	Overstock	0.757	38	0.084			
39	BestBuy	Target	0.768	39	0.087			
40	Etsy	Nordstrom	0.836	40	0.089			

Pair	Site 1	Site 2	*p*-value	Rank	BH Threshold	Unadjusted Result	BH Result	Bonferroni Result
41	Target	BedBath	0.857	41	0.091			
42	Walmart	Target	0.877	42	0.093			
43	Target	Overstock	0.884	43	0.096			
44	BestBuy	BedBath	0.909	44	0.098			
45	Walmart	Overstock	0.982	45	0.100			

ASSESSING INTERACTIONS

For certain kinds of experimental designs it is possible to partition the $SS_{Between}$ into independent effects. For example, factorial designs allow the independent estimation of the effects of two or more independent variables and their interactions. A significant interaction occurs when the result for an independent variable varies sufficiently depending on the level of a different independent variable. The simplest factorial design is one in which there are two independent variables, each with two levels (known as a 2×2 factorial design).

For example, consider an unpublished study in which male and female participants used the MOS-R to rate the quality of two artificial voices, one male and one female. Nass and Brave (2005) had suggested that the social psychological principle of "similarity attraction" might apply to user reactions to artificial voices such that males would prefer a male voice and females a female voice. If the similarity attraction hypothesis held, the expectation was that there would be a significant interaction between the gender of the artificial voice (Voice) and the gender of the person rating the voice (Rater).

Fig. 10.8 illustrates some of the patterns of results that can occur given this type of factorial study. If there were a main effect of Voice but no main effect of Rater or any interaction, the pattern would look something like (a). If there were a main effect of Voice but not one of Rater and no interaction, it would be something like (b). The pattern in (c) results from significant main effects for both independent variables and their interaction. The pattern in (d) is a special case known as a crossed interaction—there is no main effect for either independent variable but there is a significant interaction. For this study, if similarity attraction has a strong effect on how listeners perceive artificial voices, we would expect a crossed interaction (Fig. 10.8d).

For factorial designs, the formulas for computing SS_{Total}, $SS_{Between}$, and SS_{Within} are the same as those from the previous section of this chapter. The general formulas for computing the SS for the independent (main) effects and their interaction are:

$$SS_{Var1} = \sum \frac{(\Sigma \text{ for each level of } Var_1)^2}{n \text{ for each level of } Var_1} - \frac{(\Sigma x)^2}{n}$$

$$SS_{Var2} = \sum \frac{(\Sigma \text{ for each level of } Var_2)^2}{n \text{ for each level of } Var_2} - \frac{(\Sigma x)^2}{n}$$

$$SS_{Interaction} = SS_{Between} - SS_{Var1} - SS_{Var2}$$

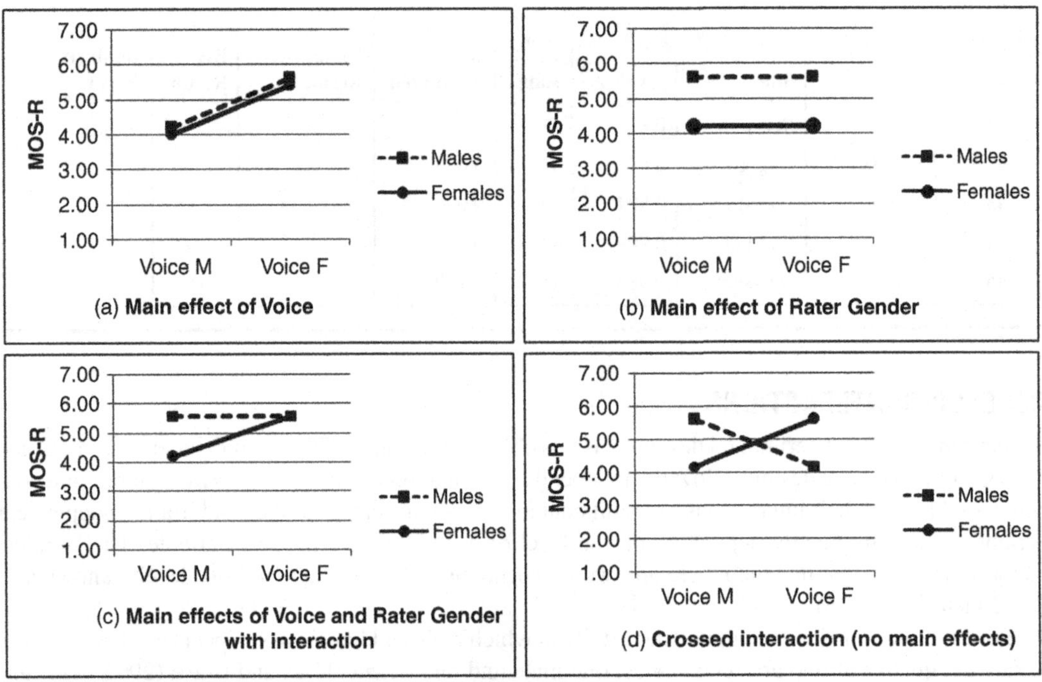

FIGURE 10.8 Some possible outcomes for a 2 × 2 factorial design

The *df* for the main effects are the number of levels of the independent variable minus 1. To compute the *df* for the interaction, multiply the *df* for each of the independent variables involved in the interaction.

Table 10.14 shows the results of the study and Table 10.15 shows the summary table. From the summary table, note that $SS_{Between}$ had three degrees of freedom. There were two levels of Voice (Voice M and Voice F), so this effect had one degree of freedom. The same was true of Rater—just two levels (Male and Female), so it also had one degree of freedom. To get the degrees of freedom for the interaction, you multiply the degrees of freedom for the associated main effects, which was $1 \times 1 = 1$. When $df = 1$, the MS is equal to the SS. If you work with more advanced forms of ANOVA, you'll find yourself carefully tracking the degrees of freedom to make sure they add up correctly.

The steps for computing the values for SS, *df*, and MS in the summary table (ignoring some small discrepancies due to round off error) are:

- $SS_{Total} = 331.4 - 5012.6/16 = 18.13$
- $SS_{Between} = 96.04 + 108.16 + 52.56 + 63.2 - 313.29 = 6.68$
- $SS_{Voice} = (19.6 + 20.8)^2/8 + (14.5 + 15.9)^2/8 - 313.29 = 6.25$
- $SS_{Rater} = (19.6 + 14.5)^2/8 + (20.8 + 15.9)^2/8 - 313.29 = 0.42$
- $SS_{Interaction} = 6.68 - 6.25 - 0.42 = 0.003$
- $SS_{Within} = 18.13 - 6.68 = 11.46$
- $df_{Total} = 16 - 1 = 15$
- $df_{Between} = 4 - 1 = 3$
- $df_{Voice} = 2 - 1 = 1$

Table 10.14 Results of the Factorial Experiment of Voice and Rater

		Voice M (Males)	Voice M (Females)	Voice F (Males)	Voice F (Females)
		3.6	6.0	4.2	4.4
		6.1	3.4	3.4	4.2
		5.7	5.7	3.2	4.6
		4.2	5.7	3.7	2.7
Computed	**Combined**				
Mean	4.43	4.90	5.20	3.63	3.98
Sum(x)	70.8	19.6	20.8	14.5	15.9
(Sum(x))^2	5012.6	384.2	432.6	210.3	252.8
((Sum(x))$^{2)}$/n	313.29	96.04	108.16	52.56	63.20
Sum(x^2)	331.4	100.3	112.5	53.1	65.5
n	16	4	4	4	4

Table 10.15 Summary Table for ANOVA of the Factorial Study of Voice and Rater

Source	SS	*df*	MS	*F*	Sig
Total	18.13	15	1.21		
Between	6.68	3	2.23		
Voice	6.25	1	6.25	6.55	0.025
Rater	0.42	1	0.42	0.44	0.52
Interaction	0.003	1	0.003	0.003	0.96
Within	11.46	12	0.95		

- $df_{\text{Rater}} = 2 - 1 = 1$
- $df_{\text{Interaction}} = 1(1) = 1$
- $df_{\text{Within}} = 15 - 3 = 12$ (these are the error/denominator *df*)
- $\text{MS}_{\text{Total}} = 18.3/15 = 1.21$
- $\text{MS}_{\text{Between}} = 6.68/3 = 2.23$
- $\text{MS}_{\text{Voice}} = 6/25/1 = 6.25$
- $\text{MS}_{\text{Rater}} = 0.42/1 = 0.42$
- $\text{MS}_{\text{Interaction}} = 0.003/1 = 0.003$
- $\text{MS}_{\text{Within}} = 11.46/12 = 0.95$ (error MS for this ANOVA model)
- The values for the *F*-tests are the mean squares of the effect divided by $\text{MS}_{\text{Within}}$

Fig. 10.9 shows a graph of the main effects and the interaction from this study. As shown in the ANOVA summary table, only the main effect of Voice was statistically significant. Interpreting a significant interaction is more important than interpreting the associated main effects (captured in the

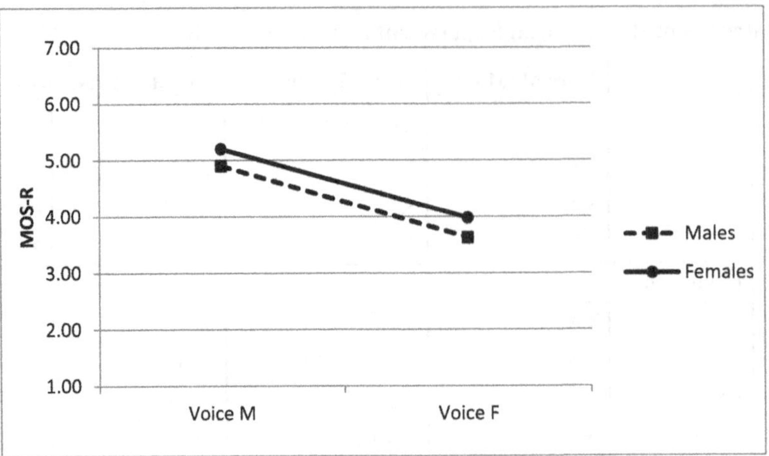

FIGURE 10.9 Graph of results from the factorial study of Voice and Rater

informal rule, "interactions trump main effects"), but in this case the interaction was not significant (for an example of a significant interaction, see the sidebar "Large-Sample Real-World Example of an Interaction Effect"). The patterns of ratings of male and female participants were about the same for each artificial voice, with both genders preferring the male voice (Voice M) over the female voice (Voice F). Note that these results do not necessarily disprove the similarity attraction hypothesis, but do suggest that if it exists, it is weaker than the difference in the quality of these artificial voices (Lewis, 2011).

Prior to the work that Fisher did at the Rothamsted Experimental Station, the most common approach to conducting experiments was to manipulate one variable at a time while trying to hold all other variables constant. One of Fisher's greatest contributions to research was demonstrating the efficiency of factorial designs relative to one-variable-at-a-time designs. As demonstrated in this section, with a properly designed factorial experiment you can study all of the variables of interest in one experiment and, in addition to assessing their individual effects, you can also assess their interactions.

LARGE-SAMPLE REAL-WORLD EXAMPLE OF AN INTERACTION EFFECT

Is there an interaction between pre- and post-brand affection and pre-existing brand affection?—From the files of Jeff Sauro

Prior attitudes with a brand, product, or website are often a powerful predictor of attitudinal metrics collected in a usability study and should be collected and analyzed when drawing conclusions. For example, we were working to understand how a new checkout experience influenced the brand affection of participants. We asked participants their overall affection toward the brand prior to checking out and then after the checkout experience. Brand affection was measured using an average from 10 items using 7-point response options (Thomson et al., 2005).

We knew that many customers had a strongly favorable attitude whereas others had a strongly negative attitude toward the brand already, so we wanted to see if the checkout experience affected these customers differently.

We found that overall, brand affection for participants in the study increased after checking out. However, the story was more nuanced once we included prior brand affection. Fig. 10.10 shows a significant interaction effect between pre- and post-brand affection. We saw that participants who had high brand affection actually slightly decreased their affection (by about 4%) after checking-out. In contrast, participants with low pre-existing brand affection actually increased their affection toward the brand substantially (18%).

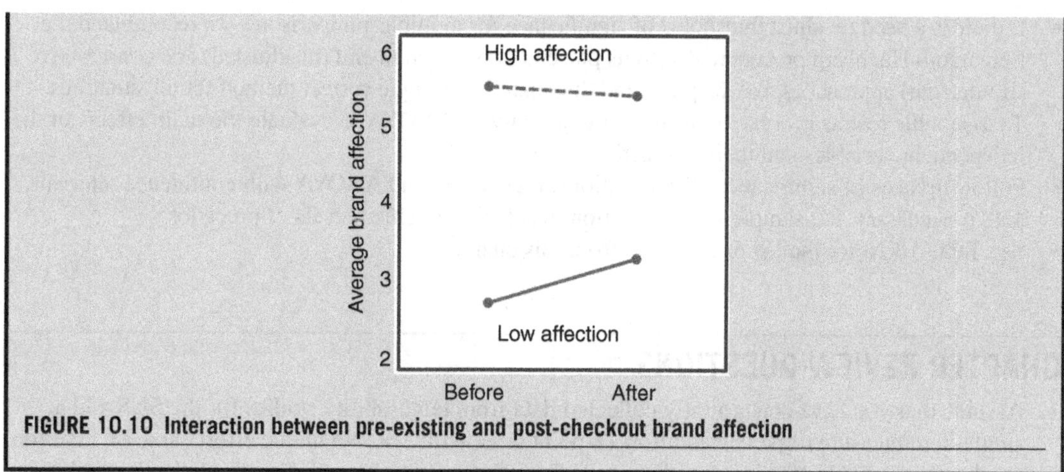

FIGURE 10.10 Interaction between pre-existing and post-checkout brand affection

CONFIDENCE INTERVALS AND SAMPLE SIZE ESTIMATION FOR ANOVA

Confidence intervals

We expect that most researchers who use ANOVA will do their analyses with a statistical computer application such as SAS or SPSS. For the various effects of interest, these programs provide estimates of the standard error. Recall that the fundamental formula for computing a confidence interval is to multiply the standard error by the appropriate value of z or t (depending on the denominator degrees of freedom for the effect) to get the margin of error, then add and subtract that margin of error from the point estimate (the mean).

Sample size estimation

The appropriate sample size estimate for an ANOVA depends on the details of the design in addition to other assumptions (e.g., magnitude of variance, equal or unequal variances for the various groups, etc.). A free resource for ANOVA sample size estimation is the G*Power application (see "Dealing with More Complex Sample Size Estimation" in Chapter 6).

KEY POINTS

- Linear correlation, linear regression, and ANOVA are variations of the General Linear Model.
- Use correlation to assess the extent to which two variables are related or independent (and be sure to graph the relationship).
- Guidelines for interpreting the magnitude of correlations are: small ($r = 0.10$), medium ($r = 0.30$), and large ($r = 0.50$).
- Correlation alone does not prove causation.
- For binary data, use phi correlation.
- Use linear regression to model the relationship between two variables.
- Be cautious when using a regression equation to extrapolate (estimate beyond the ends of the observed values).
- To compare more than two means, use a one-way ANOVA combined with multiple comparisons.

- If there is a need to adjust thresholds of significance for multiple comparisons, we recommend the Benjamini–Hochberg procedure due to its placement between liberal (unadjusted) and conservative (Bonferroni) approaches, but keep in mind that there is no single correct method for all situations.
- To assess the results of a factorial study, use a two-way ANOVA to evaluate the main effects of the independent variables and their interactions.
- Follow up tests of significance of correlations, regression, and ANOVA with confidence intervals and, if necessary, use sample size estimation to achieve specified levels of precision.
- See Table 10.16 for the list of formulas from this chapter.

CHAPTER REVIEW QUESTIONS

1. Assume that you have concurrently collected data from ten usability studies for the SUS and a single-item measure of perceived effort (7-point scale with 1 = "No undue effort" and 7 = "Far too much effort"). Table 10.17 shows the means from the ten experiments. You think they're probably correlated, but you're not sure to what extent. For this question (a) calculate the correlation and assess its statistical significance, (b) then determine the 95% confidence interval around the estimated correlation, and (c) compute and interpret the coefficient of determination.
2. Based on the results from Question 1, you've decided that you'd like to establish a company-wide target for future usability tests that use the perceived effort item. It is common to set a target for the SUS to 80, which is an A- on the Sauro–Lewis curved grading scale (Table 8.5 in Chapter 8). For this question, (a) determine the regression equation that would allow prediction of Effort from SUS, (b) use the equation to compute the value of Effort that corresponds to a SUS of 80, and (c) compute the 90% confidence interval around that estimated Effort value.
3. Suppose you wanted to control your estimate of the appropriate Effort target to within 0.1. Given the results in (2) and continuing to use 90% confidence, what sample size (number of studies with concurrent collection of SUS and Effort) would you probably need?
4. Convert the values in Table 10.17 (shown in Question 1) to binary data where SUS scores greater than 79.9 are "1" and all others are 0, and Effort scores greater than 5.5 are "1" and all others are 0. Then compute phi to estimate the correlation between SUS and Effort and assess its statistical significance.
5. Suppose you have used a survey to collect SUS scores from respondents who have used a major hotel website or mobile app to book a reservation, with the results shown in Table 10.18. Does the omnibus *F*-test for a one-way ANOVA indicate that at least one of the means is different from the others? Which one(s)?
6. Continuing to use the data from Question 5, switch to a two-way ANOVA to assess the main effects of Company (A vs. B) and Channel (website vs. mobile app) and their interaction. Interpret the results.

ANSWERS TO CHAPTER REVIEW QUESTIONS

1. First, inspect a graph of the data to check for any clear nonlinear patterns. As shown in Fig. 10.11, there appears to be a strong linear component.

Table 10.16 List of Formulas from the Chapter

Type of Evaluation	Basic Formula	Notes
Correlation (r)	$r = \frac{SS_{xy}}{\sqrt{(SS_{xx})(SS_{yy})}}$	Where $SS_{xx=\Sigma(x_i-\bar{x})^2}$ $SS_{yy=\Sigma(y_i-\bar{y})^2}$ and $SS_{xy=\Sigma(x_i-\bar{x})(y_i-\bar{y})}$
Significance of r (transform r to t)	$t = \frac{r}{\sqrt{\frac{1-r^2}{n-2}}}$	Use this to conduct a test of significance of r with $df = n - 2$
r to z'	$z' = 0.5 \ln[(1+r)/(1-r)]$	This is a step in the process of computing a confidence interval for r
Margin of error for r	$d = \frac{z_{(1-\alpha)}}{\sqrt{n-3}}$	This is a step in the process of computing a confidence interval for r (used to set bounds around z')
z' endpoints back to r	$r = \frac{\exp(2z')-1}{\exp(2z')+1}$	This is a step in the process of computing a confidence interval for r
Sample size estimation for r	$n = \frac{z^2(1-r^2)^2}{d^2} + 1 + 6r^2$	Decide the level of confidence (for 95% confidence $z = 1.96$), the size of the critical difference (also known as the margin of error, d in the equation) and the expected value of r (if you have no idea what to expect, then set r to 0 to maximize the estimated sample size)
Phi (φ)	$\varphi = \frac{ad-bc}{\sqrt{(a+b)(c+d)(a+c)(b+d)}}$	The letters a, b, c, and d refer to cells in a 2 × 2 contingency table
Phi to chi-squared (Significance of φ)	$\chi^2(1) = n\varphi^2$	Use this to conduct a test of significance using χ^2 with $df = 1$
General form of regression equation	$\hat{y} = b_0 + b_1 x + e$	Shows prediction of dependent variable ($\hat{y}$) by adding the intercept (b_0) to the slope (b_1) times the value of the independent variable (x) plus error (e)
Regression slope	$b_1 = r\frac{s_y}{s_x}$	r is the correlation between X and Y, and s_x and s_y are the standard deviations of the x-and y-values
Regression intercept	$b_0 = \bar{y} - b_1\bar{x}$	$\bar{x}$ and $\bar{y}$ are the means of the x- and y-values, and b_1 is the slope
Standard error of regression slope	$SE = \frac{\sqrt{\frac{\Sigma(y_i-\hat{y}_i)^2}{(n-2)}}}{\sqrt{\Sigma(x_i-\bar{x})^2}}$	y_i is the value of the dependent variable for observation i, $\hat{y}_i$ is the estimated value of the dependent variable for observation i, x_i is the observed value of the independent variable for observation i, $\bar{x}$ is the mean of the independent variable, and n is the sample size—to compute a margin of error for a confidence interval multiply this by the value of t for the level of confidence using $n-2$ degrees of freedom

(*Continued*)

Table 10.16 List of Formulas from the Chapter (*cont.*)

Type of Evaluation	Basic Formula	Notes
Standard error of predicted value	$SE = \sqrt{\frac{\Sigma(y_i - \hat{y}_i)^2}{(n-2)}}\sqrt{\frac{1}{n} + \frac{(x-\overline{x})^2}{\Sigma(x_i - \overline{x})^2}}$	y_i is the value of the dependent variable for observation *i*, $\hat{y}_i$ is the estimated value of the dependent variable for observation *i*, x_i is the observed value of the independent variable for observation *i*, $\overline{x}$ is the mean of the independent variable, and *n* is the sample size—to compute a margin of error for a confidence interval multiply this by the value of *t* for the level of confidence using $n-2$ degrees of freedom—the intercept is the special case where $x = 0$
Sample size estimation based on the slope	$n = \frac{t^2 s_e^2}{d^2 s_x^2} + 2$	You need an estimate of the population variability of *x* (s_x^2), an estimate of the population variability of *e* (s_e^2), the desired level of confidence (used to determine the value of *t*), and the smallest difference between the obtained and true value that you want to be able to detect (*d*), then solve iteratively for *n*
Sample size estimation based on the intercept	$n = \frac{t^2 s_e^2 \left(1 + \frac{\overline{x}^2}{s_x^2}\right)}{d^2} + 2$	You need an estimate of the population variability of *x* (s_x^2), an estimate of the sample variability of *e* (s_e^2), the desired level of confidence (for the value of *t*), the target difference between the obtained and true value to detect (*d*), and an estimate of the mean value of *x* ($\overline{x}$), then solve iteratively for *n*—to estimate a specific value of *x* other than the *y*-intercept, replace $\overline{x}^2$ with $(x - \overline{x}^2)$
ANOVA SS_{Total}	$SS_{Total} = \Sigma x^2 - \frac{(\Sigma x)^2}{n}$	The *df* for the total SS are $n - 1$—the MS is the SS/*df*
ANOVA $SS_{Between}$	$SS_{Between} = \frac{(\Sigma x_1)^2}{n_1} + \frac{(\Sigma x_2)^2}{n_2} + \cdots + \frac{(\Sigma x_k)^2}{n_k} - \frac{(\Sigma x)^2}{n}$	The *df* for $SS_{Between}$ are $k - 1$—the MS is the SS/*df*
ANOVA SS_{Within}	$SS_{Within} = SS_{Total} - SS_{Between}$	The *df* for SS_{Within} are $n - k$— the MS is the SS/*df*
ANOVA $SS_{MainEffect}$	$SS_{Var1} = \Sigma\frac{(\Sigma \text{ for each level of } Var_1)^2}{n \text{ for each level of } Var_1} - \frac{(\Sigma x)^2}{n}$	The *df* for a main effect are the number of levels of the variable minus 1—the MS is the SS/*df*
ANOVA $SS_{Interaction}$	$SS_{Interaction} = SS_{Between} - SS_{Var1} - SS_{Var2}$	This is for two independent variables—to compute interaction *df* multiply the *df* for the main effects
F-test	$F = \frac{MS_{Effect}}{MS_{Error}}$	To evaluate *F* you need to know the numerator and denominator *df* (df_1 and df_2)—for the designs presented in this chapter, MS_{Error} is the same as MS_{Within}

Table 10.17 Data for Review Question 1

Experiment	SUS	Effort
1	68.1	4.0
2	50.0	4.2
3	70.8	4.0
4	85.2	6.4
5	92.4	6.6
6	69.9	3.9
7	45.7	3.5
8	82.3	6.2
9	78.6	5.8
10	55.5	4.0

Table 10.18 Data for Review Question 5

Company A (website)	Company A (mobile)	Company B (website)	Company B (mobile)
72.5	62.5	82.5	100.0
85.0	72.5	72.5	80.0
70.0	77.5	87.5	90.0
80.0	57.5	70.0	80.0
60.0	82.5	80.0	85.0
80.0	50.0	75.0	80.0
80.0	67.5	97.5	92.5
85.0	70.0	57.5	75.0
65.0	52.5	70.0	100.0
75.0	82.5	85.0	77.5

Table 10.19 shows the calculations needed to compute the correlation, its statistical significance, the 95% confidence interval, and the coefficient of determination. The linear correlation is statistically significant ($r(8) = 0.858$, $p = 0.003$). The 95% confidence interval ranges from 0.498 to 0.966. The coefficient of determination, R^2, is 73.7%, suggesting that variability in mean SUS accounts for much of the variability in mean Effort, but with about 27.3% of variability left unexplained (either due to error, the effect of some other variable(s), or systematic nonlinear components).

2. Table 10.20 shows the calculations needed to compute the regression slope and intercept for predicting Effort from SUS, which is Effort = 0.122 + 0.068(SUS). The predicted value for Effort after setting SUS to 80 is about 5.5. The 90% confidence interval around that predicted value ranges from 5.1 to 6.0.

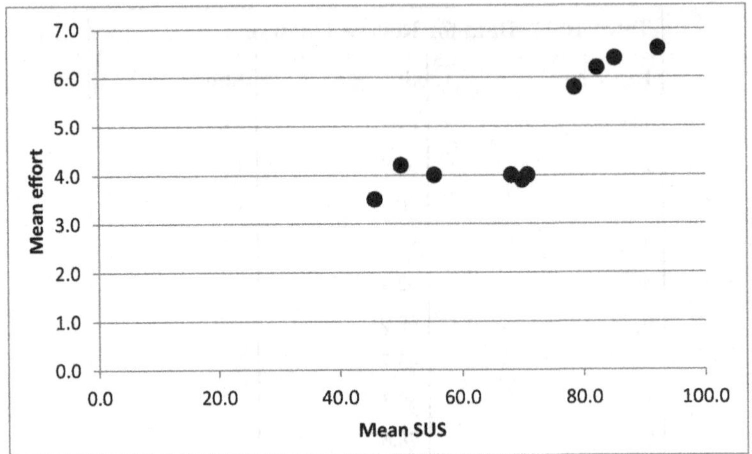

FIGURE 10.11 Scatterplot of hypothetical SUS and effort means

3. As shown in Table 10.21, if you want to control the estimate of Effort to within 0.1, assuming everything except the sample size stays the same, you'd need data from about 146 studies. You might need to learn to live with a bit more uncertainty.
4. Table 10.22 shows the conversion of the rating data to binary values based on whether the scores were above or below the targets discussed in Review Question 2. Table 10.23 shows the summary of the data in a 2 × 2 matrix. The resulting value of phi is a statistically significant 0.802 ($\chi^2(1) = 6.43$, $p = 0.01$).

$$\varphi = \frac{ad - bc}{\sqrt{(a+b)(c+d)(a+c)(b+d)}}$$

$$\varphi = \frac{3(6) - 1(0)}{\sqrt{(3+1)(0+6)(3+3)(1+6)}}$$

$$\varphi = \frac{18}{22.45} = 0.802$$

$$\chi^2(1) = n\varphi^2$$

$$\chi^2(1) = 10(0.802)^2$$

$$\chi^2(1) = 10(0.643) = 6.43$$

5. Table 10.24 shows the computations; Table 10.25 is the summary table. The significant F-test ($F(3, 36) = 5.576$, $p = 0.003$) indicates that at least one of the means is different from at least one of the other means. Table 10.26 shows the observed significance levels (p-values) for the six comparisons and, using $\alpha = 0.05$, the results for multiple comparisons without adjustment, using the Benjamini–Hochberg adjustment, and using the Bonferroni adjustment ($\alpha/6 = 0.008$). For the Benjamini–Hochberg method the p-values from the six comparisons were ranked from lowest to highest. The new statistical significance thresholds were created by dividing the rank by the number of comparisons and then multiplying this by alpha (0.05). For six comparisons, the

Table 10.19 Calculations for Review Question 1

Study	SUS	Effort	x_i-x	y_i-y	$(x_i-x)^2$	$(y_i-y)^2$	$(x_i-x)(y_i-y)$
1	68.1	4.0	−1.8	−0.9	3.06	0.74	1.51
2	50.0	4.2	−19.9	−0.7	394.02	0.44	13.10
3	70.8	4.0	1.0	−0.9	0.90	0.74	−0.82
4	85.2	6.4	15.4	1.5	235.62	2.37	23.64
5	92.4	6.6	22.6	1.7	508.50	3.03	39.24
6	69.9	3.9	0.1	−1.0	0.00	0.92	−0.05
7	45.7	3.5	−24.2	−1.4	583.22	1.85	32.84
8	82.3	6.2	12.5	1.3	155.00	1.80	16.68
9	78.6	5.8	8.8	0.9	76.56	0.88	8.23
10	55.5	4.0	−14.4	−0.9	205.92	0.74	12.34
Mean	69.9	4.9					
Std Dev	15.5	1.2		SS	2162.83	13.50	146.71
						r	**0.858**
						t	4.734
						df	8
						p	0.001
						R^2	73.7%
						z'	1.287
						$d95$	0.741
						$z' + d$	2.028
						$z' - d$	0.547
						r_{Upper}	0.966
						r_{Lower}	0.498

lowest p-value (with a rank of 1) is compared against a new threshold of (1/6)*0.05 = 0.008, the second is compared against (2/6)*0.05 = 0.017, and so forth. Two comparisons were statistically significant without adjustment and when using the Benjamini–Hochberg method (A Mobile vs. B Mobile and A Web vs. B Mobile). Only one comparison (A Mobile vs. B Mobile) was significant when using the Bonferroni adjustment. There are other comparisons that also have relatively low values of p (all but A Web vs. B Web) that might bear consideration, especially for a researcher working in an industrial context in which Type II errors are as or more important than Type I errors.

6. The calculation of Total, Between, and Within SS is the same for one-way and two-way ANOVAs. Table 10.27 shows the additional computations needed for the two-way ANOVA to partition the SS Between into the SS for main effects and their interaction, Table 10.28 shows the resulting

Table 10.20 Calculations for Review Question 2

Study	SUS	Effort	$\hat{y}$	$y_i - \hat{y}$	$(y_i - \hat{y})^2$
1	68.1	4.0	4.75	−0.75	0.57
2	50.0	4.2	3.52	0.68	0.46
3	70.8	4.0	4.94	−0.94	0.88
4	85.2	6.4	5.92	0.48	0.23
5	92.4	6.6	6.41	0.19	0.04
6	69.9	3.9	4.88	−0.98	0.95
7	45.7	3.5	3.23	0.27	0.07
8	82.3	6.2	5.72	0.48	0.23
9	78.6	5.8	5.47	0.33	0.11
10	55.5	4.0	3.90	0.10	0.01
Mean	69.9	4.9			
Std Dev	15.5	1.2		SS	3.55
				Slope	0.068
				Intercept	0.122
				$\text{Effort}_{\text{Pred}}$	5.5
				SE	0.256
				$t_{.10}$	1.860
				d	0.476
				$\text{Effort}_{\text{Upper}}$	6.0
				$\text{Effort}_{\text{Lower}}$	5.1

Table 10.21 Calculations for Review Question 3

Iteration	d	d^2	t	df	t^2	$\bar{x}$	$\bar{x}^2$	varp(x)	varp(e)	n	Roundup
1	0.1	0.01	1.645	na	2.706	69.9	103.02	216.283	0.355	143.89	144
2	0.1	0.01	1.656	142	2.741	69.9	103.02	216.283	0.355	145.76	146
3	0.1	0.01	1.656	144	2.741	69.9	103.02	216.283	0.355	145.73	146

ANOVA summary, and Fig. 10.12 depicts the interaction. For this hypothetical study, the main effect of Company was significant ($F(1,36) = 10.58$, $p = 0.002$), the main effect of Channel was not ($F(1, 36) = 0.01$, $p = 0.939$), and they interacted significantly ($F(1, 36) = 6.14$, $p = 0.018$).

When main effects do not interact, the interpretation of results focuses on the main effects. When their interaction is significant, the interaction becomes the focus of interpretation.

Table 10.22 Binary Conversion of SUS and Effort

Study	SUS	Effort
1	0	0
2	0	0
3	0	0
4	1	1
5	1	1
6	0	0
7	0	0
8	1	1
9	0	1
10	0	0

Table 10.23 Table of Corresponding and Noncorresponding SUS and Effort Values

	SUS	
Effort	**1**	**0**
1	3 (*a*)	1 (*b*)
0	0 (*c*)	6 (*d*)

Inspection of Fig. 10.12 shows that the Web experiences are about the same for the two companies, but the mobile experience for Company A is poorer than the mobile experience for Company B. To analyze the interaction, you could use an approach similar to that in the previous exercise, but with four rather than six comparisons, specifically, Company A Web versus Company A Mobile, Company B Web versus Company B Mobile, Company A Web versus Company B Web, and Company A Mobile versus Company B Mobile.

Table 10.29 shows the results of these multiple comparisons without adjustment (all using $\alpha = 0.05$), with Benjamini–Hochberg adjustment, and with Bonferroni adjustment (0.05/4 = 0.013). For the Benjamini–Hochberg method, the *p*-values from the four comparisons were ranked from lowest to highest. The new statistical significance thresholds were created by dividing the rank by the number of comparisons and multiplying by alpha (0.05). For four comparisons, the lowest *p*-value, with a rank of 1 is compared against a new threshold of (1/4)*0.05 = 0.013 and so forth. In this example, all three methods (unadjusted, Benjamini–Hochberg, and Bonferroni) indicated that only the comparison of Company A Mobile versus Company B mobile was statistically significant.

Table 10.24 ANOVA Computations for Review Question 5

		Company A (website)	Company A (mobile)	Company B (website)	Company B (mobile)
		72.5	62.5	82.5	100.0
		85.0	72.5	72.5	80.0
		70.0	77.5	87.5	90.0
		80.0	57.5	70.0	80.0
		60.0	82.5	80.0	85.0
		80.0	50.0	75.0	80.0
		80.0	67.5	97.5	92.5
		85.0	70.0	57.5	75.0
		65.0	52.5	70.0	100.0
		75.0	82.5	85.0	77.5
Computed	**Combined**				
Mean	76.63	75.25	67.50	77.75	86.00
Sum(x)	3065.0	752.5	675.0	777.5	860.0
$(\text{Sum}(x))^2$	9394225.0	566256.3	455625.0	604506.3	739600.0
$((\text{Sum}(x))^{2})/n$	234855.63	56625.625	45562.5	60450.625	73960
Sum(x^2)	240350.0	57256.3	46800.0	61581.3	74712.5
n	40	10	10	10	10

Table 10.25 ANOVA Summary Table for Review Question 5

Source	SS	*df*	MS	*F*	Sig
Total	5494.38	39	140.88		
Between	1743.13	3	581.04	5.576	0.003
Within	3751.25	36	104.20		

Table 10.26 Observed Significance Levels for the Six Comparisons

Comparison	*p*-value	Rank	BH Threshold	Unadjusted Result	BH Result	Bonferroni Result
A Mobile versus B Mobile	0.001	1	0.008	Sig.	Sig.	Sig.
A Web versus B Mobile	0.014	2	0.017	Sig.	Sig.	
A Mobile versus B Web	0.062	3	0.025			
B Web versus B Mobile	0.089	4	0.033			
A Web versus A Mobile	0.108	5	0.042			
A Web versus B Web	0.58	6	0.05			

Table 10.27 Additional Computations for the Two-way ANOVA

Computed	Company A	Company B	Website	Mobile
Sum	1427.5	1637.5	1530.0	1535.0
Sum-sq	2037756.3	2681406.3	2340900.0	2356225.0
n	20	20	20	20
(Sum-sq)/n	101887.813	134070.3125	117045	117811.25

Table 10.28 ANOVA Summary Table for Review Question 6

Source	SS	*df*	MS	*F*	Sig
Total	5494.38	39	140.88		
Between	1743.13	3	581.04		
Company	1102.50	1	1102.50	10.58	0.002
Channel	0.63	1	0.63	0.01	0.939
Interaction	640.00	1	640.00	6.14	0.018
Within	3751.25	36	104.20		

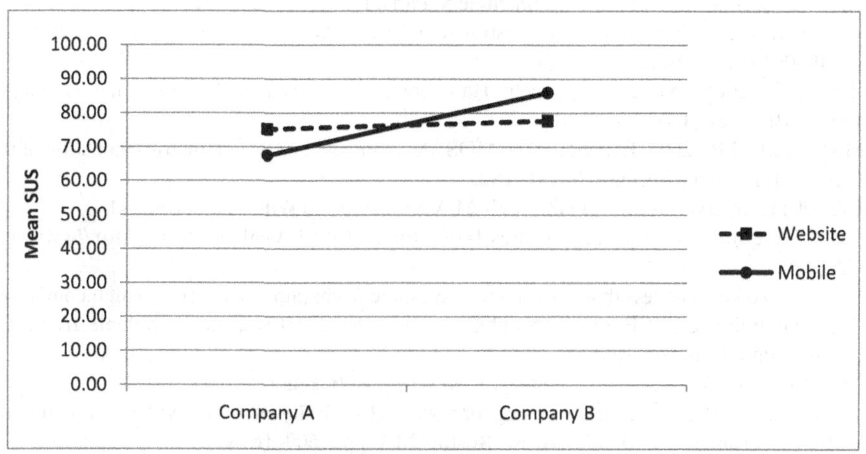

FIGURE 10.12 Graph of interaction for Review Question 6

Table 10.29 Analysis of Interaction for Review Question 6

Comparison	p-value	Rank	BH Threshold	Unadjusted Result	BH Result	Bonferroni Result
A Mobile versus B Mobile	0.001	1	0.013	Sig.	Sig.	Sig.
B Web versus B Mobile	0.089	2	0.025			
A Web versus A Mobile	0.108	3	0.038			
A Web versus B Web	0.58	4	0.050			

REFERENCES

Abelson, R.P., 1995. Statistics as Principled Argument. Lawrence Erlbaum, Hillsdale, NJ.

Benjamini, Y., Hochberg, Y., 1995. Controlling the false discovery rate: a practical and powerful approach to multiple testing. J. R. Soc. Ser. B 57 (1), 289–300.

Bobko, P., 2001. Correlation and Regression: Applications for Industrial Organizational Psychology and Management, second ed. Sage Publications, Thousand Oaks, CA.

Cohen, J., 1988. Statistical Power Analysis for the Behavioral Sciences, second ed. Lawrence Erlbaum, Hillsdale, NJ.

Cohen, L., Manion, L., Morrison, K., 2011. Research Methods in Education, seventh ed. Routledge, New York, NY.

Cowles, M., 1989. Statistics in Psychology: An Historical Perspective. Lawrence Erlbaum, Hillsdale, NJ.

Gladwell, M., 2008. Outliers: The Story of Success. Little, Brown, and Company, New York, NY.

Lewis, J.R., 2011. Practical Speech User Interface Design. Taylor & Francis, Boca Raton, FL.

Lewis, J.R., Sauro, J., 2016. Excel and R Companion to "Quantifying the User Experience": Rapid Answers to Over 100 Examples and Exercises, second ed. Create Space Publishing, Denver, CO.

Lewis, J.R., Utesch, B.S., Maher, D.E., 2013. UMUX-LITE—when there's no time for the SUS. In: Proceedings of CHI 2013, Association for Computing Machinery, Paris, France, pp. 2099–2102.

Moinester, M., Gottfried, R., 2014. Sample size estimation for correlations with pre-specified confidence interval. Quant. Methods Psychol. 10 (2), 124–130.

Nass, C., Brave, S., 2005. Wired for Speech: How Voice Activates and Advances the Human–Computer Relationship. MIT Press, Cambridge, MA.

Polkosky, M.D., Lewis, J.R., 2003. Expanding the MOS: development and psychometric evaluation of the MOS-R and MOS-X. Int. J. Speech Technol. 6, 161–182.

Rutherford, A., 2011. ANOVA and ANCOVA: A GLM Approach. John Wiley, Hoboken, NJ.

Sauro, J., 2010. Were most software millionaires born around 1955? Available from: http://www.measuringu.com/1955.php

Sauro, J., 2011. Are women paid less than men in UX? Available from: http://www.measuringu.com/ux-gender.php

Sauro, J., 2013. Usability & Net Promoter benchmark report for retail websites. Available from: http://www.measuringu.com/products/retailReport

Sauro, J., 2015. Customer Analytics for Dummies. John Wiley, Hoboken, NJ.

Sauro, J., Lewis, J.R., 2009. Correlations among prototypical usability metrics: evidence for the construct of usability. In: Proceedings of CHI 2009, ACM, Boston, MA, pp. 1609–1618.

Tabachnick, B.G., Fidell, L.S., 2012. Using Multivariate Statistics, sixth ed. Pearson, New York, NY.

Thomson, M., MacInnis, D.J., Whan Park, C., 2005. The ties that bind: measuring the strength of consumers' emotional attachments to brands. J. Consum. Psychol. 15 (1), 77–91.

APPENDIX: DERIVATION OF SAMPLE SIZE FORMULAS FOR REGRESSION

The purpose of this appendix is to document the derivation of the sample size formulas for regression given a focus on estimating the slope or estimating the intercept. If you have no interest in the math, just skip this appendix.

BASED ON CONFIDENCE INTERVAL FOR REGRESSION SLOPE

$$\mathrm{SE} = \frac{\sqrt{\dfrac{s_e^2}{n-2}}}{\sqrt{s_x^2}}$$

$$d = \frac{t\sqrt{\dfrac{s_e^2}{n-2}}}{\sqrt{s_x^2}}$$

$$d^2 = \frac{\dfrac{t^2 s_e^2}{n-2}}{s_x^2}$$

$$d^2 s_x^2 = \frac{t^2 s_e^2}{n-2}$$

$$d^2 s_x^2 (n-2) = t^2 s_e^2$$

$$n-2 = \frac{t^2 s_e^2}{d^2 s_x^2}$$

$$n = \frac{t^2 s_e^2}{d^2 s_x^2} + 2$$

BASED ON CONFIDENCE INTERVAL FOR REGRESSION INTERCEPT

$$\mathrm{SE} = \sqrt{\frac{\mathrm{SS}_e}{(n-2)}}\sqrt{\frac{1}{n} + \frac{(\bar{x})^2}{\mathrm{SS}_x}}$$

$$d = t\sqrt{\frac{ns_e^2}{(n-2)}}\sqrt{\frac{1}{n} + \frac{\bar{x}^2}{ns_x^2}}$$

$$d^2 = t^2 \frac{ns_e^2}{(n-2)}\left(\frac{s_x^2}{ns_x^2} + \frac{\bar{x}^2}{ns_x^2}\right)$$

$$\frac{d^2}{t^2} = \frac{ns_e^2}{(n-2)}\left(\frac{s_x^2 + \bar{x}^2}{ns_x^2}\right)$$

$$\frac{d^2}{t^2} = \frac{s_e^2}{(n-2)}\left(\frac{s_x^2 + \overline{x}^2}{s_x^2}\right)$$

$$\frac{d^2}{t^2} = \frac{s_e^2}{(n-2)}\left(1 + \frac{\overline{x}^2}{s_x^2}\right)$$

$$\frac{s_e^2}{n-2} = \frac{d^2}{t^2\left(1 + \frac{\overline{x}^2}{s_x^2}\right)}$$

$$\frac{n-2}{s_e^2} = \frac{t^2\left(1 + \frac{\overline{x}^2}{s_x^2}\right)}{d^2}$$

$$n-2 = \frac{t^2 s_e^2\left(1 + \frac{\overline{x}^2}{s_x^2}\right)}{d^2}$$

$$n = \frac{t^2 s_e^2\left(1 + \frac{\overline{x}^2}{s_x^2}\right)}{d^2} + 2$$

For sample size estimation other than the special case of the intercept, replace $\overline{x}^2$ with $(x-\overline{x})^2$. For the special case when $x = \overline{x}$, the formula simplifies to

$$n = \frac{t^2 s_e^2}{d^2} + 2$$

CHAPTER

WRAPPING UP

11

INTRODUCTION

"One of science's defining characteristics is that new ideas are developed and that both new and old ideas are tested empirically. ...Just like any other science, what you want to know about any statistical technique is the degree to which it might give you a wrong answer and whether there are other methods around that give you a better chance of getting things right. There aren't rules, laws, and commandments about this, you just have to know the latest research data" (Vickers, 2010, p. 140).

In this book, we've shared decades of research in what we believe to be the best statistical approaches to solving the most common issues that arise in user research, including modifications to our current practices based on recent published research in binomial confidence intervals and the analysis of 2 × 2 contingency tables. We've covered the three major statistical questions—the precision of estimates (confidence intervals), tests against benchmarks, and comparison of products. The chapters on sample size estimation include classical statistical methods and new sample size formulas derived from recently published research, some presented for the first time in the first edition of this book. We've provided a comprehensive review of standardized usability questionnaires, and a discussion of enduring controversies in measurement and statistics that affect usability practitioners and researchers. In the Appendix, we have a crash course in fundamental statistical concepts, based on years of teaching short courses at professional conferences that cover a semester of introductory statistics in about a half hour.

GETTING MORE INFORMATION

We believe we've addressed the major issues that most usability practitioners and researchers encounter, but we have not covered more advanced and specialized topics, such as:

- **Advanced analysis of variance (ANOVA)**: Chapter 10 in this edition of the book covered the basic one- and two-way ANOVAs. We did not, however, cover more advanced forms of ANOVA and experimental designs such as Latin squares, split plots, and fractional factorials. We also did not cover designs for within-subjects experiments, which are considerably more complex in ANOVA than those for between-subjects experiments.
- **Analysis of many-way contingency tables**: For this book, we restricted our analyses to 2 × 2 contingency tables. For larger, more complex contingency tables, the most common analytical method is the chi-squared test, which extends easily from 2 × 2 tables. Another approach is to use an advanced method called log-linear analysis.
- **Advanced correlation and linear regression**: This edition of the book introduced correlation and linear regression in Chapter 10. As with ANOVA, there are more advanced forms of correlation

Quantifying the User Experience. http://dx.doi.org/10.1016/B978-0-12-802308-2.00011-4

and regression analyses that were not covered, such as partial correlation, canonical correlation, principal components analysis, factor analysis, and advanced multiple regression.

- **Nonparametric data analysis**: These are tests that make fewer initial assumptions about the underlying data than z- or t-tests, often by converting raw data to ranks or through resampling methods (e.g., jackknife or bootstrapping). Although we did not cover rank- or resampling-based procedures (for which the jury is still out as to whether they are advantageous when applied to typical user research data), the following procedures included in this book are generally considered nonparametric:
  - Binomial Test (Chapter 4)
  - Chi-Square Test and $N-1$ Chi-Square Test (Chapter 5)
  - Two-Proportion Test and $N-1$ Two-Proportion Test (Chapter 5)
  - Fisher Exact Test (Chapter 5)
  - McNemar Exact Test (Chapter 5)
- **Card sorting and analysis**: Card sorting is a user research method used to develop models of mental organization of information, applied to the design of menu structures and information architectures. Methods used to analyze the data from a card-sorting study include cluster analysis, multidimensional scaling, and path analysis.
- **Analysis of eye-tracking data**: The use of eye tracking has become more common in user research as the equipment has become less expensive and more reliable. Common analyses of eye-tracking data include "heat maps," "look zones," and scan paths.

For information on advanced ANOVA, correlation, regression, and nonparametric data analysis, you can consult standard statistics textbooks. It is possible to spend a lifetime learning advanced methods in general linear modeling and nonparametric statistics, but for most practical user research, there is rarely a need. For a quick introduction to card sorting and analysis of eye-tracking data, we recommend *Eye Tracking in User Experience Design* (Bergstrom and Schall, 2014) and *Measuring the User Experience* (Tullis and Albert, 2013, which also includes valuable information on collecting and presenting a wide variety of user research data with brief descriptions of correlation and ANOVA).

If you're new to the measurement of usability, in addition to the Tullis & Albert book, we recommend *A Practical Guide to Measuring Usability* (Sauro, 2010) which addresses the most commonly asked questions about quantifying usability. For a comprehensive review of the System Usability Scale, including discussions of other standardized usability questionnaires, we recommend *A Practical Guide to the System Usability Scale* (Sauro, 2011). Finally, if you expect to use these statistical methods frequently in your day-to-day work, we recommend Lewis and Sauro (2016), a companion book which contains detailed information on how to use an Excel calculator (or a custom set of functions written in the R statistical programming language) to solve the over 100 quantitative examples and exercises in this book.

Any book must eventually come to an end (publishers insist on this), but research on statistical methods for user research will continue. For late-breaking developments in usability research and practice, there are a number of annual conferences that have usability evaluation as a significant portion of their content, including occasional papers on statistical methods for user research published in their proceedings. These major conferences are:

- ACM Special Interest Group in Computer–Human Interaction (CHI) (www.acm.org/sigchi/)
- Human Factors and Ergonomics Society (hfes.org/)
- User Experience Professionals Association (www.uxpa.org/)

- Human–Computer Interaction International (www.hci-international.org/)
- INTERACT (held every two years; (e.g., see www.interact2015.org/)

You can also get information on statistical methods for user research from the magazines and journals produced by professional organizations such as ACM, HFES, and UXPA. For example, you will find references in this book to:

- *Ergonomics in Design* (www.hfes.org/publications/ProductDetail.aspx?ProductId=36)
- Interactions (interactions.acm.org)
- *Journal of Usability Studies* (www.uxpajournal.org)
- *Human Factors* (www.hfes.org/Publications/ProductDetail.aspx?ProductID=1)
- *International Journal of Human-Computer Interaction* (www.tandf.co.uk/10447318)
- *IEEE Transactions on Professional Communication* (ieeexplore.ieee.org/xpl/RecentIssue.jsp?punumber=47)
- *IEEE Software* (www.computer.org/web/computingnow/software)
- *Behaviour & Information Technology* (www.tandf.co.uk/journals/tf/0144929X.html)
- *Behavior Research Methods* (www.springer.com/psychology/cognitive+psychology/journal/13428)
- *Communications of the ACM* (cacm.acm.org)
- *Applied Ergonomics* (www.elsevier.com/wps/find/journaldescription.cws_home/30389/description)
- *Computers in Human Behavior* (www.elsevier.com/wps/find/journaldescription.cws_home/759/description)
- *Interacting with Computers* (www.elsevier.com/wps/find/journaldescription.cws_home/525445/description)
- *International Journal of Human-Computer Studies* (www.elsevier.com/wps/find/journaldescription.cws_home/622846/description)

The following journals provide more technical coverage of statistical issues that occasionally relate to methods for user research:

- *The American Statistician* (www.amstat.org/publications/tas.cfm)
- *Journal of the American Statistical Association* (www.amstat.org/publications/jasa.cfm)
- *The American Psychologist* (www.apa.org/pubs/journals/amp/index.aspx)
- *Psychological Bulletin* (www.apa.org/pubs/journals/bul/index.aspx)
- *Psychological Science* (www.psychologicalscience.org/index.php/publications/journals/psychological_science)
- *Current Directions in Psychological Science* (www.psychologicalscience.org/index.php/publications/journals/current_directions)
- *ACTA Psychologica* (www.elsevier.com/wps/find/journaldescription.cws_home/505579/description)
- *Educational and Psychological Measurement* (epm.sagepub.com)
- *Journal of Experimental Psychology* (www.apa.org/pubs/journals/xge/index.aspx)
- *Statistics in Medicine* (onlinelibrary.wiley.com/journal/10.1002/(ISSN)1097-0258)
- *Biometrics* (www.biometrics.tibs.org)
- *Biometrika* (biomet.oxfordjournals.org)

- *Technometrics* (www.amstat.org/publications/tech.cfm)
- *Journal of Mathematical Psychology* (www.elsevier.com/wps/find/journaldescription.cws_home/622887/description)

> **STAY TUNED FOR FUTURE RESEARCH**
>
> **How to sign up for the measuringu.com newsletter**
>
> We plan to continue investigating and publishing our findings on statistical methods for user research. Probably the best source for updates on our research is the website:
>
> measuringu.com
>
> The easiest way to stay informed is to subscribe to the newsletter by clicking the Email Updates link in the upper right corner of the home page. The website also contains online tutorials and courses that cover many of the concepts in this book using visualizations and interactive demonstrations.

GOOD LUCK!

We wish you the best of luck as you collect and analyze user data in support of the goal of making products easier to use and, as a consequence, making life better for your users. As you do your research, keep in mind that statistics provides "the world's most specific way of saying maybe" (Searles, 1978). The use of statistical methods does not guarantee 100% correct decisions, but it doesn't have to be perfect to be effective. It is important, however, to understand its strengths, limitations, and leading practices when applied to user research to ensure its most effective use. It is our sincere hope that this book has helped in the development of that understanding.

KEY POINTS

- This book includes discussion of the most common issues that arise in user research.
- Topics not covered in this book are more advanced or specialized subjects such as advanced analysis of variance, advanced correlation, advanced linear regression, nonparametric data analysis, card sorting, and eye tracking.
- A good resource for an introduction to several of the topics not covered here is the second edition of *Measuring the User Experience* by Tom Tullis and Bill Albert (2013).
- Sources for monitoring future developments in statistical methods for user research include the proceedings of major conferences and a variety of scientific publications.
- For up-to-date information on our future research, visit measuringu.com and sign up for the newsletter.

REFERENCES

Bergstrom, J.R., Schall, A.J., 2014. Eye Tracking in User Experience Design. Elsevier, Boston, MA/Amsterdam.

Lewis, J.R., Sauro, J., 2016. Excel and R Companion to "Quantifying the User Experience: Practical Statistics for User Research": Rapid Answers to Over 100 Examples and Exercises, second ed. Create Space Publishers, Denver.

Sauro, J., 2010. A Practical Guide to Measuring Usability. Create Space Publishers, Denver, CO.
Sauro, J., 2011. A Practical Guide to the System Usability Scale. Create Space Publishers, Denver, CO.
Searles, D., 1978. PSI burn: a study of physiological deterioration in parapsychological experimentation. Omni Mag. 1 (3), 108–110, <Satire with amusing definitions of statistical terms>.
Tullis, T., Albert, B., 2013. Measuring the User Experience: Collecting, Analyzing, and Presenting Usability Metrics, second ed. Morgan Kaufmann, Waltham, MA.
Vickers, A., 2010. What is a *p*-value Anyway? Addison-Wesley, Boston, MA.

Appendix

A CRASH COURSE IN FUNDAMENTAL STATISTICAL CONCEPTS

INTRODUCTION

Throughout the book we've attempted to provide as much statistical background as possible without letting it get too overwhelming. In this appendix we review some fundamental statistical concepts and provide pointers to chapters where the concepts are covered in greater detail. If you've never had an introductory statistics class or don't remember basic concepts such as measuring central tendency and variability, then you can use this appendix for a quick review.

TYPES OF DATA

The first step in using statistics to make better decisions is obtaining measurements. There are two major types of measurements: quantitative and categorical. Task time, number of usability problems, and rating scale data are quantitative. Things like gender, operating system, and usability problem type are categorical variables.

Quantitative data fall on a spectrum from continuous to discrete-binary, as shown in Fig. A.1. Note that the extreme discrete end of this spectrum includes binary categorical measurements such as pass/fail and yes/no. The more discrete the data, the larger the required sample size for the same level of precision as a continuous measure. Also, you'll usually use different statistical tests for continuous versus discrete data (Chapters 3–6).

Discrete data have finite values, or buckets. You can count them. Continuous data technically have an infinite number of steps, which form a continuum. The number of usability problems would be discrete—there are a finite and countable number of observed usability problems. Time to complete a task is continuous since it could take any value from 0 to infinity, for example, 178.8977687 s.

You can tell the difference between discrete and continuous data because discrete can usually be preceded by the phrase "number of...," for example, number of errors or number of calls to the help desk.

You can convert categorical data into discrete quantitative data. For example, task passes and failures can be converted to 0 for fail and 1 for pass. Discrete data don't lend themselves well to subdividing (you can't have half an error) but we're often able to analyze them more like continuous data because they can potentially range from 0 to infinity. Questionnaire data that use closed-ended rating scales (e.g., values from 1 to 7) do have discrete values, but because the mean rating can take an infinite number of values we can analyze it like continuous data.

There are other ways of classifying measurements, such as the famous and controversial hierarchy of Nominal, Ordinal, Interval, and Ratio data discussed in Chapter 9. For most applied user research, the major useful distinctions are between categorical and quantitative data and, within quantitative data, between continuous and discrete.

Quantifying the User Experience. http://dx.doi.org/10.1016/B978-0-12-802308-2.00012-6

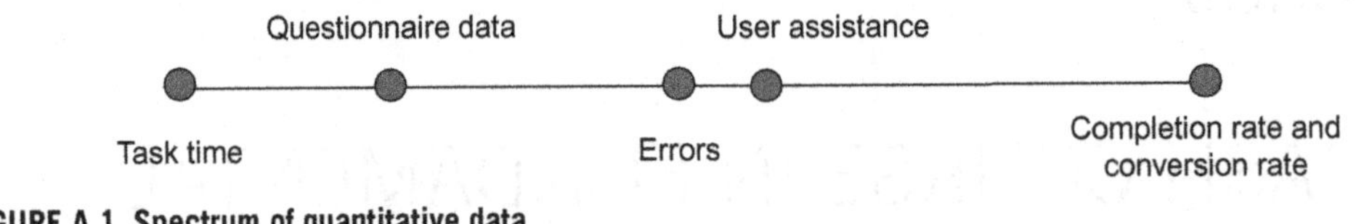

FIGURE A.1 Spectrum of quantitative data

POPULATIONS AND SAMPLES

We rarely have access to the entire population of users. Instead we rely on a subset of the population to use as a proxy for the population. When we ask a sample of users to attempt tasks and we measure the average task time, we're using this sample to estimate the average task time for the entire user population. Means, standard deviations, medians, and other summary values from samples are called statistics. Sample statistics estimate unknown population parameters. Population parameters (like the mean task time and standard deviation) are denoted with Greek symbols (μ for mean and σ for standard deviation) and sample statistics are denoted with Latin characters ($\bar{x}$ for mean and s for standard deviation).

SAMPLING

The most important thing in drawing conclusions from data, whether in user research, psychology, or medicine, is that the sample of users you measure represents the population about which you intend to make statements. No amount of statistical manipulation can correct for making inferences about one population if you observe a sample from a different population.

Ideally, you should select your sample randomly from the parent population. In practice, this can be very difficult due to (1) issues in establishing a truly random selection scheme or (2) problems getting the selected users to participate. It's always important to understand the potential biases in your data and how that limits your conclusions. In applied research we are constrained by budgets and the availability of users but products still must ship, so we make the best decisions we can given the data we have. Where possible seek to minimize systematic bias in your sample but remember that representativeness is more important than randomness. In other words, you'll make better decisions if you have a less-than-perfectly random sample from the right population than if you have a perfectly random sample from the wrong population. See Chapter 2 for more discussion on Randomness and Representativeness.

MEASURING CENTRAL TENDENCY

MEAN

One of the first and easiest things to do with a set of data is to find the average. The average is a measure of central tendency, meaning it is a way of summarizing the middle value (where the center of the data tends to be). For a set of data that is roughly symmetrical, the arithmetic mean provides a good center value. To calculate the mean, add up each value and divide by the total number in the group. For example, here are ten SUS scores from a recent usability test (see Chapter 8 for more on SUS).

90.6, 34.4, 34.4, 87.5, 75.0, 62.5, 100.0, 65.6, 71.9, 53.1, 34.4, 37.5, 75.0, 87.5, 12.5, 46.9

The mean SUS score is 60.55. You can use the Excel function =AVERAGE() to find the arithmetic mean.

MEDIAN

When the data you're analyzing aren't symmetrical, like task times, the mean can be heavily influenced by a few extreme data points and thus becomes a poor measure of the middle value. In such cases the median provides a better idea of the most typical value. For odd samples, the median is the central value; for even samples, it's the average of the two central values. Here is an example of task-times data from a usability test, arranged from fastest to slowest:

84, 85, 86, 103, 111, 122, 180, 183, 235, 278

For these data, the median is 116.5 (the mean of 111 and 122). In Excel, you can find the median with the function =MEDIAN().

GEOMETRIC MEAN

The median is by definition the center value. In a small sample of data (less than 25 or so), the sample median tends to do a poor job of estimating the population median. For task-time data we've found that another average called the geometric mean tends to provide a better estimate of the population's middle value than the sample median (see Chapter 3 for more discussion on using the geometric mean with task times). To find the geometric mean, transform the raw times to log-times (using the Excel function =LN()), find the arithmetic mean of these log-times, then convert this mean of the logs back into the original scale (using the Excel function =EXP()). The geometric mean for the task times shown previously is 133.8 s. You can also use the Excel function =GEOMEAN() on the raw task times. Fig. A.2 shows the various "average" times for this example.

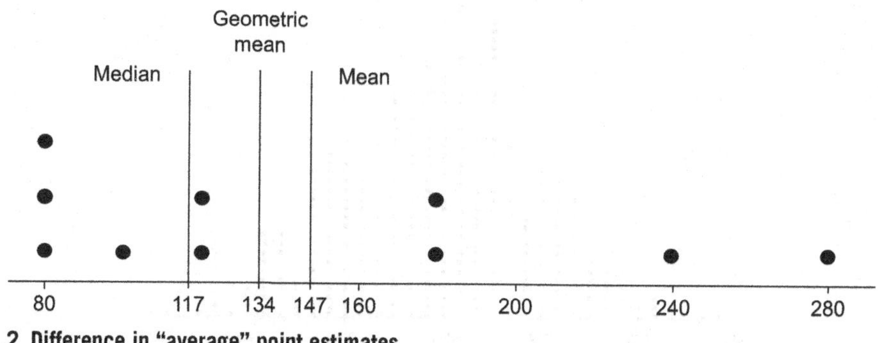

FIGURE A.2 Difference in "average" point estimates

STANDARD DEVIATION AND VARIANCE

In addition to describing the center or most typical value in a set of data, we also need a measure of the spread of the data around the average. The most common way to do this is using a metric called the standard deviation. The standard deviation provides an estimate of the average difference of each value from the mean.

If, however, you just subtract each value from the mean and take an average, you'll always get 0 because the differences cancel out. To avoid this problem, after subtracting each value from the mean, square the values then take the average of the squared values. This gets you the average squared difference from the mean, a statistic called the variance. It is used a lot in statistical methods, but it's hard to think in terms of squared differences. The solution is to take the square root of the variance to get the standard deviation—an intuitive (and the most common) way to describe the spread of data. A narrated visualization of the standard deviation is available online at http://www.usablestats.com/tutorials/StandardDeviation.

THE NORMAL DISTRIBUTION

Many measures when graphed tend to look like a bell-shaped curve. For example heights, weights, and IQ scores are some of the more famous bell-shaped distributions. Fig. A.3 shows a graph of 500 North American men's heights in inches. The average height is 5 ft. 10 in. (178 cm) with a standard deviation of 3 in. (7.6 cm).

Over the past century, researchers have found that the bulk of the values in a population cluster around the "head" of the bell curve. In general, they've found that 68% of values fall within one standard deviation of the mean, 95% fall within two standard deviations, and 99.7% fall within three standard deviations. In other words, for a population that follows a normal distribution, almost all the values will fall within three standard deviations above and below the mean—a property known as the Empirical Rule (Fig. A.4).

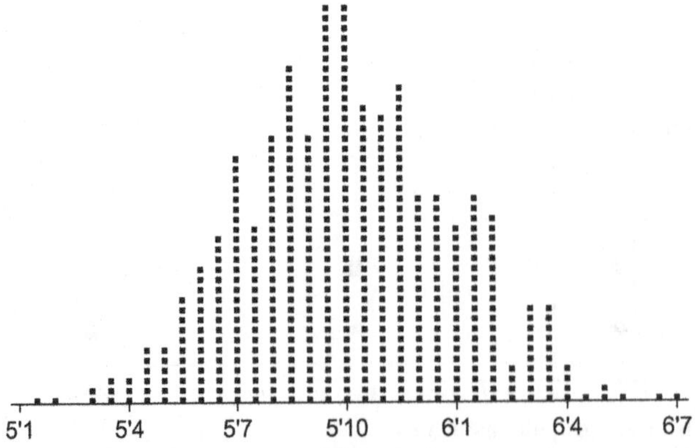

FIGURE A.3 Distribution of North American men's heights in inches

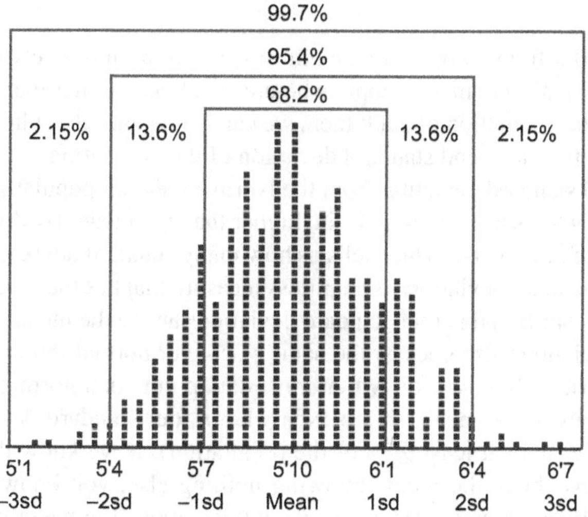

FIGURE A.4 Illustration of the Empirical Rule

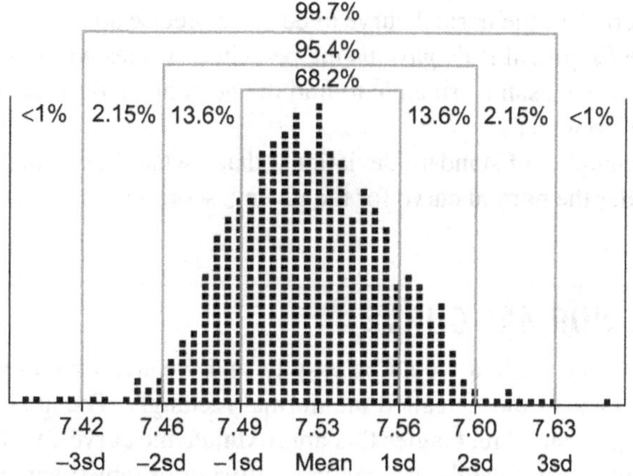

FIGURE A.5 Weights of 2000 Euro coins

As you can see in Fig. A.4, the bulk of the heights fall close to the mean with only a few further than two standard deviations from the mean.

As another example, Fig. A.5 shows the weights of 2000 Euro coins which have an average weight of 7.53 g and a standard deviation of 0.035 g.

Almost all coins fall within three standard deviations of the mean weight.

If we can establish that our population follows a normal distribution and we have a good idea about the mean and standard deviation, then we have some idea about how unusual values are—whether they are heights, weights, average satisfaction scores, or average task times.

z-SCORES

For example, if you had a friend who had a height of 6 ft. 10 in., intuitively you'd think he was tall. In fact, you probably haven't met many people who are as tall as or taller than him. If we think of this person as one point in the population of adult men, we can get an idea about how unusual this height is. All we need to know is the mean and standard deviation of the population.

Using the mean and standard deviation from the North American population (5 ft. 10 in. and 3 in., respectively), someone who is 6 ft. 10 in. is 12 in. higher than the mean. By dividing this difference by the standard deviation of 3, we get 4, which tells us how many standard deviations this point is from the mean. The number of standard deviations is a unitless measure that has the same meaning regardless of the dataset. In this case, our friend is four standard deviations above the mean. When used this way, the number of standard deviations also goes by the name *z*-score or normal score.

Based on the Empirical Rule, we know that most data points in a normal distribution fall within three standard deviations of the mean, so a person who is four standard deviations above the mean is very tall indeed (taller than at least 99% of the population). If we know that a toddler's height is four standard deviations above the mean, knowing nothing else, you know that he is very tall for his age. If a student's IQ score is four standard deviations above the mean you know that her score is well above average. If you know a company's loyalty ratings are four standard deviations above the mean, this is compelling evidence that their scores are among the highest (and they have a very loyal following).

We can use the properties of the normal curve to be more precise about just how tall, smart, or loyal someone is. Just like the Empirical Rule gave us the percent of values within one, two, and three standard deviations, we can use the same principle to find the percent we'd expect to fall between any two points and how extreme a point is.

We already have the number of standard deviations (that's what the *z*-score tells us), so all we have to do is find the area under the normal curve for the given *z*-score(s).

AREA UNDER THE NORMAL CURVE

If the normal curve was a rectangle it would be easy to find the area by multiplying the length times the width—but it's not, or it would be called the normal rectangle. The area of curved shapes is essentially found by adding up small rectangles that approximate the curves, with this process smoothed through the use of calculus. Fortunately, we can use software or tabled values to spare us all the tedious calculus.

One of the most important things to remember about using the normal curve as a reference distribution is that the total area under the curve adds up to 1 or 100% (Fig. A.6).

You can think of it like a big pie-chart—you can have as many slices as you want but they all need to add up to 100%. The same principle applies to the normal curve. Unlike a pie chart though, the normal curve theoretically goes on to both positive and negative infinity, but the area gets infinitesimally small as you go beyond four standard deviations from the mean.

If you have access to Excel, you can find the percent of area up to a point in the normal curve by using the function =NORMSDIST(*z*), where *z* is the number of standard deviations (the *z*-score). For example, a *z*-score of 1.28 provides the area from negative infinity to 1.28 standard deviations above

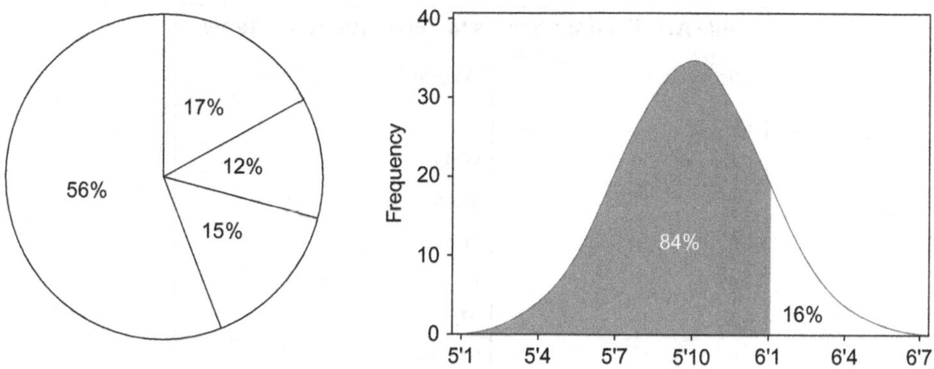

FIGURE A.6 Like a pie chart, the area under the normal curve adds up to 100%

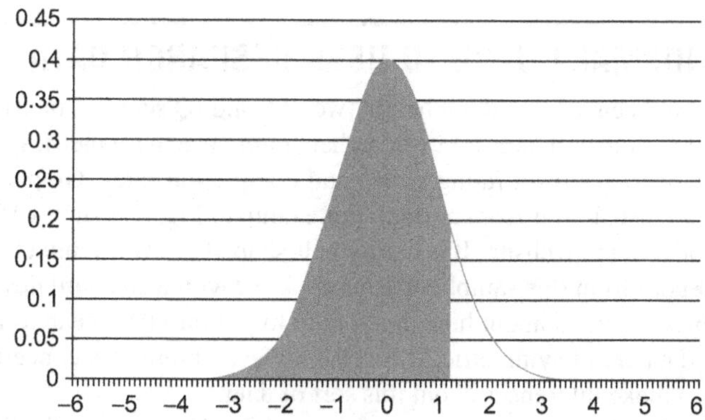

FIGURE A.7 Illustration of an area under the normal curve

the mean and accounts for about 90% of the area. The shaded region in Fig. A.7 shows you 90% of the area from negative infinity to 1.28 standard deviations above the mean. We can use the area under the curve as a percentile rank to describe how typical or unusual a value is.

A person who is four standard deviations above the mean would be in the =NORMSDIST(4) 99.997th percentile in height (very unusual!). Most statistics books include a table of normal values. To find the percentile rank from the table, you find the *z*-score that's closest to yours and find the area. For example, Table A.1 is a section from a normal table. There isn't an entry for 1.28 but we can see it falls somewhere between 88.49% and 90.32% (closer to 90.32%).

Because the total area must add up to 100% under the curve, we can express a *z*-score of 1.28 as being higher than 90% of values or less than 10% of values (100% minus 90%).

Table A.1 Partial z-Scores to Percentile Rank Table

z-Score	Percentile
1.0	84.13
1.1	86.43
1.2	**88.49**
1.3	**90.32**
1.4	91.92
1.5	93.32
1.6	94.52
1.7	95.54

APPLYING THE NORMAL CURVE TO USER RESEARCH DATA

The examples so far have been mostly about height, weight, and IQ scores—metrics that nicely follow a normal distribution. In our experience, user researchers rarely use these metrics, more typically using measurements such as averages from rating scales and completion rates. Graphs of the distributions of these types of data are usually far from normal. For example, Fig. A.8 shows 15 SUS scores from a usability test of the Budget.com website. It is hardly bell-shaped or even symmetrical.

The average SUS score from this sample of 15 users is 80 with a standard deviation of 24. It's understandable to be a bit concerned about how much faith to put into this mean as a measure of central tendency because the data aren't symmetric. It is certainly even more of a concern about how we can use the normal curve to make inferences about this sort of data.

It turns out this sample of 15 comes from a larger sample of 311 users, with all the values shown in Fig. A.9. The mean SUS score of these data is 78.

Again, the shape of this distribution makes you wonder if the normal curve is even relevant. However, if we take 1000 random samples of 15 users from this large population of 311, then plot the

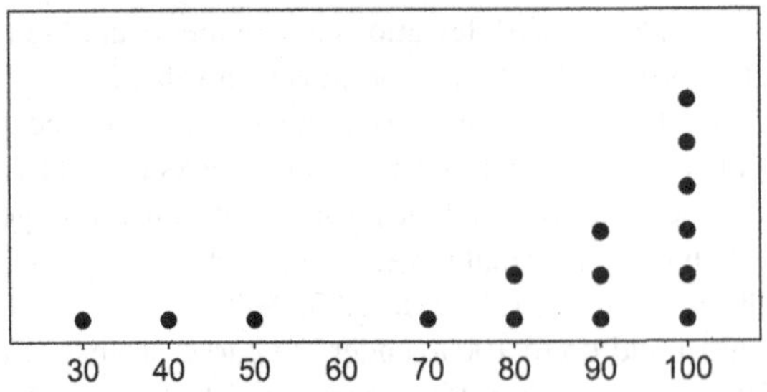

FIGURE A.8 Graph of 15 SUS scores

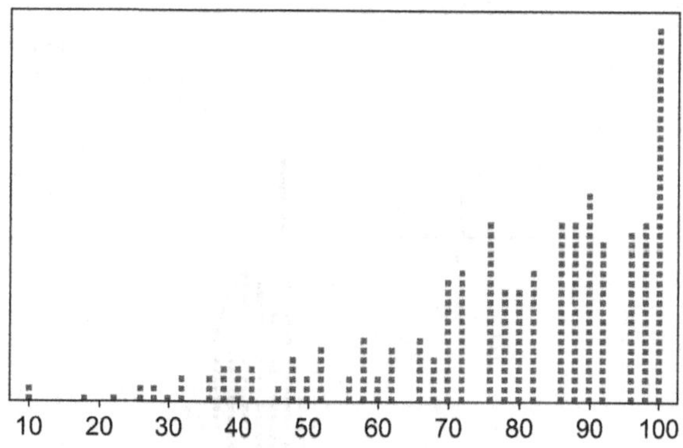

FIGURE A.9 Graph of 311 SUS scores

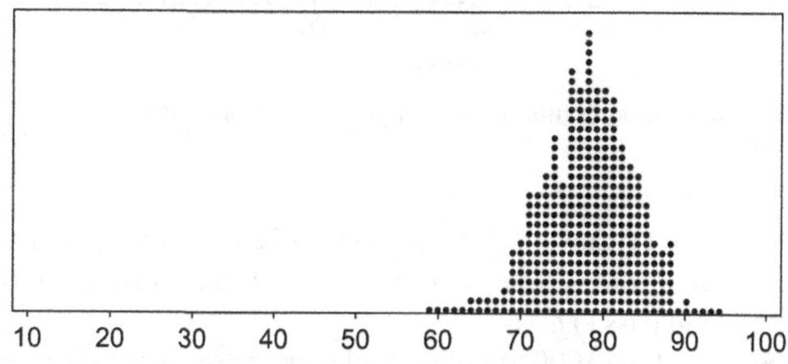

FIGURE A.10 Graph of 1000 means of random samples of 15 SUS scores

1000 means, you get the graph shown in Fig. A.10. Although the large sample of 311 SUS scores is not normal, the distribution of the random means shown in Fig. A.10 does follow a normal distribution. The same principle applies if the population we draw randomly from is 311 or 311 million.

CENTRAL LIMIT THEOREM

Fig. A.10 illustrates one of the most fundamental and important statistical concepts—the Central Limit Theorem. In short, this theorem states that as the sample size approaches infinity, the distribution of sample means will follow a normal distribution regardless of what the parent population looks like. Even for some very nonnormal populations, at a sample size of around 30 or higher, the distribution of the sample means becomes normal. The mean of this distribution of sample means will also be equal to the mean of the parent population.

For many other populations, like rating scale data, the distribution becomes normal at much smaller sample sizes (we used 15 in Fig. A.10). To illustrate this point with binary data, which has a drastically

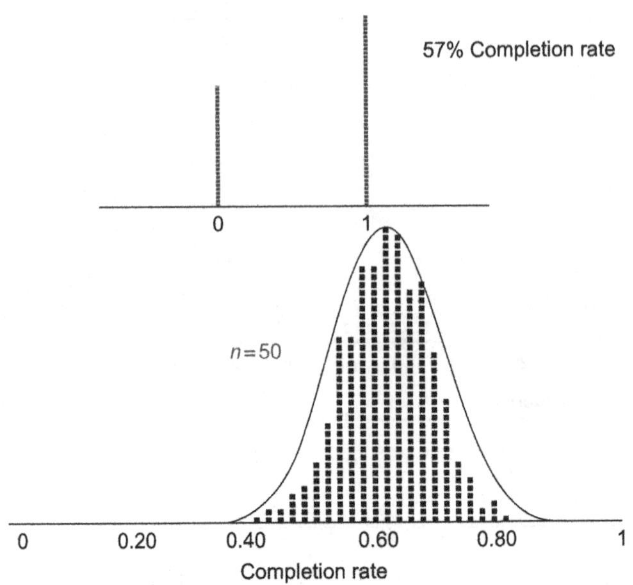

FIGURE A.11 Illustration of distribution of binary means approaching normality

nonnormal distribution, Fig. A.11 shows 1000 random samples taken from a large sample of completion rate data with a population completion rate of 57%. The data are discrete-binary because the only possible values are fail (0) and pass (1).

The black dots show each of the 1000 sample completion rates at a sample size of 50. Again we can see the bell-shaped normal distribution take shape. The mean of the sampling distribution of completion rates is 57%, the same as the population from which it was drawn. For reasonably large sample sizes, we can use the normal distribution to approximate the shape of the distribution of average completion rates. The best approaches for working with this type of data are discussed in Chapters 3 through 6.

STANDARD ERROR OF THE MEAN

We will use the properties of the normal curve to describe how unusual a sample mean is for things like rating scale data and task times. When we speak in terms of the standard deviation of the distribution of sample means, this special standard deviation goes by the name "standard error" to remind us that that each sample mean we obtain differs by some amount from the true unknown population mean. Because it describes the mean of multiple members of a population, the standard error is always smaller than the standard deviation. The larger our sample size is, the smaller we would expect the standard error to be and the less we'd expect our sample mean to differ from the population mean. Our standard error needs to take into account the sample size. In fact, based on the sample size, there is a direct relationship between the standard deviation and the standard error. We use the sample standard deviation and the square root of the sample size to estimate the standard error—how much sample means fluctuate from the population mean.

$$\frac{s}{\sqrt{n}}$$

From our initial sample of 15 users we had a mean of 80 and a standard deviation of 24. This generates a standard error (technically the estimate of the standard error) of 6.2.

$$\frac{s}{\sqrt{n}} = \frac{24}{\sqrt{15}} = 6.2$$

MARGIN OF ERROR

We can use this standard error just like we use the standard deviation to describe how unusual values are from certain points. Using the Empirical Rule and the standard error of 6.2 from this sample, we'd expect around 95% of sample means to fall within two standard errors or about 12.4 points on either side of the mean population score. This 12.4-point spread is called the margin of error. If we add and subtract the margin of error to the sample mean of 80, we have a 95% confidence interval that ranges from 67.6 to 92.4 (see Chapter 3 for more detail on generating confidence intervals). However, we don't know the population mean or standard deviation. Instead, we're estimating it from our sample of 15 so there is some additional error we need to account for. Our solution, interestingly enough, comes from beer.

t-DISTRIBUTION

Using the Empirical Rule and *z*-scores to find the percent of area only works when we know the population mean and standard deviation. We rarely do in applied research. Fortunately, a solution was provided over 100 years ago by an applied researcher named William Gossett who faced the same problem at Guinness Brewing (for more information, see Chapter 9).

He compensated for flawed estimates of the population mean and standard deviation by accounting for the sample size to modify the *z*-distribution into the *t*-distribution. Essentially, at smaller sample sizes, sample means fluctuate more around the population mean, creating a bell curve that is a bit fatter in the tails than the normal distribution. Instead of 95% of values falling with 1.96 standard deviations of the mean, at a sample size of 15, they fall within 2.14 standard deviations.

For most small-sample research, we use these *t*-scores instead of *z*-scores to account for how much we expect the sample mean to fluctuate. Statistics textbooks include *t*-tables or, if you have access to Excel, you can use the formula =TINV(0.05,14) to find how many standard deviations account for 95% of the area (called a critical value). The two parameters in the formula are alpha (1 minus the level of confidence $(1-0.95 = 0.05)$) and the degrees of freedom (sample size minus 1 for a one-sample t), for which $t = 2.14$.

Therefore a more accurate confidence interval would be 2.14 standard errors (6.2*2.14) which generates the slightly wider margin of error of 13.3. This would provide us with a 95% confidence interval ranging from 66.7 to 93.3. Confidence intervals based on *t*-scores will always be larger than those based on *z*-scores (reflecting the slightly higher variability associated with small sample estimates), but will be more likely to contain the population mean at the specified level of confidence. Chapter 3 provides more detail on computing confidence intervals for a variety of data.

SIGNIFICANCE TESTING AND *p*-VALUES

The concept of the number of standard errors that sample means differ from population means applies to both confidence intervals and significance tests. If we want to know if a new design actually improves task-completion times but can't measure everyone, we need to estimate the difference from sample data. Sampling error then plays a role in our decision. For example, Fig. A.12 shows the times from 14 users who attempted to add a contact in a CRM application. The average sample completion time is 33 s with a standard deviation of 22 s.

A new version of the data entry screen was developed and a different set of 13 users attempted the same task (Fig. A.13). This time the mean completion time was 18 s with a standard deviation of 10 s.

So, our best estimate is that the new version is 15 s faster than the older version. A natural question to ask is whether the difference is statistically significant. That is, it could be that there is really no difference in task-completion times between versions. It could be that our sampling error from our relatively modest sample sizes is just leading us to believe there is a difference. We could just be taking two random samples from the same population with a mean of 26 s. How can we be sure and convince others that at this sample size we can be confident the difference isn't due to chance alone?

HOW MUCH DO SAMPLE MEANS FLUCTUATE?

Fig. A.14 shows the graph of a large dataset of completion times with a mean of 26 s and a standard deviation of 13 s.

Imagine you randomly selected two samples—one containing 14 task times and the other 13 times, found the mean for each group, computed the difference between the two means, and graphed it. Fig. A.15 shows what the distribution of the difference between the sample means would look like after 1000 samples. Again we see the shape of the normal curve.

We can see in Fig. A.15 that a difference of 15 s is possible if the samples came from the same population (because there are dots that appear at and above 15 s and −15 s). This value does, however, fall in the upper tail of the distribution of 1000 mean differences—the vast majority cluster around 0. Just how likely is it to get a 15 s difference between these sample means if there really is no difference?

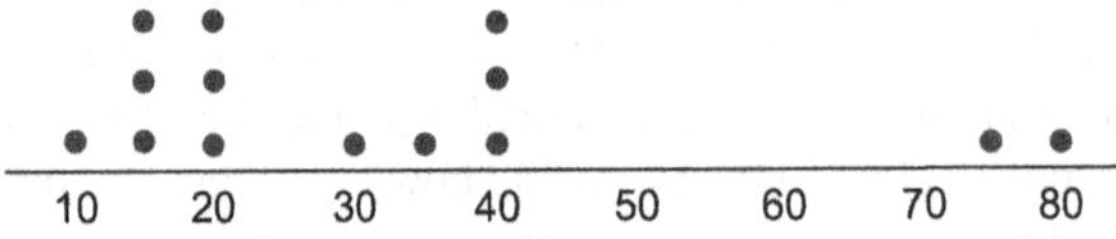

FIGURE A.12 Task completion times from 14 users

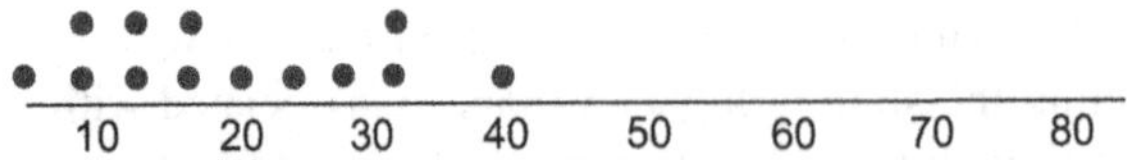

FIGURE A.13 Task completion times from 13 other users

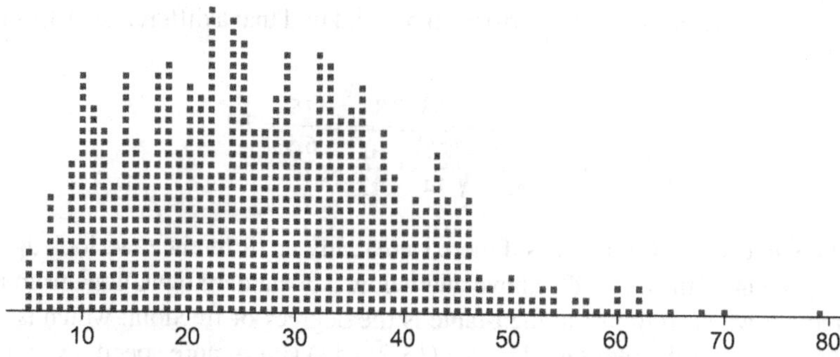

FIGURE A.14 Large dataset of completion times

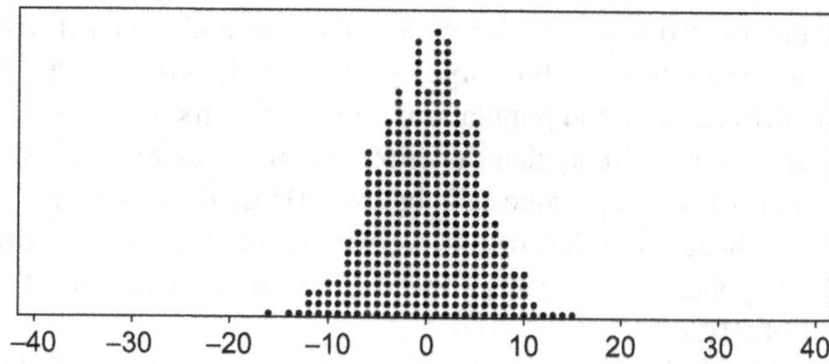

FIGURE A.15 Result of 1000 random comparisons

To find out, we again count the number of standard errors that the observed mean difference is from the expected population mean of 0 if there really is no difference. As a reminder, this simulation is showing us that when there is no difference between means (we took two samples from the same dataset) we will still see differences just by chance.

For this two-sample *t*-test, there is a slight modification to the standard error portion of the formula because we have two estimates of the standard error—one from each sample. As shown in the following formula for the two-sample *t*, we combine these estimates using a weighted average of the variances (see Chapter 5 for more detail):

$$t = \frac{\hat{x}_1 - \hat{x}_2}{\sqrt{\frac{s_1^2}{n_1} + \frac{s_2^2}{n_2}}}$$

where $\hat{x}_1$ and $\hat{x}_2$ are the means from sample 1 (33 s) and sample 2 (18 s),
s_1 and s_2 are the standard deviations from sample 1 (22 s) and sample 2 (10 s),
n_1 and n_2 are the sample sizes from sample 1 (14) and sample 2 (13), and
t is the test statistic (look up using the *t*-distribution based on the sample size for **two-sided area).**

Filling in the values, we get a standard error of 6.5 s, and find that a difference of 15 s is 2.3 standard errors from the mean.

$$t = \frac{\hat{x}_1 - \hat{x}_2}{\sqrt{\frac{s_1^2}{n_1} + \frac{s_2^2}{n_2}}} = \frac{33-18}{\sqrt{\frac{22^2}{14} + \frac{10^2}{13}}} = \frac{15}{6.5} = 2.3$$

To find out how likely this difference is if there were really no difference, we look up 2.3 in a t-table to find out what percent of the area falls above and below 2.3 standard deviations from the mean. The only other ingredient we need to use in the t-table is the degrees of freedom, which is approximately two less than the smaller of the two sample sizes (13-2 = 11) (for a more specific way to compute the degrees of freedom for this type of test, see Chapter 5). Using the Excel function = TDIST(2.3,11,2) we get 0.04, which is called the p-value. A p-value is just a percentile rank or point in the t-distribution. It's the same concept as the percent of area under the normal curve used with z-score. A p-value of 0.04 means that only 4% of differences would be greater than 15 s if there really was no difference. Put another way, 2.3 standard errors account for 96% of the area under the t-distribution (1 − 0.04). In other words, we expect to see a difference this large by chance only around 4 in 100 times. It's certainly possible that there is no difference in the populations from which the two samples came (that the true mean difference is 0), but it is more likely that the difference between means is something more like 5, 10, or 15 s. By convention, when the p-value falls below 0.05 there is sufficient evidence to conclude the difference isn't due to chance. In other words, we would conclude that the difference between the two versions of the CRM application indicates a real difference (see Chapter 9 for more discussion on using the p-value cutoff of 0.05).

Keep in mind that although the statistical decision is that one design is faster, we have not absolutely proven that it is faster. We're just saying that it's unlikely enough that the observed mean differences come from populations with a mean difference of 0 (with the observed difference of 15 s due to chance). As we saw with the resampling exercise, we occasionally obtained a difference of 15 s even though we were taking random samples from the same population. Statistics is not about ensuring 100% accuracy – instead it's more about risk management. Using these methods we'll be right most of the time, but at a 95% level of confidence, in the long run we will incorrectly conclude 5 out of 100 times (1 out of 20) that a difference is statistically significant when there is really no difference. Note that this error rate only applies to situations in which there is really no difference.

THE LOGIC OF HYPOTHESIS TESTING

The p-value we obtain after testing two means tells us the probability the difference between means is really 0. The hypothesis of no difference is referred to as the null hypothesis. The p-value speaks to the credibility of the null hypothesis. A low p-value means the null hypothesis is less credible and unlikely to be true. If the null hypothesis is unlikely to be true then it suggests our research hypothesis is true—specifically, there is a difference. In the two CRM designs, the difference between mean task times was 15 s. We've estimated that a difference this large would only happen by chance around 4% of the time, so the probability the null hypothesis is true is 4%. It seems much more likely that the alternate hypothesis, namely, that our designs really did make a difference, is true.

Rejecting the opposite of what we're interested in seems like a lot of hoops to jump through. Why not just test the hypothesis that there is a difference between versions? The reason for this approach is at the heart of the scientific process of falsification.

It's very difficult to prove something scientifically. For example, the statement, "Every software program has usability problems," would be very difficult to prove or disprove. You would need to examine every program ever made and to-be made for usability problems. However, another statement, "Software programs never have usability problems," would be much easier to disprove. All it takes is one software program to have usability problems and the statement has been falsified.

With null hypothesis testing, all it takes is sufficient evidence (instead of definitive proof) that a 0 difference between means isn't likely and you can operate as if at least some difference is true. The size of the difference, of course, also matters. For any significance test, you should also generate the confidence interval around the difference to provide an idea of practical significance. The mechanics of computing a confidence interval around the difference between means appears in Chapter 5. In this case, the 95% confidence interval is 1.3–28.7 s. In other words, we can be 95% confident the difference is at least 1.3 s, which is to say the reduction in task time is probably somewhere between a modest 4% reduction (1.3/33) or a more noticeable 87% reduction (28.7/33).

As a pragmatic matter, it's more common to test the hypothesis of 0 difference than some other hypothetical difference. It is, in fact, so common that we often leave off the difference in the test statistic. In the formula used to test for a difference, the difference between means is placed in the numerator. When the difference we're testing is 0, it's left out of the equation because it makes no difference.

$$t = \frac{\hat{x}_1 - \hat{x}_2 - \mathbf{0}}{\sqrt{\frac{s_1^2}{n_1} + \frac{s_2^2}{n_2}}} = \frac{\hat{x}_1 - \hat{x}_2}{\sqrt{\frac{s_1^2}{n_1} + \frac{s_2^2}{n_2}}}$$

In the CRM example, we could have asked the question, is there at least a 10-s difference between versions? We would update the formula for testing a 10-s difference between means and would have obtained a test statistic of 0.769 (as shown in the following formula).

$$t = \frac{\hat{x}_1 - \hat{x}_2 - \mathbf{10}}{\sqrt{\frac{s_1^2}{n_1} + \frac{s_2^2}{n_2}}} = \frac{33 - 18 - 10}{\sqrt{\frac{22^2}{14} + \frac{10^2}{13}}} = \frac{5}{6.5} = 0.769$$

Looking this up using the Excel function =TDIST(0.769,11,2) we get a p-value of 0.458.

A p-value of 0.458 would tell us there's about a 46% chance of obtaining a difference of 15 s if the difference was really exactly 10 s. We could then update our formula and test for a 5 s difference and get a p-value of 0.152. As you can see, the more efficient approach is to test for a 0 difference and if the p-value is sufficiently small (by convention less than 0.05, but see Chapter 9) then we can conclude there is at least some difference and look to the confidence interval to show us the range of plausible differences.

ERRORS IN STATISTICS

Because we can never be 100% sure of anything in statistics, there is always a chance we're wrong—there's a "probably" in probability, not "certainty." There are two types of errors we can make. We can say there is a difference when one doesn't really exist—called a Type I error – or we can conclude

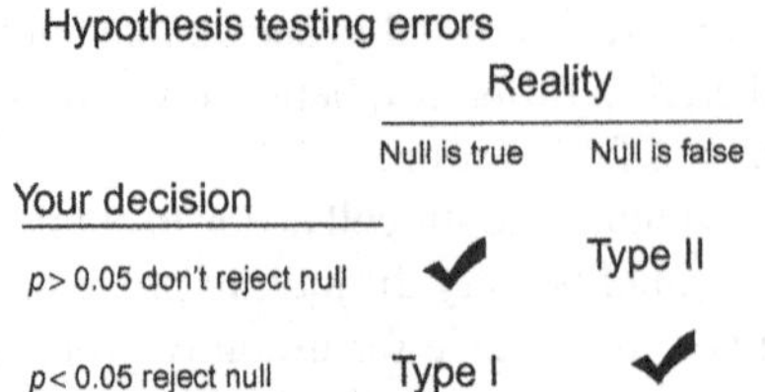

FIGURE A.16 Statistical decision making: two ways to be right; two ways to be wrong

no difference exists when one in fact does exist—a Type II error. Fig. A.16 provides a visualization of the ways we can be wrong and right in hypothesis testing, using $\alpha = 0.05$ as the criterion for rejecting the null hypothesis.

The *p*-value tells us the probability we're making a Type I error. When we see a *p*-value of 0.05, we interpret this to mean that the probability of obtaining a difference this large or larger if the difference is really 0 is about 5%. So over the long run of our statistical careers, if we only conclude designs are different if the *p*-value is less than 0.05, we can expect to be wrong no more than about 5% of the time, and that's only if the null hypothesis is always true when we test.

Not reported in the *p*-value is our chance of failing to say there is a difference when one exists. So for all those times when we get *p*-values of, say, 0.15 and we conclude there is no difference in designs, we can also be making an error. A difference could exist, but because our sample size was too small or the difference was too modest, we didn't observe a statistically significant difference in our test. Chapters 6 and 7 contain a thorough discussion of power and computing sample sizes to control Type II errors. A discussion about the importance of balancing Type I and Type II errors for applied research appears in Chapter 9.

If you need more background and exposure to statistics, we've put together interactive lessons with many visualizations and examples on the measuringu.com website.

KEY POINTS

- Pay attention to the type of data you're collecting. This can affect the statistical procedures you use and your interpretation of the results.
- You almost never know the characteristics of the populations of interesting data, so you must infer the population characteristics from the statistics you calculate from a sample of data.
- Two of the most important types of statistics are measures of central tendency (e.g., the mean, median, and geometric mean) and variation (e.g., the variance, standard deviation, and standard error).
- Many metrics tend to be normally distributed. Normal distributions follow the Empirical Rule—that 68% of values fall within one standard deviation, 95% within two, and 99.7% within three.
- As predicted by the Central Limit Theorem, even for distributions that are not normally distributed, the sampling distribution of the mean approaches normality as the sample size increases.
- To compute the number of standard deviations that a specific score is from the mean, divide the difference between that specific score and the mean by the standard deviation to convert it to a standard score, also known as a *z*-score.

- To compute the number of standard deviations that a sample mean is from a hypothesized mean, divide the difference between the sample mean and the hypothesized mean by the standard error of the mean (which is the standard deviation divided by the square root of the sample size), which is also interpreted as a z-score.
- Use the area under the normal curve to estimate the probability of a z-score. For example, the probability of getting a z-score of 1.28 or higher by chance is 10%. The probability of getting a z-score of 1.96 or higher by chance is 2.5%.
- For small samples of continuous data, use t-scores rather than z-scores, making sure to use the correct degrees of freedom (based on the sample size).
- You can use t-scores to compute confidence intervals or to conduct tests of significance—the best strategy is to do both. The significance test provides an estimate of the likelihood of an observed result if there is really no effect of interest. The confidence interval provides an estimate of the size of the effect, combining statistical with practical significance.
- In significance testing, keep in mind that there are two ways to be wrong and two ways to be right. If you conclude that there is a real difference when there isn't, you've made a Type I error. If you conclude that you have insufficient evidence to claim a difference exists when it really does, you've made a Type II error. In practical user research (as opposed to scientific publication), it is important to seek the appropriate balance between the two types of error—a topic covered from several perspectives in Chapter 9.

Subject Index

D

E

F

G

H

I

K

L

M

T

U

V

W

Y

Z

Printed in the United States
By Bookmasters